P9-CDC-842

PENGUIN BOOKS

TERROR INC

'A history of terror which extends far beyond the current Islamic threat
. . . she ranges across the whole world to describe the terrible, entangled
business of money and violence that she calls the "new economy of
terror" . . . to build a terrifying picture' *Literary Review*

'Economist Loretta Napoleoni comes up with a startling conclusion that
the "New Economy of Terror" is a fast growing international economic
system, with a turnover of about $1.5 trillion, twice the GDP of the
United Kingdom' *Wall Street Journal*

'Rather than look at terrorism from a political or religious standpoint,
Napoleoni approaches it as an economist, which she was before becoming
a writer. The business of terrorism is now so large and the financial networks
supporting it so complex, she says, that if the flow of money to terrorists
were suddenly cut off, the drop in liquidity could have a serious impact
on the Western economies' *Newsweek*

'Napoleoni traces fifty years of Western economic and political dominance
in developing Muslim countries – backing repressive, corrupt regimes,
fighting the Cold War by Proxy and blocking the legitimate economic
ascendancy of millions. "As in the Crusades", in which Napoleoni finds
many modern parallels, "religion is simply a recruitment tool; the real
driving force is economics" ' *Publisher's Weekly*

'Most recent books on terrorism attempt to locate its motivation in history,
culture, or religion. Napoleoni focuses on economics and therefore adds
a useful new layer to the study of terrorism. The book's strength is its
determination to "follow the money", highlighting the consequences of
economic dependency and providing detailed accounts of how terrorist
organizations are funded' *Choice*

ABOUT THE AUTHOR

Loretta Napoleoni holds an MPhil in terrorism from the London School of Economics and advises the Homeland Security on terrorism. She has conducted numerous interviews with former members of the Red Brigades and other Italian and South American terrorist organisations. More recently she has met and collected data on members of Islamist armed groups. She has written extensively on the subject and her work has appeared in many journals and publications, including several European newspapers. She holds a Masters in International Relations and Economics from John Hopkins University, School of Advanced International Studies and has worked for several international organisations including the IMF, the UN and the European Bank for Reconstruction and Development.

Terror Inc

Tracing the Money Behind Global Terrorism

LORETTA NAPOLEONI

PENGUIN BOOKS

PENGUIN BOOKS

Published by the Penguin Group
Penguin Books Ltd, 80 Strand, London WC2R ORL, England
Penguin Group (USA), Inc., 375 Hudson Street, New York, New York 10014, USA
Penguin Books Australia Ltd, 250 Camberwell Road,
Camberwell, Victoria 3124, Australia
Penguin Books Canada Ltd, 10 Alcorn Avenue, Toronto, Ontario, Canada M4V 3B2
Penguin Books India (P) Ltd, 11 Community Centre,
Panchsheel Park, New Delhi – 110 017, India
Penguin Group (NZ), cnr Airborne and Rosedale Roads, Albany,
Auckland 1310, New Zealand
Penguin Books (South Africa) (Pty) Ltd, 24 Sturdee Avenue,
Rosebank 2196, South Africa

Penguin Books Ltd, Registered Offices: 80 Strand, London WC2R ORL, England

www.penguin.com

Published under the title *Modern Jihad* by Pluto Press 2003
Published under the current title and with new material in Penguin Books 2004

3

Typeset by Palimpsest Book Production Limited, Polmont, Stirlingshire
Printed in England by Clays Ltd, St Ives plc

To my husband

Contents

Part III The New Economy of Terror

Foreword
John K. Cooley

An allegorical lover in a couplet of the Persian poet Omar Khayám complains: 'There was a door for which I had no key/ There was a veil through which I could not see.' Loretta Napoleoni's book hands the reader a magic key, which is her grasp of a shadowy world of global covert and semi-covert finance. It opens wide a door of understanding which has remained largely veiled for us, despite the many studies of international organized crime and of terrorism by individuals, groups and states, published and otherwise.

Her exhaustive and careful research unearths and analyzes thousands of documentary and human sources. Napoleoni shows how great historical movements, such as the medieval Crusades and the twentieth-century Cold War between the United States and the former Soviet Union had economic roots and motivations, leading those concerned into outlaw patterns of violence, funded by rogue finance. 'Terrorism' or terror, as embodied in the horrendous attacks on the US of September 11, 2001, and as described by the presidents, dictators and commentators of our own age, especially violence masquerading or legitimizing itself in the eyes of its supporters as liberation or freedom movements, cannot thrive without a constant supply of ready cash. Part I of her book explains this.

Terror Inc. then shows us how such movements, from the successful anti-Soviet, CIA-managed campaign by Muslim zealots to expel the Red Army from Afghanistan in 1979–89 to the Algerian armed struggle to end 130 years of French colonial rule, newer Muslim insurgencies in Central Asia, the perennial Irish conflicts or the present bloodthirsty internecine wars in Africa, gain and keep essential financial support. This enables them to proliferate and go on to new campaigns, like that of al–Qaeda against the West, once their primary mission ends. She describes a 1.5 trillion dollar system which grows daily. Traffic in drugs, oil, arms, precious stones, and human beings; as well as donations which respectable banks and other financial institutions often believe they are channeling to foundations with solely charitable aims, are vital parts of this system. Napoleoni depicts all of this in the second part of her book, aptly titled 'The New Economic Disorder.'

Central to her arguments in the third part, 'The New Economy of Terror,' is her discussion of such groups as al–Qaeda, which as a consequence of the wars in Afghanistan and their blowback, has become a global terror network in every sense of the word. These are not only driven by real economic forces in the Third World, especially in Muslim states from Morocco to Indonesia, but also by accomplices and complicities in the heart of the West. These complicities – and she is here, as in other arguments of her book, detailed and specific – reach into the sacrosanct bastions of Western capitalism: Wall Street; the City of London; Hong Kong's moguls of finance, as well as into the shadowy world of the *hawala* in Arabia and South Asia.

Without passion or polemics, Napoleoni steers us away from the many current heated debates about religion and politics, which she sees as creating a dark mist veiling the true mechanics of global violence and terror, and concentrates on economy. Her narrative is artfully woven, holding our interest with the force of a first-rate thriller novel. Her truths may not be stranger than fiction, but they are told with such precision and clarity that much fiction about the same subjects seems boring by comparison. Perhaps some university will add the book to its graduate studies program as the text for a course in 'The Economics of Terrorism 1001.'

This meticulous and well-written work should be read, studied, and preserved as a guide and reference. In this twenty-first century the democratic values we in the West profess to cherish are already being threatened by violence. This is generated partly by the inequities of our own civilization, and partly by politicians, criminals and outlaws seeking their own power and profit. Apart from its appeal for the general reader, the book is a valuable tool for the specialist who must deal with the problems it describes.

John K. Cooley
Athens
June 19, 2003

Introduction

George Magnus

The term 'new economy' was used erroneously by many economists to describe the impact of the information and communications technology revolution on the global economy. More recently, it has been deployed more aptly in trying to understand the economic implications of shifting geo-political tectonics in the early years of the new century. Loretta Napoleoni has applied the phrase in a chilling and insightful way to depict a critical phenomenon in this period of our history.

The New Economy of Terror, the size of which she estimates to be approximately 5% of world GDP, is both the result of historical processes and a feeding structure that sustains and nurtures global terror. This new economy, she argues, has an interdependent relationship with western market economies but is, simultaneously, in a state of increasing tension with them. This irony is one of many developed in the book as we try to grasp a major contemporary conundrum.

The book is a time-tapestry in which state-sponsored terrorism during the Cold War evolves into self-financed armed groups relying on crime and then into organisations which use and manage sophisticated business techniques and financing vehicles in order to promote their goals. Some have established themselves as 'state shells' with formal links to full nation states and their financial institutions and it is in this context that the New Economy of Terror exists in earnest.

A further and poignant irony emerges. The New Economy of Terror is in fact a product of globalisation and, in particular, of the rapid pace of globalisation that emerged after the fall of the Berlin Wall. Globalisation allowed non-state entities to promote a variety of liberal causes, social change and economic advancement but has also facilitated the networking of terrorist movements like al-Qaeda and the growing sophistication of the 'terror economy'. Privatisation, deregulation, openness, the free movement of labour and capital, technological advances – all hailed as the key ingredients of economic success in the last twenty years have been exploited by and adapted into the terror economy in a macabre form of geo-political ju-jitsu. In other words, the very strengths of legitimate economies have been turned into double-edged swords. Non-state organised, diffuse and decentralised economic networks might well be regarded as typically Reaganite or Thatcherite but for the fact that the subject matter here is the privatisation of terror organisations not telecommunications companies.

Loretta Napoleoni's New Economy of Terror could not have existed before the end of the Cold War. There are of course, many examples of local uprisings and terror campaigns, many of which proved successful against despotic or imperial powers. And they all needed money and some form of economic organisation to succeed. Ms. Napoleoni's central thesis about the global nature of the terror economy today is linked inextricably to the post-Cold War globalisation and, in particular, to the latter's mirror image of fragmentation. As the world has fragmented and broken up into smaller units of organisation, it has allowed groups – especially those with strong appeals to religious bonds and radical Islam in particular – to develop into state shells. These shells simultaneously substitute for the economic failures of legitimate states, for example by providing education and financial support and aspire to displace them. A further irony, of course is that many of the states that the terror economy seeks to displace are, themselves, the sources, directly or indirectly, of arms, logistics, refuge and, importantly, finance. The oldest adage in the world about money making the world go round finds a disturbing echo in this context. The US dollar, the world's reserve currency printed legitimately by the Federal

Reserve is the terror economy's main currency. Western and, more recently, Islamic banks are the vehicles through which this currency is transacted. Small, informal businesses are often the agents. Progressive and more liberal laws pertaining to immigration and capital movement and ease of access to arms and ammunitions have clearly been available for exploitation.

Finally and fundamentally, the rhetoric of terror groups and their sympathisers may be no more than that. The real issue, according to Loretta Napoleoni, is the growing tension between a dominant western capitalist system and a populous Muslim nation in which an emerging class of merchants and bankers is finding development is checked or frustrated. A sort of twist, if you will, on medieval times in which a dominant Islam was challenged by the rising tide of a European economic class and ultimately the Crusades. There will inevitably be much more debate among economists and political scientists as to the legitimacy and implication of this assertion, Ms. Napoleoni's belief that this is what 'Modern Jihad' is about merits serious attention. It certainly jives with the consensus view, for example, that al-Qaeda's principal villain is not even so much US military and economic primacy, per se, as Islamic states with which it is in a state of ambivalent tension. For western nations, the implication is that the fight against global terror needs also to be waged increasingly on an economic front. This is one in which the role of the state must be bigger, the role of the market and vested interests smaller. It is one in which there may well be significant financial costs to those that have profited from 'new economy' links to the terror economy.

George Magnus
Chief Economist
UBS Warburg
June 2003

Preface

Terrorism has become part of the fabric of modern life. It dominates newspaper headlines, parliamentary debates and dinner table conversations. Yet few people have a clear understanding of what constitutes 'terrorism', despite the many definitions of it available to the reader. History provides limited help. The word comes from the Reign of Terror which followed the French revolution, but one can find references to terrorism as far back as the Roman Empire. Politicians, the public, academics and members of armed groups variously employ a literal, propagandistic[1] or academic definition of what is in essence the same phenomenon.

Academics agree that any definition of terrorism must include its three main characteristics: its political nature, the targeting of civilians and the creation of a climate of extreme fear.[2] Yet libraries are bursting with books that focus exclusively on one or other of these elements. Members of armed organisations and politicians freely use the propagandistic definition of terrorism -- what Chomsky summarised as 'violent acts committed by enemies against "us" or "our allies"'.[3] When, in the early 1990s, I interviewed members of Italian left- and right-wing armed organisations, what struck me most was their consistent use of the word 'terrorist' to describe both each other and the state they attacked.

Political perception is the yardstick most people use to define terrorism. After 11 September 2001, I interviewed several Italians about their reactions to the attack on the World Trade Center. Many were sympathetic, but others were indifferent about the suffering of Americans. 'Why should I be supportive of the US?' one woman, a professional banker, challenged me. 'Have we forgotten what the Americans have done in Serbia, when they bombed all the bridges of Belgrade, terrorising the population? No, I cannot empathise with a nation that has brought death and despair to the world. Now they know what it means to be the target of terrorist aggression.'

Governments' use of the word 'terrorism' is often dictated by foreign policy considerations. In 1998, following attacks by the Kosovo Liberation Army (KLA) against Serbian police and civilians, the US accused the KLA of being a terrorist organisation. The British followed suit. Then, in March 1999, foreign policy in the US and UK underwent a radical shift. Both governments condemned the Serbs. Suddenly, members of the KLA were no longer 'terrorists' but 'freedom fighters'. Their new status was short-lived. As soon as the KLA supported an Islamist insurgency against the government of Macedonia – a US ally – it was once again listed as a terrorist organisation by the US State Department.[4]

The truth is that terrorism is a political phenomenon and, as long as it remains in the domain of politics, no worldwide consensus will be reached as to its definition. This is the main limitation of the political analysis. To get around this obstacle and shed some light on what has become a global menace, I will conduct an economic analysis of what is commonly known as terrorism. To underscore that no tools belonging to the domain of politics have been used, and to avoid falling into the trap of political definitions, I have chosen to use the word 'terror' instead of 'terrorism' to describe the recourse to violence by armed groups to achieve political goals. I must stress that although this is the first attempt to approach political violence from a new angle – to describe the economics of terror – this is not an academic book. Rather, it has been written in the belief that the ideas behind it should be accessible to everybody. Terror threatens the man on the street as much as academics and politicians. Its causes and the methods of its deployment should be understood by all.

This book aims to show that, over the last 50 years, members of armed organisations have been hunted down like criminals at home by the same political forces that have fostered them abroad; the final aim being to serve the economic interests of the West and its allies, Muslim oligarchies and of the East, for example the former Soviet Union in the past and Russia at present. This duality provided terror organisations with the motives to strike back and the opportunity to build their own economy. I have defined this phenomenon as the New Economy of Terror, an international network linking the support and logistical systems of armed groups. Today the New Economy of Terror is a fast-growing international economic system, with a turnover of about $1.5 trillion, twice the GDP of the United Kingdom, and is challenging Western hegemony. What we are facing today is the global clash between two economic systems, one dominant – Western capitalism – the other insurgent – the New Economy of Terror. As we shall see, this scenario is reminiscent of the Crusades, when Western Christendom rebelled against the domination of Islam. Behind the religious conflagration, economic forces initiated and sustained the Crusades, enabling the West to repel Islam and begin its march to dominance.

Over the last 50 years, the economic and political dominance of the West has hindered the expansion of emerging economic and financial forces in the Muslim world. These forces have forged alliances with Islamist armed groups and hard-line religious leaders in a campaign to rid Muslim countries of Western influence and domestic oligarchic rulers. As in the Crusades, religion is simply a recruitment tool; the real driving force is economics.

The New Economy of Terror has become an integral part of the global illegal economy, generating vast amounts of money. This river of cash flows into traditional economies, primarily to the US, where it is recycled. It has devastating effects on Western business ethics, but above all it cements the many links and opens new ones between the New Economy of Terror and legal economies.

11 September was a rude awakening for the world. It has triggered a war against a phenomenal enemy, who will attack whenever possible. What the world has not realised is that this enemy is the product of policies of dominance adopted by Western governments and their allies – the oligarchic powers of the Middle East and Asia – and its monetary lifeline is deeply intertwined with our own economies. The essence of its being is the New Economy of Terror.

Acknowledgements

I started researching this book many years ago, when terrorism was not a current affairs topic and nobody was interested in publishing a book on the economics of it. My deepest thanks go to those people who, before 9/11, have supported and encouraged me in continuing my work: Prof. Paul Gilbert, friend, mentor and PhD supervisor, with whom I spent precious days discussing my ideas; Noam Chomsky, whose invaluable advice and suggestions, through hundreds of emails across the Atlantic, have guided my research; Anna Maresso, fellow PhD student from LSE, who read the first proposal and suggested the title, Modern Jihad; my remarkable agents, Roberta Oliva and Daniela Ogliari, who never doubted my professional abilities and backed me all the way, selling this book to so many European publishers; Alexander Schmid, of the United Nations, who edited the finished manuscript and provided so many useful references. Special thanks go to my Italian publisher, Marco Tropea, who financed my research and even agreed to let me write this book in English; and to Pluto Press, my English-language publisher, who is investing in its promotion in the US, the UK and other English-speaking countries.

A special mention for John Cooley for writing the foreword, so neatly summarizing my message, and for George Magnus, my long-time friend and former colleague, who in the introduction managed to explain so well the 'economics' behind it.

My most sincere thanks go to my research assistants, young and enthusiastic post-graduate students Natalie Nicora, Rati Tripathi and Sam Calkins, who have done a fantastic job and have always been at the end of a phone or on-line for me; to my friend and editor, Elizabeth Richards, who held my hand for over a year, read and re-read my writings and polished my English – I could not have gone through chapter by chapter without her professional and gentle advice; to my other editor, Mehvish Hussein, who, time and time again, from Pakistan, checked the accuracy of my information and data; to Marta Ceccato, who translated important material from French into English. Without my sources, hundreds of people whose names I cannot mention and who, through a decade of research, have pointed me in the right direction, _Modern Jihad_ would not exist. My gratitude goes also to those who have contributed their professional knowledge to the making of this book: Dean Baker, Emily Bernhard, Scott Burchill, Jason Burke, Mustafa Gundogdu, Kitty Kelly, Damien Kingsbury, Susan Johns, Peter Mallinson, Greg Palast, Tuncai Sigar, Kate Snell, Bob Wilkinson, Richard Trigle, Cecilia Zarate. Special thanks to Raymond Baker, of the Brookings Institution, who unveiled for me the murky world of money laundering.

To my economist friends – Siobhan Breen, Francesca Massone, Bart Stevens, Grant Woods – who not only supplied data and literature, but also read the drafts of the book and made important suggestions, a very, very special thanks. Many thanks are due also to my lawyer friends – David Ereira and Bruce McEvoy – who _made sure nobody could sue me_.

Much gratitude to the many readers – Ikaty Ammar, Akram Aslam, Jean Arthur, Sean Bobbit, Gregg Glaser, Michael Ezra, Anthony Kenney, Abe Koukou, Henry Porter, Kenneth Bernhard, Venetia Morrison, Eugenia and Bogdan Patriniche, Lynn Sellegren, Bella Shapiro, Marc Vitria. A special thanks goes to my invaluable friend and former partner, Lesley Wakefield, who read the manuscript twice, once to check the contents and once to check the proof reading. Thank you also to Fredda Weinberg who is promoting the book on the web.

Thank you to all my friends who for two years have been listening to me talking about this book – Giovanna Amato, Mario Barbieri, Amanda Deutch, Sabina de Luca, Howard Fogt,

Martina and Tonino Giuffre', Carole and Martin Gerson, Roberto Giuliani, Antonio Guadalupi, Cecilia Guastadisegni, Nick Follows, Sally Klein, Melinda Levitt, Bettina Mallinson, Nami Marinuzzi, Silvia Marazza, Elisabetta Porfiri, Mauro Scarfone. Thanks to Deb Thompson for being a very special friend and supplying valuable information and contacts.

For the paperback edition, my deepest thanks go to Stephen Craturo, Nick Fielding, Simon Marazza and Valerio Nobili.

To my children, Alexander and Julian, and step-children, Andrew and Leigh, who had to put up with me working all the time, to my family in Rome, who hardly saw me for two years and to my husband, who has been, as usual, wonderful, thank you.

Prologue

On the morning of 11 September 2001, Paolo Salvo[1] woke up and, for a split second, wondered where he was. For the past 20 years, he had been awakened by the harsh voices of the guards and inmates of various Italian high-security prisons. To shut out those painful memories, he closed his eyes. The soothing sound of the sea, breaking on the sandy beaches of Calabria, murmured in the background. Suddenly he remembered that he was on parole and jumped out of bed. He dressed quickly and walked to the *Miramare*, a local café, for his breakfast. Sitting on the pavement of the *lungomare*, he gazed at the beauty of the bay.

Paolo Salvo had been born in a similar place. When I first interviewed him in the early 1990s, he fondly recalled how he had learned to swim and fish before kicking a football or riding a bike. The sea had been his playground, fishing his favourite pastime. His father was a fisherman, like his grandfather and his great-grandfather before him. For generations the sea had nurtured his family and it was understood that it would also provide for him – until he discovered politics. Even today, after so many years spent revisiting his past, Paolo cannot pinpoint the exact moment when he turned his back on his destiny to embrace political violence.

On one occasion his mother asked him if he had been coerced – 'brainwashed' was the word she used. Apparently, a journalist had written that he did not fit the profile of a terrorist. 'Of course I did not fit the mould of a terrorist!' Paolo told me and explained why, using the dogmatic rhetoric of a Marxist militant. 'I was a fighter, a soldier. When I joined my group, I became part of an army, the armed community. Terrorism was something else. Terrorism was what the US government had done in Chile, in Central America and in the Middle East, the systematic slaughtering of whoever opposed its imperialistic rule.'[2]

On 11 September, Paolo finished his coffee, stood up and scanned the horizon. Painful memories flooded into his mind, memories of a life tainted by political violence. In the early 1980s, soon after his arrest, he was taken to Trani, a high-security prison on the desolate and rugged coast of Puglia. 'A prison-fortress floating in the sea' is how the inmates describe it. When Paolo first saw it, from the military helicopter that had transported him there, he understood why. The prison perched at the end of a high promontory that extended into the sea. How ironic, he thought, to be so close to the sea and yet be unable to touch it. Trani was populated exclusively by members of armed gangs and high-ranking criminals. Mafia, Camorra and Sacra Corona Unita, all were well represented. Right- and left-wing armed groups were not fully segregated from the common criminals; though they did not share cells, they used the same prison facilities. Trani was the closest Paolo ever came to a living hell. Life was so unbearable, he confided to me several years ago, that when in December 1980 the inmates staged one of the bloodiest prison revolts in Italian history, death did not seem a bad option. Yet, for him, the most painful memory of those years was neither the savage beating from the guards after the revolt, nor the nights spent lying naked and bruised on the freezing floor of an isolation cell. It was the summer breeze from the Balkans. In late summer, the salty scent of freedom, similar to that which rises from the cliffs of Calabria, permeated the prison-fortress and tormented the inmates.

At Trani, the Balkan wind had stirred Paolo's memories, a few of them happy, but most painful. Images of lives smashed in the name of ideals that now seemed irrelevant. Flashbacks of his own acts of violence committed against strangers, of the endless sufferings imposed on his family, even on his friends.

Had it been worth it? I asked him a long time ago.

He did not answer but simply looked at me and slowly shook his head.

At exactly 15:46 on 11 September the owner of *Miramare* rushed out into the street shouting something to a group of fishermen busy mending their nets on the beach. The men stopped working and ran towards him. From a distance, lying on the beach, Paolo watched them disappear inside the bar and wondered what had happened. When one of them rushed back outside and signalled to the few people on the beach to join him, he followed them.

'As I entered the dim-lit room of the *Miramare*,' he told me, 'I took off my sunglasses and saw a group of people staring at an old television set on a shelf above the bar. Standing on a chair, the owner was frantically twiddling the volume knob to adjust the audio, which had suddenly gone quiet. I raised my eyes to the screen and watched the silent image of a thick cloud of smoke and fire engulf one of the towers of the World Trade Center. Mesmerised, I wondered what the nature of such a bizarre programme could be. A new Hollywood blockbuster? A documentary? A tragic accident, broadcast live across the world? A couple of men, annoyed by the lack of sound, impatiently exhorted the owner to hurry up and fix it. The man was about to turn towards them and answer when a plane appeared on the right-hand side of the screen and everyone fell silent. The room plunged into an eerie stillness. As the cockpit of the Boeing penetrated the glass hip of the building, I had the chilling realisation that we were witnessing live the biggest terror attack in modern history.'

The cry of the commentator, from the television set, inexplicably audible again, stirred a loud chorus of voices in the bar. People expressed disbelief, despair, horror and fear. Others rushed into the *Miramare*, pushing their way towards the TV screen. Women and children started searching for their loved ones, calling their names, as if the tragedy was unfolding on their doorstep instead of thousands of miles away.

'I instinctively retreated into a corner, near the entrance,' Paolo admitted. 'Immediately next to me a woman began sobbing. She was worrying about her relatives – she knew they lived near New York City, but did not know where they worked. An old woman clutched her hand and invoked the Virgin Mary repeatedly, bending forwards at each invocation. On the other side of the room, a baby was crying hysterically in the arms of his father . . . it was total chaos!'[3]

When the commentator broke the news that on a third hijacked plane a man had phoned his wife to say goodbye, people looked at each other in anguish. 'Are there other planes?' they asked one another. Images of men and women running through the streets trying to escape the two towers flashed on the screen. The reporter began lamenting the tragic fate of the passengers on board the suicide planes. Suddenly, Paolo was gripped by the memory of an execution he had witnessed. He knew too well the mixture of disbelief and panic etched on the faces of those running for their lives in New York City. 'Why are you taking my life?' That was the question that he had seen many times before in people's eyes.

'In war men and women are willing to run the risk of becoming a casualty,' a former member of an Italian right-wing armed group had explained.[4] 'They know that a bomb, a bullet, a mine can terminate their life because they are at war. The armed struggle, on the contrary, has never been granted the status of conflict. Instead, it has been dismissed as terrorism, a cruel, unlawful, irrational attack against innocent people.'

Inside the *Miramare* it began to emerge that the hijackers had taken control of the planes and used them as bombs. They were 'suicide bombers'. Paolo had never met one of them. He had had contact with the Arab armed community, mostly with

Palestinians linked to the PLO, with whom every European armed group dealt in weapons. They smoked, drank and enjoyed sex. He had never seen them praying, let alone fasting during Ramadan. His knowledge of the Islamic Jihad and of its followers was limited to what he had learned from the media. He was unable to relate to them as fellow fighters. Their willingness to die as martyrs, to enter a life of joy and pleasure in a holy warrior paradise, seemed absurd.

'Why throw away the life of a good soldier like that?'[5] he once challenged me. What bothered him most, though, was the killing of ordinary civilians; his armed organisation, he claimed, would never have targeted them. On the contrary, its members risked their lives to target the right person, those who exploited the people he had fought for. When I reminded him that the Italian armed community had killed far more *Carabinieri* and policemen, mostly young working-class men, than corrupt politicians, he dismissed my point by saying that those were the lives of soldiers at arms.

Until the afternoon of 11 September there had been only one form of 'terrorism' for Paolo Salvo: the one sponsored by the United States. Now, he was not so sure any more. Were the Islamic hijackers soldiers, freedom fighters or holy warriors? Or did they belong to a new breed of terrorists? A good soldier, he had learned, considers death a likelihood; voluntarily committing suicide was another matter.

'When you are at war death is part of the game,' he told me. 'To take a life you must be prepared to lose your own.' Yet Paolo Salvo had always struggled with this concept until the revolt at Trani, where for the first time he had fought the guards without fear, ready to die. 'I crossed the threshold of humanity,' he explained, 'like many others before me. I was blind to life, detached from it; killing and dying meant nothing to me. I felt soulless, like the American soldier in *Apocalypse Now* who is high on LSD and machine-guns the Vietnamese fishing boat, killing all the passengers.'

'How did that happen?' I asked him.

'I have never been able to answer that question,' he admitted, 'but I suspect that my readiness to die sprang from the loss of a reason to live, not from the hope of a better life after death.'

Suddenly, one of the twin towers collapsed, 'like a house of cards blown away by a child's breath,' was how Paolo described it. 'Tons and tons of glass, steel girders, cement and people ground to dust. Thousands of lives vanished.'

'Thousands of innocent lives,' I added.

He nodded. 'I was confused,' he admitted. 'Civilians had never been a target. Violence had always been a means, never an end in itself.'[6]

I told him that this was not what the average Italian believed during the *Anni di Piombo*, when Italy was caught in a deadly spiral of political violence. On the contrary, public opinion had denounced members of armed organisations as perpetrators of crimes against civilians.

'What is the difference between past and present terror?' I finally challenged him.

He looked at me in distress before answering. 'I rushed out of the *Miramare*,' he began. 'I needed some air. When I turned towards the bar and glanced once more at the screen the other tower was collapsing, burying Lower Manhattan under a cloud of dust. I was suddenly overwhelmed by the significance of what I was witnessing . . . I fell to my knees and started to cry . . . The truth is that there is no difference between past and present terror!'

Buried beneath the debris of the twin towers there was also something which had belonged to Paolo: the dreams and illusions of a generation that had embraced the armed struggle, that had killed, injured and maimed in its mission to wage war against an oppressive power. Islamist terror was its most recent manifestation.

Part I
The Cold War Years: The Economic Dependency of Terror

1. The Dilemma of Terrorism: War or Crime?

'We are terrorists, yes we are terrorists, because it is our faith.'

Abu Mahaz, Palestinian extremist, to CNN, 1993

On 31 August 1992, Ramzi Yousef left Peshawar for Karachi en route to New York City. Accompanying him was Ahmed Mohammad Ajaj, a former Domino's Pizza deliveryman from Houston, Texas. The two had probably met in Afghanistan at one of the training camps run by Osama bin Laden, or at the infamous University of Dawa and Jihad, a war training school located in Pakistan. As neither of them had a regular entry visa, Yousef bribed a Pakistani official with $2,700 to arrange boarding cards for flight PK-703 to New York.[1] Twenty hours later, a well-groomed Yousef disembarked from the first-class cabin of the plane and approached the immigration desk manned by Martha Morales. Calmly and politely he applied for political asylum. He claimed he was being persecuted by the Iraqi military and said that he faced certain death if his application was refused. Although his boarding card and passport bore two different names and a third identity emerged when Morales posed the routine question 'What is your name?' Ramzi Yousef was allowed to enter the US to await his asylum hearing.

A different destiny awaited his companion, Ajaj, who was carrying Yousef's bomb-building manuals. He produced a fake Swedish passport. When the immigration officer peeled off the badly glued photograph from the document, he became aggressive, shouting that he had a Swedish grandmother. Eventually, he was asked to step into the immigration office for questioning, where his luggage was searched. Officers were stunned to discover what he was carrying: manuals and videotapes on the making of explosives, detonators and even a video of the suicide bombing of an American embassy. He was immediately taken into custody.

While immigration officials questioned Ajaj, Yousef took a taxi and headed for the al-Kifah refugee centre, the New York City headquarters of Islamist terror, on Atlantic Avenue in Brooklyn. There, he was welcomed by Mahmud Abouhalima, a 33-year-old Egyptian Yousef had met in Afghanistan in 1988. At the time Abouhalima was working as a chauffeur for the Islamist religious leader Sheikh Omar Abdul Rahman, better known as the Blind Sheikh. The Egyptian introduced Yousef to Rahman as 'a friend from Afghanistan, a guy who will do anything'.[2] Abouhalima's description could not have been more accurate. In just six months, Yousef conceived, masterminded and executed the first bombing of the World Trade Center, the biggest attack on American soil prior to the Oklahoma bombing and 11 September 2001. As Yousef himself explained in 1995 to the FBI agents who escorted him back to the US from Pakistan, his plan was to have one of the World Trade Center towers collapse into the other. The bomb was intended to destroy the support columns that held the towers together. Monetary constraints, he admitted, had forced him to drop another plan to use chemical substances with the explosion.[3] Luckily, Yousef's plan did not work to perfection: the van with the explosives was parked several metres away from the 'ideal' spot, where it would have caused maximum damage, and parts of the bomb failed to detonate. Nevertheless, six people lost their lives in the attack and hundreds more were physically and psychologically injured.

The investigation that followed unveiled a terrifying scenario. Yousef and his companions were part of a conspiracy headed by Sheikh Omar, who was planning to bring Jihad to the heart of America. It soon emerged that more deadly attacks were intended for major US institutions, including the Pentagon. Under the noses of the FBI, the CIA and the US government, a dangerous phenomenon had taken root and grown for over a decade in America's own backyard. Veterans from the anti-Soviet Jihad had turned their hatred against their old ally, the United States. Astonishingly, these discoveries did not raise any national security concerns, nor was the threat posed by Islamist armed groups ever properly addressed. Why? The answer lies partly in the decision of the US administration to deal with political violence as a threat to civil order rather than as an assault on national security and partly in the 'special' relationship that exists between the US and Saudi Arabia.

By the early 1990s, the danger represented by Islamist radical groups was well known to the FBI and the CIA. Soon after the first attack on the World Trade Center, Dale Watson, head of the FBI's International Terrorism Section, Division of National Security, wrote that, at the time, members of Hamas, Hizbollah, al-Gama and al-Islamiyya were not only present in large numbers in the US, but had been particularly active for some time. Several Iranian students belonging to the Anjoman Islamie, the Iranian Islamist group, had enrolled in American universities. Their task was to monitor US policies towards the Middle East and coordinate future terror attacks. Watson also identified the existence of several cells planted in specific places, often bankrolled by countries such as Iraq, Iran and Sudan, and a plethora of Internet sites used for propaganda, recruitment and fundraising. Islamist armed groups, he stressed in his report, regarded New York as the optimal target because it was host to so many national and international organisations.[4]

There is plenty of evidence that, in the early 1990s, the FBI was monitoring militant Islamist groups, knew their *modus operandi* and had a clear idea of their strategies. Towards the end of 1992, Emad Salem, a former lieutenant colonel in the Egyptian army and an informant for the FBI, had warned the Bureau that militants very close to the Blind Sheikh were looking for

explosives and planning attacks in New York City. But the FBI
ignored Salem's warning in the belief that he was exaggerating
the threat Islamist extremists posed to New York, and suspended
his monthly salary of $500.[5] Had they taken him seriously, Ramzi
Yousef would probably have failed to carry out his plan.

The question that comes to mind is why such warnings
were ignored. The answer is very simple: there have been
constraints imposed by all post-Cold War US administrations
on investigating the Saudis. On BBC2's *Newsnight*, Greg Palast
interviewed an FBI agent who admitted that there was a
plethora of evidence

tied in with the Saudi royal household which appears to be involved
in the funding of terrorist organisations or organisations linked to
terrorism . . . Now the problem was the investigations were shut down.
There were problems that go back to Father Bush; when he was head
of the CIA, he tried to stop investigations of the Saudis; [the problems]
continued on under Reagan, Daddy Bush and . . . under Clinton too
. . . I have to add it was also the CIA and all the other international
agencies . . . I have to say that the sources are not just the FBI trying
to get even with the agencies, but in fact the other agencies. The information was that they were absolutely prohibited, until September 11,
at looking at Saudi funding of the al-Qaeda network and other terrorist
organisations.[6]

A great deal of circumstantial evidence gathered after the first
attack on the World Trade Center pointed in the direction of
Osama bin Laden, who at that time was living in exile in Sudan.
Several of the convicted conspirators had strong links with him.
The Saudi terror tycoon was also financing the Office of
Services, a group based in Pakistan aimed at organising and
promoting Jihad worldwide. From 1993 to 1995, when he was
finally captured, Ramzi Yousef had resided on and off in Peshawar
at the Bayt Ashuhada (House of the Martyrs), one of the guest
houses financed by bin Laden.[7] However, the trail that could

have led to bin Laden and his al-Qaeda network was never fully investigated, nor was the loophole in the immigration system – so successfully exploited by Yousef – ever closed. In fact, the 11 September hijackers exploited that same weakness to gain entry into the United States.

TERRORISM AS A CRIME

'In retrospect, the wake-up call should have been the 1993 World Trade Center bombing,' admitted Michael Sheehan, counter-terrorism coordinator at the State Department during the Clinton administration.[8] However, the US administration continued to ignore all the warning signs. The president chose to follow in his predecessor's footsteps, believing that political violence was a civil crime to be prosecuted and punished, not a threat to national security to be prevented or an enemy to be reckoned with. Following this strategy, law enforcement agencies were tasked with prosecuting the members of armed organisations as common criminals, using the instrument of the law. Political violence had so little salience on Clinton's agenda that he never even visited the World Trade Center, nor did he shake the hands of the victims' families in front of the cameras. To mollify public opinion, Congress passed legislation to tighten immigration, but the rules were never fully implemented. Astonishingly, nobody considered the perils of porous borders.

Perhaps the White House reaction would have been different had Yousef succeeded in killing thousands of people. The first World Trade Center attack 'wasn't the kind of thing where you walked into a staff meeting and people asked, what are we doing today in the war against terrorism?' Clinton's first-term adviser for policy and strategy, George Stephanopoulos, told the *New York Times*.[9] When in 1995 a van full of explosives was driven into the Alfred P. Murrah Federal Building in Oklahoma City, killing 168 people, the reaction was completely different.

Clinton not only flew to the site for a memorial service, he also issued orders to intensify the fight against terrorism. However, no clear strategy was drawn up to accomplish this objective.

Is it possible that politicians and anti-terrorism bureaucracies alike had no idea of the magnitude of the danger? That may well have been the case. 'Prior to September 11, a lot of people who were working full time on terrorism thought it was no more than a nuisance.'[10] But why? Again the answer lies in treating political violence as a crime against individuals and property rather than a threat to the state, as well as in the politics of curbing further investigation into who was funding Islamist terror.

The FBI and the agencies had very little room for manoeuvre. In the late 1990s, a Saudi diplomat who defected to the United States brought 14,000 documents with him. 'He offered [them] to the FBI but they would not accept them,' revealed a former FBI officer.

The low-level agents wanted this stuff because they were tremendous leads. But the upper-level people would not permit this, did not want to touch this material. That is quite extraordinary. We don't even want to look. We do not want to know. Because obviously going through 14,000 documents from the Saudi government files would anger the Saudis. And it seems to be policy number one that we don't get these boys angry.[11]

This approach hamstrung professionals, who were prevented from acting on vital inside information. For example, in the spring of 1996 the CIA interrogated Ahmed al-Fadl, who had been involved in a plot to kill US soldiers in Somalia in 1992. He described bin Laden's vast network, al-Qaeda; his dream of attacking the US and his attempts to purchase uranium. Al-Fadl's shocking revelations were passed on to every anti-terrorist organisation in the US, yet the State Department did not add al-Qaeda to its list of foreign terrorist organisations.[12] In 1997 another wake-up call went unheeded when a member of al-Qaeda walked into the US embassy in Nairobi and unveiled a plot to bomb several American embassies in Africa. The CIA dismissed his story as unreliable. On 7 August 1998, the US embassies in Kenya and Tanzania were simultaneously bombed. A string of bombing incidents against US targets around the world followed, including sites in Sri Lanka, Uganda, Israel and South Africa. In the aftermath of these attacks, instead of launching a massive investigation, the White House undertook an unsuccessful covert operation to kill bin Laden.[13]

During his two terms as president, Clinton's overall approach to political violence remained unchanged: it was regarded as criminal activity, not as a threat to national security. Understandably, after the first attack against the World Trade Center, anti-terrorist agencies were looking for isolated groups of criminals operating mostly outside the US, not for international armed organisations plotting to strike inside US borders. This mistake gave Osama bin Laden and his network eight more years to expand and establish cells all over the world. According to Dr Laurie Mylroie, an American expert on terrorism and Iraq, the US government was unable simultaneously to address the national security question of state sponsorship of violent acts and the criminal question of the guilt or innocence of individual perpetrators.[14] After the first World Trade Center bombing, for example, once the arrests had been made, the organisation of the defendants' trials took bureaucratic priority over everything else. The Justice Department was in charge of the entire investigation and its brief was to prosecute and convict criminals, not to hunt down 'terrorists'. More important, because a rift exists between the Justice Department (including the FBI) on the one hand and the agencies of national security (the National Security Agency, the CIA and the Defense Department) on the other,[15] the investigation was carried out behind closed doors. Access to information was systematically denied, even to the CIA, for fear of 'tainting the evidence'.

As reported by the *New York Times*, former CIA director James Woolsey admitted during an interview that important leads pointing overseas had not been shared with the CIA due to the rule of secrecy of the grand jury.[16] 'The US judiciary is conceived to operate strictly according to its routine,' an American criminal lawyer explained. 'Its final aim is to prove beyond reasonable doubt that the defendant is innocent or guilty, regardless of the type of crime committed. It is not equipped to track "terrorist cells" around the world.'

In the specific case of the 1993 World Trade Center attack, confining a terror attack within the straitjacket of criminality, rather than adopting a war model, served to undermine national security. The trial of Ramzi Yousef succeeded in proving his involvement in the first bombing of the World Trade Center, but failed to answer important questions such as who was backing him financially and ideologically. Knowing the answers to questions such as this and having the freedom to investigate the Saudis might have prevented the attacks of 11 September and the present threat of international terror. Although the FBI and the CIA succeeded in tracing some of Yousef's money to Germany, Iran, Saudi Arabia and Kuwait, without a confession or a major breakthrough it was impossible to discover the identity of the sources.[17] Yousef insisted that the whole operation cost no more than $15,000 and that more than half of that came from friends and family. The court did not press him to reveal his financial sources because they were not considered vital in establishing his innocence or guilt during the trial. So he never explained how he paid for the vast expenditures incurred in carrying out other deadly attacks in Asia, including the ambitious Bojinka plot.[18]

Today, it is well accepted that 11 September was a copycat of the Bojinka plot, a plan to blow up several jumbo jets simultaneously, killing thousands of people. The plan died a sudden death in 1995 when a fire broke out in the flat rented by Ramzi Yousef and his associates in Manila. In the rush to escape, Yousef forgot his laptop, which contained vital information. Abdul

Hakim Murad, one of the accomplices, was sent to recover the computer, but was arrested by the police. He later admitted to being a qualified pilot recruited by Yousef to carry out a suicide mission. According to Murad's confession, Yousef intended to hijack several commercial flights in the US and crash the planes into the CIA headquarters and the Pentagon.[19] The decoding of the data in the laptop revealed a link between Ramzi Yousef and al-Qaeda through Riduan Isamuddin, better known as Hambali, regarded by the Filipino authorities as the regional head of al-Qaeda (and one of the men suspected of having masterminded the Bali bombing in October 2002). In 1995 Hambali was a director of Konsojaya, a Malaysian company bankrolling the Islamist terror cells operating in the archipelago. He may also have been involved in the planning of the 11 September attacks. In January 2000, he met Khalid al-Midhar and Mawaf Alhazimi, two of the hijackers of the plane that struck the Pentagon. Malaysian officials confirmed that this meeting took place in Malaysia.[20] Eight months later, Hambali had a meeting with Zacarias Moussaoui, the Moroccan accused of being part of the 11 September conspiracy.[21] Although this information was shared with the US authorities, once Yousef was safely behind bars no major investigation was launched to track down his accomplices still at large. Aida Fariscal, the former police inspector of the Filipino inquiry, believes that had the US paid more attention to the data contained in Yousef's laptop, the 11 September attacks could have been prevented.[22] The truth is that 11 September was not an intelligence break-down; it was much more than that. 'There is no question we had what looked like the biggest failure of the intelligence community since Pearl Harbor, but what we are learning now is that it wasn't a failure, it was a directive.'[23] The general feeling is that the White House prevented the intelligence community from digging deeply into Islamist extremism in order to protect the Saudis. As long as America was safe, they were left alone.

THE WAR ON TERROR

This policy ended abruptly on 11 September 2001. At the same time, terrorism ceased to be a criminal activity and became an act of war. President Bush's immediate reaction was to describe the strike as 'a national tragedy'. That evening, in a televised address to the nation, he referred to the attack as 'an act of war against the United States'. In the immediate aftermath, the president and his administration behaved as if the nation was under military attack. As in a Hollywood blockbuster, all airports were closed, planes were grounded, borders sealed, schools, offices and shops shut down; Americans were told to go home and wait while the White House took care of the damage. On 12 September, in a meeting with his national security team, the president admitted that 'the American people need to know that we are facing a different enemy than we have ever faced'. A few days later, in a presidential directive, George W. Bush created the Homeland Security Advisory System, 'the foundation for building a comprehensive and effective communication structure for the dissemination of information regarding the risk of terrorist attacks to all levels of government and American people'. 'Terrorism' was assigned its own institutional watchdog. Less than a month later, on 7 October, America declared war on the Taliban regime. The official justification was that it was harbouring Osama bin Laden and the al-Qaeda international terror network.

While Clinton's and Bush's reactions could not have been more different, the similarities between the two World Trade Center attacks are striking. Both aimed at killing the maximum number of people, both targeted one of the greatest symbols of modern America and Western capitalism and both were part of a conspiracy to bring Jihad to the heart of America. Neither of the groups that carried out the attacks had adequate means to finance the schemes themselves. In both cases, the money trails led to the same countries in the Middle East. The perpetrators were former Arab-Afghans, Muslim volunteers who had fought in the anti-Soviet Jihad, Mujahedin who had strong links with Osama bin Laden's network. Yousef and the 11 September hijackers knew full well the weaknesses of the immigration system and exploited them to enter the US. Finally, Yousef's Bojinka plan was the blueprint for the second attack. The sole crucial difference was that the bombing of the World Trade Center failed to destroy the towers, while the second succeeded.

On 11 September the world was told that, confronted with the scale of the damage, the number of victims and the warlike dynamics of the strike, the US government could no longer dismiss the perpetrators as common criminals. Clearly, America's national security was under attack and war had suddenly become an option. The picture that emerged was that of a state engaged in a conflict with a new type of enemy: a conglomerate of armed organisations and terror states, the core of a vast international network of terror. This, the White House stressed, was a unique phenomenon.

Western citizens had been brutally confronted with a reality that not only escaped any previous Western definitions of political violence, but also posed challenging new questions as to how such an enemy had emerged in the first place. As the media frantically searched for clues to answer these questions, it became clear that the new enemy was a well-known foe, one that had been nurtured for decades in the bosom of US foreign policy. Its birth and evolution are the essence of the New Economy of Terror.

2. The Macroeconomics of Terror

*'Yes, I am a terrorist and I am proud of it. And I support terrorism as
long as it was against the United States government and against Israel,
because you are more than terrorists; you are the ones who invented
terrorism and are using it every day. You are butchers, liars and hypocrites.'*

Ramzi Yousef, during the trial for the 1993 bombing of the World
Trade Center

In the years immediately after the Second World War, while
Britain and the United States were busy containing Soviet
expansion in Eastern Europe, France was engaged in a vicious
war in Indochina. To prevent communists from taking over its
colonies, which included Vietnam, Laos and Cambodia, the
French government dispatched contingents of regular troops to
South East Asia. In response, the communists launched a guerrilla war. Within the dense jungle of Indochina, French troops
soon discovered that hunting down guerrilla fighters was an
impossible task. Organised in small commando units scattered
throughout the jungles and mountains of northern Vietnam, the
guerrillas attacked villages and French garrisons with rapid and
well-planned incursions. They also used terror tactics to drive
a wedge between the local population and the French administration, publicly executing tribal chiefs and elders who opposed
them. The successes of guerrilla warfare were soon apparent:
communist influence and support in Indochina grew exponentially and the French government ultimately had to admit
that conventional warfare offered an inadequate response.

As early as 1949, the French developed a new strategy. They

began training hill tribesmen and religious minorities as intelligence agents, saboteurs and radio operators. Criminals such as the Nung pirates, who operated in the Gulf of Tonkin and the Binh Xuyen, gangsters and river pirates located near Saigon, were also recruited as guerrilla fighters.[1] Once trained, the men were organised into groups of about 3,000, known as *maquis*, and infiltrated the territories controlled by the communists. The *maquis* were the mirror-image of the communist commandos; they fought using the same terror tactics as the enemy.

Throughout the conflict, the main problem for the French government was funding. The war in Indochina was unpopular and it was extremely difficult to raise money in France. In particular, the Service de Documentation Extérieure et du Contre-Espionage (SDECE, the French body ultimately responsible for the *maquis*)[2] struggled to sustain its operations. The communists, also facing a serious cash shortage, were the first to spot a local funding opportunity. In 1952 they confiscated Laos's opium crop, sold it on the open market in Thailand and used the profits to buy arms from China. Once again the French took a leaf from the enemy's book, and formulated 'Operation X'. The SDECE secretly negotiated to buy the next year's entire Laotian opium crop from local tribes, who welcomed both the revenue and the opportunity to strike back at the communists. Soon after harvesting, the opium was loaded on to a French DC-3 and transported to South Vietnam. From there it was taken by truck to Saigon and handed over to a gang of criminals well known to the SDECE for refining drugs. Some of the opium was sold directly in Saigon opium dens and shops, some was purchased by Chinese merchants, who exported it to Hong Kong, and the rest was sold to the Union Corse, the Corsican Mafia, who smuggled it to France[3] and various European and North American markets. Thus, the SDECE netted a handsome profit that was used to finance the *maquis*.

The Americans were well aware that the French were using narcotics to finance the *maquis*, but chose to turn a blind eye.

When Colonel Edward Lansdale, a CIA official, learnt of the existence of 'Operation X', he reported immediately to Washington that the French military were involved in illegal drug trafficking in Indochina. 'Don't you have anything else to do?' was the response. 'We do not want you to open this can of worms since it will be a major embarrassment to a friendly government. So drop your investigation.'[4]

THE DOCTRINE OF COUNTER-INSURGENCY

The French response to communist guerrilla warfare in Indochina became known as counter-insurgency. A new concept in political warfare, counter-insurgency effectively legitimised state-sponsored terrorism:[5] the financial support by a colonial power for guerrilla warfare as a means of confronting insurgency, dissent and subversion.[6] Exporting warfare to an unconventional battlefield, the new doctrine required the formation of special units, paramilitary elite groups and a powerful, centralised intelligence agency under military control. As the world plunged deeper into the Cold War, counter-insurgency became the most effective means of maintaining the status quo and preventing direct confrontation between the two superpowers.

In 1961 President John F. Kennedy officially legitimised the new doctrine and brought it into the open. 'The free world's security can be endangered not only by a nuclear attack,' Kennedy told Congress on 28 March 1961, 'but also by being nibbled away at the periphery . . . by forces of subversion, infiltration, intimidation, indirect or non-overt aggression, internal revolution, diplomatic blackmail, guerrilla warfare or a series of limited wars.'[7] Six days after his nomination, his administration presented the National Security Council with a proposal for an immediate budget allocation of $19 million (equivalent today to about $100 million) as part of an ambitious counter-insurgency programme, including an expansion of the US Army's Special Forces from a few hundred to 4,000 men. A new foreign aid infrastructure, comprehensive of military and civilian agencies, was developed to manage guerrilla forces.

In November 1961, a special secret group was set up to deal exclusively with Cuba, a Marxist enclave in the US sphere of influence. Under the code name 'Mongoose', 400 Americans and 200 Cubans were given a private fleet of speedboats and a $50 million annual budget to undermine Castro's regime. The group was partly run by the Miami station of the CIA, in open violation of the Neutrality Act[8] and of legislation prohibiting the CIA from operating within the United States territory.[9] 'Mongoose' was merely one of the many unconventional military initiatives undertaken by the Kennedy administration. By 1963, the year the president was assassinated, American counter-insurgency groups were operating in 12 countries and three continents: Africa, Asia and Latin America.

Counter-Insurgency Doctrine had by then become the ideology underpinning Washington's unconventional warfare. The Special Forces constituted its army. Almost overnight, from the jungles of South East Asia to the high mountains of South America, American warriors became Cold War heroes for the political elite at home and abroad. Their most powerful weapon was counter-insurgent terror, the mirror-image of guerrilla terror. This principle was employed in Vietnam in 1961, in Colombia in 1962 and in Central America in 1966.[10] Eventually, these soldiers became specialists in training others in the art of unconventional warfare, passing on their knowledge to foreigners.

In the early days, one of the most successful counter-insurgent terror operations carried out was 'Operation Black Eagle'. US agents trained selective Vietnamese troops in the art of assassination and organised them in small commando units known as death squads. The task of the death squads was to kill high-ranking Viet Cong. Within days of the launch of

'Black Eagle', leaders of the Viet Cong underground organisation were found dead in their beds. On their corpses the assassins had left a drawing of a human eye. The same image was found on the doors of the victims' houses,[11] a warning to whoever supported them. Similar groups were trained in Central America during the civil war in El Salvador; again the human eye was used as a symbol. Psychological warfare – terrorising the enemy – was a central tenet of counter-insurgency strategy. Fear was a weapon, especially powerful in the underdeveloped world. During the 1966–67 military campaign in Guatemala, known as '*el Contra-Terror*', as many as 8,000 people[12] – most of them civilians – were slaughtered by the army in two provinces as a warning to stop others from collaborating with the guerrilla movement.[13]

The USSR and her allies were also heavily involved in state-sponsored terrorism, but the Soviet attitude towards it was somewhat ambiguous. This sprang from a contradiction within Soviet foreign policy during the Cold War. While adhering to the principle of avoiding any direct confrontation with the West, the USSR upheld Lenin's position on war and civil war. Like von Clausewitz, Lenin believed that war was 'a continuation of politics by other means'. When merged with the Marxist principles of perpetual struggle between the classes and between capitalism and communism, this concept held devastating consequences for the Third World. Outside the 'safety net' afforded by the Cold War (NATO and Warsaw Pact countries enjoying a period of relative peace and stability),[14] Moscow envisaged clusters of nations in Africa, Asia and South America caught up in a state of perpetual war. In a speech delivered in 1965, Soviet foreign minister Andrei Kosygin summarised the contradiction of his country's foreign policy:

The policy of peaceful coexistence . . . proceeds from the inadmissibility of the application of force in solving disputed questions among states. But this in no case means the rejection of the right of peoples, arms in hand, to oppose aggression or to strive for liberation from foreign oppressors. This right is holy and inalienable and the Soviet Union without fail assists people [who seek to assert it].[15]

Following Lenin, the communist leadership placed great importance on unconventional warfare and the training of Special Forces, better known as *Spetsnaz*. In 1979, for example, the Soviets deployed them and the Alpha anti-terror group as cover units to penetrate Afghanistan[16] ahead of its conventional army. Moscow was particularly keen on moulding Marxist Cold War fighters into *Spetsnaz* across the world. Therefore, the free training of Marxist armed groups became a form of indirect financial support. In the 1970s, to strengthen its influence in the Middle East, Moscow established a school of sabotage in Prague where East German and Russian instructors trained select members of the Palestinian al-Fatah.[17] The course lasted six months, after which the men were sent to another camp in Kosice, Czechoslovakia, to complete their training.[18] At the Lenin Institute and Patrice Lumumba University in Moscow, Soviet and foreign students learned techniques of psychological warfare and media manipulation along with Marxist ideology.[19] Among its 'distinguished' students was Carlos the Jackal, a beneficiary of a Soviet scholarship. Once the course was completed, students moved to training camps across the USSR: in Baku, Tashkent, and Odessa, in Simferopol in the Crimea and elsewhere in the Eastern Bloc.[20]

A third party generally mediated the Soviet financing of Marxist armed groups. East Germany and Bulgaria, for example, had the task of channelling Soviet support to armed groups in Europe, the Middle East and Africa. In his memoirs, the head of East German foreign espionage, Markus Wolf, admitted having supplied weapons and financial aid to Marxist armed organisations; however, he claimed that the recipients were 'legitimate'.[21] While the Americans used Counter-Insurgency Doctrine to justify state-sponsored terrorism, the Soviets concealed their involvement in the same game by extending the concept of 'international solidarity' to what they called 'progressive forces' in the Third World. Among them were PLO fighters who operated within the occupied territories and targeted Israeli military and strategic outposts.

EL SALVADOR: A GUERRILLA WAR ECONOMY

With the nuclear threat ever present during the Cold War, confrontation between the two blocs was to be avoided at all cost. However, the two superpowers constantly undermined each other, creating armed uprisings on the fringes of their spheres of influence. The Cold War was an unconventional war in many aspects: it was fought at the periphery, in foreign territories and by state-sponsored armed groups. For over a decade, for example, the US and the Soviet Union fought a war by proxy in El Salvador, a country already in the grip of a civil war between the right-wing dictatorial regime and the Marxist revolutionary movement. In 1980, the political situation in El Salvador became critical. Economic and natural disasters coupled with guerrilla warfare in the countryside resulted in great social unrest and poverty. From 1979 to 1981 GDP declined by 18 per cent. Over the same period productivity and capital income fell by 20 and 26 per cent, respectively. From January 1980 to August 1981, employment dropped 27 per cent in manufacturing, 56 per cent in construction, 25 per cent in commerce and 33 per cent in transport.[22] By 1981 all investment had ceased and industrial production fell by 17 per cent. At that point, the US intervened to sustain the economy and the government of El Salvador, prompted not so much by altruism as by the spectacular victory of the Sandinistas in neighbouring Nicaragua. Simultaneously, using Cuba and Nicaragua as intermediaries, the Soviets backed Marxist guerrillas in the country with funds, arms, military training and political support.[23] Thus El Salvador became one of the many battle-fields of the Cold War.

From the beginning of American and Soviet involvement in El Salvador, it was apparent that the health of the national economy would decide the outcome of the civil war. This was a view shared by the guerrilla leadership, who believed that 'the key is to break the capacity of the economy to sustain the war'.[24] Indeed, from 1981 to 1984, the FMLN (Farabundo Martì National Liberation Front — a coalition of five Marxist revo-lutionary groups) targeted the economy and launched a fierce campaign to sabotage its infrastructure, hitting telephone and electrical systems, power stations, dams, bridges, water supplies and agriculture. Fearing that the socio-economic structure would collapse, President Reagan convinced Congress of the need to increase aid to El Salvador from $64 million in 1980 to $156 million in 1981, of which $35 million was allocated for military purposes. In 1982 this figure rose to $302 million ($80 million in military aid).[25] The aim was to support the govern-ment by using American money to bridge the discrepancy between government revenues and expenditures. So, while the FMLN's strategy was to bring about the collapse of the economy, the government and the US were desperately seeking to stabilise it.

The impact of the economic sabotage[26] was twofold: it weakened the government and strengthened the FMLN. The guerrilla group benefited from the erosion of the economy, mostly because it had detached itself and its support system from the national economy. Its strongholds were isolated rural regions, such as Morazan and Chalaltenango. Sabotage of the main economic infrastructures had no impact in these areas. Ravaged and impoverished by the civil war, they were completely cut off from the rest of the country. Without tele-phone lines, electricity or running water, the population survived thanks to the economy generated by the FMLN guerrilla activities. This 'guerrilla war economy'[27] was based on subsistence and external assistance, i.e. foreign aid, such as the arms and funds provided by the Soviets to the *guerrilleros*. It was in the countryside that the guerrilla war economy had its core and from which the FMLN drew its strength and support: 95 per cent of guerrilla combatants came from the countryside and were of peasant origin.[28] The group was regarded as the saviour and protector of the *campesinos* against the abuses of the right-wing regime. In December 1980, *New York Times* reporter Raymond Bonner asked newly elected President José Napoleón Duarte 'why the guerrillas were in the hills'. Duarte's reply surprised Bonner: 'Fifty years of lies, fifty years of injustice, fifty years of frustration. This is the history of people starving to death, living in misery. For fifty years the same people had all the power, all the money, all the jobs, all the education, all the opportunities.'[29]

The US government was conscious of the dangers of a prolonged FMLN campaign against economic targets and well aware of the FMLN's final aim: to destroy the economy of El Salvador and replace it with its own. Therefore, in tandem with military aid, the US designed an ambitious programme to remodel the social and economic structure of the country. Along with agrarian reform aimed at winning over new farmers, the US encouraged a shift in exports from agricultural products towards non-traditional items, such as textiles. Bypassing the government, which showed some resistance to this plan, funds were channelled to the Foundation for Economic and Social Development, an organisation with close links to the private sector. Between 1984 and 1992, $100 million were channelled from the US to operations in El Salvador through this organisation. Thanks to this initiative, private business, especially big business, was allowed to develop independently of the government framework, taking over functions no longer carried out by the state. At the same time, new businesses became powerful partners for the United States.[30]

The end of the Cold War brought the conflict in El Salvador to an end without a clear victory for either side. The ARENA government[31] remained in power. Although the United States managed to prevent a Marxist revolution, the FMLN was undefeated and was allowed to participate in the elections. The presence of the army was still visible, but the country was largely demilitarised. The civilian population paid the greatest cost for the internationalisation of the civil war: 75,000 people died, a quarter of the population were made refugees and the bulk of the countryside was destroyed. The transition from war to peace failed to bring an end to sporadic violence, which has become endemic. This was the most lethal legacy of the Cold War years. During the civil war an average of 6,250 people a year were killed, in 1995 there were 8,500 'peacetime murders'. Although these assassinations seem unrelated to the Cold War politics of El Salvador, they are 'the expression of a violent political economy'.[32]

STATE-SPONSORED TERRORISM

Unlike the Americans, who became involved on the battlefield in Indochina, the Soviets were reluctant to commit troops in support of anti-colonial warriors, armed organisations and Latin American Marxists groups – a strategy abandoned in 1979 with the invasion of Afghanistan. Financial aid from the USSR predominantly took the form of arms supplies and training. Even in the aftermath of the Second World War, when the Kremlin was trying to lure countries like Greece into the Eastern Bloc, Moscow maintained its detachment. From November 1949 to the summer of 1950, Greek communists received a steady flow of weapons but no direct military support. Czechoslovak arms reached Albania where Greek communists collected them. Not all shipments were intended for the Greeks. A considerable number went further south, to Palestine, Egypt and Kenya, via Djibouti. Ethiopia, an old Soviet customer and partner in a regular arms trade agreement, became the port of entry for the supply of arms to the Mau Mau rebels fighting British rule in Kenya. In the aftermath of the Second World War, the Middle East also became a regular beneficiary of Soviet arms shipments. Well before the formation of the state of Israel, the Kremlin, determined to eradicate British colonial power in the region, offered its support to both the Palestinian Arabs and the Jews against the British. Czechoslovak weapons were shipped to both the Jewish Agency and the Palestinians.[33]

Overall, the Soviets lacked a well-defined strategy. They provided weapons and formative training, sometimes even charging for it, to any warrior fighting or willing to fight the West. This seems to have been their sole criterion for granting assistance. Indeed, with the exception of Cuba, Soviet-sponsored revolutions failed to produce a single worthwhile ally; Egypt, Ethiopia, Mozambique and Zimbabwe all proved to be unreliable. Others, such as Angola under Dos Santos, were far too independent.[34]

However, the two superpowers were not the only states engaged in sponsoring armed organisations. By its nature, state-sponsored terrorism is a means available to anyone able to fund it. After the first oil shock and subsequent recycling of petro-dollars,[35] Arab leaders had to manage huge export revenues almost overnight. With overflowing current accounts, many indulged in the sponsorship of armed groups. Muammar Gaddafi was one such leader. Having come to power through a revolution in 1969, he felt compelled to promote anti-imperialist movements across the world. In the 1970s, he began channelling part of Libya's energy surplus towards what he regarded as revolutionary armed groups. From the PLO to the IRA, from the Angolan Liberation Movement to the ANC in South Africa and the KANAK of New Caledonia, international armed organisations were showered with Libyan oil revenues. As Libya's oil surplus increased, reaching $22 billion in the 1980s, Gaddafi became increasingly generous. He even set up a kind of bonus system for particularly risky and prestigious operations. For example, members of Black September who participated in the terror action at the 1972 Munich Olympics were given bonuses ranging from $1 million to $5 million.[36] International hitman Carlos the Jackal was given a $2 million bonus after kidnapping OPEC oil ministers in Vienna in December 1975. Hans-Joachim Klein, one of the men in Carlos's commando unit, received compensation of $100,000 for being shot in the stomach during the kidnapping.[37] The Libyan leader's generosity earned him the nickname 'godfather of terrorism'.

In 1973, Gaddafi took advantage of the civil war in Chad to further his dreams of expansion. Offering his support to the military leader Goukuni Oueddei against dictator Hissene Habre, Gaddafi occupied the Aouzou strip in the north of Chad, a region rich in manganese and uranium. He saw Aouzou, which borders the southern tip of Libya, as a natural bridge to Central Africa. His long-term plan was to establish a Saharan Republic, to include Tunisia, Mauritania, Algeria, Niger, Chad and Western Sahara, all under Libyan leadership. Not surprisingly, his actions provoked immediate retaliation from the French, who feared a destabilising effect in the region. President Mitterrand sent 3,500 soldiers to back Hissene Habre, who succeeded in crushing Oueddei. The latter took refuge in Libya, where he acted as a head of state in exile. The war dragged on for years and cost Libya dearly. In 1985, when Libyan annual oil revenues declined to $8.5 billion, the war became cause for great resentment among the population. Eventually, unable to sustain the campaign financially, Gaddafi withdrew from Aouzou.

THE SAFARI CLUB

In the early 1980s, Muhammad Hasseinine Haykal, an Egyptian author, stumbled upon a well-kept secret. While researching the imperial archives in Teheran he discovered the original copy of an agreement signed on 1 September 1976 by the heads of counter-espionage agencies of several countries.[38] With increasing excitement, Haykal read some of the signatures, which included Count Alexandre de Marenches, head of French counter-espionage, and Kamal Adham, head of the Saudi intelligence agency. The agreement marked the birth of a secret Cold War organisation whose task was to carry out anti-communist operations in Africa and in the Third World on behalf of the West. Haykal named it the 'Safari Club', the headquarters of which were in Cairo, in a building donated by Egyptian President Anwar al-Sadat. France provided the sophisticated technical equipment and some of the personnel.

The Safari Club is a perfect example of how Counter-Insurgency Doctrine was adapted to a new international political landscape. Humiliation in Vietnam and the anti-war movement at home had forced the Americans to reassess their exposure in unconventional warfare. To shield the US from criticism at home and abroad, indirect state-sponsored support for anti-communist forces, i.e. monetary and military aid via a third party, was now considered a more feasible option than direct involvement. Consequently, Henry Kissinger, Secretary of State under Richard Nixon, promoted the idea of using friendly parties to carry out vital operations to contain the spread of Marxist movements. A list of friendly states was compiled, including France, Morocco, Egypt, Saudi Arabia and Persia. An invitation was also extended to Algeria, but the self-declared Islamic socialist regime of Boumedienne declined to participate.

One of the Safari Club's first operations was to rescue Siad Barre, the Somali dictator, then at war with Ethiopia over control of the Ogaden territory. At the eleventh hour, the Soviets, who had been sustaining Barre's regime for some time, switched their support to the Ethiopian government. Barre turned to the Safari Club for help. Members agreed that Egypt should sell him some of its stock of Soviet-made arms.

Accordingly, $75 million of old Soviet weapons, obtained from Czechoslovakia during Nasser's rule, were promptly shipped to the Somali army. The bill was footed by Saudi Arabia, whose greatest problem at the time was an overflowing current account. Confronted with such generosity, Barre severed all remaining ties with Moscow and placed his country and himself under the protection of the Safari Club and, indirectly, the US.

However, he soon discovered that, in the changing climate of the Cold War, America's support was as volatile as the Soviet Union's. In 1977, US Secretary of State Cyrus Vance showed reluctance to commit additional financial help to Somalia's dictator in his war with Ethiopia. Under mounting pressure from Barre, the Shah of Iran, Reza Pahlavi, stepped in and sent him German mortars (purchased from Turkey) and anti-tank weapons. Ironically, when the Somali troops discovered that the anti-tank weapons bore an Israeli stamp of manufacture, they refused to use them. Soon after, in return for the Soviet Union's guarantee not to get involved in the transition from white to black rule in Rhodesia, the US agreed to stop supporting Somalia in the Ogaden territorial dispute. The Safari Club followed suit and abandoned Barre – another pawn sacrificed on the Cold War chessboard.[39]

Only on rare occasions did the Soviets get involved in direct support of Third World insurgencies. Cuba was one of these. In 1959 Fidel Castro came to power, thanks largely to Soviet funding. However, in a gesture of accommodation from a 'new neighbour', Castro offered to allow the US to continue conducting business in Cuba, provided the Americans agreed to comply with new local legislation. Hoping to cripple the economy and put an end to the communist regime, the US government granted economic aid, but under the most rigid conditions. Castro immediately turned to the USSR, which set up a heavily subsidised oil-for-sugar deal.[40] In a few years, the steady flow of money brought economic stability to Cuba and strengthened the revolution. Castro also enjoyed a generous

direct line of credit from Moscow, money supposedly offset
by trade transactions. However, as all commercial exchanges
within the Soviet bloc were cleared in convertible roubles, a
currency that existed only for accounting purposes,[41] it was
easy to inflate or deflate the value of the loans or even to
wipe them off the books.

CUBA, THE SOVIET REPRESENTATIVE IN LATIN AMERICA

Direct Soviet financial aid to Cuba was motivated by the island's
strategic role in Cold War politics. Havana was Moscow's *de facto*
representative in Latin America, with the task of nurturing Marxist
movements in the region. In the 1980s, the Soviet Union was
funnelling an estimated $4 billion a year through the Caribbean
island, the bulk of which was used for training guerrilla groups.[42]
The military base of Guanabo, in the northern coast of Cuba,
became one of the most popular communist training camps.
Trainees arrived from Nicaragua, El Salvador, Colombia, the
Middle East, Angola and many other countries. Cuba's main role,
however, was not to produce guerrilla fighters, but to unite the
various groups under a common ideological umbrella and to
help them coordinate their strategies. At Guanabo, ideology played
a key role. Unlike the American-trained Vietnamese death squads,
communist guerrilla fighters spent a great deal of time attending
political lectures and, apparently, not enough training in the field.
Often the result was poor military performance. On 6 June 1982,
during 'Operation Peace for Galilee',[43] Israeli soldiers reported
that the Palestinians showed limited tactical skills and a scant
knowledge of their weaponry and equipment. They did not fight
as an army, remarked the Israelis, but as a group of individuals,
using tanks as artillery equipment instead of as highly mobile
forces.[44] Soviet-trained fighters in the Rhodesian war displayed
a similar lack of tactical knowledge.[45]

Behind an ideological mask, Moscow and Havana treated armed insurgency as a commercial enterprise. Contrary to popular belief, the Soviet Union did not hesitate to charge armed organisations for its services. The PLO, for example, was often asked to pay in hard currency for arms and training.[46] Other sponsors, such as Saudi Arabia and Libya, provided the funds. Cuba had a similarly mercenary approach. Castro sent thousands of Cuban troops, travelling as 'construction workers', to help communist armed groups from Angola to Nicaragua, Mali to Grenada. For this he charged a fixed monthly rate.[47]

COVERT SPONSORSHIP: THE CONTRAS AFFAIR

By the end of the 1970s, it was apparent that direct financial support for foreign armed groups had become the least popular means of exercising power at the periphery of the superpowers' spheres of influence. Western democracies required strong backing from the population in order to grant aid. In the United States, for example, Congressional approval was required for all financial aid to foreign countries. Thus, in the early 1980s, President Reagan had to embark on a campaign to convince Congress of the need to support the Contras in Nicaragua. The Contras' struggle to overthrow the Sandinista regime was portrayed as a 'war of liberation', a patriotic stand to halt the spread of Marxist governments in Central America. In reality, the Contras were an armed organisation created by the US to fight its own war by proxy in Central America.

In his book, *In Search of Enemies*, John Stockwell, the highest-ranking CIA official ever to leave the agency and go public, describes the birth of the Contras as follows:

To destabilise Nicaragua, we began funding this force of Somosa's ex-national guardsmen, calling them the Contras (the counter-revolutionaries). We created this force; it did not exist until we allocated money. We've armed them, put uniforms on their backs, boots on their feet, gave them camps in Honduras to live in, medical supplies, doctors, training, leadership and direction as we sent them in to destabilise Nicaragua. Under our direction they have systematically been blowing up granaries, saw mills, bridges, government offices, schools, health centers. They ambush trucks so the produce can't get to market. They raid farms and villages. The farmer has to carry a gun while he tries to plough, if he can plough at all.[48]

In 1984 the Reagan administration managed to raise a $24 million aid package to arm 2,000 men.[49] Although this figure was increased every year thereafter until the Iran–Contra scandal erupted,[50] it was too little to sustain the increasing costs of the US war by proxy in Nicaragua. Other forms of financing were required to bridge the widening gap between funding and expenditure. Thus, in parallel with the official pro-Contra campaign, the Reagan–Bush administration set up a spectacular covert operation to raise money to undermine the Sandinista government. A web of thousands of people and hundreds of companies and foundations contributed to the plan. In the end American taxpayers were defrauded of billions of dollars, money used to finance not only the Contras, but also their American sponsors.[51]

According to Al Martin, a retired US Navy lieutenant commander who was part of the Contras affair,[52] in July 1984, a secret memorandum written by Colonel Oliver North and Donald Gregg, then the vice-president's national security adviser, set a target of $1 billion a month to supply the Contras. This target was to be achieved via illegal financial operations inside the US.[53] North initiated several schemes: fraudulent insurance transactions, illegal bank loans, fake security sales, insurance fraud, money laundering, etc. Five thousand people, an army of right-wing supporters, became involved in raising money for the 'Cause', as North defined it. At the top of the pyramid were political organisations and foundations, primarily used for their tax-exempt status. For example, donor contributions of $10,000 to the American Eagle Foundation, set up by North, could be written off for tax purposes.[54] To encourage donations, contributors received a card bearing the number of a direct line to the White House where a North employee was always available 'for help'. This 'soft' money was then laundered from the foundation's books and channelled to the Contras.

The base of the pyramid consisted of subcontractors, former CIA agents, military staff, politicians' assistants, and others. These people operated in several fields – oil and gas, gold bullion or gold mining, real estate, stock brokerage, etc. – to generate money illegally. Ultimately, most of these operations were aimed at defrauding American banks where officers sympathised with the 'Cause'. Insurance companies were also defrauded. In his book *The Conspirators*, Al Martin reveals that in 1984 Major General John K. Singlaub set up the World Anti-Communist League to raise money to support Republicans and anti-communists.[55] People donated small planes in return for tax concessions. Certain types of aircraft were passed on to a subsidiary of the League. These planes were then sold to small private airlines such as DeVoe Airlines, Rich Aviation, Southern Air Transport and Polar Avions because of their suitability for smuggling narcotics out of South America. All other planes were hidden in Joplin, Missouri, and reported stolen. The insurance companies paid the premium: a $100,000 aircraft, for example, would fetch $300,000. Some of the money went to the League as donations, while the rest found its way back to the owners.

By the end of 1985 North's accomplices were almost reaching the $1 billion a month target. Some of this money ended up in the pockets of Republican politicians; part headed south to pay for the Contras' fighters and arms; and a considerable amount went to finance direct American involvement in unconventional warfare in Central America. This happened in 1985 when North mined Cordoba Harbour, the most important port in eastern Nicaragua and the port of entry for Soviet ships carrying supplies for the Sandinistas. The operation required the use of Titan Mark 4 Sea Mines, which were controlled by satellite communication. Since the mines could not be bought from the US Navy without clearance from the National Security Council, an alternative purchase route had to be found. Defcon Armaments Ltd. of Lisbon bought the mines directly from US inventories. In turn, the Portuguese company sold them to Stanford Technologies Overseas, a company controlled by Major General Richard Secord, one of North's men.[56] Through Secord the mines reached the Contras.

The collapse of the Soviet Union may have ended the Cold War, but it did not terminate state-sponsored terror. In the early 1990s, the US supplied Turkey with 80 per cent of the arms used to crush the Kurdish insurgency, which resulted in the death of tens of thousands of people, 2–3 million refugees and the destruction of about 3,500 villages.[57] It was soon apparent that outside the framework of the Cold War the clarity of Counter-Insurgency Doctrine had blurred, leaving state-sponsored terrorism without an ideological underpinning. Following the Gulf War, as the tragedy of the Kurds unfolded, the story of the exodus of hundreds of thousands of civilians was broadcast live in Western countries. People were confused about the identity of aggressors and victims alike. The Turks and the Kurds accused each other of being terrorists, of conducting a deliberate campaign of terror. Without an enemy at its gates, Western public opinion became uneasy at the slaughter of civilians. The melting of the Cold War had left the landscape of US foreign policy, along with that of its allies, scarred with the evidence of their involvement in foreign civil wars.

THE COMMERCIAL WAR ECONOMY OF SENDERO LUMINOSO

The most devastating consequence of superpower intervention in the affairs of other nations has been the destabilisation of entire regions and the collapse of their economies. The legacy of state-sponsored terrorism in Latin America was the proliferation of armed groups and the subsequent birth of terror-run microeconomies. In the 1980s, parts of El Salvador, Nicaragua, Honduras, Colombia and Peru fell under the military control of guerrilla groups. This happened to the people living in the Upper Huallaga valley in Peru. The valley, also known as Selva Alta, ranges from an altitude of 1,500 to 6,000 feet on the eastern slopes of the north-east Andes. The region was restructured under the agrarian reforms of the late 1960s, but this turned out to be a great failure. Due to the harsh climate, none of the crops did well and the local population was soon on the brink of starvation. Only one marketable plant appeared to be sufficiently resilient to thrive at such an altitude: *Erythroxylum Coca*. Local people have chewed its leaves for centuries to gain energy and suppress hunger. Therefore, when the Colombian drug traffickers came to the valley to buy coca, the impoverished farmers welcomed their arrival. Almost overnight, subsistence farmers became commercial growers, catering for more than their own needs, and almost as quickly they fell victim to the exploitation of the powerful Medellin cartel.

In 1978, under mounting US pressure, the government of Francisco Morales Bermudez attempted to eradicate coca production. The programme was extremely unpopular and never took off. Despite military intervention, coca planting in Selva Alta increased to supply the booming drug trade. In 1980, militants from the Sendero Luminoso armed group (*Senderistas*) moved to the Upper Huallaga valley and began living with the locals. They soon discovered that the population was being harassed by both the drug traffickers and the police. So the

Senderistas launched a two-pronged campaign: to undermine government policies – an easy task among a population constantly threatened by Lima – and to defend growers from the Colombian cartel.

In the same year, the Peruvian government introduced another project for coca eradication in the Upper Huallaga valley. The residents were apprehensive about the new agrarian programme which would deprive them of their only viable means of survival. Capitalising on these fears, the *Senderistas* visited villages and small towns to sympathise with the people and to denounce the United States as the initiator of the reforms. They explained that cocaine was not a threat to Peru, but to the US. However, Americans did not want to start a war against their own drug dealers and stop the monetary flow generated by the laundering of drug money. Therefore, they were putting pressure on the Peruvian government to curb coca production. Neither Washington nor Lima, stressed the *Senderistas*, cared that the entire valley was economically dependent on the coca crop. The Sendero Luminoso offered protection against the military, who were about to enforce the new programme, and against the cocaine syndicate, which had been exploiting the growers. The people rallied round the *Senderistas* with enthusiasm. 'They are professional agitators,' Hector John Caro, Peruvian Army General and former chief of the secret police, said dismissively 'they are always prepared to act.'[58] Under Sendero Luminoso's supervision the growers were organised into unions, a move which allowed them to negotiate better prices.

Employing terror tactics, Sendero Luminoso began taking military control of the entire valley. A common ploy was to move into a town accompanied by at least 30 armed men, gather the inhabitants together, lecture them and proceed with interrogations to find out who was working for the local author-ities or gangs. These individuals were then publicly executed and local authority was replaced by general assemblies composed of the *Senderistas*. Once an area was 'liberated', the *Senderistas* moved on to the next town. By 1985, the group had established a strong military presence throughout the entire region. Bridges were blown up to prevent regular troops entering the valley and road blocks were established to search every vehicle approaching along the Marginal Highway, the sole communication link to the outside world. Selva Alta soon became a 'no-go' area for police and government troops.

Meanwhile, the growers were content that the valley was under the control of the *Senderistas* because they felt protected from the drug traffickers and criminal gangs as well as from the government's agrarian reforms. Interestingly, the cocaine producers and drug traffickers also welcomed the change because discipline among growers boosted production. By 1988, 211,000 hectares of the valley were covered with coca plants. In addition, under Sendero Luminoso's rule, shipment procedures were streamlined. It was Sendero Luminoso's responsibility to protect airstrips scattered through the valley, a task it continued to carry out in 2002 without interference. As a result, shipping by small aeroplane became not only easier, but more efficient.

Sendero's activities were not limited to the control of coca production. In some areas they also took over other businesses, for example, foreign exchange. In Xiòn, local banks stopped changing dollars into Peruvian intis for the intermediaries of the Medellin Cartel. Instead, Sendero Luminoso, for a small commission, provided the Colombians with domestic currency to pay growers. Naturally, bankers were extremely unhappy about this arrangement, but there was nothing they could do because Sendero Luminoso was the *de facto* governing authority in the valley. Control of foreign exchange allowed the *Senderistas* access to a considerable amount of hard cash in a country starved of foreign exchange. Part of the money was used to maintain Sendero's authority in Selva Alta and other enclaves; part was allocated to buy weapons to promote the group's Maoist vision for Peru.

Sendero Luminoso was – before the Colombian FARC – by far the best-armed group in Latin America. Between February and September 1989, for example, it successfully undermined the government's efforts to eradicate drug trafficking in the valley. In retaliation for the use of the herbicide 'Spike', which destroyed coca plantations, members of Sendero Luminoso assaulted a military garrison in the town of Uchiza and shot dead the 50 soldiers who had surrendered after being outnumbered by the *Senderistas*. That same year the government declared the Upper Huallaga valley a military emergency zone.[59]

In the Upper Huallaga valley, the Sendero Luminoso succeeded in creating a terror-run economy, which formed the core of a micro-state. As will be described in chapter 5, Selva Alta is one of the many 'state-shells', *de facto* state entities created around a war economy generated by the violent activities of armed groups. Sendero Luminoso's model is that of a 'commercial war economy', based on the commercialisation of local resources, such as coca plantations, and trafficking in illegal products, such as narcotics. In this model

armed groups create economic sanctuaries by gaining military control of economically profitable areas [such as Selva Alta] and develop commercial networks with third parties, i.e. the Colombian drug cartels; they even work in collusion with rival groups. The impact can be positive by contributing to . . . the protection of illegal sectors, [for example coca production].[60]

Some of these economies can generate vast amounts of income, as is the case in the Upper Huallaga valley. In the late 1980s, total revenues for Peruvian coca leaves and coca paste yielded an estimated $28 billion from the United States alone. Of this, the share of Peruvian paste producers and local traffickers was $7.48 billion, equivalent to 20 per cent of Peruvian GNP, which in 1990 was $35 billion. Growers received $240 million for cultivating coca. Sendero Luminoso's share of this business in

Selva Alta was estimated at $30 million,[61] sufficient to purchase arms and expand its protection racket and extortion across Peru. The benefits of the commercial war economy were also apparent among the population. The 66,000 families living in the Upper Huallaga valley enjoyed annual average earnings of $3,639, more than three times the $1,000 per capita average income in the rest of Peru.

The international ramifications of terror-run economies, such as that in the Upper Huallaga valley, are staggering. On a global scale, billions of dollars generated by narcotics are laundered in the United States; between 30 and 40 per cent enter the US economy,[62] while the rest is pumped into the international illegal economy and, as will be explained later, used to fuel the New Economy of Terror.

3. The Privatisation of Terror

'No, I am not a professional killer. It isn't easy to shoot somebody in the eye when he's looking at you, especially if you've killed four people in less than ten seconds as I did . . .'

Carlos the Jackal

In the summer of 1981, while I was a Fulbright student in the US, a friend invited me to spend a few days at Cape Cod as a family guest. I was immediately struck by how strict the parents, wealthy Irish Catholics from Boston, were towards their children, all in their early to mid-twenties. The three daughters were forbidden to wear bikinis on the beach and the boys could not smoke in the presence of the parents. One evening, after dinner, as we sat on the porch looking at the sunset, the mother asked about my views on abortion. I told her that being able to choose when to have a child was a great achievement for women. Clearly disappointed, she shook her head and replied: 'It is a terrible crime, an unforgivable sin.' The next morning, on the beach, I noticed three pale young men cruising the shore and stopping to chat with almost everybody. As they approached our group my friend's parents welcomed them and invited them in for lunch. When I enquired about them, my friend explained that they were from Ireland and were collecting money for the IRA. I must have shown my surprise because he repeated the answer twice. 'Your parents,' I remember telling him, 'they are so Catholic, so strict, and yet they have lunch with the IRA!' 'We are Irish,' he replied softly, 'they are our people.'

Traditionally, Irish-Americans have represented a generous source of income for the IRA. It was the American branch of the Fenian Brotherhood (founded in 1858 in New York) that financed the Irish insurrection of the late nineteenth century. In the 1960s and 1970s, money flowed across the Atlantic thanks to the work of three IRA veterans, Jack McCarthy, John McGowan and Michael Flannery. In the 1960s they set up Irish Northern Aid, better known as Noraid. The headquarters was in the Bronx, at 273 East 194th Street.[1] Its voice was the newspaper *The Irish People*, distributed across the United States. The success of the venture was almost immediate: Noraid latched on to the existing network of Irish-American organisations – various union branches of the police and dock workers on the East Coast, for example – reaching a wide range of people. By the late 1970s, it had 5,000 members and 30,000 followers.[2] Money came in from all over the US and was collected in many ways: from the sale of publications, in Irish-American bars like O'Neil's in Chicago and Wednesday's in New York, at raffles, during dances and parades, as well as along the sunny shores of Cape Cod. A large proportion of funds came from working-class Irish-Americans. Several unions even paid a fixed weekly sum into Noraid accounts. Donations were also collected by well-known Irish public figures touring the country. In 1969, Bernadette Devlin raised $650,000 while visiting the US for the Northern Ireland Civil Rights Association (NICRA).[3] Within a decade Noraid had achieved a budget of $7 million and was able to fund more than 50 per cent of the IRA's cash requirements.[4]

Noraid's mission was to secure political power as well as financial sponsorship, to be a lobby powerful enough to influence the US government in its handling of the relationship between Ireland and the UK. Like professional lobbyists, Noraid organised fundraising events, the most important being a New Year's Eve dinner held in several cities across America. In New York the venue was always the Waldorf Astoria. The events were attended by distinguished politicians and union members, paying as much as $400 a ticket. They raised an average of $20,000–30,000 and increased people's awareness of the Irish cause.

Initially, Noraid funds reached Ulster via the Northern Aid Committee, a Belfast-based organisation set up in 1969 after the Londonderry riots. When this organisation was taken over by An Cumann Cobrach (ACC), a modern version of the 1920s Prisoners' Dependants Fund, money began flowing to the ACC, which shared a Dublin office with Sinn Féin. The ACC then transferred the cash to the Green Cross in Belfast, officially a support organisation for the families of Republican prisoners, but in reality a financial vehicle for funding the IRA. Interestingly, the Green Cross had no address or phone number, did not publish accounts and was not registered as a charitable organisation with the tax authorities.[5] Although Noraid insisted that its Irish-American sponsors sent money to clothe and feed the homeless of Northern Ireland, the charitable work was a cover for the Provisional IRA. In 1982, during a court case against Noraid, the US Department of Justice stated that 'since its inception, Noraid has acted as the agent in [Ireland] of the provisional wing of the Irish Republican Army, its political arm Sinn Féin and their affiliates'.[6] A considerable percentage of the money raised by Noraid in the US went to purchase weapons and smuggle them to Ulster. In 1982, for example, the FBI unveiled an arms smuggling operation in New York City valued at $1 million.[7] Andrew Duggan, one of the two men who orchestrated it, was a member of Noraid.

Although direct financial aid from independent organisations such as Noraid has fewer strings attached than state sponsorship, armed groups are equally conditioned by it. The assassination of Lord Mountbatten in 1979 and the 1983 Christmas bombing of the Harrods department store in London drew the attention of the US public to the campaign of terror that the IRA was waging in England. This caused a distinct chill in the relationship between the IRA and Irish-Americans. Against this background, Noraid struggled to portray the British as invaders of Irish soil. In the eyes of many Irish-Americans, the IRA was no longer fighting foreign occupying forces; it was killing innocent civilians in England. Except in 1981, when Bobby Sands, Raymond McCreesh and a number of other members of the IRA went on hunger strike and died in the Maze Prison in protest against living conditions there and to underscore their status as political prisoners, Noraid's support declined. Irish-American politicians and organisations began keeping their distance, deserting its venues and parades. In 1983, the Irish government, the New York Roman Catholic Archdiocese and many Irish-American politicians even boycotted New York's St Patrick's Day parade. Suddenly Noraid faced a new reality: the romantic vision of Irish freedom fighters had been irredeemably sullied by the IRA's acts of terror in England. As an Irish-American friend living in London commented to me in 1984, if they can bomb Harrods at Christmas, no one is safe. Political violence had come dangerously close to home.

The shift in sentiment among Irish-Americans dried up Noraid accounts and showed the limits of foreign sponsorship. These limitations were particularly poignant in the context of the IRA's new strategy, outlined by Gerry Adams in 1977. In what became known as 'the ballot and the bullet programme', the IRA was to expand and develop a legitimate political base without abandoning its fierce campaign of violence. To secure funds to support Adams's strategy, the IRA relied more and more on illegal operations such as contraband, tax avoidance and fraud. The 270-mile border between the Republic of Ireland and Ulster offered ideal terrain for smuggling. IRA supporters in the Irish Republic took advantage of Common Market export subsidies for Irish agricultural products to the UK – of which Northern Ireland is a part – to raise money. Pigs were exported from the Republic to IRA supporters in Northern

Ireland to collect the subsidy (equivalent to £8 per pig) and
smuggled back to the Republic. This operation was repeated
again and again with the same animals, producing a considerable amount of cash and some very tired pigs. According to
British intelligence, in 1985 Thomas Murphy, a member of the
IRA border unit ASU and owner of a farm ideally positioned
on the border of the two countries, deposited as much as £8,000
a week in IRA coffers, earned through the pig-smuggling business. Annually, Murphy alone managed to raise as much as $2
million. When Brussels removed the subsidy on animals, the
IRA switched to other products, such as grain, which
commanded a £12 per ton subsidy. Although it is difficult to
calculate the total amount generated by the subsidy fraud, an
indication is provided by the Court of Auditors of the European
Commission, which in 1985 set the figure in terms of losses
for the Common Market at £450 million.[8]

Another profitable illegal business was the exploitation of
different tax rates, specifically Value Added Tax (VAT), between
the Republic and Northern Ireland. VAT on luxury goods such
as colour televisions was 35 per cent in the south but 15 per
cent in the north. Goods were smuggled from the north to
the south and sold well below market prices. Overall, contraband cost the Dublin government $100 million in lost revenue
each year.[9]

While Gerry Adams organised the IRA's transition into
mainstream politics, large tranches of IRA revenue were
diverted to finance Sinn Féin's political campaigns. According
to the British government, Adams's political dreams cost three
times as much as it had cost to run the IRA as an armed organisation.[10] During the 1983 political campaign in which Adams
was elected, for example, the cost of security alone was estimated
at £1.30 per vote, a total of £137,000,[11] which was largely funded
by the IRA's criminal profits. In 1985 the Irish government
uncovered an illegal transfer of $2 million to the IRA, part of
which was earmarked to finance the council election campaign.

The money had been extorted from Associated British Foods to dissuade the IRA from carrying out violent acts such as kidnapping and bombings in the Irish Republic. Tracking the money trail, Irish investigators and US Customs were able to reconstruct the movement of the funds and unveil the complexity of the financial operation. From Switzerland, the money was deposited in a New York account at the Bank of Ireland. Alan Clancy, a New York bar owner and member of Noraid, travelling on a false passport, carried the cash to Ireland, depositing it at the bank's branch in Navan. When he later tried to withdraw the funds, however, he was arrested.[12]

Using covert operations to finance legitimate political campaigns is a common recourse for armed organisations attempting to make the transition into mainstream politics. Unfortunately, the partnership with crime ends up permeating the ethics of these groups, even after the transition is complete. Sinn Féin and Adams have a similar approach to funding. In 2001 alone, the IRA raised £7 million through criminal activities. Tobacco smuggling from Eastern Europe was the largest source of income. Lorries loaded with cigarettes travelled to England and the Irish Republic from Eastern Europe. Evading duties, the IRA resold them, netting profits of up to £400,000 per lorry.[13] In mid-2002, while the IRA was considering disarmament within the framework of the peace process, three of its members were arrested in Colombia for training the FARC (Fuerzas Armadas Revolucionarias de Colombia), the largest Colombian armed group, in the use of explosive devices. One of them, Martin McCauley, was the director of elections for Sinn Féin. Their defence lawyer, Ernesto Amezquita, said that they had visited the area under control of the FARC as 'eco-tourists'. The head of the FARC, Manuel 'Sureshot' Marulanda, backed the explanation, describing the armed group's stronghold as a sort of tourist 'ecological attraction' for VIPs. 'Various parties and political movements from Europe and the United States have come to visit us,' he asserted. 'We have even had the president of the New York Stock Exchange and the Queen of Jordan . . . The Irishmen were here to discuss international relations.'[14] Gerry Adams, on the other hand, refused even to admit any links between the three men and Sinn Féin, and the three men were later acquitted of these charges. However, it is not unreasonable to assume that the money generated by them was meant to finance Sinn Féin and Adams's political campaigns.[15]

For many armed groups, partnership in crime was the easiest alternative to state-sponsored terrorism, the first step in breaking away from the conditioning and manipulation of foreign powers. In the mid-1970s, as political violence intensified and gained momentum, armed organisations began to disengage from the old structures of the Cold War. Having absorbed their sponsors' methodologies in covert and illegal operations to raise money, they found it easy to set up their own illegal businesses.

THE PRIVATISATION OF TERROR

On 23 July 1968, an El Al passenger plane en route to Tel Aviv from Rome was hijacked and diverted to Algiers. All the passengers were released except 12 Israeli men. The hijackers held them captive for 39 days while their demand – the exchange of the hostages for 15 Palestinians jailed in Israeli prisons – was processed. The El Al hijacking became a milestone in terror tactics and financing. For the first time Israeli nationals had been targeted outside Israel. Although al-Fatah and Arafat expressed public disapproval of the attack, insisting that it was not their policy to attack Israeli civilians, the operation was applauded across the Arab world. Its perpetrators, the Popular Front for the Liberation of Palestine, gained instant notoriety among Arab guerrillas and armed groups.

The El Al hijacking was the brainchild of Wadi Haddad, a Palestinian graduate in medicine from the American University of Beirut. Haddad founded the Movement of Arab Nationalists

(MAN) with some of his university friends, among them George Habash and Kuwaiti-born Ahmad al-Khatib. In 1968 Haddad and Habash transformed the MAN into the Popular Front for the Liberation of Palestine (PFLP). The two leaders disagreed with al-Fatah's strategy, which concentrated on striking strategic targets inside Israel such as water supplies, pipelines and railway tracks. Haddad and Habash wanted to widen the struggle. However, their immediate concern was to gain economic independence from Arab sponsors and to differentiate themselves from al-Fatah, the group in control of the PLO. The El Al hijacking achieved both these goals.

The attack was a runaway success and immediately became a prototype. Following the hijacking, several airlines willingly paid protection money to prevent further attacks. Suddenly, Haddad was receiving monthly payments amounting to about $1 million from a number of armed groups.[16] Protection money soon became a valuable source of revenue for the international armed community. The payment was regarded as a sort of insurance premium by airlines against hijacking. Lufthansa, for example, joined the scheme in 1972 after one of its planes was hijacked in Aden by the PFLP, which had cornered the market in this form of extortion. The yearly cost of the insurance ranged from $5 million to $10 million. The money was divided among various PLO members (who by then had dropped their opposition to hijacking), including the PFLP.[17]

The business of extorting protection money soon extended to the oil industry. In 1972, after Black September attacked a number of oil facilities in Rotterdam, many major oil companies joined the 'insurance scheme'. ARAMCO, the Arabian-American Oil Company, followed suit after a group of its employees was attacked at Rome airport. OPEC was not immune either. In December 1975, Illich Ramirez Sanchez (better known as Carlos the Jackal) and a commando unit of the PFLP seized the OPEC headquarters in Vienna. According to the CIA, after the attack, OPEC paid Haddad and the groups that had backed the operation $100 million to safeguard OPEC interests. In addition, it placed $120 million in the PLO Chairman's Secret Fund.[18]

At times, the desire to gain independence from foreign interference was strong enough to justify very unlikely partnerships among armed groups, like the one between the PLO and the Christian Phalange in Lebanon. At the beginning of January 1976, Bashir Gemayal, leader of the Israeli-backed Christian militia, and Abu Hassan Salameh, head of security for al-Fatah, struck an extraordinary alliance. After fighting with each other savagely for years, they called a 48-hour truce to rob the British Bank of the Middle East in downtown Beirut.

Early in the morning of 20 January 1976, commandos of al-Fatah and the Christian Phalange sealed the business district of the city. The area, which housed most of the financial institutions active in the Middle East and several diplomatic residences, covered the area around Place de Martyrs and was controlled on the south by the Phalange and to the north by al-Fatah. On the morning of 20 January, bank employees, currency dealers, embassy staff and visitors approaching the square were stopped, told to go home and not to return for two days. By midday the entire area had been emptied and cordoned off. A team of PLO and Phalange militants entered the Catholic Capuchin church, adjacent to the British Bank of the Middle East, and negotiated with the monks to break through the wall of the church to reach the vault of the bank. To avoid damaging the church, no dynamite or explosives were used; picks and axes were employed instead. While the team went to work, PLO and Phalange members patrolled the area, exchanging jokes, smoking and eating together. Two days later, workers approaching their offices were once again sent back; the PLO and Christian Phalange were still inside the Capuchin church hammering their way through the wall. When they finally reached the vault they had to concede defeat, admitting to each other that they were unable to open it. 'We are fighters,' one of them protested, 'not robbers.' So a team of demolition experts from the Corsican Mafia were flown over to solve the problem. They succeeded in opening the vault using a massive amount of dynamite.

It took two days to loot the bank. Gold bullion, stock certificates, jewellery and bags of hard currency were removed and loaded into trucks. The robbery earned a small fortune[19] and entered the *Guinness Book of Records*.[20] The loot was split among the PLO, the Phalange and the Mafia. The Corsicans chartered a DC-3 and took home their cut: one-third in gold, jewellery and cash. The Phalange spent most of their money on arms, but the PLO invested theirs abroad.[21] Their share was loaded on to another chartered plane and flown with Arafat, Abu Iyad and Salameh[22] to Switzerland, where it was deposited in various Swiss bank accounts.

Generating money from criminal activities was relatively easy. Laundering and reinvesting it to produce a regular income, however, proved much more difficult. Although as early as the 1970s several armed organisations understood that their survival depended on a skilful handling of finances, only a few succeeded in establishing long-term legitimate investments. The PLO was one of these. In the months following the robbery of the British Bank of the Middle East, the PLO, acting as a financial operator on the secondary market, sold the stocks and bonds stolen from the bank's security boxes for 20–30 cents to the dollar. Many were repurchased by the owners, who feared disclosure of the extent of their wealth and its dubious origins. According to several sources, the profits were bigger than the robbery itself. Again, Arafat shipped the cash by chartered plane to Switzerland.[23]

ETA'S PREDATORY ECONOMY

Over the last 30 years, Arafat has been one of the most imaginative terror leaders in laundering and reinvesting money. His adviser is a well-known financier, Nabil Shaath, president of TEAM, a management consultancy firm based in Cairo. Before becoming Arafat's adviser, Shaath was a professor of corporate finance at the prestigious Wharton School of Business at the University of Pennsylvania.[24]

To manage their finances, successful armed groups had to develop sophisticated accountancy structures. In 1986, the discovery in a secret room below the Sokoa factory in Hendaya, France, of the financial headquarters of ETA (Euskadi Ta Askatasuna), a nationalist armed group fighting for the independence of the Basque region, brought to light the complex bookkeeping techniques used by the group to balance its budget.[25] Inflows and outflows were recorded in a fashion similar to the balance of payments of legitimate states, some in Spanish pesetas, the rest in French francs (85 per cent of ETA's budget is in Spain and the rest in France). Revenues were raised predominantly through kidnapping, extortion and armed robbery; the latter had netted only about 800 million pesetas in over a decade and was abandoned in the mid-1980s due also to the poor return for the high risk involved. Kidnapping, on the other hand, became an extremely lucrative business over the years. The 50 million pesetas generated in 1970 had jumped to 1.5 billion pesetas ($15 million) in 1997. In fact, the crime became so widespread that in 1984 the Spanish government passed legislation to prosecute people who acted as intermediaries and froze the bank accounts of victims and their families to prevent the withdrawal of funds to pay the ransom,[26] a strategy pioneered in Italy.

Extortion from businessmen and industrialists was also a sizeable source of income. Often it took the form of protection against acts of vandalism and violence. ETA members regarded it as a 'revolutionary tax' imposed on the wealth of the population. Nationalist arguments backed the levy: 'Considering that all people from the Basque region have the legal and moral responsibility to sustain the resistance against the oppressor [the

Spanish government], ETA forces the fulfilment of such responsibility [of paying] in the same fashion that governments of independent states impose the payment of a tax upon their citizens.'[27] According to the documentation found in the Sokoa factory, the total inflow generated by extortion between 1980 and 1986 was a staggering 1.2 billion pesetas ($12 million). Financial contributions from militants and sympathisers added to the income. The accounts found at Sokoa, for example, showed a 5 per cent tax levied on the salaries of Basque nationals working abroad, especially in France, which was collected through the Basque committee for refugees. No inflows from foreign countries were recorded. Aid from the Soviet Union, its East European allies and the PLO was limited to the supply of arms and training, and therefore difficult to quantify in terms of cash. ETA's strong links with the Spanish Communist Party served logistical and tactical purposes rather than as a source of income.[28] ETA predominantly supported itself. From 1978 to 1997, its average yearly inflow was above 400 million pesetas ($4 million).[29]

The consequences of ETA's self-financing activities in the Basque countries were disastrous for the local economy. The Basque population represented a small minority in Spain. In the early 1980s there were about 1.5 million Basques living in Spain and 200,000 in France, while the total population of Spain was 37 million. Francisco Franco's[30] policy of relocation had generated massive flows of immigrants from the poorest parts of Spain to the Basque region, tilting the region's ethnic balance. Immigrants were attracted by the industrial wealth of the region; steel mills, mines and shipyards were a magnet for anyone willing to work. In the 1960s, before the outbreak of terror, industry was booming in the area. The average income of the Basque region was at a par with that of the Benelux countries and personal income was the highest in Spain (in Bilbao it was about 40 per cent higher than in the rest of the country). This economic prosperity was shattered by the campaign of terror mounted by ETA to finance its armed struggle against Madrid. Paradoxically, ETA's nationalist dream depleted resources, impoverished the region and drove away wealthy patriots. Factories closed. Basque industrialists fled in fear of ETA's fundraising methods: kidnapping, beating, extortion, bank robberies, higher and higher revolutionary taxes. 'What's keeping me here?' a businessman asked author Claire Sterling during her research on ETA. 'My brother's wife and child were held at gunpoint until he cleared out his bank balance for ETA; now he is gone. My uncle got sick of paying through the nose month after month, so he is gone. I am sick of paying through the nose; and what's more, I have no intention of forcing my five kids to learn a false history in school or speak a dead language that does not even have a written alphabet. So you can assume that the next time you come, I will be gone.'[31]

This exodus of wealthy people forced ETA to look outside the region to finance its fight. In 1985, militants' monthly salaries were expressed in French francs, confirming that ETA had shifted its activities across the border. During the same year, 65 per cent of the expenditures were also recorded in French francs, indicating that more money had been spent in France. From 1985 onwards most of the yearly outflows of ETA were recorded in French francs. The change of currency is a strong indication that the organisation had to move to the French side of the Basque region to raise money.

As far as expenditures were concerned, cash availability was paramount in determining ETA salaries. Average yearly outflow in the 1980s and 1990s was 600,000 French francs ($120,000)[32] equivalent to only 10 per cent of ETA's total outflows.[33] On average, in the 1990s, ETA paid a salary of 1,200 French francs ($240) per married person plus 200 French francs ($40) per child, while young, single people received 700 French francs ($140). These wages were considerably lower than the average monthly salary in Spain (the average per capita GDP per month in Spain was 5,400 French francs, about $1,080). The group paid minimal subsistence salaries to its members, forcing them to rely on the help of sympathisers and supporters or on financial aid from their own families. Priority was given to strategic expenses: the purchase of arms and explosives and the establishment of safe hideouts.

Disbursements to militants abroad were also conditioned by cash flows. Payments were arranged in various ways. For instance, ETA paid its members in Nicaragua (who had been sent to help the Sandinistas) via Larreàtegui Cuadra, a Basque gang. Banknotes were hidden between the pages of magazines and sent by post. In Nicaragua, ETA salaries were $20 a month until 1989 rising to $100 after the payment of the ransom of Emiliano Revilla, a businessman kidnapped in 1988, which brought in an estimated 1,200–1,500 million pesetas ($12–15 million). Other outflows were represented by domestic political infrastructure, international aid to other armed organisations such as the Sandinistas (34 per cent) and operational expenditures (57 per cent), which included purchase of arms and explosives and financial support for members in prisons. The average yearly total expenditures of ETA from 1978 to 1997 ranged from 300 to 400 million pesetas ($3–4 million), a figure slightly lower than total revenues.[34]

The discovery of the accountancy structure of ETA unveiled the existence of a basic economy centred on terror, similar to a war economy. ETA's self-financing was based on a variation of the model of the 'predatory war economy', where 'armed groups relate to local population and economic resources through violence [and] predation . . . While efficient as a short-term survival scheme, this type of political economy results in the progressive exhaustion of resources and diminishing political support . . . This war economy has a dramatic impact on populations resulting in massive displacement, destitution and death.'[35]

As happens in wartime, exploitation of the legitimate economy was not only allowed, it was actively encouraged. Indeed, the mainstream economy represented the sole source of sustenance. Therefore, while the legitimate economy was depleted, there was no redistribution of wealth in the region. Money spent on arms and ammunition left the monetary circuit of the Basque region instead of creating new wealth. As a result, the population was impoverished. 'After terrorism became endemic to the region, fears of violence, extortion and kidnapping by ETA separatists were responsible, on average, for a 10 per cent drop in the area's per capita GDP.'[36] ETA's parasitic drain of resources could not last forever. Eventually the organisation had to move on to another region to generate income.

There is no denying that the economic and financial haemorrhage caused by terror economies can lead to the collapse of the legitimate economy. Nevertheless, the population may not experience the full impact of such an event. In certain circumstances the terror economy simply takes over the mainstream economy. When this occurs, the legitimate economy becomes progressively dependent on the terror economy. This happened in Lebanon during the civil war. In 1982, while Israeli troops were besieging Beirut, Arafat took refuge inside the vault of the Banque Nationale de Paris, one of the international banks that managed the PLO deposits. From there he transferred all the PLO accounts out of Lebanon to other Arab banks. The amount of cash withdrawn was so great that it accelerated the collapse of the Lebanese pound.[37] By 1984, when the PLO and the Palestinians were forced out of Lebanon, the Lebanese pound had suffered a massive devaluation reaching 270 to $1.

THE BIRTH OF NARCO-TERRORISM

At dawn on 10 March 1984, Colombian police helicopters appeared in the sky near the river Yari, about 700 miles south of Bogota. They landed on the riverbank and opened their bellies. A commando unit of elite anti-terrorist agents leapt out, quickly moving to attack a complex of buildings which was believed to be a hideout for local drug barons. As they advanced towards the target, the men were ambushed by heavy gunfire from the jungle surrounding the clearing. It took them two hours to reach the compound and take control. Inside, they found 13.8 tons of cocaine with a street value of about $1.2 billion.[38]

The operation was successful in many respects. It destroyed an important drug base in the jungle, it inflicted huge financial losses on the drug barons and, more importantly, unveiled a dangerous liaison between the FARC and the buoyant Colombian drug business. Investigators soon learned that the gunfire directed against the police at Yari had come from a commando unit of 100 FARC men. Documents found inside the buildings confirmed that the FARC was providing drug barons with armed protection.

The alliance of terrorism and drugs is a recent and deadly phenomenon. Until 1980, the FARC and M19 (Movimiento 19 Abril) were struggling to survive on income from armed robbery and the kidnapping of local businessmen. The number of their followers had dropped to 200, a handful of hard-core militants; recruitment was at a standstill because there was no cash for salaries, and the leaders of the two organisations feared their demise. However, they soon learned that in the vast jungle of Colombia there was an immense source of wealth waiting to be tapped. In 1981, Colombia produced 2,500 metric tons of coca leaf;[39] by 1986 this figure, fuelled by North America's insatiable appetite for drugs, had risen to a staggering 13,000 metric tons.[40] In the mid-1980s, the drug economy contributed $5 billion a year in cash to the Colombian balance of payments.[41] Revenues from cocaine exports well exceeded revenues from coffee and cut flowers, the country's other two largest foreign exchange earners. The bulk of the drugs business was under the control of a handful of men running powerful cartels. In 1981 the FARC and M19 struck a deal with the Colombian drug mafia: they would provide armed protection against the army in exchange for a share in the coca profits.

The FARC levied a 10 per cent protection tax on all coca growers in areas under its control, which alone netted a monthly income of $3.3 million.[42] By 1984, the FARC and M19 earned $150 million a year from the business of protecting drug smugglers and traffickers. A large percentage of the profits was spent on recruitment, so that by 1988 both groups commanded a combined militia of 10,000 people, large enough to be feared by members of the government.[43] Another percentage was used to bribe top politicians to ensure that entire areas of Colombia came under rebel control, regions into which the regular Colombian army could no longer venture. In the grip of the FARC and M19, the economy of these territories was quickly reduced to drug production and its armed defence. Coca was the single export and source of foreign exchange or income. Business became either ancillary to it or an indirect beneficiary of its profits.

As the alliance between the drug barons, FARC and M19 was consolidated, the narco-terror business expanded and partnership was extended to fourth parties. A deal was struck with the Cuban authorities whereby Colombian vessels could use Cuban ports as a stopover for the shipment of drugs to the US. In exchange, Cuba received as much as $500,000 in cash for each vessel and the right to sell the Colombians arms for the FARC and M19.[44] The dynamics of the operation were explained by David Perez, an American drug dealer, at his trial in Miami in 1983. The Colombian cargo left Colombia bearing its own flag. When it entered international waters, however, it hoisted Cuban colours and radioed Cuba with an estimated time of arrival. Once in Cuban waters, several small boats sailed to the ship. The drugs were loaded on to these boats and smuggled to Florida. Often this procedure resulted in barter deals whereby drugs were exchanged for arms. Profits for the Cubans varied from cargo to cargo, depending on the type of drugs; for example a $10 per pound tax was levied on each cargo of marijuana. For a vessel of methaqualone (known in the US as Mandrax), Havana received a third of the profits.[45] In the 1980s, Castro's regime netted an annual $200 million in foreign currency from the Colombian drugs and arms smuggling businesses alone.

Domestically, the impact of the Colombian narco-terrorist economy has been tragic. Widespread political corruption, coupled with assassinations, curtailed any serious effort to fight the narco-traffickers. The massive amount of hard cash generated by the cocaine trade tilted the country's balance of payment into surplus and inevitably sustained business growth. As the drug barons' rivers of cash flowed into the economy, it became more and more difficult to attack them as criminals. In the mid-1980s, President Betancour[46] attempted to fight back, only to be faced with the drug barons' threat to close down 1,800 businesses and assemble an army of 18,000 people.[47] The weakness of the Colombian government in dealing with the phenomenon of narco-terror is underlined by its unsuccessful attempts to negotiate a peace treaty with the FARC, a desperate gesture which stresses the power this group has attained.

The extraordinary growth of the Colombian drug cartel affected not just the home front, but also produced a serious spillover into neighbouring countries. In Peru, as we saw in chapter 2, Sendero Luminoso was able to gain strength and eventually control large regions by mediating between local coca growers and Colombian drug traffickers. It also affected the United States: in the mid-1980s, the Colombian drug smuggling trade contributed about $15 billion a year to the economy of Florida. This huge injection of cash was mostly generated by the laundering of drug money,[48] money that inevitably corrupted Florida's financial establishment. Cash-hungry banks welcomed highly liquid businesses and did not ask awkward questions. They were legally required to report deposits of over $10,000 in cash, but seldom did so, silently recycling the money.[49]

ODD ALLIANCES

Armed groups' buoyant economies inevitably have an impact on their neighbours. In exceptional circumstances, as in the case of the PLO and Israel before 1987, they can even create a symbiotic relationship. In the summer of 1987, a young Palestinian man with a suitcase approached the Allenby Bridge, the transit point between Israel and Jordan. The Israeli patrol stopped him and asked to search the suitcase. Without hesitation, the man opened it. Inside there was $999,000 in cash, in US-denominated banknotes. The man was taken into custody and the border patrol contacted their superiors to ask what to do. Eventually Adi Amorai, the Israeli deputy finance minister, consulted Shmuel Goren, the coordinator of activities in the occupied territories of Gaza and the West Bank. Goren suspected that the money was destined to support the Palestinian infrastructure in the occupied territories, for the payment of teachers' and nurses' salaries, rather than to purchase arms. Amorai was of the same opinion, since covert funds were shipped by the PLO discreetly, via bank accounts and financial channels, not across the Allenby Bridge in a suitcase. Amorai was also concerned about the stagnant Israeli economy and rising inflation, then running at 40 per cent. He knew that the Palestinian courier needed to convert the dollars into Israeli shekels and that injections of hard currency were much needed by Israel's economy. In addition, he was certain that a large proportion of the money would be spent in Israel. Therefore, he decided to let the Palestinian proceed with the delivery.[50]

The strange symbiosis between the PLO and Israel is part of the financial cost sustained by Israel for its occupation of the Gaza Strip and the West Bank. It also outlines the economic power of the PLO, an armed organisation that through the years has survived and prospered exclusively in a war economy and through foreign contributions. The key to the success of its leadership rests on its remarkable ability to tap into alternative sources of growth. An economic parasite, the PLO has moved from the depletion of one resource to another, landmarks in the Palestinian diaspora. Perhaps the best example of its leaders' skill is the carving up of the Lebanese economy.

THE LEBANESE ECONOMY AND THE PLO

In 1970, King Hussein expelled the PLO from Jordan as he feared an attempt to take over his country. The organisation resettled in Lebanon, where it immediately forged an alliance with the Lebanese National Movement (LNM). The LNM wanted to transform Lebanon into a pure Arab state, a goal that fully complemented Arafat's hidden agenda. While politically backing the LNM and its fight against the Christian militia, the PLO concentrated on penetrating the Lebanese economy. 'The road to Palestine passes through Lebanon' was Abu Iyad's favourite slogan.[51] Lebanon, like Jordan before it, was a vehicle for a victorious return to the homeland. And in Lebanon, as in Jordan, Arafat and his followers' ultimate goal was twofold: to free themselves from dependence on Arab countries and to guarantee a steady flow of money to maintain the PLO. Since the early 1960s, Arafat had been attempting to break away from state sponsorship, which he despised. His armed organisation, al-Fatah, was created by the secret services of Egypt and Syria. They had supplied funds, arms and training. However, it was apparent to Arafat that al-Fatah was no more than an instrument in the hands of its sponsors and that they would not hesitate to withdraw their support the moment it ceased to be useful to their own domestic politics. It was to avoid this scenario

that Arafat joined the PLO coalition and later took control of
it, turning the organisation into the *de facto* political and
economic government of the Palestinian people.

In Lebanon, the first step towards economic independence
was to establish territorial control. Ports and strategic regions
such as the southern Bekaa valley were targeted by the PLO's
military apparatus. The ports of Tyre and Sidon, for example,
were attacked and occupied by PLO commandos. Arafat then
appointed Asmi Zarir, a former Jordanian army officer, as
commander of the Tyre region. The second step was to replace
regional and local authorities with the PLO's own institutions.
The same strategy was carried out in the refugee camps situated around the capital. The Lebanese authorities appointed
to administer them were progressively replaced with PLO officials. In Beirut, the Fakhani section where the headquarters
of both the PLO and al-Fatah were located was also under
PLO jurisdiction. These enclaves soon became 'no-go' areas
for the Lebanese police, who were unable to enter them without
engaging in armed clashes. In some areas, the PLO forged
alliances with other armed organisations. The port of Tripoli,
for example, was managed in conjunction with al-Tauchid
(Islamic Unification), the Sunni militia headed by Sheikh Sa'id
Sha'aban.

Territorial control gave the PLO leadership the power to levy
taxes.[52] These took various forms, ranging from protection fees,
similar to those levied by ETA, to import–export duties.
Interestingly, smuggled items commanded higher fees. Among
other tasks, Asmi Zarir collected taxes for the PLO on goods
passing through the ports of Tyre and Sidon. Zarir soon realised
the advantages of entering the smuggling business and set up a
joint venture with the Tyre fishing association whereby profits
were split between the PLO and the smugglers. Between them
they monitored the movement of goods to and from the region.[53]

The third step was the maximisation of the exploitation of
resources, which included illegal and criminal businesses. Illegal

activities ranged from petty theft to drug smuggling. Bank robbery was so widespread in Lebanon that all major banks were forced to move their funds out of the country. Even the Banque du Liban, the central bank, shipped its assets abroad, keeping only funds necessary for daily transactions. But apart from the successful looting of the British Bank of the Middle East in 1976, bank robbery was not the most profitable source of income for armed groups. Looting of national properties proved to be more lucrative. During the civil war the Christian Phalange looted the port of Beirut, collecting $715 million in goods, which they sold mostly to Iraq.[54] Smuggling of drugs was also a highly profitable business. Lebanon was a major processing area for hard drugs from Asia, while the Bekaa valley was a large producer of hashish. Extending over 4,280 square kilometres east of Lebanon, the valley borders Syria to the east and Israel to the south. When the PLO gained control of the southern part of the valley, Arafat negotiated an agreement with the growers and smugglers. In exchange for a promise not to interfere with the drug trade, the PLO was allowed to levy a tax of 10 per cent on the whole business, estimated at $1.5 billion, netting about $150 million per year. According to Neil Livingstone and David Halevy, co-authors of *Inside the PLO*, other forces received a cut of the business, among them Crown Prince Hassan of Jordan, Rifat, brother of Hafez el-Assad of Syria and the Maronite Christian clan headed by Bashir Gemayal, all fierce enemies of the PLO. The loose commercial association with them, however, did not bother Arafat.[55]

When civil war broke out in Lebanon, the Bekaa valley became the playground of warlords and armed groups. The 40,000 Syrian soldiers and myriad terror groups engaged in the civil war used it as their gateway to Lebanon. Fruit and vegetable plantations were quickly replaced by fields of cannabis, a crop whose high return was used to finance the various armed organisations. Drug production spread from the north to the south and by the beginning of 1981 the Beirut–Damascus

highway was surrounded by fields of cannabis. Estimated production figures for the early 1980s ranged from 700 to 2,000 metric
tons. Facilitated by the decline in policing in Lebanon, drug
smuggling boomed, pushing annual foreign exchange earnings
well above $10 billion. Since the PLO controlled many of the
major drug routes, it naturally collected a considerable share of
this figure in road taxes. Arafat's involvement with the drug trade
continued well after his deportation from Lebanon. In 1983, for
example, members of the PLO were reported to have sold 4.3
tons of 'Lebanese Gold', a top quality hashish, to British dealers,
who loaded it on to their boats to smuggle to Europe. The
street value of the hashish was $12 million.[56]

In Lebanon the PLO founded and consolidated its economic
and financial empire, gaining independence from Arab sponsors. Gone were the humiliations of the early days, when the
PLO leadership had to tour Arab countries begging for financial help. Gone was the image of an organisation without real
structure, surviving on a day-to-day basis. By the time the PLO
left Lebanon, it was a financial giant managing the wealth of
a nation in exile. A few statistics give an idea of the amount
of money the PLO commanded. In 1982, a few days before
the fall of Beirut to the Israeli army, $400 million was with-
drawn from Lebanese banks and moved to Switzerland and
other Arab countries. Soon after, Arafat paid $2.4 million in
cash for the boats that made the Tripoli exodus possible. He
rewarded every captain and sailor who successfully completed
the journey with $5,000 and $3,000 in cash, respectively. The
55-day battle of Tripoli[57] cost $26 million, of which about
$580,000 came from PLO bank accounts in cash every day.[58]

The Israeli invasion of Lebanon did not destroy the financial expertise and complex structure of the PLO; it only
dismantled a part of its economic infrastructure, which was
soon rebuilt in the Arab countries that hosted Palestinians. In
the 1980s the PLO continued to prosper independently of its
Arab sponsors. The 1988 'overt' budget shows total revenues

at $674.5 million, of which direct contributions from Arab states amounted to $216 million. Total expenditures were $395 million, leaving an 'overt' surplus of $280 million, more than the direct contribution of Arab states.[59] These figures do not include the Chairman's Secret Fund.[60] Clearly, the PLO had managed to become self-sufficient.

THE IRAN–CONTRA AFFAIR

The PLO's exploitation of the Lebanese economy turned that country into an ideal breeding ground for armed groups. The progressive weakening of the state provided the necessary resources for many armed organisations seeking economic independence, an achievement that gave them a new status. Iran, the newly formed Islamic state, eager to get involved in the business of sponsoring terrorism in the Middle East, offered financial support to some of these groups. In the early 1980s, Islamic Jihad managed to establish control over parts of Lebanon and embarked on a vicious kidnapping campaign with Teheran's full economic backing. This alliance led to the biggest scandal in post-war America since Watergate: the Iran–Contra affair (discussed in chapter 2).

In 1986, the American public were shocked to learn the details of the scandal. Not only had the US broken its own embargo on the sale of arms to Iran, it had profiteered from it and used the revenues to finance the covert operations of the Contras in Nicaragua and El Salvador. As the details of the Iran–Contra affair unfolded, it became apparent that the US had been taken to ransom as early as 1979 by the Iranian government. To free the hostages in Teheran, the administration had secretly released the funds frozen in the US at the outbreak of the Iranian revolution and most of the $3.5 billion in property held by the Shah in the US.[61] In the mid-1980s, unable to get to grips with the hostage situation in Lebanon, the administration had turned to Iran to act as mediator with the Islamic Jihad, the armed group that held the US hostages captive in Beirut. Following an agreement between the two governments, the CIA shipped $12 million of Defense Department weapons to Iran via Israel from January to September 1986, including TOW anti-tank missiles. Israel acted as a broker during the entire operation. Given the level of mistrust between Iran and Israel, though, an Iranian middleman, Manucher Ghorbanifar, was brought in to secure the help of Saudi Arabia. Saudi businessman Adnan Khashoggi provided a bridging loan of $5 million as guarantee for the Israelis that the Iranians would honour the contract.[62] With the knowledge of the Iranians, the Israelis sold the arms to Iran at a premium ranging from $10 million to $30 million above their actual cost and pocketed the profit. The CIA received $12 million plus the cost from the Iranian sale. The extra funds were transferred to a Swiss account nominated by Oliver North. The account was controlled by the Contras.[63]

One outcome of the PLO's long fight for economic independence was the disintegration of the state monopoly on the sponsorship of armed groups. In the international political arena, new, self-financed armed groups were formed, new alliances forged, new fronts opened, new sponsors involved. Terror was no longer the exclusive domain of the superpowers and their close allies; it had become an autonomous business.

4. Terror Reaganomics

'Fifty thousand people or perhaps eighty thousand people might have been killed during the war in Timor . . . It was war. Then what is the big fuss?'

Adam Malik, Indonesian foreign minister
during a press conference in Jakarta

I met Akmed, a Palestinian student who was studying engin-eering in West Germany, in 1978. We were both stranded in Istanbul during the violent demonstrations against the regime of Bülent Ecevit.[1] Unable to go outside, we spent hours in the cafeteria of the youth hostel discussing politics. During one of our conversations, Akmed admitted that a few months earlier he had travelled to Lebanon with the intention of joining the PLO. Like many students in the West who had come of age during the anti-Vietnam era, he had a romantic and idealistic image of the PLO. For Akmed the fedayeen were freedom fighters, coura-geous and honourable warriors struggling to reconquer Palestine. It was to answer their call to arms, he explained, that he had abandoned his studies and headed for Beirut.

But as soon as he arrived there, Akmed was submerged in a surreal world of violence. 'When I got to Beirut,' he told me,

I was shocked by the militarisation of the society. The city is divided into war zones, with roadblocks and militia patrolling the bound-aries. Behind a façade of normality, a strong undercurrent of violence prevails. War is so deeply intertwined with life that violence seems the sole possible reality. People's identity is defined exclusively by their role in the fight. The fedayeen are the core of Muslim society. A cluster of people: mothers, fathers, spouses, children, surround them – mere human accessories of the Arab warriors. In Beirut you are no one unless you belong to an armed group.

When Akmed went to visit some relatives in East Beirut, a fedayeen arrived a few minutes later. 'He was a tall, lean man with an M16 rifle slung on his shoulder,' Akmed described. 'My uncle introduced him as the commander of their street. He shook my hand and immediately recruited me.' That evening Akmed was handed a PLO membership card. Two days later, while visiting other relatives a few streets away, he was stopped by three armed men. After enquiring about his origins, they invited him to join their group. When he explained that he had already been recruited, they held him at gunpoint and frisked him. Eventually, they found his membership card and let him go. Two months later, at a loss in this surreal society, Akmed returned to Germany.

Akmed was one of the many Palestinian students scattered around European and North American university campuses who, in the late 1970s, answered the call of the fedayeen. This army of young intellectuals poured into Lebanon, intrigued and seduced by the successes of the PLO. Under the rule of Arafat, a man who actively sought independence from state sponsorship, the PLO was consolidating its grip on the Lebanese economy while working towards the constitution of a Palestinian state. By flocking to Lebanon, the students were also making a strong statement against what they saw as the superpowers' dirty game of state-sponsored terrorism. To many, victory over the US warriors of the Cold War seemed not only feasible, but also imminent.

As soon as the students arrived in Lebanon, PLO commanders rushed to recruit them. Recruitment was of paramount importance because Arafat allocated funds according to the number of members controlled by the commander of each of the various groups. Recruitment was the engine of the PLO war machine and money its fuel. Members received a monthly salary ranging from 700 to 1,000 Lebanese pounds, equivalent to the average wage of a local agricultural worker. If they were married, their wives and children below the age of 16 were also granted monthly stipends of 650 and 25 Lebanese pounds respectively. At the age of 16, boys were expected to join the PLO, at a starting salary of 650 Lebanese pounds.[2] To fund such an army the PLO had to build a strong financial and economic base.

On the financial side, as discussed in chapter 3, most of the money generated from illegal or criminal activities was cleverly invested abroad to produce income. Although it is difficult to estimate the size of its financial empire, the extent of the PLO's portfolio can be appreciated thanks to the discoveries of a hacker who broke into the PLO computer system in 1999. The hacker found documentation for $8 billion held in accounts in New York, Geneva and Zurich. Smaller accounts were located in North Africa, Europe and Asia. From downloaded records it transpired that the PLO also owned shares in the Tokyo and Paris stock exchanges, and real estate in expensive areas in London, Paris and other European capitals. The hacker unveiled a list of companies that fronted for the PLO in international financial markets. He also discovered stock held in Mercedes-Benz, shares in the national airlines of Guinea-Bissau and the Maldive Islands and several other financial holdings totalling about $50 billion.[3]

Funds were also used to lay the foundations of a legitimate Palestinian economy. In 1970 in Jordan, the PLO established the Palestine Martyrs Work Society, better known as Samed. Originally, Samed had the task of providing vocational training to Palestinian orphans. However, when the PLO was ousted from Jordan and relocated in Lebanon, Samed was reorganised. As we shall see in chapter 5, Samed was instrumental in creating the economic infrastructure of the future Palestinian state.

Under the direct supervision of Arafat, Samed channelled the workforce of the refugee camps towards the creation of a solid social and industrial infrastructure. Its ultimate goal was to make the Palestinians self-sufficient and the PLO independent of donations from Arab countries. The success of this initiative was extraordinary. By 1982, Samed controlled 35 factories in Lebanon and five in Syria and owned several businesses abroad, exporting regularly to East European and Arab countries. The same year, its turnover was estimated at $45 million.[4] Economic growth was also sustained by a 5 per cent tax levied on all Palestinians working in Arab countries. According to the CIA, by 1999 the PLO had accumulated between $8 billion and $14 billion in assets from this tax alone.[5]

SUHARTO'S COUP IN INDONESIA

The privatisation of political violence was aimed primarily at escaping the restrictions imposed by sponsors as a form of economic dependency. State sponsorship limited the scope of the armed struggle to the maintenance of the Cold War status quo and, therefore, disregarded the right of self-determination of nations. Alejandro Reuss reports Henry Kissinger's memorable remark on the political situation in Chile: 'I do not see why we have to stand by and watch a country go communist due to the irresponsibility of its own people.'[6] The USSR had a similar approach, using the various armed groups in the Middle East as pawns in a chess game with the US. Arafat grasped this reality very early on and concentrated on making the PLO financially independent; for him the road to Jerusalem did not go through Moscow; it ran straight through Zurich's Bahnhofstrasse.

What is the difference between self-financed armed struggles and state-sponsored war by proxy? In the latter, a foreign power decides which political, nationalist or insurgent group to support, as in the creation of the Contras by the CIA, described in chapter 2. In the privatisation of political violence model, on the other hand, the armed group develops its own strategy, sets its goals and targets a sector of society for support; that is, it has a popular constituency rather than a state as backer. Naturally, this model depends on the ability of the group to generate enough money to underwrite the armed struggle.

Ultimately, foreign sponsorship of armed or insurgent groups[7] tended to safeguard Western economic interests in developing countries to the detriment of the local population. This is what happened in Indonesia. In the 1950s and early 1960s, the US and its Western allies became increasingly concerned with the regime of President Sukarno. In 1964 the US ambassador to Malaysia summarised these fears in a cable to Washington: 'Our difficulties in Indonesia stem basically from deliberate, positive GOI [Government of Indonesia] strategy of seeking to push Britain and the US out of Southeast Asia.'[8] Western powers disapproved of Sukarno's decision to join the non-aligned movement and adopt a militant anti-Western stance. In particular, the West dreaded the rise of the Communist Party of Indonesia, the Partai Kumunis Indonesia (PKI), the largest Asian left-wing party outside the Eastern Bloc and China. These fears mounted when Sukarno got involved in an anti-colonial confrontation with the Netherlands over the status of Papua New Guinea. At that point it became clear to the US administration that some action had to be taken to defend Western economic interests (Indonesia being rich in natural resources, particularly petroleum).

A US report stressed that Sukarno was pursuing 'wrong priorities'.

The government occupies a dominant position in basic industry, public utilities, internal transportation and communication . . . It is probable that private ownership will disappear and may be succeeded by some form of production-profit-sharing contract arrangements to be applied to all foreign investment . . . Indonesia's objective is to 'stand on their own feet' in developing their economy, free from foreign, especially Western influence.[9]

Against this backdrop, the US administration decided to strengthen Western influence in the region by supporting the army with a programme of military assistance. Financial aid and training in the US were offered to Indonesian officers.[10] The decision to promote the military as a leading political force bore fruit in October 1965 when Sukarno was ousted in a violent coup led by General Suharto. In the following six months the PKI was exterminated and as many as 1 million people died. A dictatorial regime took over the archipelago.

The new regime abandoned Sukarno's non-aligned, anti-colonial policy and opened the doors to Western investment. Corporations flocked to what was described as an investors' paradise.[11] In exchange, Suharto received financial and military aid and a free hand in the pursuit of an aggressive expansionist policy in the region. In December 1975, Indonesia invaded the former Portuguese colony of East Timor, then in the process of decolonisation.[12] The United States and Australia condoned the invasion. Australian ambassador Richard Woolcott even recommended a 'pragmatic course of Kissingerian realism', in other words, an invasion in the style of the CIA-sponsored coup that brought General Pinochet to power in Chile. It was Woolcott's opinion that, rather than an independent state, an Indonesian-controlled East Timor would provide a better opportunity for the West to exploit the country's rich oil resources.[13] Australia would, therefore, be assured of the right to explore and exploit the oil and gas fields in the Timor Sea, the stretch of water that separates East Timor and Australia.[14]

Two days after the invasion, the Revolutionary Front for the Independence of East Timor (Fretelin) broadcast the unfolding tragedy in a desperate radio appeal. 'The Indonesian forces are killing indiscriminately. Women and children are being shot in the streets. We are all going to be killed. I repeat, we are all going to be killed . . . This is an appeal for international help.'[15] A few days later, the UN passed a resolution which strongly condemned the invasion and called for urgent action to protect the territorial integrity of Portuguese Timor and its population's right to self-determination. Yet no action was taken. Seventy-two countries rejected the decision to condemn Indonesia for violating the UN Charter, only ten voted against the aggression of the Suharto regime while 43, including the US, the UK and most of Western Europe, abstained.

Although heavily armed and financed by the Carter administration and its Western allies, Indonesia none the less had to struggle for several years to gain control of East Timor. To win the island, the army committed appalling atrocities. By the end of 1979, about a third of the entire population of East Timor had lost their lives in the conflict. US bombers and counterinsurgency aircraft supplied by the Western champion of human rights and future Nobel Peace Prize winner, President Carter, helped Suharto to take control of the island.[16] A few die-hard members of Fretelin, however, refused to give up the fight. They regrouped using guerrilla tactics and continued to fight the occupying forces. Suharto's regime of terror, meanwhile, greatly benefited from Western generosity ($3.15 billion in 1987 and $4.01 billion in 1988). Western leaders even showered the general with praise and declared him 'our kind of guy'.

In some of the frontier regions of the Cold War, armed groups fought in total isolation, waging war by proxy for the two superpowers. With the exception of Cuba in Latin America, the superpowers' policy of sponsorship promoted fragmentation, with each group fighting only and exclusively its opponent. Thus the Fretelin's desperate appeal remained unanswered by the Asian armed organisations. It was only in the 1980s, during the anti–Soviet Jihad, that would-be warriors started migrating to join a multi-ethnic Muslim army. As discussed in chapter 9, this was a by-product of the economic self-sufficiency of armed groups. Before then, cooperation among them was limited to arms purchases and the exchange of information.

THE INTERNATIONALISATION OF ARMED GROUPS

Attempts to forge strategic alliances among armed organisations date back to the early 1970s. In Lebanon in 1972, George Habash hosted one of the first international summits to form a common front against Zionism and Western imperialism.[17] Representatives came from the Japanese Red Army, the Iranian Liberation Front, the IRA, the Bader-Meinhof and the Turkish Revolutionary People's Liberation Front.[18] The participants agreed to set up an international network which included economic and financial cooperation, the exchange of intelligence, sharing safe houses, joint training programmes and arms purchases.

Partnership in arms dealings and smuggling was particularly popular; given that it was one of the major activities of armed groups, joint ventures in this field soon blossomed. In 1994, I interviewed a former member of the Red Brigades who had a passion for sailboats. He admitted that his maritime expertise had come in very handy in the late 1970s and early 1980s when his beautiful 50-foot yacht was used to smuggle arms and ammunition. His last journey was particularly memorable. He sailed to Lebanon with one of the leaders of the Red Brigades. 'It was late summer and the sea was warm and friendly,' he told me. 'As usual, the Mediterranean was packed with boats and yachts; no one paid attention to us, two holidaymakers on a sailboat.'[19] The crossing was smooth and pleasant. When they finally entered Lebanese waters, a delegation of PLO members met and escorted them to a fishing village. There, they were welcomed by a group of fedayeen. At dawn, after arms and ammunition had been loaded on to the boat, they sailed back.

Eventually, the cargo was divided among the Red Brigades, the IRA and the separatist Sardinian group, Barbagia Rossa. In another similar journey, Mario Moretti, the leader of the Red Brigades, brought back machine guns, heavy Energa anti-tank mines, grenades, SAM 7 Strela missiles, etc. These weapons were shared with the IRA, ETA and German underground groups.[20] Due to the geographical position of Italy, with its 7,600 kilometres of coastline and its proximity to the Middle East, it was easy for Italian armed groups to play the role of courier to and from the Middle East.

In the 1970s, civil war turned Lebanon into the hub of the international illegal arms market and the Palestinians into its main brokers and dealers. Weapons were smuggled in and out of Lebanon's spectacular Mediterranean coastline using ingenious techniques, for example, by exploiting tides and currents. This is an unusual method that the PLO continues to use to supply the occupied territories with arms. In the spring of 2002, a group of children playing on the Gaza beach found a black-painted oil barrel on the shore. On opening it, they discovered that it contained grenades, Kalashnikov rifles and mortar shells. Apparently, about 25–30 miles off the coast of Gaza, there is a natural pool, known as *al-birkah*, where the currents converge to head towards the Gaza beaches. 'The currents of the sea are like the roads in the desert,' an informer told journalist Robert Fisk. 'People know the right time to drop stuff over the side of a ship, how long it will take to reach Gaza – less than a week. These are professionals – they know how to get the guns in.'[21] Arms were even smuggled in using duty-free shops. In 1985, front men for the PLO took over several duty-free shops in Africa and used them to ship arms, explosives and ammunition. Trucks carrying goods for the duty-free shops were used to cache the weapons.[22]

In the early 1980s, Patrizio Peci, the first *pentito*[23] (repentant) from the Red Brigades, linked the assassination of former Italian prime minister Aldo Moro to the Palestinian arms trade. He confessed that the machine gun, a Czechoslovakian Skorpion, used to kill Moro had been picked up in the Middle East by Mario Moretti during one of his shopping trips to Lebanon. Although Peci did not identify the source, it is very likely that the supplier was the PFLP (Popular Front for the Liberation of Palestine). In the late 1970s and early 1980s, the PFLP was the main weapons broker for European armed groups. The Italians handled most of the shipping. In 1979, the police arrested Daniele Pifano, leader of Autonomia; at the time he was carrying two Strela missiles. In court he insisted that he was simply doing George Habash a favour; Habash had asked him to be his courier. The PFLP not only confirmed this statement, but it asked for the missiles to be returned as they were the property of Habash.[24]

The Palestine Resistance Movement in Western Europe had played a similar role to that of the Cubans in Latin America. The Soviets provided arms, ammunition, technical know-how and military and strategic training; the Palestinians brokered these to European armed groups. 'The USSR set up a chain of terrorist Do-It-Yourselfs across the Middle East,' an Italian magistrate explained to me, 'and gave it to the Palestinians to manage.'[25] This was a more subtle form of state sponsorship as compared to the direct involvement of American soldiers in foreign countries.

Reducing economic dependence on sponsors necessitated a constant sourcing of funds. 'We were always short of cash,' admitted a former member of the Red Brigades. 'Although we lived an extremely frugal existence and did not need much to survive, we needed cash, a lot of it, to finance our fight.'[26] Leaders of armed organisations are in a permanent state of anxiety about funding. A glance at some of the expense accounts of the Red Brigades explains why. The estimated cost of a 'regular', full-time member of the Red Brigades who had gone underground was about $15,000 a year, including salary,[27] rent, food, clothing and personal weapons. Therefore, to run an organisation with as few as 500 regulars, the Red Brigades needed to raise about $8 million a year. In the 1970s and 1980s, this figure rose in line with the high rate of inflation. On top of running costs, the organisation had to provide for the extras: plane tickets, special weapons purchases, the cost of sailing trips to the Middle East, high-tech equipment, etc. Author Claire Sterling estimates that the cost of running the Red Brigades alone was close to $10 million a year (equivalent to $100,000 million today).[28] The cost of running Italian armed groups as a whole, inclusive of right- and left-wing groups, was at least three times this figure.[29]

To generate and administer such a large amount of cash required a high degree of professionalism and managerial skill. Only multi-million dollar bank robberies and kidnap ransoms could provide such funding. Gone were the days of the super-market 'expropriations' of Curcio and Franceschini, two of the founders of the Red Brigades.[30] Armed organisations like the Red Brigades had to be run along the lines of a business cor-poration. No money was to be wasted. In the late 1970s, the Red Brigades discovered that the banknotes of a kidnapping's ransom had all been stained with yellow ink and were therefore unusable. Unwilling to give the money up, they washed it. 'Three people spent days washing the banknotes one by one and drying them with a hair dryer in a damp Milan basement flat.'[31]

All expenses had to be accounted for, itemised and eventu-ally checked and double-checked by the organisation. When the police raided the hideout in via Gradoli where Moro had been held captive, they found receipts for 3,000 lire for petrol and 6,000 lire for marker pens and stationery.[32]

TERROR BUSINESS MAVERICKS

While sponsored by a state, armed groups had simply been the recipients of funds and therefore had had the luxury of focusing exclusively on fighting. Under the self-financing scheme, however, their first priority lay in finding ways to support themselves. The new entrepreneurial tasks changed the structure of armed groups and revolutionised the natural selection of its leaders. Heads of armed organisations were now required to display managerial and entrepreneurial skills; financial acumen became more valued than military genius. Business mavericks appeared on the scene. Some, like Arafat, used their talent to climb the greasy pole of large armed organisations, while others, like Abu Nidal or Carlos the Jackal, put their skills to work for themselves. For the latter the armed struggle was just a business. According to several sources, Abu Nidal had no specific knowledge of guerrilla warfare or terror tactics. Indeed, many people even questioned his political motivation and his courage as a fighter, stopping just short of calling him a coward. In May 1984, for example, while Nidal was visiting Gaddafi in Tripoli, Libyan intelligence unveiled a plot by the National Front for the Salvation of Libya to assassinate the Libyan leader. The hideout of the rebels was attacked and a fierce gun battle ensued. Abu Nidal was in a nearby villa waiting to leave for the airport. The shooting sent him into a total panic. He began shouting to his right-hand man, Abd al-Rahman Isa, to get him out of Libya. Apparently he relaxed only when he was out of the country.[33]

The search for economic independence turned the armed struggle into a multi-million dollar business and freedom fighters into entrepreneurs. Abu Nidal, a man who not only managed to exploit Arab state sponsorship to his own advantage, but also succeeded in 'milking rich Arabs' via extortion, became the stereotype of the terror wheeler-dealer. From 1974 to 1991 he was hosted by Iraq, Syria and finally Libya. There, he received financial and logistical support and a safe haven from which to launch his attacks. His career started in the early 1970s. While residing in Baghdad as the PLO's representative, he succeeded in branching out and setting up his own group. In exchange for his unconditional support of Saddam Hussein, he received $4 million of al-Fatah assets from the Iraqis, about $15 million of arms and a bonus of $5 million when the al-Fatah leadership sentenced him to death.[34]

By skilfully playing one power against another, he proceeded to create his own multinational of terror. According to the Iraqis, he made millions acting as an intermediary between the Iraqi government and the armed groups it supported. He brokered weapons and services. He also profiteered from wars in the Middle East. At the outbreak of the Iran–Iraq conflict, for example, the Iraqis were ready to get rid of him and his organisation. However, Nidal offered to carry out assassinations abroad for the Iraqis, to maintain a secret channel of communication with Syria and to act as a middleman in arms deals. Saddam welcomed the proposal and paid handsomely for his services, allowing him to remain in Baghdad.

Abu Nidal's ability to exploit his sponsors to the full was renowned in the Arab world. In the early 1980s he offered to supply Saddam Hussein with Polish T72 tanks. The Iraqis paid $11 million as down payment, a sum that Nidal immediately deposited in a Swiss bank account. Soon afterwards the Iraqis decided that they did not need the tanks after all, they wanted to strengthen their artillery instead. Abu Nidal could be of no help in this matter. However, when he was asked to return the down payment he ignored the request. Eventually, he was asked to leave Iraq.[35] From Baghdad, he went to Damascus where he continued to profit from the Iran–Iraq conflict, mostly by selling arms to both sides. The supply came from East European countries, especially Bulgaria. He bought weapons from state corporations at cut-rate prices and sold them for high profits, often using the Eastern Bloc as a refuge. His total profits from the Iraq–Iran war are estimated at $280 million.[36]

While living in Syria, Nidal also extorted money from oil sheikhs and the Gulf rulers. His tactics were simple: he sent his victims threatening messages on tape. If they did not agree to pay, he sent another message containing an explicit death threat.

If this message remained unanswered, Nidal took action, as he did with Sheikh Zayid bin Sultan, ruler of Abu Dhabi. The sheikh was a generous supporter of the PLO and the Palestinian cause, but he had never given money to Abu Nidal or any of his organisations. When Nidal threatened him, Zayid refused to comply. On 23 September 1983, a Gulf Air Boeing 737 from Karachi to Dubai crashed a few kilometres from the Abu Dhabi airport killing all passengers and crew. A defector from the Arab Revolutionary Brigades, the fictional group that claimed responsibility for the crash, confirmed that Abu Nidal had masterminded the attack. A few months later, on 8 February 1984, the ambassador of the United Arab Emirates was shot dead in Paris. On 25 October 1984, another diplomat from the United Arab Emirates was assassinated in Rome. In both cases the Arab Revolutionary Brigades claimed responsibility. Eventually, Sheikh Zayid gave in and agreed to pay Abu Nidal $17 million.[37]

During the 1973–74 oil crisis, the Arab ruling class became conscious of the power of their resources and developed a taste for economic supremacy, as discussed in chapter 2. Money started to flow freely and some of it trickled down to Arab populations. Very few people were immune to the seductive power of wealth, including members of the armed groups. Some capitalised on the knowledge of arms and combat and became 'guns for hire', selling their expert services to the highest bidder.

At the end of the 1970s, after the second oil shock, monetarism and deregulation swept through the West and shaped a new generation, the children of Thatcherism and Reaganism, producing traders devoted exclusively to the accumulation of wealth. At the same time, the Middle East was taken over by a new breed of mercenaries, warriors who professed loyalty to only one cause: money. Armed groups abandoned state sponsorship and financed themselves using market and business techniques. It was the beginning of the Reaganomics of terror.

GUNS FOR HIRE

In the summer of 1988, Ahmed Jibril, the leader of the Popular Front for the Liberation of Palestine – General Command (PFLP-GC), realised that he was nearly broke. Libya had just suspended its annual payment of $25 million and Jibril did not know how to support his followers, 400–600 Arab fedayeen. Since the 1960s Jibril, a well-known figure among Arab leaders of armed groups, had succeeded in selling his services to the major sponsors of terrorism. For more than a decade he had been Moscow's front man in the Middle East, enjoying direct relations with the KGB, acting as a mediator between the Kremlin and Syria, brokering Soviet terror products, such as arms and services, and promoting the role of Bulgaria in the development of the European web of terror. It was to serve Moscow better that he had left George Habash and the PFLP, whom he judged to be too focused on the export of the Palestinian cause to Europe. His organisation was instrumental in sabotaging Palestinian peace attempts through diplomacy and in maintaining a state of permanent military confrontation between Israel and the Arabs. Other Arab leaders, who sponsored Jibril, shared this aim. Gaddafi paid the PFLP-GC salaries, supplied arms and financed several terror operations. Training facilities and housing were also provided by the Libyan leader. In exchange, Jibril carried out terror attacks and supplied Gaddafi with his own fighters in the war in Chad.[38]

For two decades, the Russians, Syrians and Arab leaders, such as Gaddafi, had paid through the nose for his services. However, in the summer of 1988, Ahmed Jibril and his army of mercenaries had nowhere to turn. Then, on 4 July 1988 the USS *Vincennes* accidentally shot down an Iranian jetliner with 290 people on board. As soon as the news reached Jibril, he laid out his plan. He contacted the Iranians and offered – at a price, of course – to carry out a retaliatory attack against the US. He suggested a US jetliner, possibly a Boeing 747, as a likely target.

The same month Jibril dispatched one of his key men, Hafeth el-Dalkamuni Abu Mohammad, to Teheran. With the help of the Iranian interior minister, Machtashimi Four, an old friend of Dalkamuni, the PFLP-GC cut a deal. The Iranians agreed to meet the group's financial requirements for that year in exchange for Jibril's services. As a sign of their goodwill the Iranians deposited $2 million in PFLP-GC accounts.

In September 1988, Dalkamuni was arrested in West Germany. The police discovered a hideout where bombs and explosives had been stored, clearly meant to be carried on board an airplane. Unfortunately, the police did not pursue the matter further and never discovered a second hideout in the suburbs of Frankfurt. From there two people, a bomb maker and a 'charmer', a Palestinian who had the task of duping someone into carrying the bomb on board, completed the mission. On 21 December 1988, Pan Am flight 103 exploded in mid-air over Lockerbie, Scotland. The bodies of the 259 people on board littered the ground below. Two days after the disaster, the Iranians transferred the balance of payment to the PFLP-GC accounts.[39] This evidence contradicts the official view that Libya was responsible for the bombing.[40] The failure to see the Lockerbie bombing as part of a global phenomenon of terror is partly due to the deep antagonism that the UK and US government felt at the time towards Gaddafi.

Opportunities for making money – considerable sums of it – by capitalising on terror knowledge and expertise also appealed to Westerners. In the 1970s, two ex-CIA men, Edwin Wilson and Frank Terpil, profiteered through terror. Terpil, who had been involved in the Bay of Pigs and in Vietnam, was fired from the CIA in 1971 and soon after set up a company called Oceanic International Corporation, which was put to the service of President Idi Amin of Uganda. Exploiting his contacts, Terpil supplied arms, torture devices, military equipment, explosives and bombs to the Ugandan dictator. He was paid well for these services. For example, the contract with the

State Research Bureau, Uganda's secret service, alone netted him $3.3 million. Amin was so pleased with the services of the Oceanic International Corporation that he introduced Terpil to Gaddafi.[41]

Meanwhile, Edwin Wilson, who had gained his experience in the Middle East and Bangladesh, left the CIA in 1976. Wilson used his contacts to broker arms for various dictators, including Augusto Pinochet. Terpil contacted Wilson and together they set up an advisory board for Gaddafi. They supplied weapons and equipment, most of which they bought at knock-down prices in the oversupplied US market. Their margins were extremely high. In the late 1970s, for example, they sold US military equipment to Libya for $900,000, which they had purchased for only $60,000. The equipment was shipped using forged State Department export documents.[42] In the 1980s alone, tax court files on Wilson's dealings with Libya show that his business had generated a gross income of $22.9 million. More than half this figure came from a contract to supply small arms to the Libyan Armed Forces.[43]

In 1977 Wilson and Terpil decided to expand their activity to training. They recruited ten former Green Berets for whom the payment structure was as follows: the leader of the team received $140,000 and each man $100,000. The package included cover for health care in Europe and an insurance scheme that paid $250,000 in case of death and $125,000 for the loss of a limb. After recruitment, each man was given $1,000 in cash and a plane ticket to Zurich, where Wilson received them. From Switzerland, the group travelled to Tripoli. In Libya the former Green Berets trained Gaddafi protégés in terror tactics, including the use of explosives. To this purpose, a stock of 20 tons of C4 was shipped by air from Houston, Texas, to Tripoli at a cost of $300,000. Trainees were also paid a salary: Africans and Arabs $400 a month, all other nationalities $1,000.

Terpil and Wilson established several training camps for Gaddafi. They also carried out assassinations and attempted coups in Chad on his behalf. They had a price list for such services: killing an American, for instance, demanded a 40 per cent premium. Eventually, Wilson was arrested in the US for tax evasion. The Internal Revenue Service demanded $21 million in unpaid taxes and penalties for an estimated income of $51 million he had earned from 1977 to 1981.[44]

The advent of financial mavericks into the armed struggle triggered the fragmentation of the larger armed organisations. New groups and new leaders emerged, such as Ahmed Jibril – people with their own political agendas. This trend was global. In 1970, the IRA split over a major political issue: the repudiation of the armed struggle. Under the leadership of David O'Connell, Rory O'Brady and Gerry Adams, a section of the IRA refused to give up arms and broke off to become the Provisional IRA. In 1974, Seamus Costello, one of the official IRA's leading personalities, was expelled for criticising the organisation and violating the cease-fire with a series of violent attacks carried out by his group, the People's Liberation Army, an armed wing within the official IRA. Consequently, Costello and 80 other delegates formed the Irish Republic Socialist Party. Soon after, the People's Liberation Army was restructured and renamed the Irish National Liberation Army (INLA). Throughout the 1980s, the process of fragmentation continued within INLA and IRA factions.

In other parts of the world, flirtations with capitalism eroded terror mavericks' commitment to their cause and transformed some of them into mercenaries and guns for hire, as was the case with Abu Nidal. At a certain stage, their loyalty could be bought even in the course of terror operations. During the 1995 kidnapping of OPEC ministers, Carlos the Jackal cut a deal and freed the hostages, including Sheikh Yamani, whom he was supposed to execute. 'Carlos sold out', was the comment by the people close to him. For a ransom payment, he called the whole operation off and retired to a life of leisure and luxury in Eastern Europe.[45]

For a time, this corruption obscured the political aims of the armed groups and vilified the fighters in the eyes of their supporters. But then spontaneous popular uprisings, such as the Intifada in the occupied territories of Palestine, brought fresh blood and new impetus to the international armed struggle.

Part II
The New Economic Disorder

5. The Birth of the Terror State-Shell

'I have benefited so greatly from the Jihad in Afghanistan that it would have been impossible for me to gain such benefit from any other chance . . . What we benefited from most was [that] the glory and myth of the superpower was destroyed not only in my mind, but also in the [minds] of all Muslims.'

Osama bin Laden to CNN journalist
Peter L. Bergen, May 1997

In December 1987, the Palestinians living in the Gaza Strip and the West Bank launched the Intifada. The spontaneous uprising marked a distinct shift in Israeli policy. The Israeli government no longer tolerated 'unofficial' inflows of money into the occupied territories, like the $999,000 in cash discovered at the Allenby Bridge. Police were ordered to stop money being smuggled across the transit points. In the following year, over $20 million were confiscated. This measure did little to curb the PLO's economic support of the occupied territories, however. Money was plentiful and came in via more sophisticated routes. What the Israelis soon discovered was that Arafat had transformed a loose confederation of armed groups into a complex economic organisation. Acting like a legitimate state, the PLO generated annual revenue in excess of the gross national product of a number of Arab countries, including Jordan. Thanks to this windfall it effectively ran Gaza and the West Bank.

The PLO's 'overt' budget covered the day-to-day expenditures of Palestinian enclaves. In 1988, for example, this budget totalled $674 million. Almost half of it came from investment income ($300 million). PLO activities were funded through the Palestinian National Fund (PNF), which had been constituted in 1964 for this specific purpose. Initially, the PNF depended on donations from Arab countries; however, a clever policy of long-term investment coupled with close control of expenditures produced a solid asset base. By the late 1980s, the PNF was independently wealthy and managed an estimated portfolio of $6 billion. Welfare organisations scattered inside the occupied territories received money directly from the Palestinian Welfare Association (PWA), which was set up in 1983 by a group of rich Palestinians. The PWA collected donations from Palestinians and sympathisers to their cause across the world.

In tandem with the 'overt' budget, the PLO also had a 'covert' one: the Secret Chairman's Budget (SCB) which was part of the Chairman's Secret Fund, controlled exclusively by Arafat. Unlike the PLO's other financial resources, the SCB's revenues and portfolio have always been kept secret. Revenues generated by illegal and terror activities were channelled into this fund and, by the end of the 1980s, the SCB controlled an estimated $2 billion in assets. The SCB financed terror activities and arms purchases, provided for the chairman's security and covered the costs of Arafat's personal vendettas within the PLO. Occasionally, the Secret Chairman's Budget was used to meet exceptional expenditures, such as part of the high costs incurred by the PLO during the exodus from Lebanon. According to the CIA, by 1990 the total wealth of the PLO was between $8 billion and $14 billion.[1] If we take these figures as an indicator of its GNP, it was higher than the yearly GDP of other Arab countries such as Bahrain ($6 billion), Jordan ($10.6 billion) and Yemen ($6.5 billion).[2]

With economic independence came a higher degree of political freedom and the opportunity for armed organisations to develop their own foreign policy. Thus, at the onset of the Gulf

War, Yasser Arafat could afford to take a stand against his Arab benefactors by supporting Saddam Hussein. Arafat's defiance of Arab leaders was symptomatic of a new reality: as soon as armed groups were able to dispose freely of their income, they developed a taste for real power and started building the infrastructure of their own state. However, with money but no political recognition, they could create only the shell of a state. This is different from the model of nationalism in which the economy and its infrastructure are built after the process of self-determination leads to political integration. I have called this new model the state-shell[3] model.

In the state-shell, political integration may even be absent; the state is constructed around the economics of war generated by the armed struggle. Thus, in the assembly of a state-shell, the economy comes first because it is needed to sustain the war. 'War is our way of life,' declared a Northern Alliance fighter from the Shomali plain in Afghanistan.[4] Other than poppy production and smuggling, 'there is nothing else to do but fight in this region since there is no industry, no commerce, no agriculture, not even the embryo of an economy'.[5] But a fighter in Afghanistan, prior to the fall of the Taliban, could earn up to $250 a month and have access to food and cigarettes. Because state-shell leaders construct the socio-economic infrastructure of the state exclusively around the war, they offer employment to fighters, provide military services and levy taxes to buy arms and ammunition, etc.; in short, they create an economy and its infrastructure to keep on fighting.[6] 'There is no shortage on the front line,' admitted Mohammad Haider, an Afghani fighter.[7] State-shells are entities in a constant state of war, run by military elites, under a permanent political curfew, where popular political participation is either prohibited or limited in scope.

According to Professor Christopher Pierson,[8] professor of politics at the University of Nottingham, a modern state displays nine main characteristics. Of these the state-shell shares four:

a monopoly on the means of violence; territoriality; taxation; and public bureaucracy. The remaining five – sovereignty; constitutionality; the rule of law; impersonal power; and the legitimacy of authority and citizenship – are absent.

Applying this classification, a pertinent example of how a state-shell is built can be seen in the transformation of the PLO into the *de facto* governing body of the Palestinian people in Lebanon. In the enclaves it controlled, it exercised the monopoly of violence. Violence was the sole tool used to conquer and maintain a firm grip on the territories it occupied. At the same time, violence legitimised the use of force inside those enclaves. Thus the PLO resorted to physical violence to displace the Christian population in Lebanese villages and continued to rely on it to protect the Palestinian refugees who repopulated them. To fund its war economy, the PLO imposed various taxes. Of significance for the state-shell model is the Palestinian liberation tax, a 5–6 per cent levy on the salaries of all Palestinians working abroad. In a fashion similar to the US, the PLO taxed people on the basis of their nationality, regardless of where their income was generated. The task of collecting the liberation tax and remitting the money to the PLO fell on Arab governments. These were not small revenues: in 1985, it generated about 6 per cent of the PLO's total income. The largest yield came from Kuwait, where Palestinians represented a quarter of the population.[9] Finally, the PLO created ad hoc institutions, the equivalent of modern state public bureaucracies, which were assigned the task of developing the socio-economic infrastructure of the Palestinian state-shell.

SAMED: THE BIRTH OF THE PLO STATE-SHELL

Paramount to the development of the Palestinian state-shell was Samed. Acting as the economic arm of the military force, Samed shared Arafat's main priority of making the PLO independent of its Arab sponsors. To fulfil this objective, in the 1970s it actively participated in the creation of a Palestinian state inside Lebanon. Among other tasks, Samed took charge of the resettlement of refugees in strategically vital areas. In the village of Damour, 20 kilometres from Beirut, for example, after PLO fighters had brutally displaced the Christian population, Samed moved in to fill the economic void. It immediately laid the foundation for the economic infrastructure required to support the Palestinian refugees sent to settle there. It set up workshops to manufacture clothes, blankets and woollen and metal products to provide for employment and meet the demands of PLO fighters.[10]

In 1973, Samed became independent of the PLO's Social Affairs Department and was reorganised into four main divisions: industrial; information (print and films); agricultural; and general commerce. Samed had a dual function: to train and find employment for individuals and to provide products at accessible prices for the Palestinian population. As it fulfilled these functions during the course of the diaspora, it transformed itself from a social welfare institution into the core of the new Palestinian economy.

Since the main goal was to guarantee self-sufficiency for the Palestinian community, the industrial sector initially produced military uniforms, textiles and clothing for the PLO. Soon, however, it expanded its commercial line and began exporting. In 1981, for example, it exported 100,000 shirts and 50,000 pairs of trousers to the Soviet Union.[11] By that year, purchases from the PLO represented only 35 per cent of all Samed sales. Of the rest, 8 per cent were from Lebanon, 30 per cent from Arab countries and 27 per cent from other world markets. Overall, prior to the Israeli invasion of Lebanon, the annual turnover of the industrial sector was about $18 million.[12]

In 1981, Samed employed more than 5,000 permanent workers in Lebanon, 200 in Syria and 1,800 in Africa. An additional 6,000 employees worked part-time in Lebanon and as

many as 12,000 received regular training before setting up their
own businesses.[13] Samed controlled 46 factories in Lebanon
and five in Syria.[14] In every Palestinian camp there was at least
one Samed factory. Workers enjoyed various benefits; if married
they were given allowances for their wives and children. They
also received productivity bonuses and life insurance.

In the agricultural sector, Samed ran poultry and dairy farms
in order to satisfy Palestinian food demand. In the early 1980s,
this sector generated a yearly income of $16 million. Samed
also set up cooperatives in several African countries including
Sudan, Somalia, Uganda and Guinea. As direct involvement in
the occupied territories was prohibited, it was forced to find
ways of circumventing the Israeli discrimination against
Palestinian products. The Israelis imposed severe water rationing
in the region, crippling agricultural production, and required
a special licence for Palestinian products to be exported to
Israel. By contrast, Israeli goods were freely sold in the occupied territories. The competitiveness of Israeli agriculture was
further boosted by its tax-free status, while Palestinian products were heavily taxed. To overcome this economic barrier,
Samed acted as an interest-free broker and organised export
and import agreements for Palestinian producers. In 1981, for
example, it brokered the sale of 250,000 tons of Gaza citrus
fruit to Arab states.[15]

Samed did not enjoy a fixed budgetary allocation from the
organisation. It was largely self-financed, but could apply for
interest-free loans from the PLO when they were needed. It
also received funds from abroad. The Belgian Oxfam Society,
for example, granted Samed $250,000 in 1981.

The Israeli invasion of Lebanon in 1982 was a blow to Samed,
but failed to dismantle its economic infrastructure. According
to Ahmed Quary, Samed's chairman at the time, the invasion
generated losses of $17 million.[16] The factories in the camps of
Burj el-Shamali, Ein El-Hilweh and Mijeh wa Mijeh were
destroyed. However, all the others were left untouched and

continued to operate. Gross revenues show how quickly Samed was able to recover. In 1986 these amounted to $39 million, down by only $6 million from 1982 and by 1989 they had rebounded to $70 million.[17] Samed's ability to survive was partly due to the diversification of its activities and expansion into other countries. According to an Arab diplomat, by the end of the 1980s, the PLO owned so many poultry farms in Africa that it could have supplied eggs to the armies of all the Arab states.[18] It held investments and had branches in more than 30 countries in the Middle East, Africa, Eastern Europe and Latin America and employed 12,000 people. Its investments in these countries were estimated at $50 million.[19]

THE ARAB BANK, THE CENTRAL BANK OF THE PLO

On 9 June 1982, following the Israeli invasion of Lebanon, three Israelis visited the Arab Bank in Sidon. Since the bank was well known in the Middle East as one of the leading financial institutions managing PLO funds, the manager understandably assumed that the Israelis were agents from Mossad seeking to penetrate the complex financial structure of the PLO. It soon emerged that the Israelis had a detailed list of the accounts they wanted to investigate and that they had put in a similar request at the Banque du Liban, the Central Bank of Lebanon. However, strict Lebanese banking legislation prevented managers at both banks from complying with the Israelis' request. After a lengthy exchange, the men agreed to leave and return the following day. As soon as they had left, the bank manager contacted the governor of the Central Bank, Michel Khoury, who called Bashir Gemayal, the elected president of Lebanon. Gemayal telephoned Menachem Begin, the Israeli prime minister, reminding him of the Swiss-like rules of secrecy of the Lebanese banking system and the full commitment of the government and the central bank to respect them. The three Israelis never returned.[20]

The Israelis were right to visit the Arab Bank. It was the sole bank fully trusted by the PLO and the one that managed most of the organisation's accounts. Founded before the Second World War in Palestine, it shared the misfortunes of the Palestinian people. In 1948, when the exodus began, it lost three branches in Haifa, Jerusalem and Jaffa, all of which were taken over by the Israelis. To prove its loyalty to the Palestinians, the bank honoured all the branches' deposits, a gesture greatly appreciated and never forgotten. In 1967, during the Arab–Israeli war, the bank lost six additional branches in the West Bank and one in Gaza. However, it was able to transfer almost all its funds to Amman before the Israelis took over its banking network.

The move to Jordan was very successful. Within two decades, the Arab Bank, acting as the financial arm of the PLO, established a strong presence inside the Jordanian economy. According to a Jordanian banker, in the mid-1980s the PLO controlled as much as 70 per cent of the country's national economy.[21] The PLO owned textile factories, fruit plantations and transport and construction companies. It was an economic and financial force visibly present in Jordan, wielding tremendous influence on business decisions. Once, when a bank in Amman wanted to erect a high-rise building, the PLO threatened to withdraw its funds from it unless its own construction company was hired. More than once, the Arab Bank came to the rescue of the debt-ridden Jordanian monarch, King Hussein. The bank also supervised the PLO's capital outflow into other countries, mostly via the Arab Bank for Economic Development and the Arab African Bank. When Arafat withdrew money from Lebanon at the outset of the 1982 Israeli invasion, it used the Arab Bank to disperse its funds across the Middle East, Europe and the United States.

The bank and the PLO are products of the Palestinian diaspora. Their destinies are intertwined. Abdul-Majeed Shoman, son of Arab Bank founder Abdel Hamid, is the chairman of the Palestine National Fund and the man who masterminded the PLO investment programme. This extraordinary partnership transformed the bank into one of the largest financial organisations in the world, with assets in the 1980s in excess of $10 billion and branches all over the globe. It helped turn the PLO into the richest terror group on earth.[22]

While building the Palestinian state-shell, the PLO relied on the Arab Bank as its investment and commercial bank. However, at times, the bank also acted as the Central Bank of Palestine. In July 1988, for example, the Jordanian government renounced its claim to sovereignty over the West Bank and almost overnight stopped paying the wages of 18,000 Palestinian civil servants working there. The PLO stepped in and guaranteed all the salaries. It appointed the Arab Bank as the body responsible for disbursing the monthly $6 million required to pay the employees.[23]

In addition to a complex and comprehensive economic infrastructure, the PLO provided social welfare to Palestinians in a manner similar to any sovereign territorial state. Money was spent to guarantee free schooling and medical care inside the occupied territories and in PLO enclaves scattered around the Arab world. In a report published by the PLO's Occupied Homeland Department, it was stated that, from 1979 to the end of February 1987, $487.5 million had been spent in the occupied territories (including $109.4 million on education and culture and $101 million to improve transport).[24] The PLO economy, which centred on militant armed opposition to Israel, also extended into the welfare system. Comprehensive insurance coverage was granted to the families of people killed or injured while fighting Israel.

THE CHRISTIAN MILITIA STATE-SHELL

The PLO example is not unique. Several armed organisations have been able to create their own state-shells. Given their dependency on war economics, state-shells flourish in the anarchy created by political violence. Their primary characteristic is the war economy that sustains their own fight. State-shells can vary in size, being as small as towns or districts of large cities, as was the case with the Christian militia in Beirut. Often their size depends on the scale of the conflict in which they are engaged. In the late 1970s, a cluster of state-shells run by armed groups proliferated in Lebanon. Inside the territories they controlled, each group acted as a state-like ruling power. The Christian militia, for example, led by the Phalange Party of President Amin Gemayel, ran the Christian enclave north and east of Beirut. The militia levied its own customs fees at several ports of entry, costing the Lebanese government – already crippled by war – $300 million yearly in lost revenue. Under the protection of the Phalange, Christian entrepreneurs ran large and profitable smuggling businesses, from which the militia received a percentage. Inside the enclave, the Phalangists imposed their own taxation system, comprising both direct and indirect taxes (a petrol surtax of 10 cents a gallon, a monthly residence tax of $3 per flat, a 2 per cent tax on restaurant bills and several monthly corporate taxes, some as high as several hundred dollars).

The money raised was used to support the militia in its fight against the PLO. An estimated 10,000–15,000 soldiers were on active duty at any given time. However, revenues also went to improve the living conditions of the residents. The Phalange provided all public services, including street cleaning, transportation, planting of trees, retail price control, street patrols, etc. They built car parks and ran radio campaigns to keep the city clean (including suggestions on how to tie rubbish sacks to avoid spillage); they even enforced noise regulations to ensure that late-night parties did not disturb neighbours. 'They replaced the state,' said Nada Klink, a young Phalangist supporter.[25] Most residents of East and North Beirut were happy enough with the arrangement.

HAMAS'S STATE-SHELL

Economic independence facilitated the fragmentation of armed groups, as discussed in chapter 4, as did the environment of political anarchy within which they operated. The proliferation of armed organisations boosted the growth of state-shells. Not all survived. Those that were able to integrate their independent revenues with outside sponsors had a better chance of survival and development. This has been the case with Hamas, the Islamist militant group. When, at the onset of the Gulf War, Arafat supported Saddam Hussein, Saudi Arabia retaliated by terminating all financial assistance to the PLO. Money sent to the occupied territories went to fund Hamas instead.[26] Emerging during the Intifada in the 1980s, Hamas countered the PLO's moderate politics with a mixture of Islamic fundamentalism and democratic principles. Since the group took inspiration from the Muslim Brotherhood and the Islamic Jihad in Egypt and Jordan, it developed strong links with these and other Islamic fundamentalist armed groups, such as the Lebanese Hizbollah. Its political agenda is in sharp contrast to that of the PLO. For instance, Hamas does not recognise the right of the PLO to create a secular state and therefore does not accept its role in peace negotiations with Israel. Because of its opposition to the PLO, Hamas was initially welcomed by Israel. 'Hamas is a creature of Israel,' affirmed Arafat, 'which at the time of Prime Minister [Yitzhak] Shamir gave it money and more than 700 institutions among them schools, universities and mosques.'[27] However, in line with other fundamentalist groups, Hamas calls for the destruction of the state of Israel and its replacement by a Palestinian pan-Islamic state stretching 'from the Mediterranean Sea to the River Jordan'.

The Hamas leadership used the unexpected income to strengthen its self-financing capability and to challenge Arafat's leadership in the Gaza Strip and the West Bank. When Arafat's support for Saddam caused the expulsion of thousands of PLO workers from various Arab countries, Palestinians began looking to Hamas as their new leader. As money flowed in, Hamas offered socio-economic protection to its members and followers. It provided bewildered Palestinians, inside and outside the occupied territories, with an alternative state-shell.

Hamas's improved financial status was followed by a sharp increase in its armed activities. During the first ten months of 1992, the organisation carried out 192 attacks against Israel, as compared to 140 in the whole of 1991. By the end of the 1990s, Hamas had a near-monopoly on terror activity in Israel. According to Israeli intelligence, in the 16 months prior to May 2002, the Saudis provided $135 million to meet Hamas's expenses. Ad hoc charities set up by Arab countries also channelled funds to the group for various purposes. For example, some of these contributed an average of $5,000 per martyr to the families of suicide bombers.[28]

Over the last decade, Hamas's greatest economic effort has been to establish itself as the leading political power inside the occupied territories. In doing so it has carved out its own state-shell. Following in the footsteps of similar violent Islamic movements in Algeria and Jordan, Hamas took root in the political milieu of Gaza and the West Bank. It poured money (and continues to do so) into an extensive social services network which supports schools, orphanages, mosques, health-care clinics, soup kitchens and sports leagues in the poorest areas. As a result, its popularity is particularly high in the shanty towns of the Gaza Strip, where its followers number in the tens of thousands. 'Among the poverty and desolation of these areas,' explained a Hamas sympathiser, 'Hamas's violent and radical message has been the only voice of hope.'[29] The group has also gained support from trade unions and agricultural cooperatives, within hospitals and among student unions. Today, it is the second strongest group inside the occupied territories after al-Fatah. Its main activities are in the sectors of education and social welfare, areas where it can nurture its future martyrs. According to Martin Kramer, an Israeli specialist on Islamic fundamentalism, Hamas takes care of Palestinians from birth to death.[30]

Hamas's budget in the occupied territories is estimated at $70 million,[31] of which about 85 per cent comes from abroad; the rest is raised among Palestinians in the occupied territories. However, these figures represent only a small fraction of Hamas's wealth. Though it still receives about $20–30 million a year from Iran and various ad hoc donations from Saudi Arabia (in April 2002 a telethon in Saudi Arabia raised $150 million for the Palestinians under siege in the occupied territories), more and more money is raised through Palestinian expatriates, private donors in Saudi Arabia and other oil-rich Gulf states. In 1998, after being freed by the Israelis, Sheikh Ahmed Yassin, the spiritual leader of Hamas, set off on a four-month tour of Arab capitals. He was welcomed as a hero and collected donations of over $300 million.[32]

While the PLO achieved economic independence by investing illegal funds in mainstream finance, Hamas's self-financing model resembles Oliver North's Contras fraud scheme, discussed in chapter 3. A network of charities in the United States, Canada and Western Europe with a privileged tax status offers a variety of tax breaks to Muslim contributors. The Holy Land Foundation for Relief and Development (HLF) even stated in its brochure that it collected 'tax-deductible donations for charitable causes in the occupied territories'.[33] Founded in 1992 with a large cash infusion from Hamas,[34] the foundation collected $42 million from 1994 to 2000, according to its tax returns.[35] In 2000 it raised an estimated $13 million in the US alone ($6.3 million in 1999 and $5.8 million in 1998).[36] The HLF also received money from other charitable institutions across North America. In December 2001, for example, South African intelligence unveiled a contribution to the HLF from the Jerusalem Fund, a Canadian aid organisation.[37]

The HLF supported medical clinics, orphanages, schools,

refugee camps and community centres in the West Bank and
Gaza Strip. While charities such as the HLF provided funds,
holding companies such as the Beit-el-Mal Holdings carried
out the construction work. It was thanks to these organisations
that Hamas managed to build its own state-shell inside the
socio-economic vacuum created by the Palestinian Authority
in the occupied territories. The Beit-el-Mal Holdings was a
public investment company with offices in East Jerusalem fully
controlled by Hamas. The majority of the shareholders were
members of Hamas or had strong links to it. According to the
Palestinian Authority, the holdings supported socio-economic
and cultural organisations run by Hamas activists. Beit-el-Mal
also owned a 20 per cent stake in the Al-Aqsa International
Bank, the financial arm of Hamas. In December 2001, these
three organisations were shut down by the authorities because
they were suspected of helping Hamas recruit and train suicide
bombers. However, their role within the armed organisation
went well beyond the financing of Hamas terror attacks; they
were instrumental to the formation of its state-shell.

Over the years, Hamas has been very careful to keep its
covert and overt activities separate. This distinction applies also
to its financing. Donations from established charities are generally not used for military activities. Funds for the latter are
provided by other sources: offerings from businessmen and
donations gathered during conferences held in the US. These
fundraising activities can generate large revenues. In 1994, for
example, at a meeting of the Muslim Arab Youth Association
in Los Angeles, addressed by Sukri Abu Baker, chief executive of
the Holy Land Foundation, $207,000 were collected for the fam-
ilies of Hamas warriors.[38] During Thanksgiving 2000 the Islamic
Association for Palestine, the voice of Hamas in the US, organised a conference to raise $200,000 for the Palestinian martyrs.[39]
A steady income is also generated in Western countries through
complex financial schemes such as money laundering through
real estate. For instance, in the early 1990s, the Woodridge

Fountain, a custom-built subdivision of houses worth $300,000–500,000 in DuPage County, was used by the Quranic Literacy Institute to launder money from a wealthy Saudi supporter of Hamas. The scheme generated funds to purchase arms used by Hamas in several attacks inside Israel.[40]

Economic independence, therefore, not only increased the number of armed organisations attempting to build their own states, it also provided them with the opportunity of competing with each other in promoting themselves and recruiting among the population. This competition was not confined to the economic sphere; it also involved the strategic use of violence. The conciliatory attitude of the Palestinian Authority towards Israel was perceived by many Palestinians as a betrayal of their cause. Hamas capitalised on this and transformed the Intifada into the Fitna, its violent version. Part of the Fitna was made up of Palestinian 'shock committees' and death squads who interrogated and eventually killed suspected 'collaborators' inside the occupied territories and attacked members of the Palestinian Authority, thereby subverting the peace process.

CORRUPTION IN THE OCCUPIED TERRITORIES

According to Pierson's classification, the characteristics of the modern state that state-shells lack are constitutionality, defined as adherence to a set of laws, and sovereignty, which he describes as the acceptance of the existence of a sole ruler. State-shells are therefore undemocratic and highly hierarchical. Whoever controls the monopoly of violence and the war economy on which the state-shell is built sets the rules. Anybody able to conquer these monopolies by means of violence or money becomes the new ruler. Thus, Hamas's attempts to take over the PLO in the occupied territories hold dual significance: they aim to break the monopoly of the Palestinian

Authority over the use of force, and gain economic power. The former is countered with the Fitna and the death squads and the latter with Hamas's social and economic welfare programme. However, conquering these monopolies leads only to further problems. Without constitutionality and sovereignty, power in a state-shell is by definition highly precarious. A sense of uncertainty permeates its infrastructure; loyalty, a rare commodity, can be bought. Those at the top of the military and economic ladder, who enjoy great privileges, tend to accumulate large amounts of wealth to protect themselves and their families from the ups and downs of terror politics. It comes as no surprise that one of the main features of a state-shell is corruption. In a 1999 poll conducted by the Jerusalem Media and Communication Center, 83 per cent of the population in the occupied territories declared that there is corruption within the Palestinian Authority.

Mahmoud Hamdouni is one of the many victims of what some people call the 'Palestinian Mafia State'. In 1996 he bought 30 acres of land outside Jericho, built a petrol filling station and planned a housing estate. His dream came to an abrupt end when the Palestinian Authority decided to speculate in the area and needed his land. Hamdouni was accused of treason and imprisoned. Eventually, he was freed in exchange for signing over his land to the Palestinian Authority. The land was sold and a casino was built on it. As soon as it opened for business, a front company for the Authority took an undeclared 28 per cent stake in the gambling facility. Today, located across the street from the Aqabat Jabr refugee camp, the Oasis Casino rakes in a monthly $15 million in profits.[41]

The Israeli government is also heavily involved in the corruption of the Palestinian Authority. Israel uses its economic power over the occupied territories to maintain a grip on a small elite of Palestinians who are ready to compromise in land-for-peace negotiations. Many officials, for example, are awarded special VIP passes by Israel, so that they can travel freely in and out of the occupied territories, but these passes are revoked whenever they voice criticism against Israel. Corruption has remained an integral component of the peace process. Even Arafat was not immune to Israeli 'favours'. Until June 2000, Israel collected hundreds of millions of dollars in VAT and customs receipts which were channelled directly to his accounts. Arafat was free to dispense the cash as he pleased and, according to several observers, he used the money to buy political loyalty.

Corruption permeates society in a state-shell and becomes the *modus operandi* within its institutions. Many officials from the Palestinian Authority use their position to carry out unethical business practices or to take bribes.[42] In 1999, officials in charge of the 'safe passage' between the West Bank and Gaza were accused of charging double the price for travel permits, which are produced by Israel and sold to the Palestinian Authority at cost.[43] Another instance of corruption involved Jamil Tarifi, Arafat's minister of civil affairs and a key negotiator with Israel during the peace process. In the summer of 2000, Tarifi set up a pharmaceutical distribution company in the occupied territories. Israeli distributors of foreign drugs take a big cut of the profits from pharmaceuticals imported to the occupied territories. The owner of the Jerusalem Pharmaceuticals Co., Mohammad Masrouji, for example, pays heavy duties each time he imports them. They also supply the distributors of drugs to the occupied territories. However, within a single day Tarifi not only managed to register dozens of products with the Palestinian Ministry of Health, a process that would have taken Masrouji years, he also registered Egyptian pharmaceutical products, thus bypassing Israeli distributors. These products, according to industry professionals, did not meet international standards. Nobody at the Ministry of Health bothered to check them. International aid organisations have also been aware of widespread corruption in the occupied territories. However, they remained silent due to the fear that an anti-corruption campaign would destabilise Arafat's regime, thereby jeopardising

the huge sums ($3.8 billion from 1994 to 2000)[44] committed
by donors to these organisations.

THE PREDATORY NATURE OF STATE-SHELLS: THE AUC AND THE FARC IN COLOMBIA

State-shells are by nature predatory and exploitative. They lack
two further characteristics of the modern state: the rule of law
and the exercise of impersonal power, without which people
have no protection against the state. They are at the mercy of
whoever rules the land, often 'dehumanised', used or misused
as commodities. This has happened in Colombia, where civilians bear the heaviest burden of terror. During the last five
years, population displacement has increased dramatically,
reaching levels similar to Sudan and Angola. As many as 300,000
people a year are driven from their homes and become refugees.
In 2000 the death toll was 25,000, with the majority of deaths
occurring in massacres in the countryside. In the same year,
about 55 per cent of the Colombian population were living
below the poverty line.[45] 'We are tired of the war,' cried a man
at the massive demonstration held on 24 October 1999,[46] 'but
we are also tired of being hungry.'[47]

Poverty and death have plagued Colombia for two decades.
The war between two Marxist armed groups, the FARC and
the ELN (the National Liberation Army), on one side, and the
right-wing terror group AUC and the Colombian government
on the other, have ravaged the country. The FARC and ELN,
which are self-financed armed organisations, funded primarily
by illegal trade in cocaine, opium, oil, gold and emeralds, have
established their own state-shells within the country. They regularly bribe government officials, politicians and members of
the army in order to continue their operations unhindered. The
Colombian government, on the other hand, is supported by
the US. In 1999, Washington granted a $1.6 billion aid package

for the following three years. About 300–400 US 'advisers' were dispatched to Colombia as well. After Israel and Egypt, Colombia is the third largest recipient of US military aid and arms in the world.

Meanwhile, the paramilitary Colombian armed group, the AUC (United Self-Defence Forces of Colombia), is only partly self-financed. The bulk of its expenses are met by US military aid to the Colombian government. Founded in April 1997, the AUC is a composite of former narco-trafficker militia, army units and paramilitary groups, trained by the Americans in the 1960s. The AUC is solely the creation of wealthy landowners, drug cartel barons and some segments of the Colombian military. 'They created this organisation to "clear" large areas of Colombia, mostly in the north, of guerrilla fighters and sympathisers,' explained a Colombian refugee. The tactics used are traditional counter-insurgency ones: indiscriminate massacres against the rural population to undermine the social basis of the FARC and ELN.[48]

On 25 October 1997, members of the AUC and of the 4th Brigade of the Colombian army, attacked the village of El Aro, in an area reputed to be sympathetic to the FARC, the left-wing guerrillas. The army encircled the village, preventing anyone from escaping, and the AUC proceeded to exterminate the population. A shopkeeper was tied to a tree and brutally tortured before being castrated: his eyes were gouged out and his tongue severed with a knife. Eleven people, among them three children, were beheaded; all the public buildings were set on fire, houses looted and the water supply destroyed. The AUC and the 4th Brigade left with 30 people, who are now some of the thousands of missing Colombians.[49] The butchery in El Aro had a specific aim: to terrorise FARC sympathisers in an area targeted by the AUC and the army.

Carlos Castaño, the leader of the paramilitary, admitted that most of the casualties of the AUC raids are civilians. 'Do you know why?' he asked Maurice Lemoine from the *Monde*

Diplomatique. 'Because two-thirds of the effective force of the [FARC and ELN] guerrillas are unarmed and they belong to the civilian population.'[50] In the last months of 2001, the AUC was responsible for more civilian deaths than the other two guerrilla groups. As the areas are 'cleared', the AUC moves in. 'The population is increasingly inclined to reject the massacres, for most of which the AUC is responsible,' admitted Colombia's President Andres Pastrana in February 2001.[51] 'There were more than 130 dead in January alone.'

Until recently, the AUC was the *de facto* paramilitary division of the Colombian army, carrying out operations together with US 'advisers' and therefore benefiting from generous US aid packages.[52] But things changed after 11 September 2001. At last, the AUC was added to the official US list of 'foreign terrorist organisations'. According to an accountant who worked for the organisation, the AUC commands an army of 10,000 people and has an annual 'overt' budget of $8 million, mostly funded by taxation of the cocaine business. Several high-ranking members of the regular army are on its payroll, receiving monthly payments of up to $3,000.[53]

The concept of authority and legitimacy, another of Pierson's characteristics of a modern state, is also alien to the state-shell. Power is based exclusively on violence and monopoly of economic resources. Authority requires the consensus of citizens and no such element exists in the state-shell model. Inside state-shells, people have no political identity. In 1998, the Colombian government demilitarised an area of 42,000 square kilometres – the size of Switzerland – which included five municipalities: San Vicente del Caguan, La Macarena, Vista Hermosa, Mesetas and Uribe. The area, which became known as *Despeje*, was given to the FARC as a gesture of goodwill in reaching a peaceful conclusion to the country's civil war. Nobody bothered to ask what the residents thought of this. Overnight, the population of *Despeje* was handed over to the FARC state-shell authority. They were treated as commodities.

Citizenship is the last characteristic of the modern state that state-shells lack. Their people have no voice. Thus in the *Despeje* new rules were imposed on the population by the FARC, rules of war. In the mining towns, for example, the FARC imposed curfews: miners were prohibited from drinking alcohol and meeting after dark. The death penalty was imposed on whoever attempted to challenge the new rulers. Theft carried a minimum sentence of three months' hard labour.[54] As expected, the crime rate dropped and with it the number of violent deaths. In San Vincente, for example, the number of deaths fell from six a week to six a year. As a result two funeral directors had to close shop.[55]

The FARC also carried out social and public works in the *Despeje*. It built and paved new roads and improved the town's communal areas utilising forced and hard labour. It provided people with security, a luxury they had lacked for a long time. Several residents welcomed the change even if the price they had to pay was their own liberty. Many Palestinians in the occupied territories display the same kind of feelings towards Hamas. Similar sentiments will also be found among the population of Selva Alta with regard to Sendero Luminoso.

The PLO, the Christian Phalange, Hamas, FARC and Sendero Luminoso have all created their own state-shells. These pseudo-states have met some of the basic needs of the populations under their rule. Indeed, one of the publicised aims in the propaganda slogans of armed groups running state-shells is the improvement of living conditions of the people residing in the enclaves under their control. The same cannot be said, however, for the AUC and the Contras in Nicaragua. They did not enjoy strong support among the population and are instruments in the hands of their sponsors. In Colombia, a country with an extraordinarily unequal distribution of wealth (the top 10 per cent of the population earns 60 times more than the bottom 10 per cent), the army is fighting a war against left-wing armed groups to make the country safe for businesses conducted by the super-rich. Thus, over the last ten years, the AUC has killed about '15,000 trade unionists, peasants and indigenous leaders, human rights workers, land reforms activists, leftwing politicians and their sympathisers'.[56] The AUC is *de facto* acting as a 'hired' death squad. 'Once we have achieved a peace agreement [with the FARC],' admitted Andres Pastrana, the Colombian president, 'the AUC will cease to have any reason to exist.'[57]

An immediate conclusion can be drawn from this comparison: self-financed armed organisations, with a wide popular or nationalist base, such as the PLO and the IRA, are less exploitative and predatory towards the populations under their rule than armed groups sponsored by foreign states, as are the Contras, and/or by domestic and foreign economic interest groups, as is the AUC.

6. Towards a New World Disorder

'There were 58,000 dead in Vietnam and we owe the Russians one.'

Congressman Charles Wilson commenting
on US sponsorship of the war in Afghanistan

The plane, a huge C-141 Starlifter, always flew non-stop from
Washington DC to Islamabad. To cover the 10,000 miles, it had
to refuel in mid-air, utilising KC10 tanker aircraft based in
Europe and the Middle East. The journey was long, but William
Casey, head of the CIA since 1981 and President Reagan's chief
adviser on intelligence matters, did not mind. In the luxurious
VIP area of the Starlifter, Casey prepared for his biennial
meeting with General Akhtar and top Inter-Services
Intelligence (ISI) officials, the men in charge of logistical support
for the Mujahedin inside Afghanistan.[1] Nicknamed the Cyclone
for his outspoken anti-communism, Casey had embraced with
enthusiasm and passion the idea of manipulating Islamic
ideology to fight the Soviets. Along with many American politicians, he considered the Soviet occupation of Afghanistan to
be the long-awaited opportunity to avenge America's humiliation in Vietnam. Casey was happy to conceal the United States'
involvement from the Muslim warriors, while supplying
weapons that would be used to kill Soviet soldiers and local
guerrillas sponsored by the USSR. It was of no concern to
him that at the outset of the war the Soviets had as many as
90,000 men stationed in Afghanistan. On the contrary, the more
Russians the Mujahedin managed to engage and kill with the
help of the US, the better.[2]

Though the decision to launch a massive covert operation
to arm the Mujahedin and to use Pakistan as a middleman had
been taken by the Carter administration, it was thanks to Reagan,
Casey and their followers that the Afghan war evolved into the
biggest covert operation in US history.[3] Casey was also instrumental in turning Pakistan, a country governed by a corrupt
and undemocratic oligarchy, into one of the war's key players
and beneficiaries. Since the cardinal rule of US involvement in
the anti-Soviet Jihad had been never to have direct contact with
the Mujahedin, the CIA delegated the job of supplying and
arming the Muslim warriors to the ISI, the Pakistani secret
service,[4] which handled the whole operation from the start. Far
more powerful than the CIA was in the US, the ISI was a
parallel structure to the Pakistani state, able to influence all
sections of government and enact independent policies. At the
height of the Afghan war it employed 150,000 people.[5] The ISI
not only welcomed the special link established with the CIA,
it enjoyed doing the dirty work for the Yankees.[6]

With Saudi Arabia matching every dollar allocated by the
CIA, the ISI soon found itself managing a huge flow of arms,
ammunition, equipment and cash through a network of couriers
that became known as the 'Afghan Pipeline'. Depending on
whether the weapons were shipped by sea or air, the pipeline
ran from Karachi or Rawalpindi to Afghanistan. From 1983 to
1987 the annual shipment of weaponry funnelled through it
rose from 10,000 to a steady 65,000 tonnes.[7] The CIA purchased
all military equipment directly from countries friendly to the
US, often after consulting ISI on the military needs of the
Mujahedin. The supplies were then shipped to Islamabad; from
there the ISI delivered them to the Islamic Parties, resistance
groups which directly supported the Mujahedin.[8] The Parties
took care of shipments to individual commanders as well as
the distribution inside Afghanistan. This was a monumental task
due to the treacherous Afghan terrain. Equipment was carried
across the border and deep into the gorges of Afghanistan by

every means of transportation available: car, truck, horse, mule and on the backs of the Mujahedin. For the duration of the war, a constant stream of people and weapons, similar to an infinite procession of ants, ran from Pakistan towards the north.

Aside from military supplies, the CIA also provided the ISI with large sums of cash, using special accounts mostly controlled by the ISI. This cash was essential to the smooth running of the pipeline. By the middle of the 1980s, for example, the ISI needed about $1.5 million a month to move and store goods.[9] Money was required to pay the salaries of the Islamic Parties' officers, to finance the construction and maintenance of storage facilities, to buy equipment, clothes and food rations for the fighters, to pay for transportation, etc. The Parties' monthly expenditure for shipment alone was another $1.5 million.[10] Until 1984, commanders also managed to raise money through taxes in the Afghan provinces where they operated. However, this income soon dried up as the Soviet troops destroyed villages, smashed irrigation systems, burned crops and forced survivors to flee to refugee camps in Pakistan.[11] After 1984, therefore, money was also needed to pay for the Mujahedins' salaries, which ranged from $100 to $300 a month.[12] Considering that as early as 1984 there were already 80,000 to 150,000 Islamist warriors inside Afghanistan,[13] their monthly upkeep alone was enormous. Overall, the cost of the war for the sponsors of the Mujahedin turned out to be no less than $5 billion a year.[14]

A great deal of money handled by the ISI and the Islamic Parties also went to grease the wheels of corruption. Throughout the war, bribes, nepotism and profiteering were widespread along the pipeline. Pakistani customs officers at the various borders with Afghanistan, for example, often demanded bribes to let the convoys of supplies pass. Commanders and fighters needed cash to buy their way out of jail. In Kabul, Hadij Abdul Haq (the first Mujahedin commander to meet Ronald Reagan and Margaret Thatcher) was freed from the notorious Pul-i-Charkhi prison in Kabul after his cousins paid a bribe of $7,500. The US and its allies were not immune to this trend, either. As was the case with the fraudulent covert schemes to finance the Contras, behind a façade of ideology the anti-communist crusade was for its sponsors primarily a money-spinning machine. The main source of US financing came from the black budget, hidden funds the Pentagon used to support covert operations, which rose from a yearly $9 billion in 1981 to $36 billion in the mid-1990s. William Casey used it as the CIA's private fund. The amount of disposable cash in the hands of CIA officers was therefore enormous. International arms brokers and producers, politicians – everybody fought to have a stake in the business.

The amount of money wasted was huge and it leaked all along the pipeline. Several 'friendly' countries, for example, used CIA contracts to unload old and unusable military hardware. With the exception of China, which until 1984 sold first-class equipment,[15] countries like Egypt and Turkey saw in the anti-Soviet Jihad a golden opportunity to get rid of obsolete weaponry. Purchases were also conditioned by political decisions. In 1985, against ISI advice, the CIA bought British Blowpipe surface-to-air missiles (SAMs), which were too heavy to be transported across the rugged terrain of Afghanistan by the Mujahedin. The CIA even acquired weapons that had been captured by the Israelis during the invasion of Lebanon. The Americans, however, were careful to hide their origins.[16]

To run such an operation, the CIA had to rely on an ad hoc infrastructure of international financial institutions. Casey was particularly keen on the Bank of Credit and Commerce International (BCCI). Founded in 1972 by Agha Hasan Abedi, a Pakistani businessman, the BCCI had become the world's largest Muslim banking institution with over 400 branches in 73 countries around the globe. The BCCI was nominally owned by Arab capital from the Gulf. Twenty per cent was controlled by Khalid Bin Mahfouz, the son of the founder of the National

Commercial Bank of Saudi Arabia, the bank used by the Saudi Royal Family. Another leading shareholder was Kamal Adham, a former head of Saudi Intelligence, whose business partner was the former CIA station chief in Saudi Arabia, Raymond Close.[17] Casey knew that the BCCI had acted on behalf of the Saudis in several covert operations. Money from the kingdom had reached the Contras in Nicaragua, Unita in Angola and even Noriega in Panama via secret BCCI channels.[18] Undoubtedly, these ties were a plus as Saudi Arabia was the main sponsor of the anti-Soviet Jihad. Casey was also aware that the bank had been of service to several US institutions; the National Security Council, for example, had funnelled money through its network for the Iran–Contras arms deals and the CIA regularly utilised BCCI accounts to fund its covert operations. Moreover, the BCCI was extremely well connected in the murky underworld of illegal arms. For example, a $17 million secret arms sale to Iran by the US government, brokered by the Saudi businessman Adnan Khashoggi, had been made with the cooperation of the BCCI branch in Monte Carlo.[19] It was also thanks to BCCI involvement that the Saudis got hold of Chinese Silkworm missiles.[20] The bank even brokered arms purchases for Israeli spy agencies and Western intelligence organisations.[21] Finally, while the capital was Arab, the middle and top management were Pakistani and, therefore, its core was well rooted in Karachi.[22] This detail was of great importance for the CIA. In the eyes of Casey, the BCCI had the perfect pedigree for the job.

As soon as Abedi's bank came on board, all covert operations were passed to its 'black network', virtually a secret banking institution within the bank. Its headquarters were in Karachi and it was from this city that the underground network acted as a full-service bank for the CIA. With about 15,000 employees, it operated in a similar fashion to the Mafia. It was a fully integrated organisation: it financed and brokered covert arms deals among different countries, it shipped goods using its own

fleet, insured them with its own agency and provided manpower
and security en route.[23] In Pakistan, BCCI officials knew whom
to bribe and when to do it. They also knew where to channel
the funds. Richard Kerr, the former CIA director who admitted
that the CIA had secret BCCI accounts in Pakistan, confirmed
that those accounts had been opened to distribute the CIA
funds to Pakistani officers and members of the Afghan resistance.[24] By the mid-1980s, the black network had gained control
of the port of Karachi and handled all customs operations for
CIA shipments to Afghanistan, including the necessary bribes
for the ISI. It was the BCCI's job to make sure that cargoes
of arms and equipment were discharged quickly.[25]

As the war progressed, costs soared. There was constant
shortage of money along the pipeline to supply the Mujahedin
and so the ISI and CIA began looking for additional sources
of income. One that proved viable was drug smuggling.
Afghanistan was already a large producer of opium, but it
supplied only small neighbouring regional markets. The ISI
took on itself the task of increasing production, processing
the opium and smuggling heroin to rich Western markets. As the
Mujahedin advanced and conquered new regions, they were
told to impose a levy on opium to finance the revolution. To
pay the tax, farmers planted more poppies. Drug merchants
from Iran, who had moved to Afghanistan after the revolution,
offered growers credit in advance of their crops.[26] They also
provided the expertise needed to refine opium into heroin. In
less than two years, opium production boomed. Soon the
narcotics-based economy took over the traditional agrarian
economy of Afghanistan and, with the help of the ISI, the
Mujahedin opened hundreds of heroin laboratories. Within two
years the Pakistan–Afghanistan borderland had become the
biggest centre for the production of heroin in the world and
the single greatest supplier of heroin on American streets,
meeting 60 per cent of the US demand for narcotics. Annual
profits were estimated between $100 billion and $200 billion.[27]

The preferred smuggling route went through Pakistan. The ISI used the Pakistani army to transport the drugs across the country,[28] while the BCCI provided financial and logistical support for the whole operation. Although most of it was sold and consumed in the streets of North America, no investigation from the US narcotics authorities or the DEA was ever carried out; no action was taken to stop the well-documented flow of heroin from Pakistan to the United States.[29] By 1991, yearly production from the tribal area under the control of the Mujahedin[30] had risen to an astonishing 70 metric tons of premium quality heroin,[31] up 35 per cent from the previous year.[32] In 1995, the former CIA director of the Afghan operation, Charles Cogan, admitted that the CIA had indeed sacrificed the drug war to fight the Cold War.

While heroin was smuggled out of the region, high-tech equipment was smuggled in. The ISI and the Islamic Parties took advantage of the Afghan Transit Trade Agreement, better known as the ATTA, to launch a prosperous smuggling business of duty-free goods. In 1950, Pakistan and Afghanistan had signed the ATTA to give Afghanistan, a landlocked country, the right to import duty-free goods through the port of Karachi. Duty-free goods destined for Afghanistan were loaded in sealed containers on trucks heading for Kabul. Some of the products were sold in Afghanistan, but the bulk of them never left the trucks. The goods were returned to Pakistan to be sold on the local markets. The trucks were 'taxed' at various roadblocks by corrupt Pakistani customs officers and the transport Mafia; warlords who controlled the territories they had to cross levied their own taxes and even customs officers in Kabul took their own cut. Even so, ATTA duty-free goods were available in Pakistani markets at lower prices than identical products imported legitimately into the country. What made ATTA items so competitive was the exceptionally high import duty levied by the Pakistani government on imports, especially of electronic equipment from the Far East. ATTA stereos, TVs, video recorders and CDs could be as much as 40–50 per cent cheaper. This form of smuggling gave Pakistan a limited supply of inexpensive duty-free foreign goods and the ISI an additional source of income. Throughout the 1980s the ATTA and illegal trade expanded, servicing most of communist-controlled Afghan cities and generating about $50 million per year.

The costs throughout the anti-Soviet Jihad were phenomenal; outflows were constantly higher than inflows. US and Saudi direct financing coupled with the astonishing revenues from the drug and smuggling trade were still insufficient to support the pipeline. The bulk of the cash went to keep the whole covert operation in motion. To function, the pipeline relied on complex and expensive infrastructures located around the world. To keep arms, drugs, duty-free goods, smuggled products and cash moving, money had to change hands many times, and each exchange had a cost. Financial transactions had to be handled by very expensive hidden banking structures; without them no flow of funds could be guaranteed. In addition, the entire system needed to be constantly oiled with bribes and corruption. Theft was rampant. Arms and equipment in transit in Pakistan were often stolen. In fact, as little as 30 per cent of the weapons ever reached their intended recipients.[33] According to a former fighter, for each US dollar allocated, the Mujahedin were lucky if they received 20–30 cents. Therefore, at the receiving end of the pipeline, the Islamic Parties, commanders and Mujahedin were always short of cash, ammunition and sometimes even food. 'There were times when we had nothing to eat,' confessed a former Mujahid. Supplies that did reach the fighters were often late, provisions were insufficient and money desperately short. It was thanks to the voluntary donations of rich Arab organisations and individuals that the Parties were able to bridge the gaps and overcome shortages. Since these contributions went directly to the Parties, they were not subjected to the additional costs and thefts of the pipeline. However, money went primarily to the four fundamentalist

Islamic Parties and as a result the moderate ones became less efficient.[34]

'Independent Arab money kept the anti-Soviet Jihad alive,' admitted a former Mujahid, 'and it was thanks to these funds that the war was won.'[35] Throughout the war, Islamic warriors were ignorant of the role played by the US; they did not suspect that they were fighting a war by proxy. Even a well-connected Saudi like Osama bin Laden claimed to be unaware of the extent of CIA involvement. 'Neither I,' he stated, 'nor my brothers, saw evidence of American help.'[36] Hidden behind the ISI, the CIA succeeded in avoiding any direct contact with the fighters. 'We did not train Arabs,' confirmed Milton Beardman, a high-ranking CIA officer.[37] Their training was conducted by the ISI in military camps scattered throughout the region. An estimated 80,000 people were trained in these camps during the war. When Muslim fighters discovered after the war had ended that the US had manipulated the anti-Soviet Jihad, they felt humiliated. This sentiment greatly contributed to the hate nurtured by Islamist armed groups towards America.

BREAKING THE COLD WAR MOULD

Overall, the anti-Soviet Jihad broke the Cold War mould of war by proxy. Though it was confined within a single state, it was fought by a multi-ethnic Muslim army: the Mujahedin. Thus, it had enormous repercussions throughout the Muslim world. It had two main sponsors, the United States and Saudi Arabia. Each pursued different goals. The Saudis were motivated by religious colonialism, the Americans by naked revenge. It was fought regardless of the consequences for the balance of power in Central Asia. The primary aim of the US instigators was to inflict a mortal blow to the Soviet Union, as if by doing so the US would finally find a justification for the loss of 58,000 American lives in Vietnam. It was carried out without taking into consideration the weakness of the Soviet position in Afghanistan. For example, as early as 1983, the Russians had realised their mistake and were considering withdrawing. By 1985, when Gorbachev came to power, the Politburo was in favour of pulling out within a year. The US administration, on the other hand, running high on emotion, intensified the fight. Casey even suggested that the ISI push the fight across the borders into the Central Asian regions.[38] Indeed, it was the rise in US support for the Afghan resistance that prevented the Soviets from leaving Afghanistan in 1986.[39]

The war also carried the seeds of the economic disorder that would grip that part of the world in the following years. It forged and cemented the alliance between the United States and Pakistan, a corrupt dictatorship, which exploited this privileged position to acquire nuclear power and establish a strong political presence in Asia. It accelerated the process of disintegration of the Soviet Union, which in turn destabilised vast regions at its periphery, such as Central Asia, the Caucasus and the Balkans. In addition, it led the US to underestimate Islamist insurgency and its economic power. The defeat of America's Cold War enemy blinded the US political elite to the consequences of such a victory. US foreign policy failed to adapt to the new world order.

America's foreign policy had been shaped during half a century of Cold War. A generation of diplomats had been raised in the shadow of 'Soviet containment'. The dismembering of the Soviet Union left them in a political vacuum, without specific guidelines. To fill it, American diplomacy turned to business. They became ambassadors and diplomats of the strong Washington lobbies that backed their own parties. Almost overnight, it became apparent that US foreign policy had turned into a powerful vehicle for American corporations, seeking opportunities everywhere instead of promoting international stability. Sadly, this imperialist approach is still the engine powering the foreign policy of George W. Bush.

In the early 1990s, impelled by the oil lobby, George Bush Sr underestimated the consequences of the disintegration of the economic equilibrium in Central Asia, a balance of power forged in 1945 at Yalta.[40] The dismantling of Soviet power was perceived as the beginning of a lucrative period of exploitation, with US oil companies controlling the vast energy fields of the region. So confident was the White House in this outcome that Washington did not bother to create a political framework for the region, or even issue guidelines for the post-Soviet area. In the Middle East, while pursuing alliances with regional oligarchies, i.e. Arab capitals and dictatorial Muslim countries, the US failed to notice and understand the forces of change in motion in the region. It underestimated the implications of the hostage crisis in Lebanon, the role of Iran as an Islamic state and the rise of state-independent armed groups. Above all, it ignored the political consequences of the massive transfer of wealth generated by the first oil shock, the build-up of resentment towards the United States and the disillusionment of a fast-growing Muslim population towards the Arab leaders. These events, in particular, were at the root of a massive flow of money and people towards Islamist militant groups. These phenomena, as we shall see, created an ideal habitat for the growth of a formidable adversary: the New Economy of Terror.

7. Islamist Economics

'War is . . . the continuation of politics by other means.'

Karl von Clausewitz

General Mohammad Zia ul-Haq had a dream: to head a Muslim confederation stretching from Turkmenistan to Kashmir, a powerful Pan-Islamic league under the dominance of Pakistan. Casey and the US administration encouraged him in pursuing such a fantasy. To legitimise Pakistan as a US ally and as the front line against Iran, Washington declared that Pakistan was a secular state, though Sharia law in fact superseded the written constitution. Thanks in part to Pakistan's support of US policies, Soviet power disintegrated in Central Asia. In exchange for the favour, America turned a blind eye when Pakistan began funding Islamist fundamentalist groups in the aftermath of the Afghan war, and stood aside when Pakistan acquired nuclear power.[1]

At the end of the anti-Soviet Jihad, the powerful military and intelligence network of the ISI was not dismantled; on the contrary, it remained intact, as did the ISI's special relationship with the CIA. The ISI continued to export Islamist warriors from Pakistan to Central Asia and the Caucasus. While Soviet troops began a painful retreat from Afghanistan, a stream of covert operations was launched in Central Asia. The ISI acted as 'a catalyst for the disintegration of the Soviet Union and the emergence of new republics in Central Asia'.[2] When the republics of Kazakhstan, Kyrgyzstan, Tajikistan, Turkmenistan and Uzbekistan reluctantly gained their independence from Moscow in 1991, the ISI played a pivotal role in supporting

Islamist armed insurgencies which destabilised them. The aim was the implementation of Pakistan's plans for expansion.

Following the blueprint of the anti-Soviet Jihad, the Pakistanis set up their own arms pipelines. Pakistan's arsenal, one of the richest in Asia, had been accumulated during the Afghan war when the ISI siphoned off a large portion of weapons and equipment in transit through the Afghan Pipeline. Thus, in the aftermath of the war, Pakistan emerged as the major source of weapons in Central and South Asia. Three pipelines running from Pakistan were established: one supplying Islamist rebel groups inside India; another running to South East Asia through Thailand, Malaysia and Singapore; and the third supplying Central Asia.

The ISI had two main sources of funding for covert operations in neighbouring regions: the ATTA and the narcotics smuggling trade. After 1992, contraband activities increased exponentially. New avenues had been opened by the collapse of the Soviet Union; commercial routes which linked Kabul to the new Central Asian republics. ATTA duty-free goods began reaching these countries and their emerging markets. In 1992–93, the business was worth $128 million and its growth was accelerating. By 1997 Pakistan's and Afghanistan's share alone amounted to $2.5 billion – more than half Afghanistan's estimated GDP. Over the same period, the figure for the whole Central Asian region rose to a staggering $5 billion.[3] These figures reflect the economic disarray that occurred in the region following independence. As Russian troops moved out of the newly formed Central Asian republics, local armies and politicians were left to fend for themselves. Inside the republics, import–export activity ground to a halt because Moscow demanded payment in hard currency for their exports while refusing to pay the high prices of the Soviet era for imports. Cotton, minerals and oil prices plummeted. Loans from Russia, which had been the monetary lifeline of the region, were cancelled; banks in Moscow demanded immediate repayment of all outstanding loans. The government debts of the Central Asian Republics were called in and repayment was requested promptly in US dollars. Attempts to open up the economies of the republics to the outside world failed for lack of diplomatic and economic channels. Within the economic chaos created by independence, unemployment shot up, inflation soared, living standards plummeted and shortages of products became rampant at every level, including raw materials for industry and agriculture.[4] Central Asia met all the conditions to become a hotbed of Islamist terror.

THE RISE OF THE ISLAMIC MOVEMENT OF UZBEKISTAN

As political unrest grew, the leaders of the republics – all hardline communists who had risen to power through the Soviet hierarchy – reacted by clamping down on freedom. In this repressive climate, political violence escalated. Militant Islamist groups became the sole opposition and the economy of war they generated the only source of sustenance for a large section of the population. While the ISI trained Islamist insurgents and supplied arms, Turkey, Saudi Arabia, several Gulf states and the Taliban funded them. In 1998 Tohir Abdouhalilovitch Yuldeshev and Juma Namangiani founded the Islamic Movement of Uzbekistan (IMU), with a network that extended across several Central Asian republics, and declared Jihad against the Uzbek government. The movement supported itself with a mixture of foreign sponsorship and self-finance. In 1999, for example, it received $25 million from foreign sponsors. Funds came from various sources: the Turkish Islamist leader Necmettin Erbakan sent $100,000 for 'works' in Uzbekistan. A Turkish émigré organisation in Cologne under Erbakan's patronage signed a contract with Yuldeshev for the acquisition and free transfer of weapons worth several thousand dollars.[5]

An IMU representative collected $270,000 in Saudi Arabia, while a single donor, Mohammad Amin Turkistuni, offered $260,000 for the purchase of arms.[6] Even the Taliban leader Mullah Omar contributed $50,000.[7] That same year the IMU raised about $5 million in ransom for the release of four Japanese geologists abducted in the mountains of southern Kyrgyzstan. However, the bulk of revenues originated from the rampant drug and smuggling trade in the region of which the IMU was a part. Namangiani's networks in Tajikistan and in Central Asia were used to smuggle opium from Afghanistan. It was partly thanks to Namangiani's contacts in Chechnya that heroin reached Europe. According to Interpol, about 60 per cent of exported Afghan narcotics in 2002 passed through Central Asia. The IMU controlled 70 per cent of the opium and heroin that moved though this area,[8] and set up heroin laboratories in the territories under its control.[9]

The armed group's stronghold is the Tavildara valley, located in Tajikistan. Since 1999, however, it has fought to gain control of the Fergana valley as well. The valley, 200 miles long and 70 miles wide, forms the economic heart of Central Asia. It houses the densest concentration of people in the region: about 10 million inhabitants (20 per cent of the total population of Central Asia). The Fergana valley has been a traditional hub of Islam, a place bathed in a religious aura. However, the advent of Islamist armed insurgency and IMU successes in the area should not be attributed to religious fervour alone; rather, they are a direct consequence of the poverty that has plagued the region following the disintegration of the Soviet Union. Under the Soviets, the economy had been highly integrated, with a few centralised markets serving the whole area. The birth of the republics and their detachment from Moscow set in motion a process of decentralisation, which had the effect of destroying much of the agrarian and industrial infrastructure. Following independence, borders were drawn between the republics, dividing villages, farms, sometimes even families. Passports were required to travel to local markets, which were now located in different countries. Irrigation systems were interrupted as they criss-crossed the various borders, preventing water supplies flowing from one country to another. Trade between the Fergana valley and Tashkent, the largest and most important Central Asian market, was disrupted as this market was no longer freely accessible.

Financially and militarily backed by ISI, the IMU found widespread support among the local tribes of the Fergana valley in its fight against the newly formed governments of the republics. Government neglect and corruption had turned what was once a fertile valley into a poverty-stricken area. Lack of seeds and loans had almost destroyed agriculture, while industry was crippled by a shortage of raw materials. Due to the corruption and mismanagement of the Uzbek president Karimov, the valley failed to benefit from IMF loans, one of the few monetary lifelines available. In April 2001, unable to convince Karimov of the need to introduce reforms to stabilise the economy, the IMF withdrew from Uzbekistan altogether. Since then, capital flows have been meagre. Turkey has invested hundreds of millions of dollars in a few joint ventures; the US continues to invest in mining and in the energy fields; South Korean and German companies have bought interests in the automobile industry. But sporadic foreign loans and investment are of little help to the country's chronic monetary shortage, let alone to the people of the Fergana valley. Most deals are signed and handled by Karimov himself, who pockets large shares of the money. As a result, unemployment and inflation are rampant; in the Fergana valley unemployment has reached 80 per cent in recent years. Given that 60 per cent of the valley's population is below the age of 25, it is a fertile recruitment ground for Islamist armed groups.

Following a common pattern, as IMU guerrillas gained control of the territory and declared villages and regions 'liberated', they provided sustenance to the local population, integrating them into their economy. Recruitment is the most common and popular way of doing this. Namangiani is reported to pay his men between $100 and $500 a month. 'It's the same everywhere,' explained a social worker in the Batken region in Kyrgyzstan to author Ahmed Rashid, 'the villages are empty of young men. Either they have gone to Russia to look for work or they join Namangiani because at least he pays them and there is so much poverty here.'[10] Not all recruits are sent to fight, however; the IMU has an extensive network of sleepers, terror cells in the Fergana valley waiting to be activated. Others are given the task of providing food, arms and supplies from Tajikistan and Kyrgyzstan. To ensure supplies for his men in the Fergana valley, for example, Namangiani reached an agreement with the government of Tajikistan and the local tribes. He promised not to interfere with Tajikistani politics or to revive militant Islamist movements in that country in exchange for the reopening of ancient and important trade routes.

The success of the IMU in destabilising the Fergana valley and in establishing its own state-shell in Central Asia is apparent. The IMU network encompasses the political borders of newly formed countries; it stretches across the borders of three republics and is rooted deep into their impenetrable valleys and gorges. Guerrillas purchase supplies from local villages, they pay well and provide protection to the inhabitants. After years of civil war, the IMU has brought stability and economic growth to several villages. The local population have welcomed this change. This outcome is the direct consequence of the ISI's strategy of promoting Islamist terror as a tool to pursue Pakistan's scheme of expansion.

THE NARCOTICS TRADE

The other major source of financing utilised by the ISI to fund Islamist armed insurgency was the narcotics trade. Three-quarters of the world's opium output is produced in Central Asia, in the so-called Golden Crescent. According to the United Nations, at the end of the 1990s, the overall drug turnover was as high as $500 billion, of which the Golden Crescent contributed $200 billion.[11] Between 1983 and 1992, narcotics revenues for Pakistan rose from $384 million to $1.8 billion[12] thanks to the intervention of the ISI. The agency has extensive experience in this field, having developed Afghanistan's poppy production. Former Pakistani prime minister, Nawaz Sharif, claims that the Pakistan Army Chief of Staff, General Afzal Beg, together with the Director-General of the ISI, asked Sharif's permission to smuggle heroin to fund covert operations.[13] The request was a polite way of letting him know that the ISI had begun funding Islamist guerrillas in the Punjab and Kashmir.

Arms shipments to the Punjab and Kashmir were coupled with the training of fighters in military camps controlled by the ISI inside Pakistan. During the first decade following the Afghan war, the arms trade increased dramatically. In 1987, Indian security forces on border duty confiscated 33 rifles and 92 pistols, whereas in 1997 they confiscated 16,772 Kalashnikov rifles alone.[14]

Relations between the ISI and Kashmiri guerrillas were well cemented and in the following years grew stronger. In 1989, the ISI contributed to the creation of the Jammu and Kashmiri Hizbul Mujahedin group among the Jamiat and Islamist followers.[15] In 1993 it created the Harkatul Ansar in Peshawar, an armed group of non-Kashmiri warriors composed of Islamist militants and veterans of the anti-Soviet Jihad.[16] That same year the election of Benazir Bhutto as prime minister brought the powerful anti-American Deobandi party, the Jamiat-ul-Ulema-e-Islam (JUI), into mainstream politics.[17] The JUI was the main supporter and sponsor of the Taliban in the fight for control of Afghanistan; it more than welcomed the conflict in Kashmir. It was to the north and then to the west, however, along the southern border of the former Soviet Union, that Pakistan successfully ignited Islamist armed insurgency.

DESTABILISING THE CAUCASUS

The destabilisation of the Caucasus and the emerging role of Chechnya as the stronghold against the Russians were crucial factors for Islamist insurgency. Following in the footsteps of General Zia, Bhutto had reformulated the dictator's dream: the creation of a trans-Asian axis, under Pakistani hegemony, stretching from the eastern border with China, inclusive of Afghanistan and the Central Asian republics, to the oil-producing regions of the Caspian Sea.[18] Interestingly, the drug route of Afghan narcotics to Europe cut across the same regions. In order to realise such a dream, Pakistan needed to establish hegemony in Central Asia and in Afghanistan, where the Russians were still backing the Northern Alliance. Through a shaky coalition of ethnic warlords, the Northern Alliance maintained a firm grip on Afghanistan's northern regions, from where it carried on fighting the Taliban. One Soviet-backed warlord in particular, Ahmed Shah Massoud, represented a serious obstacle to Pakistan's plans. Massoud controlled the strategic strip of northern Afghanistan that bordered Turkmenistan, Uzbekistan and Tajikistan, a tongue of land regarded by the Pakistani ruling elite as a vital geopolitical area for the implementation of the trans-Asian axis.

The growing conflict in Chechnya, then as now fighting for full independence from Russia, offered an opportunity to divert Russian attention and resources away from Massoud. The Pakistani plan was to encourage Islamist insurgency in Chechnya, forcing the Russians to fight in the Caucasus. Accordingly, in 1994 the ISI began nurturing Shamil Basayev, a young Chechen field commander. He was trained and indoctrinated along with a small group of lieutenants at the Amir Muawia camp in the Khost province in Afghanistan. The camp had been set up in the 1980s by the ISI in cooperation with the CIA and was run by the Afghan warlord Gulbadin Hekmatyar. Once the programme had been completed, the group was sent to Pakistan to undergo further training.[19] Experienced instructors, most of them veterans of the Afghan Jihad, were also sent to Chechnya to train future fighters. Among them was the Jordanian-born Khattab, whom Basayev had met and befriended in Pakistan. Khattab was a hero of the anti-Soviet Jihad; he was also close to Osama bin Laden and his funding network. In 1995, Khattab was invited to Grozny to head the training of Mujahedin fighters.

Partnerships and alliances that had proved successful during the Afghan Jihad were soon re-created in Chechnya. The master plan for Islamist insurgency in the Caucasus and Kashmir was drawn up at a meeting held in Mogadishu, Somalia, in 1996 and attended by the ISI and various Islamist armed groups.[20] Osama bin Laden and high-ranking Iranian intelligence officers were also present. General Javed Ashraf of the ISI was handed the task of providing arms and ammunition and paying for the transportation of Islamist fighters from the training camps in Afghanistan, Pakistan, Lebanon and Sudan to the new Islamist Jihad fronts in Chechnya and Kashmir.[21]

According to Soviet intelligence sources, bin Laden contributed $25 million to the fight in Chechnya.[22] Until then, the Islamist guerrilla groups had been supported by a mixture of state and private sponsorship, primarily from Pakistan and Saudi Arabia, and crime-based self-financing activities. During the first Chechen war, the Islamist insurgency had relied mainly on foreign sponsors and domestic smuggling. In 1991, for instance, a barter deal was arranged between the Armenian militia in Nagorno-Karabakh and the National Congress of the Chechen People. A Georgian paramilitary middleman, Tengiz Kitovani,[23] brokered an exchange of Armenian small arms for oil and oil-related products from Chechnya.[24] In 1995, Khattab's move to Grozny was arranged by the International Islamic Relief Organisation, a Saudi-based charity funded by mosques and wealthy donors in the Gulf.[25] The same year, Basayev, and later Khattab, linked up with criminal organisations in Russia as well as with Albanian organised crime and the Kosovo Liberation Army (KLA). These alliances proved fruitful in generating profits from the drug trade and contraband, especially that of arms. Chechnya soon became an important hub for various rackets, including kidnapping and the trade in counterfeit dollars. Basayev also benefited financially from money-laundering activities in Chechnya.[26]

While the terror economy can either break down or destroy the traditional economy, either process will produce dangerous spill-over into nearby countries, as it did in the Caucasus in the late 1990s. As Chechen war economics bled into neighbouring countries, Islamist insurgency broke out in Ingushetia, Dagestan and North Ossetia. Initially, Saudi Arabia, Lebanon and Iran were responsible for funding the spread of Islamist armed groups in the region; soon however the various armed organisations were able to link up and plug into the booming war economy of the Caucasus. In Tbilisi, for example, neon signs put up by gun dealers advertised the sale of Kalashnikovs.[27] No superpower intervened to prevent the escalation of the terror economy. Russia, the leading power in the Commonwealth of Independent States, was struggling to get a grip in its own territory. Meanwhile, the US ignored the region, leaving it an easy prey for the expansionism of Muslim countries such as Pakistan and religious colonisation by Saudi Arabia.

THE ISLAMISATION OF THE BALKANS

As envisaged by Zia and Bhutto, the opening of a new front in the Caucasus siphoned off Russian support for the Northern Alliance. Though the Alliance remained a threat to the Taliban, it was a manageable and containable menace. What the Pakistani leaders could not predict was that from Chechnya, Mujahedin fighters would continue to move west along the drug route to Albania and Kosovo, reaching the eastern frontier of Europe.

The legacy of such expansion is the buoyant contraband of narcotics into Europe. Nearly 75 per cent of the heroin that enters the Old Continent transits via Turkey. From here, a huge quantity of heroin is carried through the Balkans: Bulgaria, Greece, Kosovo, Albania and the former Yugoslavian territories, through what has become known as the 'Balkan Route'. Each month, an estimated 4–6 metric tons of heroin are shipped from Turkey via the Balkans to Western Europe.[28]

In the Caucasus and in the Balkans, the economics of terror gave Islamist insurgency a new breath of life. Armed groups no longer needed the patronage of countries like Pakistan to carry on their fight. The narcotics trade gave them the opportunity to reduce their dependency on foreign powers and achieve self-sufficiency. These goals motivated Chechen warlords to establish good relationships with the KLA in Kosovo and to set up profitable smuggling businesses. It was thanks to the mediation of Chechen criminal groups that the KLA and the Albanian mafia managed to gain control of the transit of heroin in the Balkans. The benefits were soon apparent. During the second half of the 1990s, one of the KLA's primary sources of self-financing was the smuggling of narcotics from Afghanistan. The KLA also became a key player in the drugs-for-arms trade as well as in the laundering of drug money. German anti-narcotics agencies estimate that in 1998 $1.5 billion in drug profits was laundered in Kosovo, utilising about 200 private banks and currency exchange offices.[29]

The KLA terror economy was highly integrated with Albania's growing underground economy and illegal cross-border activity. In 1992, a triangular trade in narcotics, oil and arms took root in Albania. The embargo on Serbia and Montenegro and the blockade enforced by Greece on Macedonia in 1993 and 1994 fuelled such business. In fact, the trade in narcotics and weapons prospered under the nose of a large American contingent, which had the specific task of enforcing the embargo. The West simply turned a blind eye. Oil and narcotics revenues bought arms, often by barter trade. 'Deliveries of oil to Macedonia, skirting the Greek embargo [were] used to cover heroin, as are deliveries of Kalashnikov rifles to Albanian "brothers" in Kosovo.'[30] Indeed, the embargo created the ideal conditions for the spread of the terror economy, as it contributed to the collapse of the traditional economy. As unemployment in Kosovo reached a staggering 70 per cent, thousands of young people joined the KLA.[31]

The Islamist groups empowered by Pakistan to achieve its hopes of hegemony had gained economic independence and began pursuing their own political agendas. In the second half of the 1990s, Islamist insurgency spread from the Caucasus to the Balkans, on the doorstep of Europe. As will be described in chapters 9 and 10, new sponsors would soon emerge to support such a cause, among them Islamic banks and businesses.

8. Terror Jihad: The Islamist Crusades

'The acme of this religion is Jihad.'

Osama bin Laden, reflecting on
his experience in the Afghan war

On 27 November 1095, Pope Urban II held a public session in the Cathedral of Clermont in France. People knew that a great announcement was about to be delivered and flocked to the church. Soon the church was bursting with the nobility, the clergy and the people. Outside its doors more men and women gathered, eager to share the extraordinary news. Facing such a multitude, the pope ordered to have his chair carried outside the eastern gate of the city and placed on a platform. Surrounded by a sea of heads, Urban II stood up and delivered his speech.

With eloquence and passion he began describing the sufferings of the Christian brethren in the East. 'Eastern Christendom [has] appealed for help,' he revealed. '. . . The Turks [are] advancing into the heart of the Christian land, maltreating the inhabitants and desecrating their shrines.'[1] All around him people were nodding in agreement. The pope went on to denounce the shameful conditions in which Christians lived in Jerusalem and the sufferings imposed upon the pilgrims who journeyed there. 'Let Western Christendom march to the rescue of the East,' he proposed. 'Rich and poor alike should go. They should leave off slaying each other and fight instead a righteous war, doing the work of God; and God [will] lead them.' The crowd responded enthusiastically to these words; the nobility, who were itching for war, envisaged the looting of Palestinian cities and the lands they would conquer; the clergy embraced the idea of being once again the leading force of the masses, anticipating the great wealth and power that the pope's call to arms would bring; the merchants, bankers and traders, who had been restrained in their commerce by the power of their Arab counterparts, who not only controlled the Mediterranean but were the absolute rulers of international commerce, saw in Urban's exhortation to war the long-awaited opportunity to expand their businesses; and the poor, plagued by famine, disease and poverty, thanked God for the opportunity to have daily meals once they joined the new Christian armies. Even the sinners, those who were unable to follow the Church's strict set of rules, were happy, for Urban II offered them a chance to redeem themselves. For those who die in battle, he declared, there would be absolution and the remission of sins. The masses felt as if the gates of Paradise had been flung open.

The pope stressed the sanctity of martyrdom, contrasting its rewards with the misery of life on earth, where men were constantly threatened by the Devil and his endless temptations. Life was a continuous struggle against the flesh; humanity was tormented by the needs of the body and the will to maintain the virtues of the soul. To all those who would die in battle, the pope offered a much better existence in Paradise, a happy and joyful land where men could finally rest in the friendly shadow of God. 'There must be no delay,' Urban II firmly concluded. '[Let's] be ready to set out when the summer [has] come, with God to be [our] guide.' After a few months, the First Crusade sailed for the Holy Land.

Almost a thousand years later, from the Eastern shores of Africa, Osama bin Laden launched a similar appeal to the Muslim world: 'The people of Islam [have] suffered from aggression, iniquity and injustice imposed on them by the Zionist Crusaders' alliance and their collaborators,'[2] he wrote in 1996.

To justify his call to arms he reminded his followers of the slaughter of Muslims across the world. 'Their blood was spilled in Palestine and Iraq' as well as Lebanon, Tajikistan, Burma, Kashmir, the Philippines, Somalia, Eritrea, Chechnya, Bosnia-Herzegovina and Indonesia. He denounced the occupation of Jerusalem by Israel and the sufferings of the Palestinian people trapped inside the occupied territories. 'They [the Israelis] have occupied the blessed land around Jerusalem, route of the journey of the Prophet (Allah's blessing and salutations on him),' he declared, and since they have violated 'the land of the two Holy Places [Saudi Arabia] . . . the people of Islam should join forces and support each other to get rid of the main "*Kufr*" [the infidels]'. He then stressed that unity was the foremost requirement for winning the war. Muslims should stop fighting each other, he wrote, and unite as they have done in the past. 'The sons of the land of the two Holy Places had come out to fight against the Russians in Afghanistan, the Serbs in Bosnia-Herzegovina and today they are fighting in Chechnya, and by the Permission of Allah they have been made victorious . . .' As Urban II had done a thousand years before, bin Laden announced to his followers the rewards awaiting those who would perish in battle. The martyrs of the Jihad will enter Paradise, he stated, and their sins will be washed away, their earthly life of pain and sorrow replaced by the joy of eternity and marriage to 72 beautiful virgins.

The similarities between the two documents are remarkable: the rhetoric, the motivations; the concept of religious unity which transcends nationality; the humiliation of Jerusalem and the rewards of martyrdom. Even more remarkable are the similarities between the economic climate that produced the Christian Crusades and the process of the formation of the New Economy of Terror, which fostered Islamist terror. The Crusades were a critical chapter in the expansion of Europe eastward; they were a form of colonisation and of medieval imperialism. At the end of the first millennium, the main forces in motion in Western Europe were: exceptional demographic growth coupled with harsh economic conditions, which together fuelled widespread social unrest; the decline of the power of the Papacy, requiring new strategies to reconquer the people's trust; and pressing demands for new commercial outlets posed by the new social classes of merchants, bankers and traders. As we shall see, today similar forces are fuelling the expansionary process of Islamist fundamentalism in the Muslim world.

The fall of the Roman Empire had disastrous consequences for the economics of Western Europe. The disintegration of the *Pax Romana* opened the gates to waves of looting by barbarian tribes; without the protection of Rome, entire regions were ransacked and their economies returned to pre-Roman terms. Trade and commerce inside the former territories of the Western empire came to a halt; almost overnight what had once been a prosperous and buoyant economic system vanished. Money as a means of exchange disappeared and economic transactions regressed to straightforward barter exchanges. Travel in particular became increasingly difficult and dangerous as roads and forests were infested with robbers. Using violence as the sole instrument of establishing and maintaining legitimacy, warlords began carving state-shells out of the former territories of the empire. These new rulers soon came to control patches of territory, imposing heavy road taxes on anyone wishing to cross them. Consequently, the economy of Western Europe lurched backwards to a state of subsistence based on agriculture and war.

The disintegration of the Soviet Union had a similar impact on the economies of its former peripheral territories. Central Asia and the Caucasus, which house a large Muslim population, were hard hit by the dismantling of the Soviet economy. The abolition of the convertible rouble as a means of exchange disrupted trade, while the closure of Moscow's financing facilities drained the monetary lifeline of entire nations. At a microeconomic level, the drawing of new borders between newly formed countries severed ancient trade routes, blocked irrigation systems and hindered agrarian commerce. The Fergana valley in Central Asia, for example, which for centuries had operated as a commercial unit, was split among several countries; villages were cut off from markets and tribes plunged into poverty. Economic growth, already slow, ground to a halt and economies began to decline. As we shall see in chapter 9, the GDP of most of the former members of the Soviet Union fell during the 1990s, while unemployment and poverty rose. Widespread corruption and repressive policies characterised most of the governments that emerged from the ashes of the Soviet system. In the absence of any democratic form of dissent, political opposition became increasingly polarised around Islamist radical groups, such as the IMU in the Fergana valley. In the struggle that followed, warlords and terror groups attempted to carve out their own state-shells around patches of sustenance economies based predominantly on agriculture, i.e. the production of narcotics and war.

The similarities between the Crusades and Islamist terror also extend to the economic conditions of the 'enemy', the socio-economic and political systems that they respectively set out to destroy. In the eleventh century, the desolation of Western Europe's countryside was in harsh contrast to the splendour of Arab civilisation. Baghdad, Cairo and the cities of the eastern shore of the Mediterranean sea were vibrant with culture and wealth. The decline of the Western empire was even more evident because it coincided with the spread and blossoming of Islam. In the seventh century, Islam reached the eastern shores of the Mediterranean and North Africa; over the next two centuries, it conquered southern and central Italy and Spain. The Arab colonisation was, like any colonisation, cruel and ruthless. Arab pirates infested the Mediterranean islands: they pillaged Cyprus and Rhodes, invaded Corsica and Sardinia and the Balearic islands. By the end of the eighth century, what the Romans had named '*mare nostrum*' (our sea) had become an Arab lake, 'inaccessible to Christian shipping, but open to trade from all countries under Arab sway, with staggering results in the field of Arab economy and industry'.[3] Commerce along the coasts of the Mediterranean was flourishing. Unlike the Christians of the West who, during the Middle Ages, considered trade almost a form of usury, the Muslims held it in high regard. The prophet Mohammad, who by profession was a cross-border trader of goods and commodities, had encouraged the free movement of merchandise and the development of new markets: 'The Muhammadan tradition recorded a saying of the Prophet whereby he blessed the triple resources of the faithful as agriculture, cattle raising and commerce . . . Caliphs honoured the merchants and established rigorous security on the roads for peaceful and just circulation of commerce.'[4] Commerce in turn spread Islamic culture across the world. Proof of this was the wide usage of the Arab dinar as a means of exchange worldwide. Arab coins from the seventh to eleventh centuries have been found in Russia, Scandinavia, the Balkans, Britain and Iceland.[5]

A similar scenario exists today with regard to relations between the East and the West, except that the balance of power has now switched sides. Western colonisation left deep marks on the East and planted the seeds of economic and cultural dependency. Arab leaders like Gamal Nasser[6] embraced the secularist elements of the West and applied them to force a rapid modernisation process based on the European economic model. Decolonisation maintained Western economic principles, such as capitalism and accumulation, without introducing its socio-political values, i.e. representative democracy. This led to the creation of a new, immensely wealthy oligarchy. The Muslim elite, educated and raised in the West, became the bridge between Western capitalism and Eastern resources and markets. Partnerships and joint ventures between the new oligarchy and Western capital blossomed in order to exploit the natural resources and markets of the East. There are two main trade flows controlled by this partnership: natural resources, such as oil and gas, which run from East to West, and consumer products, which flow from West to East. This alliance hindered the development of an original post-colonial Eastern culture and denuded entire nations of their wealth. In the 1990s, the decline of the East was particularly shocking when compared to the economic and financial boom of the West. As the gap widened, younger generations, in search of their political identity, began questioning the status quo.

The issue of political identity was also at the root of Western Europeans' despair in the eleventh century. With the disintegration of the Roman Empire came the chaos of the Barbarians. Christendom was the sole socio-economic anchor available to the masses. Subordination to a set of Christian beliefs granted entry into society. Therefore, the identity of medieval Europe became largely synonymous with Christendom. 'Every Christian believed he had a soul to save.'[7] Thus the call to arms by Urban II at Clermont appealed to 'Christian identity' and war was justified by the need to help the 'brethren', the Christian brothers. The real economic and political motives of the First Crusade were cleverly hidden behind religion. Had the pope presented them to the people, few would have followed him into battle. The world had to wait another 900 years for Marxism to mobilise the masses on economic issues. Urban II also portrayed the enemy in their religious persona; he carefully avoided mentioning the economic supremacy of the Caliphs, which was blocking the development of Western European commerce and the emergence of new social classes. Instead, he focused on Jerusalem and the Christians living or travelling there, on the holiness of the city where Christ died.

Today, Islamist leaders address their followers using a similar rhetoric because this is the language more easily understood by the Muslim masses. For many tribes of Central Asia, the Caucasus and Africa, the Muslims in South East Asia as well as those born in the industrial cities of Europe, Islam has become the principal referent of their identity. To be part of a community is to submit to the set of rules imposed by the Qur'an. For millions of Muslims, mosques across the world are socio-economic anchors in deeply troubled waters. Islam, for many, has become synonymous with the Muslim world. Once again the enemy is presented in its 'clerical clothes' – 'Zionist Crusaders' as defined by bin Laden. And hence, for good Muslims, fighting them is not an option, it is a duty: 'the ruling to kill the Americans and their allies – civilians and military – is an individual duty for every Muslim who can do it in any country in which it is possible to do it . . .'[8] Just as a thousand years ago Urban II used Jerusalem and the maltreatment of the Christians and pilgrims as a pretext for war, Islamist leaders point the finger at the state of Israel and its Western allies. Their discriminatory treatment of Palestinians is nothing more than the *casus belli* of the Modern Jihad, a global war against the West.

In reality, Jerusalem and Israel are only the tip of the iceberg; the real motives of the violent clash between the East and West are deeply rooted in a complex set of relations of economic dependency. Today, the conflict is between the big capital of the West and its Eastern oligarchic allies on the one hand, and the masses of the East and an emerging merchant and banking class on the other. A thousand years ago it was between the economic splendour of Islam and its commercial pillars and the desolation of Western Europe and its emerging and frustrated new social classes. Ironically, bin Laden is one of the few Islamist leaders who offer his followers a glimpse of the true nature of the conflict. In 1996 he wrote:

People are fully concerned about their everyday livings; everybody talks about the deterioration of the economy, inflation, ever-increasing debts and jails full of prisoners. Government employees with limited income talk about debts of ten thousands and hundred thousands of

Saudi riyals. They complain that the value of the riyal is greatly and continuously deteriorating among most of the main currencies. Great merchants and contractors speak about hundreds and thousands of million riyals owed to them by the government. More than 340 billion [is] owed by the government to the people in addition to the daily accumulated interest, let alone the foreign debt. People wonder whether we are the largest oil exporting country?! They even believe that this situation is a curse put on them by Allah for not objecting to the oppressive and illegitimate behaviour and measures of the ruling regime.[9]

Economic decay characterised Western European life at the turn of the first millennium, as it does the economies of many Muslim countries at the turn of the second. During the eleventh century, life for Northern European peasants was grim. The land was rendered useless during the invasion of the Barbarians and the raids of the Norsemen. Irrigation systems and dams were destroyed and in many places the land stood under water. Peasants could not use forests for food or firewood as these were the playground of the nobility and the source of their game. Any village unprotected by a lord and his castle fell prey to soldiers and armed gangs, who constantly raided the countryside. The Church attempted to protect the poor by encouraging the construction of towns, but many lords opposed this strategy because they feared these entities would reduce their power. At the same time, extraordinary demographic growth exercised a mounting pressure on villages whose holdings became insufficient to sustain the growing population. In the words of Urban II, 'in this land you can scarcely feed the inhabitants. That is why you use up its goods and excite endless wars amongst yourself.'[10] The overall scenario was made worse by floods and pestilence, which swept through north-west Europe in 1094, and the drought and famine of 1095. Migration was the primary survival option available.

Today, modern Pakistan, a nuclear power, presents several

similarities to the rapid economic decay of Western Europe at the turn of the first millennium. The country's formal economy is on the verge of collapse; with 65.5 per cent of GDP taken up by debt servicing and 40 per cent by defence, the financial year starts with a negative balance. The country's wealth has been depleted by a deeply corrupted oligarchy, which is responsible for a massive capital outflow. Over $88 billion has been deposited in American and European banks, more than the $67 billion and the $82 billion of the country's total domestic and foreign debt respectively.[11] Unemployment is rampant; of the 800,000 people who enter the labour market every year, very few find work. Tax evasion is the norm since nobody is prepared to pay the government either direct or indirect taxes for non-existent social services. Health services are disintegrating rapidly; in 2002 over 77 per cent of the population had to finance some sort of private health scheme. Every year 135,000 women die in childbirth due to the lack of medical assistance. Meanwhile, the government allocates only 0.7 per cent of GDP to the health sector, a figure insufficient to cover even the salaries of the employees. Against this bleak background, the black economy has been growing steadily and, at the end of the 1990s, was three times the size of the formal economy. Widespread smuggling has had a negative impact on every sector of the formal economy, especially industry. From 1995 to 2000, over 6,000 industrial units closed. By the end of 1999, the economy had declined by 2.4 per cent while the population was growing at a yearly rate of 3 per cent. Poverty has been on the increase for years; in the last decade the portion of the population living below the poverty line has doubled from 17.2 per cent to 35 per cent. As little as 15 per cent of the population have sanitation facilities and only 22 per cent have access to clean water. Infant mortality is among the highest in the world. Migration is extremely appealing, especially for younger generations.[12]

The Crusades offered the starving populations of Western

Europe a chance to escape death, opportunities to profit from the war and the salvation of their souls – an extremely appealing package. Today, with no future, a grim present and a past overshadowed by Western exploitation, many young Muslims regard what is on offer for those who join the new Jihad – the worldwide Islamist insurrection, which I have named the Modern Jihad – as a similarly advantageous proposal: a salary, a mission and a purpose in life, the prospect in the long run of a better life and in death the joy of martyrdom.

The real forces that set the Crusades in motion, like those that ignited the Modern Jihad, arose from the new, economically-oriented social classes. In the economic wasteland of eleventh-century Western Europe, a new class of merchants, traders and bankers was born. They had established commercial links with the East and imported silk and spices while exporting timber, iron and cloth. These new classes looked to the East as the natural habitat for expanding their businesses, but were limited by Islam's commercial supremacy. The alliance with the Church for the Crusades opened up endless commercial opportunities for them.[13]

In the mid-1970s, the first oil shock and subsequent recycling of petrodollars created a new class of Muslim businessmen and bankers. They set up trading companies and banks, but were limited in their growth by the supremacy of the West. Interestingly, the wealth accumulated by the ruling Eastern oligarchy flowed into Western rather than Arab banks. As explained in chapter 9, Islamic banks and financial organisations never became major players in the international financial system, remaining at the fringes of world finance. The fall of the Soviet Union, however, opened up new opportunities for these economic and financial forces in countries with large Muslim populations. Thus, the Islamic financial colonisation described in chapter 9 was made possible by their alliance with Wahhabism,[14] the strictest interpretation of Islam.

A millennium ago, the Church sanctified with the Crusades the unusual partnership between the peasants of Western Europe and the emerging merchant and banker classes,[15] which became the embryo of the European bourgeoisie. Similarly, today Islam has stamped the Modern Jihad with a religious seal in order to pursue the economic and political interests of the new Muslim forces, the poor as well as the entrepreneurial classes. A new, unforeseen alliance has been forged around Islam to fight Muslim oligarchic regimes and their backers, Western capitalists. These are the ultimate targets of the Modern Jihad.

9. Islamist Financial Colonisation

'We fight against poverty because hope is an answer to terror.'

President George W. Bush announcing
an increase in foreign aid

The melting of the Cold War tilted the East–West economic equilibrium and widened the gap between rich and poor countries. The battle against poverty stalled during the 1990s, except in India and China. Many parts of the world, such as Central Asia and the Caucasus, saw an increase in extreme poverty. All Central Asian republics suffered from a reduction in real GDP.[1] In Tajikistan, for example, real GDP in the year 2000 was just half that of 1989. Over the same period the percentage of the population in transitional economies living on less than $1 a day more than tripled,[2] and Africa's share of world trade shrunk to a mere 1.2 per cent.[3] According to the World Bank, during the 1990s capital outflows depleted the African continent of 40 per cent of its aggregate wealth.[4] The gravest consequence of the progressive impoverishment of large regions of the world has been the sharp increase in armed conflicts in poor countries.[5]

Many factors have aggravated poverty during the past decade. The disintegration of the Soviet Union had a devastating impact on the economic conditions of its former members. From 1990 to 2000, income inequality more than trebled,[6] a third of the world population was forced to live below the poverty line,[7] the money supply shrank and in certain regions barter replaced the old rouble as the primary means of exchange.[8] As described in chapter 7, the dismantling of the Soviet system and subsequent regrouping of states under the Russian Federation deprived many nations, such as the Central Asian republics, of the economic mechanisms needed to survive and grow as individual political entities. Along the periphery of the former Soviet Union, extreme poverty supplied armed groups with fertile ground for recruitment.[9] Secessionist movements inside the new federation, as in the Caucasus, produced ethnic conflicts, as did nationalist movements within newly formed states. Outbreaks of civil war, fuelled by armed groups, eroded the infrastructure of old communist economies. From the progressive replacement of these economies with terror economies sprang a new cluster of state-shells, inside places like Abkhazia, Chechnya, Nagorno-Karabakh, Kosovo and Albania.[10]

Following the dissolution of the Soviet system, Russia withdrew monetary support from former members. 'Resources were pulled in to save Moscow,' recalls an Italian businessman, who was living in the Russian capital during the 1990s. 'Obviously, when the struggle for economic survival broke out, the first casualties occurred at the periphery.' In these regions, foreign aid failed to compensate for the drastic reduction in Soviet capital flows, partly because Western direct investment was focused elsewhere and partly because strategic capital investment, finally released from the Cold War's straitjacket, headed towards areas with higher and safer returns. Overall, in the 1990s, foreign aid dropped 10 per cent in real terms (as a share of donors' GNP, it fell from 0.33 per cent in 1990 to 0.22 in 2000).[11] Over the same period, net long-term capital flows to poor countries rose by less than $2 billion to reach $22.2 billion, of which official flows fell from $17 billion to $13 billion;[12] capital market flows shrank from 0.5 per cent to 0.3 per cent. Only private capital investment rose significantly, from $1.3 billion in 1991 to $2.8 billion in 1999. However, money went only to a select group of nations: middle-income countries from Latin America and Eastern Europe.

Freed from the political straitjacket of the Cold War, donors' aid followed the laws of economics. Foreign direct investment (FDI) went to those nations that successfully implemented policies for the creation of a stable economy with effective regulatory regimes. Thus Mexico's admission to the North American Free Trade Agreement and China's introduction of market reforms attracted large sums of money. World Bank policy ratings also played a key role in the allocation of foreign funds. The three largest recipients of foreign direct investment, Brazil, China and Mexico,[13] enjoyed a 4.1 country rating as compared to 3.3 for other developing countries.[14]

In addition, the New Economy, the economic revolution generated by the advent of the Internet which swept through the world during the second half of the 1990s, swallowed vast amounts of capital that could otherwise have been invested elsewhere. In the opinion of a US broker, 'high-risk takers invested heavily in the New Economy. These were people who would otherwise have invested in high-risk ventures in emerging markets.' The US experienced massive capital inflow, which lasted for a decade. From 1990 to 1996, for example, net purchases of securities by foreigners rose to $150 billion from $29 billion in 1990.[15] Over the same decade, the Nasdaq composite price index showed a spectacular rise, climbing from 500 to over 5,000. The Nasdaq telecom index followed an identical path.[16] 'Foreign investors poured money into the US,' explained a former Nasdaq dealer. 'These massive inflows fuelled the dotcom revolution.' This phenomenon created a new industry in the heart of Western capitalism and produced a redistribution of wealth in favour of Internet entrepreneurs.

With the exception of a small number of transitional economies, foreign investment shunned the former Soviet Union. 'The West knocked down the Evil Empire,' explained a former European banker, 'and left the field while the debris was still falling.' Not even the oil-rich Central Asian republics appealed to Western investors. 'The few oil companies who dared invest were badly burned,' asserted a UK oil analyst, 'like

BP in Russia.' Ironically, widespread corruption proved to be a more efficient barrier to capitalism than the old Iron Curtain. Western diplomats confirm that even today the economies of Central Asia are too prone to bribery, red tape, market strangling and interference by dictatorial presidents and their entourages to attract foreign capital. For over a decade, the tyrannical leaders of the republics have blocked any form of deregulation and modernisation. In Uzbekistan, for example, President Karimov's administration still controls many prices including that of cotton, the largest export-earning commodity. Foreign exchange is rationed and highly restricted for businesses; local entrepreneurs often barter instead.[17] Western capitalism is unwilling to venture into economic environments reminiscent of the serfdoms of the Middle Ages. According to a European ambassador, in Dushanbe, the capital of Tajikistan, government officials still exercise their right to force companies to supply public works free of charge, as in the days when feudal lords extracted unpaid labour from their vassals.[18] 'Against this backdrop, nobody is willing to take the risk of financing a project,' admitted a European investment banker.

Unsurprisingly, Western banks' participation in poor countries has been guided by the same economic criteria applied to foreign direct investment. In the West, the liberalisation of financial markets, coupled with rapid growth in trade, fuelled an unprecedented expansion of banks. Cross-border bank mergers and takeovers rose from 320 in the 1980s to about 2,000 in the 1990s, with a further acceleration from 1992 to 2000.[19] Again, the greatest beneficiaries of these expansionary policies have been the middle-income countries in Latin America, East Asia and Eastern Europe.[20] In sharp contrast, Africa, Central Asia, the Caucasus and part of the Balkans have been left out; from 1989 to 2002 per capita GDP in former Yugoslavia fell by 48 per cent, in Bosnia-Herzegovina by 26 per cent, in Croatia by 13 per cent and in Macedonia by 23 per cent.[21] The sole organisations interested in these areas were Turkish, Iranian and Arab banks, i.e. Islamic banks. Unlike their Western equivalents, Islamic financial institutions were quick to come to the rescue of the cash-strapped former communist regimes which, deprived of Moscow's monetary lifelines, became highly dependent upon Islamic finance. As we shall see in the following chapters, this process prepared the ground for pan-Islamic economic cooperation between Islamic banking and state-shells. Therefore, while banking deregulation was fuelling the Western banks' expansionary presence in Latin America and East Asia, the disintegration of the Soviet Union facilitated the penetration of Islamic banking in Africa, Central Asia, the Caucasus and the Balkans.

Isolated and marginalised by Western countries, which would never have allowed Islamic financial institutions to handle large chunks of Arab wealth for fear of massive withdrawals,[22] Islamic banks had until then carried out only minor operations internationally. None of them had ever aspired to become a major global player. 'The bulk of Saudi and Arab wealth has always been managed by European and American banks,' revealed a British banker. The fall of the Soviet system, however, presented Islamic finance with the greatest opportunity for growth since its revival in 1976.[23] 'They used finance to colonise poor nations where Muslims lived,' explained a former Middle Eastern banker. 'The material support granted to the Muslim population in need was a means of imposing fundamentalist principles upon Islamic society.' Saudi Arabia, for example, used its immense financial resources to promote Wahhabi Islam. Following the blueprint of the BCCI, Islamic banks filled the monetary gap created by the fall of Moscow and Washington's apathy.

The end of the Cold War opened up new business opportunities. It removed the last political obstacles to the process of economic deregulation launched by Reagan and Thatcher's monetarism and expanded to the maximum the horizons of finance. Without 'containment' boundaries, Western and Islamic banks freely spread their wings across the world. Domestically,

Islamic banks performed exceptionally well; they provided monetary vehicles and means for informal commerce and the black economy.[24] Internationally, they pursued aggressive financial colonisation, especially in Muslim countries on the verge of economic chaos, where they attempted to maintain a monetary base on which the economy could function.

RESHAPING THE ALBANIAN ECONOMY

Albania, a poor country with just over 3 million people, 70 per cent of whom describe themselves as Muslim, provides a good example of Islamic financial colonisation. In 1992, a delegation of the Turkish Islamic Development Bank (IDB) visited Tirana and laid the groundwork for strong economic cooperation between the two countries. Soon after, Turkish trading companies dealing with fertilisers started to offer extremely advantageous conditions to Albanian importers and exporters. They aggressively gained control of the market and pushed aside the IFDC (International Fertiliser Development Center), the US advisory board formed to help agricultural trade through the transition into a market economy. The IFDC's brief was to grant loans and supervise imports and exports. This task was progressively taken over by Turkish traders backed by Islamic banks actively involved in trade financing. At the end of 1998, IFDC personnel were evacuated for fear of terror attacks. A small group of employees were relocated to Macedonia and never returned to Albania.

A few months after the visit from the Turkish Islamic Development Bank, a delegation from Kuwait travelled to Albania and offered to implement an ambitious investment plan in exchange for permission to build several mosques. The offer was readily accepted and the Kuwaitis began building mosques and religious schools across the country. According to the Helsinki Committee on Human Rights, Islamic missionaries in Albania took advantage of the spiritual and material crisis in the country to impose foreign models of extreme fanaticism. Children were encouraged to travel to Turkey, Syria, Jordan, Malaysia, Libya, Saudi Arabia and Egypt to study Islamic theology on scholarships granted by various Muslim charitable organisations.

Religious indoctrination coincided with the arrival of members of Osama bin Laden's group, former Arab-Afghan veterans of the anti-Soviet Jihad posing as aid workers for Islamic charities. Part of their job was to divert official charity funds to sustain terror groups. Defendants in the 1999 trial in Cairo against the Islamic Jihad, the Egyptian terror group, provided interesting insights into the Arab-Afghan network in Albania. Most of them were employed by Islamic charities in Tirana and contributed 26 per cent of their salaries to the Islamic Jihad. Money from Arab charities destined to help Albania was also diverted to Egypt to support the group. An employee of a Kuwaiti charity, for example, sent part of the funds allocated for Albanian orphans to sustain the families of Islamic Jihad members in jail.[25] The main task of the Arab-Afghans was far from humanitarian. They were to recruit, finance and arm fighters for the war in Yugoslavia. Jihan Hassan, the wife of Shawki Salama Mustafa, the Egyptian who headed al-Qaeda's Albanian cell, testified at the trial that her husband ran a racket in Tirana forging identities, ranging from passports to birth certificates. This was an activity that he had mastered in 1994, while they were residing in Sudan. During the same period, Shawki managed a forgery business in the basement of his house.[26] Financially, the cell could draw from a network of bank accounts fed by small transfers of up to $2,000 from abroad. Ahmed Ibrahim al-Sayed al-Naggar, the Jihad member tied to Osama bin Laden in Albania, admitted at the trial that his comrades were well looked after by the Saudi leader. 'In case the situation gets complicated in Albania, Osama bin Laden said he is ready to sponsor any member [willing to move to]

Afghanistan,' he confessed. '. . .Osama can give each family $100 a month through his contacts with the Taliban.'[27]

The cooperation between the Islamic Jihad and bin Laden in Albania was a symptom of the progressive integration of the Egyptian terror group, which was headed by Dr Ayman al-Zawahiri, inside bin Laden's network. In early 1998 the two groups eventually merged into the World Islamic Front for the Jihad Against Jews and Crusaders. The focus of the new group was to internationalise the Jihad. The proliferation of Islamist armed groups was made possible by the expanding influence of Islamic financial and economic institutions, a process that facilitated the birth of a new phenomenon: the globalisation of the terror economy. In Albania, bin Laden's followers also had the task of integrating the country into the international network of emerging economies run by armed organisations. Albanians, mostly in Kosovo and Macedonia, established links with other Islamist armed groups such as the Chechens in order to participate in the business of smuggling drugs and arms into Europe. They then established business ventures with the Italian Mafia, which took responsibility for sales and distribution of narcotics.[28] Hence, Albania became a vital transhipment point in the drug route from Afghanistan to Europe.

At the same time, bin Laden's men carried out recruitment among the Muslim population and managed to conscript 6,000 Albanians from Kosovo, Macedonia and Albania to join the Mujahedin forces, led by the Arab-Afghans, to fight in Bosnia. It was during this period that Albania became a well-known haven for radical Islamists from other countries and for members of armed organisations on the run.[29] In 1998, the country's new role in the Balkans became official when bin Laden and the Iranian Revolutionary Guards signed an agreement to use Albania and Kosovo as their main base for forthcoming armed attacks in Europe.[30]

Iranian involvement in Albania dates back to 1997 when the Iranian government judged it ripe for economic colonisation.

The country was to be part, along with Kosovo and Macedonia, of the 'Muslim Axis'[31] – an Islamic stronghold on the doorstep of Europe. At that time the Albanian economy was disintegrating. The free market reforms imposed by the West in the 1990s to promote democracy had instead accelerated corruption and theft within state institutions. An outstanding example of this failure was the collapse of a pyramid investment scheme. Seduced by the promise of astonishingly high interest rates (more than 10 per cent a month), 70 per cent of Albanian families had entrusted their savings in the pyramid scheme. As much as $1.5 billion, equivalent to one-third of the Albanian GNP (estimated at $4.5 billion in 1990) disappeared into the scheme. The inevitable collapse depleted the country of its wealth.[32] The impact of the crash also had serious repercussions in neighbouring Macedonia, where the private banking system nearly collapsed because large amounts of money had been diverted to Albania to join the scheme.[33]

After the failure of the pyramid scheme[34] Albania was in desperate need of aid. Extreme poverty was widespread and the population focused on sheer survival. Robbery, terrorism, drug smuggling, contraband arms, kidnapping and white slavery became the primary sources of income. Against this backdrop, Teheran's plan was twofold. Officially, Islamic banks were to invest money in Albania to create a support system which included banks, financial institutions, charities and humanitarian organisations, as well as the basic infrastructure necessary to sustain the economy. Secretly, Iran planned to establish a militant Islamist network in the country, within easy reach of Europe. To fulfil this scheme, Mohsen Nurbakan, the governor of the Iranian Central Bank, instructed domestic banks to invest in Albania regardless of poor profits or high risks. Iranian banking institutions soon became a primary source of hard currency in Albania. They promoted links between local importers, exporters and Islamic trading companies; they encouraged and facilitated trade with Iranian businessmen. Local banks and financial institutions were restructured to manage relations with Islamic banks. Within a few years, the Iranian presence in the Albanian domestic banking and finance sector was not merely widespread, it became part of the establishment.[35]

BANKING AS A TOOL TO PROMOTE ISLAM

Like Albania, Indonesia was a target of Islamist colonisation. In 1998, the fall of Suharto opened the door to Islamic financial institutions. Money from Arab countries began to pour in. In 2002, hundreds of import-export and investment projects were launched from Kuwait, averaging $400,000 each. During the first six months of 2002, trade between Indonesia and nine Arab countries rose by $1.95 million, of which $950,000 were Indonesian exports.[36] In September 2002, the government signed an agreement with Egypt to supply 10,000 buses over a ten-year period. In October 2002, Indosat, the Indonesia international phone company, announced the issue of 100 billion rupee ($10.1 million) 'Sharia' bonds – public bonds designed to accommodate the ban on interest imposed by Islamic law.[37] Clearly, the aim was to target Islamic investors.

'The final task of Islamic banking is to serve and promote Islam. Banks are mere instruments,' an Arab banker explained to me several years ago. Capitalism and its rules do not apply to a financial system whose ultimate task is the endorsement of a socio-political culture: Islam. For the majority of Muslims, capitalism is considered synonymous with Western culture and is seen as unethical because of its exploitative nature. Islamic militant groups have been portraying capitalist society in this light for decades, paradoxically sharing with radical Marxist movements an image of market economies as predatory and decadent. Western democracies generate a similar mistrust. 'There is no grass roots movement for democracy in the Arab world,' said Tarik Masoud, 'largely because democracy does not resonate with the average Arab. It has no basis in the Arab past and is tainted by its association with the West.'[38] Bin Laden adds that 'popular participation is incompatible with Islam'.[39]

The victory over communism was won with weapons under the leadership of God, claim the Afghan Jihadis. Democracy, modernisation à l'Americaine, had nothing to do with it. The idea that the Jihad could end and be replaced by Western diplomats engaged in nation-building – that Afghanistan and Iraq could become carbon copies of Texas – is alien, anachronistic and, above all, blasphemous to Muslim fighters. 'We fought for God to establish His rule,' confessed a former Mujahid, 'not to bring democracy Western-style.' As pointed out by Columbia University Professor Edward Said, the sole Muslim voices that are still celebrating the advent of Western models – democracy, modernisation, Western market economies and free competition – all belong to pro-Western Arab intellectuals. Never before have they been so isolated from the Muslim masses, so detached from their world.[40] 'Next to the Soviets, the biggest losers of the war in Afghanistan were the Western-minded scholars, politicians and intellectuals who had worked to build democracy and political pluralism in the Muslim world.'[41]

Indeed, looking back at the West's involvement with developing countries outside the Cold War bubble, a far from ethical picture emerges. Covert financing, smuggling of narcotics, corruption, deceit, state-sponsored terrorism and double standards have been among its main features. Unethical behaviour among Western democracies has undoubtedly helped in legitimising radical Islamic groups in the eyes of moderate Muslims. 'Who can deny that the West has double standards?' a Saudi dissident challenged me. 'Why should Iraq respect UN resolutions while Israel can do as it pleases? When Saddam was fighting the Iranians, he was allowed to develop and use chemical weapons against Iranian soldiers. When he turned against his mentors, he became an evil man.'

Non-Islamist armed groups across the world share this unflattering vision of the West. Sendero Luminoso, for example, claims that although cocaine consumption in the US is a domestic problem, Washington is unwilling to admit this for economic reasons. Banks in Florida get a large cut of the drug money laundered by Latin American drug barons. This money contributes to the US money supply and to Florida's economy. Therefore, rather than take steps to curb domestic consumption of drugs, the US puts pressure on Latin American governments to eradicate production of narcotics. The fact that, if successful, this policy would force an entire segment of, for example, the Peruvian agrarian population well below the poverty line does not appear to be a matter of concern in Washington.

WESTERN DOUBLE STANDARDS

If capitalism is perceived as an instrument of exploitation without ethical values, why should Islamic banks and Islamic leaders comply with its rules and regulations? This is the question that occupies many Muslim minds today. A glance at US relations with the Taliban underlines this argument. John Pilger, the award-winning journalist, describes them:

When the Taliban took Kabul in 1996, Washington said nothing. Why? Because Taliban leaders were soon on their way to Houston, Texas, to be entertained by executives of the oil company, Unocal. With secret US government approval, the company offered them a generous cut of the profits of the oil and gas pumped through a pipeline that the Americans wanted to build across Afghanistan. This was going to be an underground highway that would connect the rich energy fields of Turkmenistan with the coastal shores of Pakistan and India. Naturally, the US would have had full control upon it. 'The Taliban will probably develop like the Saudis did,' commented a US diplomat, summarising in this sentence the hopes of the White House. Washington envisaged Afghanistan as an American oil colony, generating large profits for the West, overlooking the absence of democracy and the legal persecution of women. 'We can live with that,' the US diplomat added. Although the deal fell through, the construction of the pipeline remained an urgent priority for the George W. Bush administration, 'which is steeped in the oil industry. Bush's concealed agenda is to exploit the oil and gas reserves in the Caspian basin, the greatest source of untapped fossil fuel on earth and enough, according to one estimate, to meet America's voracious energy needs for a generation. Only if the pipeline runs through Afghanistan can the Americans hope to control it.[42]

Western exploitation of Eastern natural resources tainted relations between emerging state-shells, such as Afghanistan, and Western companies. Business with oil companies was char-acterised by deep mistrust and manipulation. Thus the Taliban exploited the rivalry between Unocal and the Argentinean oil company Bridas, over the construction of the pipeline, to lobby Washington for political recognition and to extort large sums of money. Unocal alone is believed to have spent up to $20 million, unsuccessfully, to win over the Taliban. Niyazov, the dictatorial president of Turkmenistan, was engaged in a similar game, granting Bridas the rights of exploitation only to rescind them soon after in order to give them to Unocal, which had offered a much higher price.[43]

Double standards and lack of ethics also tainted economic relations between Western intelligence and Islamic states. Following the outcome of the anti-Soviet Jihad, Washington was confident that it could replicate the success of the Afghan covert operation in Yugoslavia. Therefore, in 1991, the Pentagon entered a secret alliance with Islamist groups in Yugoslavia. US, Turkish and Iranian intelligence set up the 'Croatian Pipeline' using the blueprint of the Afghan Pipeline. Iranian and Turkish arms were flown into Croatia by Iran Air, and later on by a fleet of C-130 Hercules transports. Saudi Arabia paid for the weapons and equipment. Other Muslim states – Brunei, Malaysia, Pakistan, Sudan and Turkey – provided money, arms and equipment. To supply the pipeline, the US intelligence service broke the UN embargo[44] against Bosnia. With the arms entering Bosnia came Iranian revolutionary guards, spies of VEVAK,[45] and Mujahedin. In April 1994, at the suggestion of Anthony Lake, future head of the CIA, and Peter Galbraith, US ambassador to Croatia, President Clinton personally approved this policy of cooperation with Iran in Bosnia, a decision that further facilitated Iranian penetration in the region.[46] 'There is no question that the policy of getting arms into Bosnia was of great assistance in allowing the Iranians to dig in and create good relations with the Bosnian government,' a senior CIA officer told Congress in a classified deposition in 1996. 'And it is a thing we will live to regret because when they blow up some Americans, as they no doubt will before this . . . thing is over, it will be in part because the Iranians were able to have the time and contacts to establish themselves well in Bosnia.'[47] The involvement of the Clinton administration went as far as the inspection of Iranian missiles destined for the pipeline.

The Third World Relief Agency (TWRA),[48] a Sudan-based fake humanitarian organisation, was used as a go-between for the suppliers and the fighters in Bosnia. According to a report produced by the US Republican Party, the TWRA had links with leading Islamists, such as Sheikh Omar Abdul Rahman, the Blind Sheikh involved in the first World Trade Center bombing, and Osama bin Laden.[49] Interestingly, during the 1991–95 war in Yugoslavia, the Iranians and the Saudis led the US to believe that they were backing its plan to redraw the map of the country.[50] Secretly, however, they had their own agenda: to spread Islamic colonisation in the region. 'If you read Bosnian President Izetbegovic's[51] writings as I have, there is no doubt that he is an Islamic fundamentalist,' said a senior Western diplomat with

extensive experience in the region. 'He is a very nice fundamentalist, but he is still a fundamentalist. This has not changed.
His goal is to establish a Muslim state in Bosnia, and the Serbs
and Croats understand this better than the rest of us.'[52] It was
only in the mid-1990s that it became clear that the US had been
duped: the pipeline had been manipulated to establish an Islamist
stronghold at the gates of Europe.[53] By then it was too late to
avoid the consequences of this policy. As happened before, during
the Gulf War, the US ended up fighting the very people it had
helped arm.

In sharp contrast, relations between state-shells, Muslim and
Islamic states tend to be cooperative and characterised by trust,
sometimes even among enemies. In the late 1990s, fierce fighting
between the Pakistan-backed Taliban and the Afghan forces of
President Rabbani, supported by Iran, threatened to damage the
Chechen drug trade. The Taliban had conquered the area around
Khost where Chechen fighters were training, and the battle-
front had moved alongside the drug route. A delegation from
both camps, including Pakistani and Iranian representatives, met
and negotiated a deal. Accordingly, a corridor was opened
between the two forces to allow the drug couriers through,
while Northern Alliance and Taliban warriors continued killing
each other.

The Islamist colonisation of Muslim countries and state-
shells provided the ground for economic cooperation outside
the economic infrastructure of the West. Under this umbrella,
special relationships were forged. According to Russian sources,
for example, in the 1990s Pakistan sold Stinger missiles to
Chechen fighters at rock-bottom prices. Islamist armed groups
used economic cooperation to spread the seeds of terror
economics wherever possible. Partnership in the Afghan heroin
trade financed Islamist groups all over Asia, including China.
Opium and heroin flooded the province of Xinjiang and also
helped to support the Uighur rebellion against the government
of Beijing.[54] Under the sponsorship of the Taliban and the

logistical support of the ISI, Uighur fighters received their training in Afghanistan before returning to their homeland. China's fears that Xinjiang, the only region with a Muslim majority, could become the Chinese Kashmir are realistic.[55] In fact, the objective of the Chinese insurrection is to create an Islamic caliphate in the region, which would include territories in Uzbekistan, Tajikistan, Kyrgyzstan and Uighur. Islamic economic cooperation, therefore, also laid the foundation for a new solidarity among Muslim countries, an ideological stronghold which, as we shall see in the following chapters, became a weapon of power in the hands of Islamist armed groups against the West.

10. The Economic Forces of Islamist Colonisation

'There are loopholes in the [Western] temporal laws that could be exploited in favour of Islam and Muslims.'

Omar Bakri Mohammed, leader of the
al-Muhajiroun to al-Sharq al-Awasat

The dichotomy between capitalism and Islamist colonisation provides an ideal framework for revisiting the BCCI affair. The Bank of Credit and Commerce International pioneered the loan-back policy – lending large sums of money to depositors without any collateral other than the deposit itself – which became an ad hoc tool to promote important clients' businesses inside the Western capitalist system. The main beneficiaries of the policy were the BCCI's own shareholders; people like Khalid bin Mahfouz, the Saudi owner of the National Commercial Bank, who received unsecured loans well in excess of his 20 per cent share in the bank;[1] Kamal Adham, a former head of Saudi Arabian intelligence; and a core shareholding group of 12 Arab sheikhs and Pakistani bankers.[2]

The benefits were by no means one-sided; the bank also gained considerably from the 'special' relationship with its shareholders and was regarded as the most important bank in the Third World. Between the 1970s and 1980s, for example, Ghaith Pharaon, a Saudi tycoon, received an estimated $500 million in unsecured loans.[3] The money was used to purchase stocks in companies including two US banks, the National Bank of Georgia and the Independence Bank of Encino in California, for the BCCI. Pharaon acted as a smokescreen against international banking regulations and auditing; the bank more than once hid behind him to avoid US banking investigations.[4] Vast, unsecured loans to major shareholders were made possible by a steady flow of deposits. As long as the cash kept coming in, the bank had no problems. But this policy inevitably drained its treasury leading to its failure.[5]

Even so, the BCCI's strategies for climbing the greasy pole of international finance were regarded as successful by Third World and Arab bankers, because they provided a viable alternative to Western capitalist exploitation. The BCCI became a prototype for future Islamic banking institutions; in fact, its failure was attributed by many to its links with Western financial institutions and not to its fraudulent management. 'The crash has not tainted the image of the BCCI in the Third World,' admitted a Turkish banker who had worked for the bank. 'In Turkey, people still remember how much BCCI has done for trade and agriculture. All along the Mediterranean coast and inland, where today farmers struggle to survive, the economy was booming. Why? Because the BCCI was the sole bank willing to finance agriculture and trade in the region.'

To businessmen and smaller depositors operating in developing countries, the BCCI offered several services. Since most of these countries have strict foreign exchange controls, the BCCI provided its clients with sophisticated and efficient schemes to take money abroad illegally. This was particularly true for the leaders of 'friendly' nations. According to Kroll, the investigative bureau, the BCCI helped Saddam Hussein skim cash from oil revenues and deposit it all over the world.[6] A similar service was provided for Panama's General Noriega. While the bank was operative, that is, until 1991, the largest capital flights originated from India, Pakistan and African countries.[7]

On a much larger scale, the BCCI supported Muslim leaders in their political aspirations, as it did in Pakistan. From the mid-1980s, the bank donated large sums of money (up to $10 million) to finance a secret science laboratory run by Dr Abdul

Qadeer Khan, the main brain behind General Zia's effort to
develop nuclear weapons.[8] The money originated from a tax-free
foundation set up in Pakistan by the BCCI and run by Pakistan's
then finance minister and future president, Ghulam Ishaq Khan.[9]
In 1987, the bank financed the purchase of highly resistant
steel[10] on behalf of General Inam ul-Haq, the man responsible
for Pakistan's nuclear armaments programme.[11]

SAUDIS' RELIGIOUS COLONISATION

In 1998, several years after the closure of the BCCI, it was the
Islamic Bank for Development (IBD), the most important
banking organ in Saudi Arabia, that helped cover the economic
penalties imposed on Pakistan for carrying out nuclear tests. The
Saudis' generosity was a direct consequence of the policy of religious colonisation and economic solidarity pursued by the house
of Saud. The Saudi regime has subordinated financial considerations to the spread of a fundamentalist interpretation of Islam,[12]
known as Wahhabism, which will be discussed in chapter 11.
According to Rifaat el-Said, general secretary of the Egyptian
opposition party Tagammu (Progressive Union), in 1993 the
Saudis offered money to Mubarak's government on the condi-
tion that it would encourage the Islamisation of Egyptian
society.[13] 'The Saudis have . . . managed to infiltrate almost
every channel of Egyptian cultural, economic and political life.'[14]
They have promoted the proliferation of Islamic investment
houses. Loans are conditional on strict adherence to Islamic
laws and traditions. One of these organisations, al-Rayan, paid
female students 15 Egyptian pounds (about $5) a month pocket
money to take the veil.[15] Similar 'encouragements' to women
have taken place in other Muslim countries.

Saudi oil revenues paid for the spreading of Wahhabism.
Ample funding ensured its dissemination. Monetary and logistical support was granted upon the introduction of religious

courts and the application of Sharia law. This form of religious colonisation took place in several countries, for example in Chechnya. The first Chechen war (1994–96) destroyed the secular institutions of the state. In the political vacuum that followed, a cluster of state-shells emerged, run by an Islamist militia and backed by Saudi money. Some, in small cities and villages, introduced Islamic courts with the task of applying Sharia law. Overall, the civilian population was hostile to this legislation. Although Chechnya had a strong secular tradition, it could do very little to counter Saudi-financed Islamist armed groups and the radicalisation of the conflict fuelled by the Russian invasion. In Chechnya, as in many other places in the Muslim world, the Wahhabi movement fostered 'a very tiny but well-financed and well-armed minority', which had the task of instilling terror 'in the hearts of the masses . . . By creating anarchy and lawlessness, these groups [enforced] their own harsh, intolerant brand of Islam . . .'[16] As Soviet institutions collapsed, due among other reasons to the restrictive economic conditions imposed by Boris Yeltsin and the IMF, Islamic tribunals replaced them. By the end of the first Chechen war, Sheikh Abu Umar[17] had been nominated chief Islamic judge and *Mufti*, the religious jurist who issues judgments and opinions on Islamic law. He was a hard-line Islamist who had arrived in Chechnya in 1995, joined the Mujahedin of Ibn ul-Khattab and indoctrinated them with the principles of Wahhabism.[18] He had no ties with or knowledge of the history and culture of the country; his job was simply to remodel it according to Sharia law.

THE FINANCING OF SAUDI ARABIA'S RELIGIOUS IMPERIALISM

Saudi Arabia's religious imperialism was financed primarily by its banking system, whose core institutions are the Dar al-Maal al-Islami (DMI) and the Dallah al-Baraka (DAB). Both banks

have vast networks of subsidiaries in the Middle East, Africa
and Asia. The DMI was founded in 1981 by Mohammad
al-Faisal, the brother of Prince Turki; today, it is chaired by Prince
Mohammad al-Faisal al-Saud, a cousin of King Fahd. This giant
banking conglomerate is the primary vehicle used by the Saudis
to finance the spreading of Islamic fundamentalism.

The Islamic banking network, like any financial network,
is an intricate, vast and almost impenetrable web. One of the
subsidiaries of the DMI is the al-Shamil Islamic Bank in
Sudan. The US State Department claimed that Osama bin
Laden controlled the bank after paying $50 million towards
its ownership;[19] however, it is more likely that he was only a
large shareholder. Jamal Ahmed Mohammad al-Fadl, a former
business associate of bin Laden, who testified at the trial against
al-Qaeda operatives responsible for the 1998 bombing of two
US embassies, revealed that bin Laden used the al-Shamil
Islamic Bank along with two other banks, the Tadamon Islamic
Bank[20] and the Faisal Islamic Bank,[21] to channel money to
his followers around the world.[22]

Until September 2001, bin Laden and his followers operated
primarily via these three institutions, which represented the core
of a multi-billion-dollar financial organisation supported by
some of the richest men in the Middle East. The Chairman of
the Faisal Islamic Bank is Prince Mohammad al-Faisal al-Saud.
Among the founders of this bank is Saleh Abdullah Kamel, the
Saudi magnate and the king's brother-in-law. According to *Forbes
Magazine*, Saleh is the 137th richest man in the world, with a
fortune worth $4 billion.[23] It was thanks to him that in 1981
the Dallah al-Baraka (DAB) holding group, the other banking
pillar of Saudi Arabia, was founded. The DAB has 23 branches
and several investment companies scattered in 15 countries.

Islamic banks apply *zakat*, the religious almsgiving required
of all Muslims, to every contract or transaction they handle.
They deduct the appropriate amounts, equivalent to 2 per cent
of personal wealth, and transfer them to Islamic charitable

organisations. *Zakat* transfers are off the balance sheets and therefore untraceable; in addition, all records are destroyed as soon as transactions are complete.[24] A Pakistani journalist who has investigated this form of money transfer claims that the *zakat* paid to charities is one of the many stratagems used to finance terror groups. Ramzi Yousef, for example, received funds which were meant to be charitable donations from a company importing Holy Water from Mecca to Pakistan.[25] *Zakat* is a large potential source of income − the 6,000 members of the Saudi royal family alone, for example, are worth $600 billion, making their *zakat* equivalent to a yearly $12 billion.[26]

Islamic banks have been the lifeline of Islamist insurgency. In 1999 the Saudi government discovered the transfer of $3 million from a privately owned Saudi bank to charitable organisations which were fronts for bin Laden's network. Among them were Islamic Relief and Blessed Relief. From the Saudi audit acquired by US intelligence, it transpired that the money originated from five top Saudi businessmen. US officials claim that these men were paying bin Laden protection money to prevent attacks against their businesses in Saudi Arabia. According to Greg Palast, the American investigative journalist, 'one international arms dealer . . . described a meeting of Saudi billionaires at the Hotel Monceau in Paris in May 1996 to decide who would pay for Osama bin Laden's operation, and how much'. ('Our information,' adds Palast in his book, *The Best Democracy Money Can Buy*, 'is that this was not an act of support for Osama but protection money to keep the mad bomber away from Saudi Arabia.')[27] Overall, there is little evidence to prove that extortion alone was at the root of the Saudis' financing of bin Laden's network.[28] Saudi businessmen also contribute voluntarily to bin Laden, a man who enjoys great popularity among all social classes in Saudi Arabia.

Part of the $3 million was sent to the International Islamic Relief Organisation in the Philippines, a Saudi charity set up in the early 1990s by Mohammad Jamal Khalifa, bin Laden's brother-in-law. Allegedly, donations were used to bankroll the Abu Sayyef armed group.[29] US intelligence investigators believe that Khalifa, who has since returned to Saudi Arabia and has criticised bin Laden, managed terror funds for his brother-in-law in Malaysia, Mauritius, Singapore and the Philippines. Vincent Cannistraro, the former CIA chief of counter-terrorism, maintains that Khalifa was also involved in the funding of the Islamic Army of Aden, the group that claimed responsibility for the bombing of the USS *Cole*.[30]

The $3 million are part of a vast network of private donations set up by Islamic financial institutions to armed groups around the globe whose ultimate task is to promote a fundamentalist vision of Islam. This is another channel used for religious imperialism in the Muslim world. In 2000, on mounting pressure from the US and in a gesture to show its willingness to stop the flow of money, the Saudi government began investigating a group of Saudi banks and bankers. However, shutting one channel had little, if any, impact on the outflows of Saudi money. Many other Islamic banks continue to use charitable donations to fund armed organisations around the world. In 2001, official donations from Saudi Arabia alone amounted to $267 million; most of the funds went to areas where Muslims were engaged in armed conflicts. 'Who did not pay for Kashmir and Chechnya? Muslims were being hurt there and people didn't ask where the money was going,' admitted a Saudi businessman to two journalists from the *Financial Times*. 'It's about defending our brethren.'[31]

The Bush administration claims that the core of bin Laden's financing network in Saudi Arabia was masterminded and run by a Saudi businessman, Wael Hamza Jalaidan, based in Jeddah.[32] 11 September 2001 did very little to alter this network. According to a UN report on the financing of al-Qaeda produced in the summer of 2002, the organisation has received $16 million from Saudi Arabia since the World Trade Center attacks.[33] It is apparent that bin Laden can draw from a large pool of supporters inside Saudi Arabia, most of whom are successful independent businessmen. Among them is Yasin al-Qadi, a Saudi magnate. According to US authorities he has transferred millions of dollars via the Muwafaq foundation, the Arab name of Blessed Relief. The charity is supported and managed by leading Saudi families. Qadi is an international businessman involved in real estate, chemicals, banking and consulting companies operating in Saudi Arabia, Turkey, Kazakhstan, Albania and Pakistan. He is the quintessential modern Saudi businessman, with activities in Muslim countries and state-shells financially colonised by Saudi capital in the 1990s, as discussed in chapter 9. In 1998, Qadi was also implicated in a money-laundering scheme for Hamas via the Quranic Literacy Institute, a Chicago-based charity whose founder, Mohammad Salah, was a front man for Hamas.[34] After 11 September 2001, Yasin al-Qadi's assets and investments were frozen in several Muslim countries. In Tirana, for example, the Albanian authorities blocked works carried out by his Karavan Construction Company on two high-rise buildings.

Due to the contradictions inherent in Saudi politics, the link between bin Laden's network and Saudi charities is still very strong. In March 2002, the Saudi government reluctantly agreed to curb donations from the Haramain Islamic foundation, a Mecca-based charity headed by Sheikh Saleh bin Abdul Aziz al-Ashaikh, minister for Islamic affairs. Consequently, funds held in the branches in Somalia and Bosnia were frozen.[35] However, in September 2002, a Saudi newspaper reported that the charity was expanding its activity in both Bosnia and Somalia and had opened an Islamic centre in Sarajevo costing $530,000.[36] It is apparent that in Saudi Arabia, as well as in several Muslim countries, the restrictions imposed on charities have had only a temporary impact on the flow of money. Governments are reluctant to curb donations for fear of being unpopular among the population, who support Islamist causes around the world.

According to a Kuwaiti newspaper editor: 'Political Islam controls the streets of Kuwait. No one wants to burn their bridges with the Islamists just yet. Not even the Interior Minister. So they leave them alone.'[37] Since 11 September 2001, ingenious new ways of bringing money to Islamist warriors have also been found. Several Kuwaiti businessmen, for example, have been flying to Pakistan carrying suitcases full of cash. They stay at expensive hotels in Karachi, away from the tribal belt, raising no suspicions since they have no beards, travel with laptops and dress in European clothes. The cash is secretly collected by the various Islamist groups and used to finance their fight.

According to several estimates, Islamic organisations, many of which are linked to armed groups, can draw from a pool of money ranging from $5 billion to $16 billion;[38] the Saudi government alone donates $10 billion via the Ministry of Religious Works every year.[39] The origins of these funds are largely unknown. The fiscal structure of Islamic countries makes it very difficult to monitor charitable organisations. In Saudi Arabia, for example, there is no tax system or internal revenue service, consequently no one is able to audit the accounts and keep track of monetary inflows and outflows. Although companies regularly pay *zakat*, the donation is not an official tax, but a voluntary payment for which records are not required.[40] The structure of the Islamic banking system is of no help either. Most transactions are in cash. 'In the Middle East, it is common to have clients walk into a bank with a suitcase that will be filled with, or emptied of, cash,' said a former Middle Eastern banker. Although oil has brought immense wealth to countries like Saudi Arabia, the kingdom is still a tribal society, with a strong cash culture.

THE ISLAMIC MONETARY SYSTEM

Former US Assistant Deputy Secretary of State Jonathan M. Winer estimates that untraceable money flows in the Middle

East amount to 25–50 per cent of total transactions. One way for such transactions to take place is the *hawala* system where cash is deposited in one country and collected in another. All records are destroyed as soon as transactions take place.[41] Originally introduced by the ancient Chinese, who called it *fei qian* – flying money – the system was adopted by Arab traders to avoid robbery on the Silk Route. In the 1960s and 1970s, waves of immigrants from developing countries and the desire to avoid the official ban on gold imports in South East Asia revamped the *hawala*.[42] Today modern *hawala* is utilised by millions of Asian and African immigrants to send money back home. Neither the sender nor the receiver is required to be identified. 'A code of words is used that will allow the recipient to collect the cash from a trusted associate of the originating *hawala* dealer (*hawaladar*).'[43] It operates 24 hours a day, seven days a week; often it takes as little as a phone call or a telex for the money to reach its destination. 'It beats Western Union . . . You don't need to present any identification, the commissions are lower and it's quicker.'[44] *Hawaladars* charge as little as 1 per cent commission for a completed transaction; profits come from currency fluctuations and fees on large sums of money, mostly from drugs and arms traffickers, smugglers or armed groups' illicit money transfers.

Secrecy and speed of transactions are the qualities of the *hawala* system that most appeal to terror groups. There are numerous reports that Islamist extremists make extensive use of this system. A Pakistani *hawaladar* was among the financiers of the attacks against the American embassies in Africa in 1998. In 2001, Indian authorities in Delhi unveiled a network of *hawala* institutions, backed by the Pakistani ISI, which funded Kashmiri armed groups.[45] Interestingly, *hawala* networks are not controlled by Arabs, but by Indians and Pakistanis who have migrated to the Gulf. Though Indira Gandhi succeeded in crippling the system in India, the *hawala* is still widely used in Pakistan. Official figures show that in Pakistan alone $5 billion move annually through its network. At the end of the 1990s there were 1,100 known *hawaladars* in Pakistan, handling single transactions as large as $10 million.[46] According to the United Nations, the *hawala* industry turnover is $200 billion a year.[47]

Outside the *hawala* system there are many others ways to move money without being detected. Money-laundering experts claim that funds are even shipped in boxes, mostly from Dubai. The city has a long and strong tradition in gold and money markets, and enjoys solid trade ties with Iran. An Iranian family based in Dubai and involved in money traffic revealed that, until the beginning of 2001, up to two flights a week were travelling from Dubai to Kandahar with boxes full of dollar bills.[48] Western companies often use similar techniques to bring untraceable cash into developing countries. A former head of a pharmaceutical plant in Africa admitted that his company had boxes of cash flown in every month to bribe warlords and government officials in order to keep production running. The shipment was shared with a large brewery just across the street from the plant. 'One month we chartered the plane and the following month they did it,' he explained. 'It worked very well.'

Islamic banks were successful in establishing financial relations even in unsophisticated markets with a low, if any, degree of monetisation. This task was particularly hard in state-shells emerging from decades of civil war. In Afghanistan and Somalia, for example, there is no traditional banking system; everything is done through the *hawala*. Until the end of 2001, in addition to the Taliban currency (which was worth almost twice the currency of the Northern Alliance) there were four different Afghan banknotes in circulation: the one issued during the rule of former king Zahir Shah and another by the government of Burhanuddin Rabbani shared the same value; a third, printed by the Russians for Uzbek warlord general Rashid Dostum, traded at about half the value of the first two; a fourth currency, issued by the Northern Alliance, also traded at a discount.[49]

Inside Afghanistan, gold was by far the most reliable means of exchange. 'People recognise gold, they trust it because it is a tangible asset,' admitted a UN official. *Hawaladars* use gold to balance their books; *hawala* dealers hold gold instead of currencies to conduct their businesses around the world. Gold also maintains its value regardless of who rules the country. In 2001, before the war against the Taliban, the afghani was trading at 60,000 to the US dollar. As the Taliban fled, the value of the currency rose and the exchange rate was 25,000 to the dollar.[50] Yet, over the same period, the price of gold remained stable.

The Islamist colonisation of the Muslim world was eased by the *hawala* system, which feeds into Islamic banks and into commodity trading in the East. Islamic banking and the *hawala* are both regulated by the same legislation: the Sharia. The body that oversees modern Islamic finance is the Sharia Supervisory Board of Islamic Banks and Institutions, better known as the Sharia committee. Today Islamic banks operate all over the world and offer their services to the international Muslim community. Over 200 banks are active in the US, thousands in Europe, Africa, the Arab countries and in Asia. In 1998 the total liabilities of Islamic financial institutions were $148 billion.[51] To grasp the magnitude of this figure, it is sufficient to point out that Saudi Arabia's GDP for the same year was $138 billion.[52]

Modern Western monetary systems are fiduciary; that is, they are based on trust, the reliance of citizens upon their rulers. The value of paper money depends entirely on the faith in the governments that issue them. State-shells lack this relationship. This was demonstrated by the Taliban's demand that taxes on opium production be paid in gold, not in cash. Indian and Pakistani trucking companies had to pay road access taxes in gold. Often donations to bin Laden and his followers reached Afghanistan in the form of gold. Boxes of gold bullion were flown from Dubai to Kandahar on Ariana, the Afghan airline, aboard regular scheduled flights.[53] According to European and

Pakistani investigators, when at the end of 2001 the Afghan regime began to crumble, al-Qaeda shipped several containers of gold to Sudan.[54] The Taliban took an estimated $10 million worth of gold out of the country. One of the couriers was the Taliban consul general in Karachi, Kaka Zada, who carried at least one shipment worth $600,000 to Dubai,[55] where the bulk of the Taliban's gold and foreign exchange was shipped before the 2001 war in Afghanistan.

Some countries were more active than others in the promotion of the Islamist cause. Dubai, for example, was by far the most important financial port of entry for the Taliban regime and for bin Laden's network. One of the most lax banking centres in the Middle East, Dubai joined Saudi Arabia and Pakistan as the only countries to recognise the Taliban as rulers of Afghanistan. According to US investigators, some of the money used to finance the 11 September bombing went through Dubai.[56] Mohammad Atta, the leader of the hijackers, received a money transfer worth $100,000 from the United Arab Emirates.[57] Dubai's involvement with illegal banking activities goes back to the 1980s when it established a close relationship with the BCCI.

The role of Islamic banks was not limited to countries where banking systems did not, or no longer, exist. Their links with armed groups and state-shells also provided a direct and secure channel into traditional economies. 'They are tapped into sophisticated monetary systems,' explained a retired Russian banker, 'from which money can be directed to finance terror activity worldwide or to profit in the capitalist world.' Correspondent banks, for example, can help hide funds. Banks use them in countries where they do not have branches. Generally, banks vet correspondent banks to make sure that payments are legal and sound. However, if the correspondent bank has received payments from a third bank, which in turn is the recipient from another bank, the vetting system is weakened.[58] The Barclays account of the Advice and Reformation

Committee, one of the organisations believed to be a front for bin Laden, for example, received funds from correspondent banks in Sudan, Dubai and the United Arab Emirates. From Barclays the money was transferred to terror cells in Western cities, including Geneva, Chicago and London. Khalid al-Fawaaz, a Saudi dissident residing in London, was the signatory of the account. He is suspected of being one of bin Laden's men in the West. Court documents show that the original document of the *fatwa* launched by bin Laden against the Americans was faxed from Sudan to Fawaaz. From the Barclays account Fawaaz ordered transactions with several Islamic centres and charities all over the world, including Bosnia, Kosovo and Albania. In an interview in 1996, bin Laden admitted that his economic and financial establishment was present in more than 13 countries – Albania, Pakistan, Malaysia, the Netherlands, Britain, Romania, Russia, Turkey, Lebanon, Iraq and several Gulf states.[59]

The disintegration of the Soviet Union opened up new opportunities for emerging Muslim merchant and banking classes. They saw an alliance with Islamist fundamentalism as an opportunity for expansion. Secular Muslims rallied round the new forces to counteract a sense of desertion and betrayal by the West. To divert these explosive energies abroad, Saudi Arabia financed the trend of Islamic colonisation, which focused in areas where Muslims were seeking answers not only to questions of identity and lost culture, but also where there was need for material aid. With the help of Islamic finance, militant Islamist movements, armed groups and state-shells, scattered along the periphery of the former Soviet Union, began constructing their own political identity, and emerged as the primary beneficiaries of the 'New World Disorder'. As will be explained in chapters 12 and 13, these new forces converged into the Modern Jihad.

11. The Mosque Network

'American people are the financiers of the attacks against us; they are watching – through their elected senators – the spending of those taxes.'

Al-Qaeda manifesto, November 2002[1]

Every Friday, at lunchtime, men flock to the mosque near Mardan, in the North West Frontier province of Pakistan, where a member of the Kashmiri Islamist armed group Lashkar-e-Taiba addresses the faithful and collects alms. Although General Musharraf has outlawed all militant fundraising, within the mosques of Pakistan collections for the various Islamist armed organisations continue unimpeded.[2] Fundraisers in Pakistan concur that 11 September has not hindered their ability to raise money. Indeed, there is very little evidence around the world that mosques have stopped financing and recruiting on behalf of armed groups. The Mosque Network is as efficient as ever and continues to be the main vehicle through which Islamist organisations, countries, state-shells, armed groups and their sponsors link up and do business with each other.

The Mosque Network is the ideological partner of the terror financial network; it complements it and is as complex and comprehensive a web as its monetary counterpart. Its emergence is directly linked to the birth of the Kingdom of Saudi Arabia.

A VERY SPECIAL PARTNERSHIP

Between the 1920s and 1930s,[3] the House of Saud succeeded in unifying the country and establishing its monarchic rule thanks to its alliance with the Arabian peninsula's religious leaders, who preached a particularly strict version of Islam, known as Wahhabi Islam. The partnership between the political and religious powers became an integral part of the legitimacy of the royal family: one of the pillars on which the king's power rests is the 'propagation of Wahhabi Islam within Saudi Arabia and throughout the world'. Ultimately, therefore, the aim of Wahhabism is to refashion Islam according to its principles. The proselytising character of this alliance greatly influences Saudi foreign policy. In the mid-1990s, for example, the powerful Saudi *Ulema*, the council of Islamic scholars, the ultimate religious authority, put pressure on the royal family to recognise the Taliban as the legitimate rulers of Afghanistan. This unique partnership also bred a great deal of ambiguity in Saudi politics, particularly in the behaviour of the Wahhabi religious elite towards the 'special' relationship Saudi Arabia enjoyed with the US. When, at the onset of the Gulf War, the Saudis let American troops enter the country, several religious leaders voiced strong objections. A decade later, US soldiers were still stationed in the kingdom and the *Ulema* had *de facto* accepted their presence. This is due to the extreme conservativism of the *Ulema*, who are reluctant to shake the foundations of the Saudi regime.

Perhaps the best example of the dysfunctional relationship that exists between the religious and political rulers of Saudi Arabia is the role that Osama bin Laden plays in Saudi politics. From an extremely privileged background, he rebelled against the Saudi political elite, claiming that in their failure to implement strict Wahhabi Islam, they had lost legitimacy as rulers of Saudi Arabia. The natural outcome of this assertion rests on the ultimate political aim of the Saudi hijackers who participated in the 11 September attacks: to bring down the

Saudi regime and rid the country of US military presence. It is unquestionable that, as far back as 1990, bin Laden has openly challenged the Saudi authority. Yet, while stripping him of his citizenship and accusing him of plotting against the regime, the Saudi royal family has made no attempt to bring him to justice. What protects bin Laden are his strong ties with the Saudi *Ulema* and with high-ranking Islamic clerics in the Muslim world, even if the *Ulema* still officially backs the House of Saud as the legitimate ruler of the country. Unsurprisingly, given the immense size of the Saudi royal family, bin Laden's popularity extends to members of it, containing those who share his political ideas and those who back him financially. According to Saudi dissidents, his popularity in Saudi Arabia has increased since 11 September and money is plentiful. Saudi charities and wealthy businessmen continue to fund Islamist armed organisations, some of which have been shown to have links with bin Laden's terror network.

PROSELYTISING WAHHABISM

Overall, the pattern of Wahhabi colonisation has been identical to that of Islamic banks. Religion and finance formed a dual track. In the early 1990s, Wahhabism penetrated deeply into the territory of the collapsing Soviet Union, reaching countries where Muslims had long been denied freedom of religious expression. Backed by Saudi money, Wahhabi mullahs preached and taught a bellicose vision of Islam inside newly built mosques and *madaris*, the religious schools where children study the Qur'an and the Quranic laws. This violent and radical message reached Muslim populations struggling with exceptional demographic growth and high unemployment. Islam is the fastest growing religion in the world: in the mid-1990s, the annual demographic growth of the Muslim population was 6.4 per cent versus a modest 1.46 per cent for the Christian population.[4]

Against this socio-economic background, young Muslims responded enthusiastically to the Wahhabi message, streaming into mosques and *madaris* from which some of them joined newly formed Islamist armed groups. Thus Wahhabi Islam became the unifying ideology for Islamist warriors in the same way as Marxism-Leninism had been for the communists. In Uzbekistan, Wahhabi preaching fomented the rebellion of 1998 under the leadership of Juma Namangiani, whose political vision was greatly influenced by Wahhabi Islam. His final goal was to substitute the corrupt and undemocratic Uzbek government with a replica of a fifteenth-century Khanate,[5] to include some of the territories of the newly formed Central Asian republics (Uzbekistan, Tajikistan and Kyrgyzstan). Osama bin Laden's political aims are very similar to Namangiani's. His long-term goal is to bring Muslim countries back to what he and his followers consider the true origins of Islam – the age of Caliphs, the successors of Mohammad, who ruled the Islamic world from the seventh to the thirteenth centuries, until the armies of the crusaders destroyed their splendid culture. According to bin Laden, the new caliphates will be modelled on the former Taliban regime in Afghanistan, which was 'among the keenest to fulfil [Allah's] laws'.

Outside the boundaries of the former Soviet Union, Wahhabi colonisation, in both Africa and South East Asia, has followed an identical pattern: Saudi money financed the religious infrastructure necessary to proselytise Wahhabi Islam. The outcome once again has been the emergence of Wahhabism as the unifying force of Islamist armed groups. In a similar fashion to Namangiani and bin Laden, Riduan Isamuddin (the leader of the Indonesian Jemaah Islamiyah who was accused of masterminding the Bali bombing in October 2002) has been preaching for a decade the use of violence to achieve a unified Islamic state, comprehensive of Indonesia, the Philippines, Malaysia and Singapore, to be ruled as a single caliphate under Sharia law.

THE WESTERN NETWORK

In non-Muslim countries, especially in the West, Wahhabi colonisation has been more discreet, with Islamic charities primarily funding schools and courses run by mosques. In the West, the Mosque Network's main operations have been recruiting and fundraising. So successful have they been in performing these tasks that several mosques have now become hotbeds of potential terror fighters, who have been fed an explosive mixture of religion and political ideology. Abu Qatada, a Palestinian living in England, who has been accused of being one of al-Qaeda's recruiters, expressed the view of many: 'the war of the Mujahedin is dictated by what the prophet said . . . The jihad is to make the word of God supreme, we call it the Islamic jihad.'[6]

True to Qatada's assertion, in Western countries recruiters tend to put more emphasis on religious motivation and therefore target certain types of individuals: young, often disillusioned Muslims adrift in Western society. French-born Zacarias Moussaoui, the alleged twentieth hijacker of 11 September, was one of these. Moussaoui reached London penniless and in search of his own identity as a Muslim. The Mosque Network provided him with both financial and emotional support. Recruiters prefer people who approach mosques 'searching for a purpose in life', explained a former MI5 agent. '[They] often know very little about Islam and trust the older men to show them the way. But they are shown the path of violence [instead].'[7] Powerful recruitment tools used to influence young Muslims include heated sermons and gruesome videos of Jihads fought by Islamist warriors. One such video, available since January 2002 in several mosques in London, is called 'The Mirror of the Jihad' and shows Taliban forces decapitating members of the Northern Alliance with knives. The video was distributed by an Islamist organisation based in Paddington, in central London.[8] The money raised from the sales went to fund Islamist armed organisations.

In the West, as in Muslim countries, the Muslim population is experiencing phenomenal growth and is plagued by unemployment and poverty among its youth. Therefore, many flock to the mosques for material rather than spiritual assistance. At Finsbury Park Mosque in London, for example, people can buy false passports and ID cards, which entitle them to collect welfare payments. According to Reda Hassaine, an Algerian journalist who infiltrated the Finsbury Park Mosque, with fake identity papers it is possible to get income support of £50 a week in addition to rent, usually a room or flat in a council estate, fully paid for by the state. One person can accumulate a number of false identities, which can generate a lucrative business.[9]

Naturally, mosques are extremely selective when approaching potential recruits, and only a few manage to join the Jihad. One of these was Mohammad Bilal, the 24-year-old from Birmingham who drove a car full of explosives into the Indian army barracks in Srinagar.[10] Birmingham is a renowned hotbed of Islamists, and mosques here have supplied suicide bombers to al-Qaeda and Islamist armed groups in Kashmir. In fact, the UK, with its large immigrant Muslim population, is one of the best recruiting grounds in the Western world. Sheikh Omar Bakri-Mohammad, the founder of al-Muhajiroun, an Islamic group based in London which recruits for the Jihad,[11] claimed that mosques and university campuses in the UK recruit a yearly average of 18,000 British-born Muslims to take part in military services in countries where Islamist armed groups are fighting.[12] Mohammad Ibrahim Azhar, the brother of Maulana Masood Azhar (founder of the Jaish-I-Mohammad, one of the leading Islamist Kashmiri armed groups) travelled at least once to Birmingham to recruit volunteers for the fight against India. He targeted the Kashmiri Muslim community, which lives in one of the ten poorest council estates in Birmingham, plagued by a very high unemployment rate. Through the Mosque Network he was able to move about freely, get in touch with potential warriors and recruit them. These young men are given money and sent to training camps in Pakistan, Afghanistan, Yemen, Nigeria and Sudan, among other countries. However, only a minuscule fraction carry out suicide missions. According to several Muslims, the truth is that though the Mosque Network gives them a cause worth living and fighting for it rarely succeeds in persuading them that it is a cause worth dying for.

Potential martyrs are precious commodities and mosques are constantly on the lookout for them. People are not only carefully selected, their background is analysed minutely, and every single detail is taken into consideration. If a candidate is judged to be suitable, he is indoctrinated, fed a special diet of religion, spiritualism and violence. Hamas, by far one of the most efficient armed groups in preparing suicide bombers, pays a lot of attention to education. Potential martyrs are targeted at a very early age and slowly forged for their final mission. Salah Shehadeh,[13] the commander of the Izz al-Din al-Qassam Brigades, the military wing of Hamas, describes the selection process for a suicide bomber:

The choice is made according to four criteria. First, devout religious observance. Second, we verify that the young man complies with his parents' wishes and is loved by his family, and that his martyrdom will not [adversely] affect family life; that he is not the head of the family and he has siblings, as we will not take an only child. Third, his ability to carry out the task assigned [to] him and to understand its gravity; and fourth, his martyrdom should encourage others to carry out martyrdom operations and encourage Jihad in the hearts of people. We always prefer unmarried [people]. It is the regional leadership of the military apparatus of the Hamas movements that proposes his [her] candidacy, and then decides whether to accept him [her].[14]

In 2001, the association of Palestinian religious scholars granted its sanction to martyrdom. They declared that suicide attacks are part of the just war because they 'destroy the enemy and put fear in the hearts of the enemy, provoke the enemy, shake the foundations of its establishment and make it think of leaving Palestine. [They] will reduce the number of Jewish immigrants to Palestine, and will make [the Israelis] suffer financially.'[15]

The Mosque Network attempts to forge suicide bombers in a much shorter time and with a smaller pool of resources than organisations such as Hamas. The importance of suicide missions is particularly striking in economic terms. A cost-benefit analysis shows suicide operations to be by far the most efficient form of terror attacks from a military point of view; they require relatively small amounts of money and can have a great impact in terms of casualties and damage. Bin Laden and his followers are well aware of these advantages. According to the head of Egyptian Islamic Jihad, Dr Ayman al-Zawahiri, 'the method of martyrdom operation [is] the most successful way of inflicting damage against the opponent and the least costly to the Mujahedin in terms of casualties'.[16] 11 September proves how the impact of a terror attack can be maximised by the use of someone willing to die while committing it. It was also the most cost-effective terror attack ever carried out: only 19 hijackers and a budget estimated at $500,000 were employed to kill almost 3,000 people and inflict a permanent scar on Western society.

The Mosque Network also provides financial support for the Jihad. In 2001, the Lashkar-e-Taiba received £2 million in donations from British Muslims. According to Indian intelligence, among the generous donors was Ahmed Nashir, from East London, who contributed up to £15,000 a month. Nashir claimed that he had raised the money for welfare work.[17] Britain is the second largest benefactor of Muslim Kashmir, after Kashmiris living in the Middle East. The Mosque Network handles the majority of the funds; mosques collect money and make sure it reaches the right destination, i.e. their armed group of choice. Behind the network are imams like Shafiqur Rehman, the imam of Oldham, who was deported for raising funds for the Lashkar, and Sheikh Abu Hamza, the radical North London cleric who was secretly filmed at a rally held in Britain inciting Muslims to kill Americans.[18] 'Kill them,' he says in the video, 'It's okay.'

THE HIZBOLLAH IN KURDISTAN

Money raised via the Mosque Network is also used to enlarge the network itself, especially in secular Muslim areas. Towards the end of the 1980s, the Turkish government encouraged Muslim charities and mosques to raise money to build mosques in Turkish Kurdistan. A Kurdish political refugee in London explains:

Villages ended up having two mosques, but no schools or sports facilities for children were built. Scholarships to study Islamic theology in Arab countries were offered to young students by various charities, yet no scholarships were made available to study subjects like medicine or engineering. Clearly the decision to flood Kurdistan with mosques was aimed at colonising the region, traditionally secular and loyal to the PKK, the Kurdish Workers Party.

In the same period the Hizbollah began appearing in the region. They were Sunni Kurds mostly trained in Iran and Lebanon by the Shia Hizbollah; some had also received military and political training in Afghanistan.[19] They came to Kurdistan to preach and recruit for the Islamic Jihad. Initially, they were backed by Islamic charities and funds, most probably from Iran. However, they soon turned to crime as a source of self-financing. The Hizbollah used mosques as sites for organisation and recruitment.[20] Politically, they were at one with Namangiani, bin Laden and Hambali: their final goal was to turn Turkish Kurdistan into an Islamic state, a caliphate ruled by Sharia law. This political goal did not prevent the Turkish military from forging an alliance with the Hizbollah to crush the PKK. Mosques became the headquarters of Islamist violence. Faik Bulut, a Turkish Middle Eastern expert, describes the role of mosques run by the Hizbollah as follows:

Very young people between the ages of 15 and 20, the ill-educated and unemployed masses, are organised in the mosques. All of them are potential murderers. They are brave people. They work as professional murder gangs. The organisation's sources of funding are unknown. Anyone who joins them becomes rich all of a sudden. This money may come from abroad or perhaps from automobile theft, extortion, ransom and smuggling.[21]

The intention of the Turkish military was to manipulate the Hizbollah to rid Kurdistan of the PKK, as the US had done with the Mujahedin against the Soviets in Afghanistan. The alliance lasted only a few years, during which representatives and sympathisers of the PKK, along with the Kurdish population, were systematically attacked and killed by the Hizbollah.

In tandem with Islamic banks, the Mosque Network has contributed to a new economic phenomenon. Under the umbrella of Islam, and stimulated by the successes of the anti-Soviet Jihad, terror groups, state-shells, Islamist countries and their sponsors have successfully established an international network of economic and financial ties as a 'predatory alternative' to the traditional world economy. As we shall see in chapter 12, one of the cohesive forces of this new economic system has been the call for Jihad.

Part III
The New Economy of Terror

12. Weak States: Breeding Ground for Terror

'Where there should be a nation-state, there is a vacuum filled by warlords. What better place for the seeds of international terrorism and lawlessness to take root?'

Walter H. Kansteiner,
US Assistant Secretary for African Affairs

When he was seven years old, Francis Bok – a Christian child in Sudan – was captured as a slave while visiting his local market. Sudanese Muslims attacked his village and shot all adult and adolescent males. Then they rounded up the surviving children, tied them on to donkeys and took them away; children too small to ride were strapped into baskets. 'You are like animals to us,' the Sudanese soldiers told Bok, who has recently regained his freedom and now lives in Egypt. 'I have seen many people killed like animals and many children sold into slavery,' recalls Bok. 'I saw people shot, killed, children who cried had their hands or legs chopped off as an example to the others.'[1] This is not a medieval tale but the story of a twenty-first-century slave in Sudan.

Sudan belongs to a group of countries in the grip of vicious and ruthless civil wars, places where law and order have ceased to exist and people are at the mercy of predatory warlords and politicians. Hassan al-Turabi's patrimonial rule in Sudan, for example, was based on the exploitation of his own citizens. Such countries are politically unstable and prone to disintegration; they are nations in turmoil, weak states. The spectrum ranges from failing states, countries such as Colombia where the central government still maintains a certain degree of control over the territory, to failed states like Sudan, where the central authority 'is no longer able or willing to perform the job of a nation-state in a modern world';[2] to collapsed states such as Somalia, where there is a total vacuum of political authority.

Any type of weak state can provide the potential breeding ground for armed groups. A failed state does not offer a better environment for armed groups than a failing state. In Sri Lanka, the Liberation Tigers of Tamil Eelam (LTTE), the separatist armed organisation, has managed to gain control of as much as 15 per cent of the territory. Sri Lanka is not a failed state, not even a failing one; 80 per cent of the population back the government and believe that it is performing reasonably well.[3] Terror flourishes also in countries where there are only pockets of political instability, regions where the central authority has failed. Pakistan is a good example of this phenomenon. Although nobody can doubt that General Musharraf is in control of the nation, there are areas, especially inside the tribal belt, where Pakistani central authority has no power. It is in these enclaves that Islamist armed groups have been fostered.

FAILED AND BROWN AREAS

Madeleine Albright, former US Secretary of State, identified as 'failed states' countries with a weak or non-existent central authority. Failed states often arise from the political and economic disintegration of traditional states. They are countries unable to act under a national government. Often, in a failed state several competing authorities exercise various degrees of power in different regions. Consequently, the country is plagued by chaos, violence and suffering and there is large-scale neglect of basic human rights.[4] Albright's example of failure was Somalia. However, if one extends the definition of 'failed states' to include regions within weak states where the central authority has ceased to exercise any power – geographical enclaves which could be called 'failed areas' – the potential turf where terror can bloom grows exponentially. Guillermo O'Donnell, director of the Helen Kellogg Institute for International Studies in Paris, defines these areas as 'brown areas', where there is minimal or zero presence of the state both functionally and territorially.[5] The highlands of Peru, Amazonia in Brazil and Southern Colombia are examples of brown areas; so is the Fergana valley in Central Asia and specific areas in Indonesia, Malaysia and the Philippines in South East Asia.

Failed and brown areas share some of the characteristics of failed states. They are ravaged by internal fights, torn apart by savage conflicts between communities (as has happened in Kosovo); their borders are uncontrolled and undefined; the ruling power (either warlords or dictators, such as Mobutu, or the ruling political elite, such as the Taliban) prey on their own citizens; corruption is endemic; per capita as well as regional GDP is falling rapidly; violence and crime are rife and uncontrollable. Anarchy is the norm. Using O'Donnell's definition, these areas are 'examples of the evaporation of the public dimension of the state and, consequently, of the odd "reification" of the state as exclusively consisting of organisations that, in those regions, are in fact part of privatised, often sultanistic, circuits of power'.[6] Trapped in political vacuums, the populations of failed areas welcome strong leaders, warlords or armed groups who win popular support based on ethnic or clan solidarity. This desire for a strong hand is echoed by the comments of a newspaper seller in Jakarta, after the October 2002 bombing in Bali. 'If things continue like this,' he said, 'the people will welcome a military government . . . Things might have been bad under Suharto but at least we were safe.'[7] In failed areas, leaders of armed groups are perceived as strong men; they symbolise power within the socio-political and economic disintegration of the community. In 1946, many Jewish residents in Palestine backed terror groups such as the Irgun and the Stern

Gang because they believed that these organisations could fill
the vacuum created by the crumbling British protectorate.[8]
Similar motivation moved the inhabitants of Selva Alta in Peru
to entrust their lives to Sendero Luminoso, which offered them
protection against exploitation by both the corrupt Peruvian
government and the Colombian drug traffickers.

It is in 'failed areas', therefore, that armed groups most easily
establish and cement their power and legitimacy, stepping into
the void created by the collapse of the central authority. As we
saw in chapter 5, this is the process by which a state-shell, the
embryo of the state, is assembled. Armed groups replace the
economic infrastructures of the old state with their own models.
In doing so they take over the economic role of the central
authority, for example, in levying and collecting taxes. In
Pakistan, between 1997 and 1998, an estimated $600 million in
customs revenues were lost due to smuggling. Armed groups,
warlords and even Taliban officials imposed road taxes on ATTA
duty-free goods travelling to Kabul from Pakistani ports and
back to Pakistan. This money went to support the groups that
controlled the contraband trails.

A similar process occurs when a state collapses. Armed groups
fill what is left of 'a mere geographical expression, a black hole
into which a failed polity has landed'.[9] They gain control of
regions, create their own infrastructure, regulate markets and
trade flows, and even attempt to establish foreign relations with
neighbouring weak states. In August 2000, the Peruvian government was implicated in an arms smuggling scandal while
supplying weapons to the Colombian FARC. It emerged that
the Peruvian military had produced a regular purchase order
to buy 50,000 Bulgarian-made AK-47 assault rifles from the
Jordanian government. The shipment was flown from Amman
on a Ukrainian cargo plane with a Russian-Ukrainian crew.
The plane flew via the Canary Islands, Mauritania and Granada
and, eventually, before landing in Iquitos, Peru, air-dropped the
arms into the Guainia region, close to the border with Venezuela

and Brazil, the territory controlled by the FARC.[10] The plane flew back with narcotics, estimated at up to 40 tons of cocaine, which went partly to Jordanian brokers and partly to the former Soviet Union. The involvement of high-ranking Peruvian government officials in the smuggling contributed to the scandal, which eventually led to the resignation of President Fujimori[11] on 20 November 2000.

THE CAUCASUS: FOREIGN POLICY CHAOS

Armed groups can benefit from the difficulties that legitimate states encounter in relating to each other and to state-shells, that is, in developing a viable foreign policy with each other. The southern territories of the Caucasus offer an example of this phenomenon. Arab fighters, along with local Islamist armed groups, move freely in the Pankisi gorge which links Chechnya, Georgia and the Kodori gorge, a valley situated between Georgia and the irredentist region of Abkhazia. Abkhazia, like similar state-shells that have risen from the ashes of the Soviet Union, lacks legitimacy. The Pankisi and Kodori gorges are the main transit routes for arms that flow from Georgia to Chechnya as well as for drugs en route to Europe from Afghanistan. The Russians and Georgians could end both illegal trades by granting Abkhazia the right to police its own borders and thereby block access to the Pankisi gorge. This decision, however, would imply official recognition of Abkhazia as a separate state. Although Abkhazia has not been recognised by international powers, it has been functioning as a *de facto* Russian protectorate since 1993. Georgia, which claims that the region is part of its state, fears that allowing Abkhazia to break away would compromise its territorial integrity. Similar motivations are at the root of the refusal to let Russian security forces undertake military action against Chechnya's armed groups and Arab warriors inside Georgia. As a result, armed groups continue to profit from a multi-million-dollar arms and drugs trade in the region.[12]

THE ADVANTAGES OF WEAK STATES

Paradoxically, a collapsed state is a less protective cocoon for the creation of a state-shell than a failed state. This is because a collapsed state does not maintain any elements of legitimacy: it lacks government and foreign policy; internationally, it is perceived as a country with a weak, or no, identity. When a state collapses, as it did in Lebanon, Somalia and Sierra Leone, pseudo-rulers emerge and take control of parts of it; they remain illegitimate and unrecognised. Failed states, instead, retain the outward elements of sovereignty; even if they cannot control their borders, as in Sudan or Afghanistan, they maintain the footprint of territoriality. A violation of their territory by an outside power is perceived as an act of war; this is why armed groups can easily hide inside the borders of a failed state, as bin Laden did in Afghanistan. The US had to invade the country in order to hunt Osama bin Laden. For many years, the Albanian port of Durres has been openly used by the Albanian mafia for illegal traffic in drugs, weapons and migrants to Europe in conjunction with Islamist armed organisations. However, no European state is willing to invade Albania to end such trade.[13] Failed states maintain diplomacy and issue passports. In 1997, during the great Albanian unrest, 100,000 passports were stolen.[14] Interpol fears that they have been used 'to smuggle' members of Islamist armed organisations into Europe. Weak states maintain armies that can legitimately purchase weapons, which can either be transferred to armed groups or stolen by them. According to Interpol, from January to March 1997, armed and criminal organisations looted Albania's state depots of tens of thousands of assault rifles, machine guns and rocket launchers.[15]

Weak states offer other advantages to those engaged in terror. They provide territory for training camps and armed bases. In the late 1990s, members of the Indonesian terror group Jemaah Islamiyah were trained by the Moro Islamic Liberation Front in a camp on the southern Philippine island of Mindanao.[16] State-shells, once established in a weak state, can become transhipment points for narcotics, weapons, dirty money and illegal immigrants. According to Italian intelligence, Albania is one of the main transhipment points of narcotics for European markets; Chechnya is another.[17] Weak states with low or non-existent law enforcement are ideal grounds for smuggling. Weak states may also offer opportunities in legitimate business: while in Sudan, Osama bin Laden purchased plantations of gum mastic, thereby acquiring a monopoly in the international trade of gum arabic, an ingredient used in the manufacture of sweets and soft drinks.

The financial equivalent of weak states are banking 'brown areas'. These are offshore centres where there is little or no control over monetary transactions. These brown areas facilitate the laundering of income generated illegally by armed groups and criminal organisations. Untraceable financial services are available in more than 60 nations. The small Pacific island of Nauru, for example, at one point hosted 400 'shell banks', whose sole function was to hide money. Likewise in the Seychelles Islands, legislation grants immunity to investors from prosecution for all crimes committed outside its territory. People can invest sums of up to $10 million or more, generated by illegal activities. All that is required is that one does not engage in illegal activities in the Seychelles.[18]

INDONESIA, AN UNUSUAL JOINT VENTURE

The ideal breeding ground for terror is, therefore, a weak state that is slipping into a failing or failed state. It is within the progressive erosion of central power, and the escalating power struggle among fading state institutions, that terror groups are able to form surprising strategic alliances. The partnership between the military and the Islamists in Indonesia offers a good example of these 'unusual joint ventures'. In the 1970s, to contain a resurgence of communism, General Suharto's dictatorship encouraged cooperation between the military and Muslim extremist organisations. This policy received Washington's blessing. At that time the US was courting Islamist groups in an effort to contain Soviet expansion. Thus, while the CIA was manipulating the Mujahedin in Afghanistan, Suharto was attempting to do the same with the Islamists in Indonesia. One offspring of this alliance is believed to be the Jemaah Islamiyah, the Islamist terror group suspected to have been involved in the October 2002 bombing in Bali.[19] Over the years, segments of the military continued to maintain links with Islamist terror groups, often working with networks of 'special operations' against Suharto's opposition. In 1997 the FPI, Front Pembela Islam (Islam Defence Front), was set up in Indonesia with the help of the military authorities to sabotage movements for democracy. The group raids nightclubs, brothels and bars, forcing owners to pay protection money to the local police.[20]

The same political ambiguity that engulfed supporters and sponsors of the anti-Soviet Jihad resurfaces in Indonesia. While, on the one hand, Islamist groups were backed by the military, on the other, prominent leaders such as Abu Bakar Bashir – the Islamic cleric who preaches that Indonesia, Malaysia and the southern Philippines should be ruled by strict Sharia law – were imprisoned by Suharto. In 1978, Bashir, who was running a school in Java to educate the future leaders of a pure Islamic state, was charged with sedition for his involvement in the Komando Jihad, an armed group aiming to establish an Islamic state in Indonesia. Released in 1985, Bashir travelled to Malaysia. There he joined other members of the exiled Indonesian *Ulema*.

Among them was Riduan Isamuddin, better known as Hambali, who took over the Jemaah Islamiyah. Together, Bashir and Hambali travelled across Malaysia to preach and recruit warriors for their cause.[21]

When Suharto fell, the military hardliners moved their network out of the country. According to Wimar Witoelar, professor at Deakin University in Australia, they became known in Indonesia as 'dark forces', extremists both inside and outside the military.[22] The dark forces reactivated the links with the Islamists' network. To overcome the erosion of their power caused by the birth of democracy in Indonesia, the military hardliners aimed at re-establishing their presence behind the scenes; Islamist groups became their shields. Through these groups they planned to achieve the progressive destabilisation of the country. In a predominantly Muslim population, the aim was to foster the proliferation of pockets of failed areas exploiting religious and racial tensions. Islamist armed organisations took advantage of this alliance to carry out their own agenda: the creation of a pure Islamist state.

Since 1998, outbursts of violence have occurred all over the country, leaving in their wake a trail of blood and despair. The 1998 May riots in Jakarta led to over 1,000 deaths. In 2000, the military allowed thousands of members of Laskar Jihad[23] to penetrate the Moluccas. The ensuing conflict between Muslims and Christians lasted until the end of 2001, claiming 4,000 lives and leaving 500,000 refugees. From the Moluccas, Laskar fighters travelled to Papua, where Muslims do not enjoy a demographic majority, and initiated a conflict. Islamist fighters are also active in the Aceh, on the northern tip of Sumatra, where Muslim separatists have been fighting for independence since 1976. Fighting continues in Poso, in Central Sulawesi where the Laskar Jihad, the Front Pembela Islam and Laskar Jundullah, which is the operational arm of Jemaah Islamiyah, are engaged in a vicious conflict with the Christians. Since 1999, 2,500 people have been killed and 80,000 made refugees on this island.[24] In the enclaves controlled by Islamist fighters, strict application of Sharia law has already been imposed.

The destabilising forces unleashed since the fall of Suharto have created a climate of great economic uncertainty. Three presidents have failed to bring about much-needed economic reforms. They have worked within the constraints of a staggering $130 billion foreign debt, with a very high total debt to GDP ratio (over 90 per cent in 2001). Political instability, coupled with economic uncertainty, is responsible for the decline in foreign investments. When I visited Bali in the spring of 2000, a European banker told me that the island was one of the few places left where it was safe to invest. This is no longer the case. Islamist armed groups succeeded in striking a powerful blow against the troubled Indonesian economy when, in October 2002, they bombed a Bali nightclub. 'Targeting Bali really hits at Indonesia's underbelly,' commented Dewi Fortuna Anwar, an Indonesian political analyst.[25] Bali is an international tourist resort, which alone contributes $7 billion in annual revenues to the Indonesian economy (about 5 per cent of the country's GDP). Anwar added that the attack was not only directed at the tourists, but was aimed at 'Indonesia's economic well-being'. The bombing was in fact followed by a crash on the Indonesian stock market, which in turn led to a fall in the exchange rate of the already weak rupiah against the US dollar. The impact on the overall economy further weakened the banking system, still not fully recovered from the 1997 crisis of the Asian markets and riddled by corruption and mismanagement.[26]

Terror groups in Indonesia are following a well-known strategy: they are targeting the legitimate economy to accelerate the destabilisation of the central authority. As we have seen with the PLO in Lebanon, Sendero Luminoso in the highlands of Peru and the FMLN in El Salvador, once the economy has collapsed, armed groups fill the vacuum with their own economy of war.

13. From Modern Jihad to the New Economy of Terror

'We are fighting a jihad and this is the first Islamic international brigade in the modern era. The communists have their own brigades, the West has NATO, why can't the Muslims unite and form a common front?'

Lieutenant General Hameed Gul, head of ISI, Pakistani Secret Service, after the Soviet defeat in Afghanistan

Over the last 50 years, the environment where terror operates has mutated. 'Traditional' armed organisations, such as the IRA or the Kurdish Workers' Party (PKK), pursued irredentist objectives and were active only in a single region or country. Today, terror is transnational; it freely moves from one weak state to another. 'Al-Qaeda exists from Algeria to the Philippines,' explained Essid Sami Ben Khemais, a member of a Milan al-Qaeda cell. 'They are everywhere.'[1]

The transnational character of Islamist armed groups is a very recent development. It would, however, be a mistake to conceive al-Qaeda as a structural and highly integrated international network similar to a multinational of crime. Not only has the habitat in which armed organisations operate been altered, their structure has also evolved. 'Al-Qaeda is a phenomenon,' explained Saudi dissident Dr Saad al-Faqih.[2] Bin Laden is more of a charismatic leader than an organiser or manager. According to the UN Security Council's report on al-Qaeda, 'many of these extremist elements look to Osama bin Laden and his Shura Majlis as a sort of "supreme council", for inspiration and sometimes also for financial and logistical support'.[3]

Yossef Bodansky, director of a US congressional committee, agrees with this interpretation. He sees bin Laden's role as inspirational rather than operational: 'Bin Laden and his key aides are of unique importance as far as the operatives' morale and theological inspiration are concerned.'[4] Independent groups and cells are in charge of the logistics of terror attacks.

AL-QAEDA, A GLOBAL PHENOMENON

Even the origins of al-Qaeda confirm this reading. At the outset of the anti-Soviet Jihad, potential Arab warriors travelled to Pakistan where they resided in guesthouses. These hostels did not keep any records and not a single organisation listed the names of the fighters, where they had gone to fight and if they had been injured or killed. This lack of vital information caused distress among relatives. At that time bin Laden was in charge of several guesthouses and was embarrassed by the hundreds of calls requesting information. Hence, he decided to keep track of whoever stayed at the hostels and that record came to be known as the Record of al-Qaeda. This is how al-Qaeda, which means the base or the scroll, was born.[5] It was only in 1988 that bin Laden began to toy with the idea of organising Muslim volunteers into an army to fight the Jihad.

According to Dr al-Faqih, head of the UK-based anti-al-Saud organisation Movement for Islamic Reform in Arabia (MIRA), it would be more correct today to speak of 'bin Laden's group' or 'network' instead of al-Qaeda. The network has a core: bin Laden and a small inner circle of supporters, people who follow him wherever he goes. The wider picture is constituted by thousands of smaller groups, armed organisations of various sizes and forms, ranging from accomplished groups to individuals. These groups have their own chain of command, logistics and targets. This is a very loose network which looks to bin Laden as a charismatic figure, someone to inspire, sanction and help finance violent actions.[6] In mid-1999, Hambali and his group put together a presentation video of a plan to blow up a bus service used by US soldiers in Singapore. They showed this to bin Laden in the hope of receiving funds for their terror activity in South East Asia. The video was found in late 2001 in Kabul, in the house of Mohammad Atif, bin Laden's military commander. In 1999, bin Laden and his network were receiving hundreds of similar requests, most of which were not granted any funding. Hambali, however, was successful and his plan was funded. Atif used a Saudi charity to transfer money to buy the four tons of ammonium nitrate required for the bombing.[7] Since then, Hambali has been linked to several attacks in South East Asia, including five simultaneous explosions in Manila in October 2002. A few days after the Bali bombing, an Indonesian Islamist arrested in Manila confessed that Hambali had funded the attacks.[8]

The strategic importance of Indonesia, a country with an overwhelming majority of Muslims, is confirmed by the fact that leading members of bin Laden's inner circle have travelled to the country. In mid-2000 Dr Ayman al-Zawahiri went to Indonesia accompanied by a young Kuwaiti man, Omar Faruq, who was one of bin Laden's men in the Philippines. During his visit, Zawahiri established contacts with Islamist leaders, including Abu Bakar Bashir. It is likely that during these meetings, bin Laden's deputy was presented with terror attack plans and asked for financial backing. A few months later, a series of bombs exploded at Christian churches in the Moluccas. Today those explosions are considered the blueprint for the Bali bombing. According to the CIA, Bashir received $74,000 from an account controlled by Sheikh Abu Abdullah, one of bin Laden's pseudonyms. The money was used to purchase three tons of explosives from Indonesian army officers.

'Groups may or may not have direct contact with bin Laden or his inner circle,' commented al-Faqih. That does not matter. What is relevant and dangerous for the West is that the network has a life of its own, with its own breeding cycle: i.e. armed groups hatch inside weak states, evolve into state-shells and move on to link up among themselves and with other terror and criminal organisations. Cells like those that have fostered the 11 September hijackers multiply even in Western cities. What the world is facing is a living transnational conglomerate of organisms, colonies of terror everywhere. The key question is, how does this system survive? The answer is simple: what breathes life into it is the New Economy of Terror.

ISLAMIST TERROR'S REAL TARGET

Before analysing the interdependence between modern terror and its economy, two points must be made. First, the collapse of the Soviet Union and subsequent lack of involvement of the West in certain regions gave modern terror new momentum; second, the primary target of Islamist political violence is not the West, but pro-Western regimes in Muslim or predominantly Muslim countries. 'According to bin Laden, the premier betrayers [of God and His Prophet] have been Islamic governments that cooperate with the United States, regimes . . . that are "morally depraved" and that he has described as "hypocrites" that "champion falsehood". . .'[9] Al-Qaeda is undoubtedly the product of these two factors. When initially conceived by bin Laden in 1988, it was going to be 'an army of young men responding to the Jihad call'.[10] According to Abu Mahmud,[11] when bin Laden shared with him this idea he never mentioned waging Jihad against Western regimes; on the contrary he was thinking of fighting the infidel governments who oppressed Muslims around the world, as in Palestine, the Philippines, Kashmir and Central Asia which was ruled by the Soviet Union.[12] It was only after the victory in Afghanistan, the dismantling of the Soviet Union and the Gulf War that a new enemy emerged. The violent opposition to Western culture is a corollary of this phenomenon; it springs from the alliance and support of Western governments for Muslim oligarchic regimes, which are seen to exploit the masses, Saudi Arabia, Pakistan and post-Soviet Azerbaijan among them. The conflagration with the West is the *conditio sine qua non* for the removal of these oligarchies, a phenomenon which will pave the way for the establishment of a confederation of Islamist states.

The exploitative nature of the alliance between the West and Muslim oligarchies is a constant source of resentment among Muslim populations around the world. In Azerbaijan, a dissident complained:

suddenly, in the mid-nineties, as the US began to formulate a NATO security policy in the post-Cold War world order, estimates of Azerbaijan's oil reserves began to climb. Out of nowhere, initial estimates compared it to the North Sea reserves of 30–50 billion barrels, but then the numbers inflated to 200 billion barrels and comparisons were made with Saudi Arabia. As a result, a large number of American oil companies and their executives descended upon Baku and began bidding with its leadership for oil exploration contracts.[13]

In 1994, a consortium guided by BP-Aramco signed a contract for the exploration of the oil fields in Charyg, near Baku. The local partner was SOCAR, the oil company controlled by 'friends' of Heydae Aliyevich Aliyev,[14] president of Azerbaijan.[15] Western and international financial institutions, including the World Bank, backed the contract. Money was distributed by the oil company to members of the government to secure the contract and execute it. 'Azerbaijan's leaders are wined and dined on oil company expense accounts, while 600,000 Azeris still live in the most horrendous conditions, in makeshift housing outside of Baku and throughout western Azerbaijan.'[16]

Terror has not escaped the 'globalisation fever' of the 1990s. Its medium- and long-term objectives are also transnational. For Islamist armed groups the aims are respectively the Jihad and the new Caliphate, a confederation of Islamist states. 'Islamist warriors will go wherever they are needed to follow the call of the Jihad,' an Algerian Mujahid explained to me a decade ago. Indeed, in 1992, veterans from the anti-Soviet Jihad arrived in Bosnia to fight. Radical groups, such as the Lebanese Hizbollah, sent trainers to prepare young and inexperienced Muslims, who flocked to the Balkans for the new Jihad. Since then, outbreaks of Jihad have multiplied. As we discussed in chapters 9 and 10, the disintegration of the Soviet Union and the new economic and political disorder that followed spurred the proliferation of wars. Along the periphery of the old Soviet system, weak states emerged. Large regions within these states soon slipped into failed areas and became prey to emerging Islamist armed groups. International abandonment by Western countries and the US, the sole surviving superpower, also made way for the spread of terror. However, before this phenomenon took place, Islamist armed organisations had already targeted traditional Muslim regimes.

THE THREAT OF ARAB-AFGHANS

In 1992 Egyptian and Algerian leaders warned Washington of the growing threat posed by Arab-Afghans. They begged the US administration to re-engage diplomatically in Afghanistan to bring peace to the region. Their pleas were ignored. Meanwhile, the Algerian regime had gathered extensive knowledge on the Algerian veterans of the anti-Soviet Jihad and their links with Osama bin Laden's network. Their partnership was threatening Algeria's political stability. In January 1992, the army cancelled the election that had produced the victory (60 per cent of the seats) of the Islamic Salvation Front (FIS) and imposed military rule. The decision was followed by a vicious confrontation between the Islamists and the army, which, by 1999, would claim as many as 70,000 lives. The FIS was eventually taken over by the radical Islamic Jihad, which in 1995 became the Armed Islamic Group (GIA), led by Algerian veterans of the anti-Soviet Jihad.[17] The GIA was part of bin Laden's master plan to destabilise North Africa and led to the growth of Islamic extremism in France. Islamists saw Algeria and Albania as entry points of terror into Europe.

Arab-Afghans had also targeted Egypt. In the early 1990s, veterans of the Afghan war reactivated the Egyptian Islamic Jihad and brought fresh blood to it. In 1993, they unsuccessfully attempted to assassinate the interior minister and, two years later, in 1995, they tried and again failed to kill the prime minister. They did, however, succeed in killing four police officers and 58 tourists in 1997, in Luxor, a popular tourist site.

Libya was another country on which Arab-Afghans had set their sights. In 1998, Gaddafi uncovered a plot to assassinate him by the al-Muqatila, an Islamist group founded in the early 1990s by Libyan veterans of the anti-Soviet Jihad. The strategy of the group was to infiltrate the territory and the population in order to engineer a coup. Like many similar Islamist organisations in the Arab world, the al-Muqatila had its headquarters in Sudan and was backed financially by Osama bin Laden. In the 1990s, bin Laden himself resided in Libya, in Jabala Larde, a village not far from Benghazi, in the eastern part of the country. The unpopularity of the Gaddafi regime was particularly appealing to the Saudi billionaire because it made Libya a perfect hideout. Sandwiched between Algeria and Egypt, the two countries in which Islamist armed groups were most active, Libya was an ideal location for his network's headquarters. On 15 April 1998, following the failed assassination attempt on his person, Gaddafi issued a warrant for bin Laden's arrest via the Interpol. It was the first of many. Until then, the most wanted man in the world was technically free. A month later, Interpol recognised its validity and issued an international warrant for his arrest.[18]

The extraordinary partnership between MI5 and al-Muqatila illustrates the degree of detachment of the West from events taking place in the Middle East and its complacency over this situation. David Shayler, former MI5 agent based in North Africa, admitted that in November 1996 the British secret service had also planned the assassination of Gaddafi in co-operation with al-Muqatila. The plan was to attack the Libyan leader during an official transfer from one location to another, but was never implemented. Ironically, after 11 September, the British secret service asked its Libyan counterpart for information on al-Muqatila terror group.[19] A delegation of high-ranking Libyan secret agents travelled to London to brief the MI5.

MODERN JIHAD

The final aim of the New Economy of Terror is to support terror; indeed this economic system is merely a by-product of the evolution of political violence during the last half-century: from state-sponsored terrorism to the privatisation of terror and the birth of state-shells. Today the Modern Jihad, the contemporary version of the Jihad, is one of the most important manifestations of political violence on earth and the primary engine of the New Economy of Terror. In the year 2000, according to the International Institute of Strategic Studies, more than two-thirds of the 32 armed conflicts which were taking place around the globe involved Muslims.[20] Under the umbrella of the Jihad, the Muslim community is moulding a new, bellicose identity. The first step in understanding the New Economy of Terror is, therefore, to grasp the meaning of the Modern Jihad. To do so one has to look at the conditions in which it took shape.

Two leading philosophers, Samuel Huntington and Francis Fukuyama, have attempted to describe the new scenario. Huntington places the causes of growing Islamic conflicts in politics. Until the fall of the Soviet Union, politics was the privilege of the two superpowers and Muslim countries survived in their shadow. Even the oil shock and the subsequent massive flow of wealth towards Arab countries failed to tilt this equilibrium. In a recent UN development report, a group of Arab intellectuals stated that the Arab world with its oil wealth is 'richer than it is developed'.[21] Petrodollars did not bring modernisation, or better, the redistribution of wealth. On the contrary, the unprecedented transfer of cash from the West to Arab countries contributed to 'freezing Arab regimes'. In the eyes of many Muslims, the end of the Cold War also marked the decline of the supremacy of Western culture. This coincided with the beginning of the liberation of Muslim countries from its grip. It was at this point that a search for new, intellectual parameters with which to define Muslim identity intensified. Islam soon emerged as a leading referent. Islamic organisations have from the beginning aimed at meeting the needs of a growing population: they have provided social and moral support, welfare, health services, education, unemployment relief, charitable help – services too often denied by Muslim governments to their citizens.[22] (One should add that some of these needs have also been met by armed groups which have created their own state-shells, e.g. the PLO in Lebanon, Hamas in the occupied territories and the IMU in the Tavildara valley.) In Tajikistan Islamic organisations of various types continue to boost the resurgence of Muslim consciousness. Islamist radical groups, on the other hand, have also constituted the only opposition to repressive and authoritarian regimes.

Huntington stresses that across the Muslim world there is grievance and hostility against Western cultural and material colonisation. However, it seems more realistic to view this resentment as a by-product of Islamic frustration *vis-à-vis* their own rulers than as an independent opposition. Especially among the new generations, the West is held responsible for the survival of repressive and undemocratic Muslim regimes, Saudi Arabia being the most noteworthy example. Huntington also lists two other causes for the spread of Islamist terror: the endemic religious, tribal, ethnic, political and cultural divisions within Muslim communities, which fuel violence among them and towards non-Muslims, and the buoyant demographic growth of the population.[23] The evolution of these factors, he concludes, will lead to a clash between civilisations, especially Islam and the West. According to Huntington, Osama bin Laden's final aim is to ignite this violent conflict, an aim which has been furthered by recent events. A 2001 report from Digos, the elite Italian police force, stated that the al-Qaeda Milan cell discovered after 11 September had Europe in their sights. This finding was based on a series of recorded telephone conversations among its members. 'God loves us because Europe is in our hands,' said Lased Ben Heini, a Libyan veteran of the anti-Soviet Jihad and a member of the Milan cell.[24]

Fukuyama, unlike Huntington, sees modern conflicts as part of the process of modernisation, a force pushing Muslim countries, and the rest of the world, towards representative regimes, i.e. democracy. Although Khomeini forced women to wear the *chador*, Fukuyamá argues that in return he was forced to grant them the right to vote.[25] Even in the light of the growth of Islamist terror, history for Fukuyama is still moving inexorably towards universal democracy.[26]

How does Islamist terror relate to these two visions of the world? Islamism, as a modern concept, emerged from the ashes of previous Islamic movements. From the Muslim Brotherhood of Hassan al-Banna, the radical armed group founded in 1928 in Egypt, Islamism took the figure of the charismatic leader and the blind loyalty of his followers. Al-Banna had in turn borrowed these concepts from Italian Fascism. Central to the Brotherhood manifesto was the marriage between the spiritual and the physical, a concept translated by Islamist armed groups into the Jihad. From the Marxist journalist Maulana Mawdudi, the founder of the Pakistani Jamaat e-Islami in the 1940s, comes the concept of Islamic revolutionary vanguards, e.g. the anti-

Soviet Jihad warriors fighting against the West and secular Islam. Finally, the Egyptian intellectual Sayyid Qutb, who while in prison became the Brotherhood's ideologist, conceived the universal nature of the Islamic movement, projecting the image of a monolithic nation, a state ruled by an Islamic party.[27] To achieve this final goal, Sayyid justified the use of violence in any form.

Islamist fundamentalism is perhaps the natural heir of early Islamic revolutionary movements, originating from both right- and left-wing Muslim thinkers. Even so, it defines its modern identity in sharp contraposition to Western culture:

this fierce Judeo-Christian campaign against the Muslim world, the likes of which has never been seen before, is [a signal] that the Muslims must prepare all the possible might to repel the enemy in the military, economic, missionary, and all other areas. It is crucial for us to be patient and to cooperate in righteousness and piety and to raise awareness to the fact that the highest priority, after faith, is to repel the incursive enemy which corrupts the religion and the world, and nothing deserves a higher priority after faith, as the scholars have declared, for this cause, it is crucial to overlook many of the issues of bickering in order to unite our ranks so that we can repel the greater Kufr [infidel].[28]

Thus Islamism possesses the seeds both of modernisation and of the violent clash of civilisations envisaged by Fukuyama and Huntington respectively. However, Islamist terror is also something different. It is, as any revolutionary force, an economic engine, fuelled by a very special source of energy, the Modern Jihad. Paradoxically, the importance that 'economics' plays in Islamist armed groups springs from the ideological background in which early Islamist revolutionary movements were conceived, a background deeply rooted in Western ideology. The cult of martyrdom of al-Banna owes more to the French and Italian right-wing anarchists of the nineteenth century than to Sunni or Shia Islam.[29] Marxist influence is paramount in the shaping of the concept of revolutionary vanguards. As clearly expressed by the Iranian academics Ladan and Roya Boroumand, Qutb's 'ideal society was a classless one where the "selfish individual" of liberal democracies would be banished and the "exploitation of man by man" would be abolished. God alone would govern it through the implementation of Islamic law. This was Leninism in an Islamic dress.'[30]

Could it be possible that the ideological seeds of Fascism, Nazism and Bolshevism are now, almost a century later, fuelling Islamism? As far as economics is concerned, the answer is yes. The aim of all these movements was to change radically an existing socio-economic system. Wrapped in ideological or religious propaganda, their appeal to the masses was based on the promise of a redistribution of wealth in their favour. The Iranian revolution won national support on these grounds. The Romanovs in the 1910s, the Shah in the 1970s and the present Saudi royal family are targeted by the masses because of the vast economic inequalities perpetuated within their countries by their regimes. Lenin, Khomeini and bin Laden are perceived by their followers as charismatic leaders, 'strong men', the revolutionaries who grant legitimacy to those in pursuit of radical changes. This characterisation is confirmed by Ayman al-Zawahiri, leader of the Egyptian Islamic Jihad, who defined bin Laden as the 'new Che Guevara'.[31]

In this context Jihad departs from its traditional meaning and assumes new significance. Loosely translated as 'struggle', the word originally refers to the existential fight of Muslims against their moral failings and weaknesses. This is Jihad Akbar or greater Jihad. Alongside this concept is that of Jihad Asghar (literally translated as 'smaller Jihad'), which refers to the fight for self-preservation and self-defence. It is the definition of Jihad Asghar that contains military and political elements and, therefore, is regulated by a host of ethical sanctions. For example, Muslims must engage in Jihad only when attacked, but must refrain if motivated only by considerations of *realpolitik*.[32] The modification of these ethical sanctions has transformed the Jihad. Modern Jihad has as its target the state of Israel and the imperialism of America and its Western allies, political entities cleverly hidden behind their religious creeds, Judaism and Christianity. But its primary targets remain traditional Muslim states as well as any government that blocks the formation of Islamist nations, for example Indian democracy in Kashmir and Megawati's democratic government in Indonesia. Thus in its modern version, Jihad no longer distinguishes between infidels and People of the Book – Muslims, Jews and Christians – against whom it is prohibited to wage war. Religion is conveniently sheltering political and economic motivations. When this shield is removed, it is apparent that the fight is not against an aggressor but against foreign and domestic powers that economically and culturally exploit the Muslim masses. 'We have the right to attack our attackers,' reads the manifesto issued by al-Qaeda in November 2002, 'to destroy villages and cities of whoever destroyed our villages and cities, to destroy the economy of those who have robbed our wealth and to kill civilians of the country which has killed ours.'[33] The dichotomy here is closer to Marx than to Mohammad. In 1989, Hashemi Rafsanjani, then president of the Islamic Parliament, summarised this concept in a Friday sermon: 'Blow up the factory. Where you work, you can take action . . . Let them call you terrorists . . . They [the imperialism of information and propaganda] commit crimes and call it human rights. We call it the defence of rights and of an oppressed people . . . They will say the president of the parliament officially incites terror . . . Let them say it.'[34]

Chivalry, another fundamental limitation imposed on the Jihad, as the absolute prohibition of laying hands on innocents and non-combatants, has also been violated.[35] Armed groups engaged in the Modern Jihad, such as Hamas, reject the concept of innocents and non-combatants. For them the citizens of

Israel are as guilty as their leaders and are therefore legitimate targets. The same rationale backs bin Laden's call to kill Americans wherever and whenever possible. Again, the rigidity of this dichotomy is reminiscent of the French and Bolshevik revolutions where the struggle was defined as between classes. No distinction was made between bad and progressive, young and old, female and male aristocrats. Being a member of the opposing class was enough to make one an enemy.

Finally, it is the destruction of their own oppressive system, identified with the oligarchic secular Muslim regimes, and the creation of a new socio-economic system which motivate Muslims to take up arms and join the Modern Jihad. 'We must destroy the laws of democracy and secularism or any other disbelief or laws, which are *Jahiliyye,* ignorant,' declared Abu Mustafa al-Shafi, the ideologist of the Ansar al-Islam, the Islamist armed group in Northern Iraq. Islam provided the institutional framework for the new system. 'We must apply the Islamic law in all aspects of life,' continued al-Shafi. 'The laws that we must apply in life must be ordered and explained in the Qur'an or by the *Sunnah* (Prophet Mohammad's behaviour and preaching).'[36] Thus the creation of an Islamist Caliphate emerges as the goal of Islamist fundamentalism. In Indonesia, Islamist leaders like Hambali openly admit that their goal is to transform the country into a fundamentalist Islamist state.[37] The aim of the Ngruki network, a loose grouping of militant Islamist Indonesian armed cells, co-founded in the 1970s by Abu Bakar Bashir, is to create a federation of strict Islamist states, a sort of Caliphate, in Indonesia and in other South East Asian countries, i.e. Malaysia, Singapore and the Philippines.[38]

Thus the Modern Jihad is a brew made up of a mixture of Islamist revolutionary ideology, Muslim search for identity and socio-economic aspirations. As such it feeds into the network of terror economies created by armed groups attempting to achieve self-sufficiency: the smuggling of drugs and narcotics, the partnership with crime, the transfer of wealth from rich

Muslims via charitable organisations, money laundering, etc. It is the desire and the possibility of becoming part of such a network and at the same time the willingness of the network to embrace all Islamic state-shells that contributes to the proliferation of the Modern Jihad. 'The terror economic network,' commented one journalist, when I explained my concept to him, 'seems like the EU of terror, a federation of states in constant expansionary mode. Every country who wants to join in gets substantial help from Brussels to do so.' The true nature of the New Economy of Terror is expansionary and ecumenical. When Ansar al-Islam was founded on 1 September 2001 from the merging of al-Tawhid and the Second Soran Unit, three Arab veterans of the anti-Soviet Jihad presented the leaders with a gift of $300,000, seed money from Osama bin Laden's terror organisation.[39] This was a gesture of welcome into the system.

Like any economic system, the New Economy of Terror has its own rules and regulations. Its members – weak states, state-shells, armed groups and cells – have to be able to assemble at least a self-sustaining economy. They have to match outflows with inflows, i.e. they must have a balance of payments.

14. Terror's Legitimate Business

'If liberating my land is called terrorism, this is a great honour for me.'

Osama bin Laden during an interview with
Robert Fisk in 1996

In November 2001, under mounting pressure from the United States, the Yemeni government froze the bank accounts of several honey dealers and shopkeepers accused of being conduits for bin Laden's network. This decision, however, did little to curb the country's honey trade. The freezing of assets 'has not affected us', admitted the manager of al-Shifa honey store, because 'a lot of our exports are bartered against other products'.[1] In the moderate heat of the Arab winter, business inside the Yemeni honey shops continued to be buoyant as ever.

Honey is widely traded and consumed in the Middle East. In Saudi Arabia, a country with a small production, families consume an average of 1 kg of honey a month. Imports originate from Yemen, Pakistan and even Afghanistan. Yemeni honey is the purest and most expensive available in the Middle East. According to Steven Emerson, who maintains a database on Islamist armed groups, bin Laden has developed strong ties with Yemeni honey companies, among them al-Nur Honey, a company based in the capital, Sanaa. One of the owners is Mohammad al-Ahdal, a former Arab–Afghan, described in 1992 in an Arab newspaper as one of the first Arabs to fight in the anti-Soviet Jihad (in 1998, al-Ahdal was detained in Saudi Arabia, charged with plotting terrorist activities against the Saudi government).[2] Honey entrepreneurs include some of bin

Laden's top aides, such as Abu Zubaydah, al-Qaeda's director of external affairs. American intelligence maintains that bin Laden himself, through a web of shell companies and associates, owns a network of shops in the Middle East.

Osama bin Laden's entry into the honey industry coincided with his move to Sudan in the early 1990s. One of his firms there, the International al-Ikhlas Company, produced honey and sweets at a factory in Kameen. Bin Laden is not alone in this business; other Middle Eastern armed organisations, the Egyptian Islamic Jihad for example, have used honey shops to fund terror activity. Honey is also considered a good product in which to conceal contraband: drugs, arms, gold, electronic equipment and cash are often smuggled in honey containers. With the tacit approval of shopkeepers, these goods are literally 'buried' in honey. 'The smell and consistency of the honey makes it easy to hide weapons and drugs,' explained a Yemeni customs officer. '[In addition,] inspectors don't want to inspect that product. It's too messy.'[3] Legitimate businesses like the honey trade therefore offer a double advantage: a legal source of revenue and useful cover for smuggling.

Armed groups' involvement in legitimate activities is not a new phenomenon. In the 1970s, the IRA acquired a monopoly over transportation in the Catholic areas of Northern Ireland. The IRA taxi companies, Falls Taxis and People's Taxis, owned 350 cabs and employed 800 drivers. The IRA also owned co-ops, supermarkets and a butcher's shop in Andersonstown.[4] Over the same period the Protestant armed group the UDA (Ulster Defence Association) maintained a monopoly of the security market. Security firms such as Task Point Security and Leader Enterprises, in Belfast, had boards of directors, paid their taxes and were run as legitimate companies. Their annual turnover, in excess of £300,000, was in line with that of a medium-sized UK firm in the 1970s. Samed, the Palestinian Martyrs Work Society created by the PLO, employed thousands of people, producing and exporting products all over the world. Prior to the Israeli invasion of Lebanon, its industrial turnover alone was $18 million.[5] Undoubtedly, the privatisation of terror and the subsequent creation of the New Economy of Terror have widened the range of legitimate businesses run by armed organisations. Today, even small cells are able to finance themselves through legal and illegal activities. This is often the case with sleepers – dormant cells or individuals waiting to be activated at any time – such as the 24-year-old Saudi, Mohammad al-Owahali. To support himself and his family while awaiting his call from bin Laden, al-Owahali ran a small fishing business in Mombasa, Kenya.[6]

Often sleepers are given a cash lump sum to get them started. According to Jonathan Winer, former deputy assistant secretary of state for international law enforcement, terror cells receive 'seed money from their sponsors to set up shop in other countries; they are otherwise expected to "live off the land" in providing for themselves'.[7] Ahmed Ressam, the member of the Millennium Plot arrested while crossing the Canadian border with bomb materials, confessed that when he finished his training in Afghanistan he was given $12,000 to return to Montreal and settle down.[8]

At the opposite end of the spectrum, armed organisations also benefit from multi-million-dollar legitimate businesses, like the ones managed by al-Barakaat and al-Taqwa/Nada Management Group. These international financial institutions run *hawala* exchanges (as described in chapter 10) all over the world. Al-Barakaat is a Somali-based international financial conglomerate with branches in 40 countries, including the US. Every year, until September 2001 when its funds were frozen by the US authorities, the US office wired at least $500 million in international profits to the central exchange office located in the United Arab Emirates. Of these revenues, bin Laden's network received a flat 5 per cent cut, equivalent to about $25 million.[9] Al-Taqwa is a bank with strong ties with Islamist groups. It was set up in Nassau in 1987 with $50 million as capital, of which two-thirds came from Islamist fundamentalist organisations; one of the most important shareholders was the Muslim brotherhood al-Islah of Kuwait. Among other activities, it has financed the political campaigns of Islamist candidates in the municipal elections in Egypt. The bank, which operates in more than 30 countries,[10] is so secretive that at times intelligence services have even doubted its existence. After 11 September, the bank's branch in Lugano, Switzerland, was investigated for speculation and insider trading on behalf of bin Laden's associates.[11]

The development of the New Economy of Terror has facilitated the expansion of cross-border terror's legitimate activities. As a business, terror activity has gone global. By far the best-developed empire is the one run by bin Laden and his inner circle. It is rooted in business acumen rather than religious rigour. In many ways the Saudi millionaire does not fit the stereotype of the Islamist leader as a primarily spiritual guide. He lacks the required religious authority: he is not a cleric like Mullah Omar, the leader of the Taliban, nor is he a messianic preacher like the Egyptian Sheikh Omar Abdul Rahman, the Blind Sheikh imprisoned in the US for plotting the first bombing of the World Trade Center. Osama bin Laden has broken the mould of the Islamist leader, shaping his role and tasks according to politics and pragmatism.

Politics plays a large role in his rhetoric. Commenting on the decision of the Saudi royal family to let American troops into the country, he said, 'This big mistake by the Saudi regime of inviting the American troops revealed their deception. They [the Saudis] had given their support to nations that were fighting against Muslims. They helped Yemen Communists against the southern Yemeni Muslims.'[12] Bin Laden is not engaged in an ideological dispute, he is extremely pragmatic in the way he addresses his followers. In the official declaration of the Jihad against Jews and Crusades, he produced a political analysis of the US policy in the Middle East. He stated:

if the Americans' aims behind these wars are religious and economic, the aim is also to serve the Jews' petty state and divert attention from its occupation of Jerusalem and murder of Muslims there. The best proof of this is their eagerness to destroy Iraq, the strongest neighbouring Arab state, and their endeavour to fragment all the states of the region such as Iraq, Saudi Arabia, Egypt and Sudan into paper statelets and through their disunion and weakness to guarantee Israel's survival and the continuation of the brutal crusade occupation of the Peninsula.[13]

It is apparent that religion is only part of the picture.

Unlike other Islamist religious leaders, bin Laden's terror actions carry specific demands such as the abdication of King Fahd, the withdrawal of American troops from Saudi soil and the political recognition of the Taliban regime.[14] Some of these requests are backed by economic arguments. For example, bin Laden declared that Americans have been profiteering from the sale of Arab oil, openly stealing its revenues. For every barrel sold over the last 25 years, he claims, they pocketed $135. The total loss of income has been calculated at a staggering $4.05 billion a day – the greatest theft in history. The magnitude of such a 'swindle', he concludes, entitles the 1.2 billion Muslims in the world to claim $30 million each in compensation from America.[15] Thus the revolutionary message of bin Laden is encrypted in his use of political and economic arguments, reminiscent of old Marxist claims, such as the denunciation of Western capitalists' pillage of poor countries. Politics, economics and nationalism, rather than religion, are his primary motivations; they constitute the ideological bounds of his network.

BIN LADEN'S LEGITIMATE BUSINESSES

Politics, economics and nationalism are also the characteristics of bin Laden's economic and financial empire, a truly transnational financial engine of terror, a considerable section of which is represented by legitimate businesses. Among the companies it consists of: in Africa, a holding company, Wadi al-Aqiq, a Sudanese construction firm, Al-Hiraj, an ostrich farm and shrimp boats in Kenya; in the Middle East, shares in the Al-Shamil Islamic Bank and large tracks of forest in Turkey; in Asia, agricultural holdings in Tajikistan; in Europe and the United States, holding companies, venture capital firms, banks and import–export companies.[16] Real estate investments are scattered around the globe to offset losses and maximise profits. The portfolio includes real estate in London, Paris and the French Riviera; dairy businesses in Denmark; wood and paper industries in Norway; and hospital equipment in Sweden. Apparently, bin Laden and his associates have also targeted the medical market in Egypt, Jordan and Iraq, which generates hundreds of millions of dollars in revenue, part of which is utilised to fund his network of cells.[17]

Bin Laden's legitimate businesses took off while he was based in Sudan. He funded the construction of the airport at New Sudan and the highway linking it to Khartoum. For the services of his construction company, Al-Hiraj, he was paid by the government in sesame seeds, which were then traded on the international market.[18] Subsequently, he secured a virtual monopoly on corn, sunflowers and sesame seeds, Sudan's leading exports. These were handled by Themar al-Mubaraka, an agricultural firm near El Damazin, and Taba Investment, a currency trading firm. In exchange for the road works, bin Laden was also given ownership of the Khartoum Tannery. By the time bin Laden left Sudan, his Sudanese empire included a bakery, a furniture company, the Bank of Zoological Resources, a cattle-breeding farm and the Laden International import–export company. He also owned shares in a factory that processed goatskin and in Qadarat Transport, a fleet of fishing boats.

One of the most profitable businesses bin Laden acquired was the Gum Arabic Company Limited, a firm which supplies

80 per cent of the world demand for this product, giving him a monopoly in the industry. Gum arabic is produced from the sap of the acacia trees that grow in Sudan. It is used to make ink stick to newspapers, to prevent sediment forming in soft drinks and to create a protective shell around sweets and pills to keep them fresh.[19] To evade international sanctions against Sudan, profits from these enterprises were channelled through banks in the Turkish section of Cyprus with whom bin Laden had developed strong financial ties.[20] In 1997, Sidi Tayyed, a Saudi financier who was one of bin Laden's treasurers, admitted having opened accounts in Europe, Africa, Pakistan and in the Central Asian republics. He also confessed that, to reduce risks, other money went through the Central Asian republics, from where it was transferred to Turkish Cyprus. According to Tayyed's testimony, a group of Turkish businessmen close to the Turkish Cypriot government had arranged the initial contact with the banks.[21]

Bin Laden's legitimate business network seems to have followed the blueprint of Arafat's PLO investment schemes; it has been shaped to fit the mould of the ideal capitalist port-folio. Funds are placed in several banks across the world, ranging from the sultanate of Brunei to European countries. The port-folio contains financial investments with different degrees of risk and return. After the collapse of the Taliban regime, about $750,000 is believed to have been placed in short-term accounts in several financial markets in the Arab peninsula; these highly liquid assets are available for use at very short notice. In 1998, through a contact at the Arab Banking Corporation, bin Laden speculated in the French stock market in shares, including stocks from BNP and Société Générale, netting $20 million profit. Short-term speculation on Western stock markets is regarded as a favourable and efficient way of accumulating funds in the West without using bank transfers, which are more easily trace-able. These funds may be used to help sleepers and cells become operative in Western countries. Terror groups prefer these types of speculation, relatively small in size and rapid, mostly because they are less noticeable than larger and more complex transactions.[22] 'As long as you can rely on a good and discreet broker,' explained an English trader, 'you are safe. Every day, millions of these small transactions take place in the world, it is virtually impossible to scrutinise each one of them.'

11 SEPTEMBER: SPECULATING IN TERROR

The sophistication of bin Laden's financial portfolio, and his network's ability to manipulate the global stock market, match those of leading capitalist corporations, which have access to vital information. Just as Worldcom was able to use accountancy techniques to tamper with its books, bin Laden's associates succeeded in utilising sophisticated insider trading instruments to speculate on the stock market prior to 11 September. A week before the attack, an unusually high volume of trading was reported in certain sectors, e.g. air transport, energy and insurance. On 6 September, the Thursday before the attack, around 32 million British Airways shares changed hands in London, about three times the normal level. On 7 September, 2,184 put options on British Airways were traded on the LIFFE (London Futures and Options market), about five times the normal amount of daily trading. Across the Atlantic, on Monday, 10 September, the number of put options on American Airlines in the Chicago Board Options Exchange jumped 60 times the daily average. In the three days prior to the attack, the volume of put options in the US surged 285 times the average trading level. A similar trend was reported in the insurance business with leading companies becoming the object of exceptional and unexpected speculation on the futures market. 'When something like this happens,' said a currency trader in London, 'you know that somebody out there had inside information and is using it to make a lot of money.'

Speculation profits can be magnified hundreds of times over using options.

The weekend following the attack, Ernst Welteke, president of the German Bundesbank, admitted that before 11 September there had been insider trading by 'terrorists' and added that the commodities markets had also been targeted.[23] Indeed, days before the attack, oil and gold experienced a sudden and inexplicable rise in price. This was followed by a surge in activity on the futures market. On 12 September, oil prices jumped by more than 13 per cent and gold prices went up by over 3 per cent. Prices continued to climb all week. Anybody who knew what was to happen on 11 September could have predicted such a trend. 'The inexplicable rise in oil and gold prices before 11 September,' admitted a gold bullion trader, 'was due to a surge in activity originating from brokers and traders buying oil contracts at lower prices to resell them forward at higher prices. It is reasonable to believe that those people knew that something exceptional was about to happen.'[24] All bin Laden and his associates needed to speculate and make a fortune across the leading stock markets was a well-established relationship with futures brokers or stockbrokers; any of the Arab or Western banks which handle money for armed organisations could have arranged and even concealed the speculation. 'The easiest way would be via corresponding banks,' explained an Italian banker.

You build a long chain of representative offices at the end of which there is a shell-company registered offshore. You are lucky if you get to the end of the chain. Financial investigations often run into a blind alley halfway through; somewhere, in a tiny offshore office, someone has misplaced a telex or lost an e-mail and you run aground. If you are lucky and identify the shell-company, 99 per cent of the time it is only a name, an empty box. The mafia uses this technique to launder money all the time. I do not see why the terrorists would not utilise it.

According to Jamal Ahmed al-Fadl, bin Laden's former accountant, the network has as many as 80 front companies scattered around the world. In addition, a complex web of numbered Swiss bank accounts and bank accounts in Sudan, Hong Kong, Monaco, Pakistan, Malaysia and London is also available. In 1999, the introduction of 'Know Your Customer' rules in the international financial markets, obliging banks and offshore centres to know the true identity of their customers, made the illicit movement of funds through these accounts and companies more difficult. Paradoxically, the same year the US Congress refused to tighten such a rule, arguing that it was a breach of civil liberties, thus leaving more room to manoeuvre for transfers of illegal money from or within the US.[25] If the perpetrators of the attack on the two towers have profiteered from it on the stock market, most likely 'nobody will ever be able to prove it', admitted a futures trader in Chicago, even with the 'Know Your Customer' rule in place. 'If, for example, they have used executing brokers, small companies or individuals who parcel together trades on behalf of a number of clients and place the trades through a long network of different banks, it would be extremely difficult to track down each investor.' Ironically, in attacking one of the symbols of Western capitalism, bin Laden may have masterminded the biggest insider trading operation ever accomplished.

In contrast to organised crime, the main concern of armed organisations is not the accumulation of wealth, but its concealment and redistribution. Armed groups are more interested in money disbursement than in money laundering; for one, revenues generated by their legitimate businesses do not need to be laundered, they need to be distributed within the network of cells and sleepers. This is why they pay a lot of attention to money manipulation, the ability to move large sums of money without being detected.[26] These crucial distinctions spring from the differing motivations of crime and terror and dictate the way armed groups and organised crime run their respective businesses.

Greed is the motor of crime. Armed groups, on the other hand, are motivated by politics. Their ultimate aim is not monetary, it is political: to substitute one form of government with another or to defend an existing regime. An interesting distinction between old and new terror rests upon the origins and use of funds. While in the state sponsorship model, money originates from foreign states and is used exclusively to support wars by proxy as happened during the Cold War, in the privatisation model funds are raised primarily via criminal activities, such as extortion and kidnapping, and go to sustain the group and its armed struggle. Contemporary Islamist terror can also count on voluntary support and revenues from legitimate businesses, legal sources of income. Legal and illegal funds are distributed among a large spectrum of groups and state-shells and are used to support the socio-economic infrastructure of the Modern Jihad.

The economics of contemporary terror organisations are, therefore, very similar to those of a state, whereby the wealth generated by the nation is distributed to keep the community going. In contrast, a criminal organisation operates like a private corporation, the ultimate goal being profit and accumulation. The monetary flows of a criminal enterprise are managed through an accountancy system regulated by balance sheets similar to those of a big corporation. These instruments are unsuited to understanding and analysing the inflows and outflows of terror organisations and state-shells. The balance of payments is a better and more comprehensive accountancy tool to use to describe their finances.

15. Terror's Balance of Payments

'For money is the oxygen of terrorism. Without the means to raise and move money around the world, terrorists cannot function.'

Colin Powell, US Secretary of State

On a cold and breezy February evening in 1999, about 200 Albanian immigrants hurried into a Brooklyn restaurant. Men dressed in traditional Balkan clothes escorted them to their seats. As they walked to their tables, the guests passed money to the ushers. This was not a gourmet gathering to sample the cuisine of the Balkans. People had come to meet Dina, a representative of the Kosovo Liberation Army (KLA). When the restaurant was full, the lights were dimmed and Dina called for a minute of silence to honour the heroes of the homeland, those who had died for its liberation. Soon after, the gathering was shown a video depicting some of the atrocities committed by the Serbs in Kosovo.

Dina's speech, delivered after the screening, was not as moving. The soldier did not have much to say; he was a fighter, not a politician. His short and simple sentences were often broken by the sudden and loud shouting of 'Ooh Che Ke, Ooh Che Ke!' the letters for the KLA. None the less, Dina's poor rhetoric did not prevent the men from opening their wallets and donating handfuls of dollars. The fact that the KLA was listed by Western powers, including the US,[1] as a terrorist organisation and that its members had committed atrocities similar to the Serbs, did not inhibit their generosity, nor did it affect their belief that the KLA was fighting a just war. The

participants regarded Dina, his comrades in arms and themselves as patriots, people who loved their country. 'What do
they expect?' asked Izet Tafilaj, who had lost his aunt, uncle
and nephew in the war. 'If they won't help us, at least let us
help ourselves.' Then he added that he had just sold his real
estate business in New Jersey and was preparing to leave for
Kosovo to join the fighting.[2]

Similar fundraising gatherings take place in the US and other
Western countries almost daily. The IRA, Hamas, the Hizbollah
and the PLO, among many armed groups, regularly lobby immigrants to fund their organisations. This is an exercise that can
pay very well. In December 1997, a group of Albanians living
in the Bronx collected about $4 million in support of Islamist
groups and sent the money via bank transfer to the homeland.[3]
In 1999, the KLA raised $10 million from immigrants in the
US, where their largest support group is among blue-collar
workers, who represent about two-thirds of the 400,000
Albanian-Americans. The majority have immigrated recently
and still have strong ties with Kosovo.[4] Supporters of the KLA
even set up a fund, 'Home Land Calling', with a bank account
at People's Bank in Bridgeport, Connecticut. 'Home Land
Calling' accounts have also been opened in Sweden,
Switzerland, Italy, Belgium and Canada; advertisements in
Albanian newspapers printed in Europe exhort people to donate
money through these channels.[5]

IMMIGRANTS' REMITTANCES

An important item in the terror balance of payments is represented by the remittances of nationals residing abroad, either
directly or via ad hoc institutions such as Noraid for the IRA.
The PLO even imposes a 5 per cent tax on the income of all
Palestinians living abroad, as mentioned in chapter 5. In a similar
fashion, in the late 1990s, Albanian immigrants in Germany and

Switzerland sent 3 per cent of their income to fund Muslim warriors in Pristina. Although remittances represent a large source of foreign exchange, immigrants' contributions do not come only in the form of cash. Albanian-Americans, for example, provided KLA fighters with radios, night-vision equipment and bullet-proof vests, bought from an American mail order catalogue.

These contributions are often not technically illegal. The truth is that the law does not, or until recently did not, have ad hoc instruments to distinguish between legitimate remittances and sponsors of armed groups. In the US, for example, people are not prohibited from collecting 'donations for rebel organisations, groups or armies, nor is it a crime for an individual or group to join [them] – except when such an organisation, group or "army" is on the list of terrorist groups and organisations prepared by the State Department'.[6] This list, one should add, varies according to the mood of US foreign policy. In recent years, for example, the KLA has been added to and removed from it twice. Only a few months after Senator Joe Lieberman had praised it, stating: 'Fighting for the KLA is fighting for human rights and American values,'[7] the KLA was reinstated in the State Department list of terrorist organisations.[8]

CHARITABLE ORGANISATIONS

Another relevant source of foreign exchange is represented by charities. Islamic charities, in particular, are conduits through which billions of dollars reach the Islamist network every year. It is reasonable to assume that a large portion of charity funds act as a sort of international pool of money, ready to be channelled to whichever armed group is in need in the Muslim world. The link between charities and armed organisations goes back to the 1970s when Irish-Americans set up charitable organisations for Catholic widows and orphans; Islamic charities blossomed during the anti-Soviet Jihad. At that time, the US was encouraging all forms of financing for the Mujahedin, including donations from Muslim countries. Once the war was over, charities continued to support Muslims fighting similar wars in other countries, e.g. in Bosnia and Chechnya. Headed by Islamist sympathisers or members of radical Islamist groups, several charities evolved from sponsorship of the Mujahedin to financial conduits for Islamist armed groups, at times even providing shelter for members of terror organisations.

Ironically, donors were often not aware that a major metamorphosis had taken place. In 1987, Adel Batterjee, a rich Saudi businessman, funded the Benevolence International Foundation (BIF), a Saudi-backed charity that had the task of bankrolling the Mujahedin. In 1993 the charity was granted tax-exempt status in the US and employed Enaam Arnaut, a veteran of the anti-Soviet Jihad who had worked in one of bin Laden's camps in Afghanistan buying and distributing arms. According to US authorities, Arnaut laundered the charity's proceeds to fund various Islamist armed groups and carefully concealed these activities from donors. He also employed Saif al-Islam el-Masry, one of bin Laden's military advisers, as the charity's representative in Chechnya. Michael Chertoff, head of the US Justice Department's criminal division in Chicago, maintains that Arnaut and el-Masry 'send hundreds of thousands of dollars to accounts overseas that are suspected of affiliation with Chechen rebels in Georgia'.[9] In 2001, Benevolence International raised more than $3.6 million and sent $2.7 million to Muslim victims of wars in eight countries, including Afghanistan, Bosnia, Pakistan and Chechnya.[10] US authorities believe that most of these funds have reached armed groups instead of Muslims in need.

Humanitarian aid is allocated by charitable organisations to a range of projects, from the construction of mosques and *madaris* to the purchase of arms and the sponsorship of terror attacks. The combination of humanitarian aid and illegal activity is typical of Islamic charities linked to terror groups. Muwafaq, better known as Blessed Relief, the Saudi charity openly supported by bin Laden,[11] ran courses in Arabic language, computers and Quranic studies in Bosnia; it also took charge of food deliveries to help the needy. However, according to a former Croatian intelligence officer, Muwafaq also supported Muslim armed groups operating in Bosnia and Albania.[12]

COVERT AND LEGITIMATE FOREIGN AID VERSUS ASSET TRANSFERS

An additional source of foreign exchange for the terror balance of payments is state sponsorship, such as the US government's covert and legitimate aid for the Contras. Today, state sponsorship plays a small part in terror finances; a much more common means of getting hold of foreign exchange from international organisations and foreign governments is asset transfer, defined as the redistribution of external assistance or existing assets in favour of armed groups.[13] Asset transfer is one of the most lucrative sources of revenue for armed groups and state-shells in Third World countries. It can assume many forms, often imaginative and unexpected. Prior to the Iraq war, US satellite surveillance has spotted 1,000 trucks, obtained by the Iraqis under the UN oil-for-food exchange programme, which had been converted into missile launchers and army vehicles.[14] During his speech to the Security Council of the United Nations, US Secretary of State Colin Powell played a tape recording of a phone conversation in which an unidentified Iraqi man asked for instructions on how to deal with the UN inspectors if they discovered the 'altered trucks'. Asset transfer is so widespread that donor countries even accept a built-in 5 per cent standard diversion of any aid, in cash or kind.

A common form of transfer is to levy 'customs duties'; armed groups and state-shells impose road taxes in the territories they control. During the war in Bosnia, for example, Bosnian Croats imposed a 27 per cent tax on international aid in transit via their territory to Central Bosnia. Another form is robbery and ambushes, and so is the imposition of overvalued exchange rates that push up the price of domestic currencies, as happened in Sudan and Somalia.[15] Remittances in foreign currencies, for example, are converted into local currencies at the official exchange rate, much higher than the black market one. Whoever controls the territory – government, armed group or state-shell – pockets the difference.

KIDNAPPING

When foreigners, either tourists or workers, are kidnapped, it can become a source of foreign exchange for the terror balance of payments if the ransom is paid in hard currency. In 1991, the IMU kidnapped a general from the Kyrgyz Interior Ministry and four Japanese geologists working for a mining company near Batken, the least developed corner of Kyrgyzstan. According to Western diplomatic sources, the Japanese government secretly paid the IMU between $2 million and $6 million in cash for their release.[16]

Since hostages are mere commodities for armed groups – like drugs, oil, gold and diamonds – anybody can bid for their lives, including terror organisations and state-shells. In this callous trade of human lives, to purchase someone's death can become a powerful political statement. At the end of 1998, Chechen Islamist rebels kidnapped three Britons and one New Zealander, engineers working for Granger Telecom, a British company installing mobile communications systems in Chechnya. The rebels negotiated with Granger a ransom of $4 million. However, just before the transfer of money was to take place, the men were beheaded. A Channel 4 investigation into the last hours of the hostages' lives unveiled the entry of bin

Laden into the negotiations. According to Channel 4 *Dispatches*, at the eleventh hour the Saudi tycoon offered £4 million for the engineers to be executed.[17] It transpired that the men were meant to pass information to the British government on Chechnya's economic situation. In a letter sent in October 1998 to Granger, the Foreign Office wrote: 'As one of the very small number of British companies involved in Chechnya and having firsthand knowledge of Grozny, we would welcome your views on the potential for investment in Chechnya.'[18] UK oil and service companies are very active in the Caucasus and Central Asia. Backed by the government, they have been trying to penetrate these areas since the fall of the Soviet Union. The four victims' heads, recovered in a ditch alongside a road in Chechnya, were Osama bin Laden's macabre warning to the UK government: stay out of the Caucasus and away from its resources. The Chechen rebels held on to the ransom.

CRIME

Criminal activities carried out abroad are also a source of foreign exchange for the terror balance of payments, generating revenue in the same manner as organised crime. 'There is virtually no financing method that has not at some level been exploited by [terror] groups.'[19] A car theft scheme operating in Ontario and Quebec to ship vehicles to Lebanon, for example, diverted 10 per cent of the proceeds to Islamist armed groups.[20] Investigations in the US and Europe have unveiled several credit card fraud and identity theft schemes, ranging from stealing luggage containing tourist's identity cards and personal information to the manufacture of fake credit cards. These crimes are masterminded by members of criminal and armed organisations (some of them Western citizens) which have infiltrated Western countries. Abdelghani Meskini and Ahmed Ressan, two of the Algerians who attempted to place a bomb at Los

Angeles airport in what became known as the Millennium plot, admitted having supported themselves and partially financed their mission through such schemes. Meskini also confessed that a third accomplice in the Millennium plot had planned to buy a petrol station to obtain credit card numbers; the plan included placing a video camera to record people punching their PIN numbers in petrol machines.

In Chicago, another group of Algerians led by Youssef Hmimssa used cab drivers and waiters in a clever fraud known as skimming, whereby the credit card number is skimmed before being charged. Mourad Madrane, a Moroccan waiter, wore on his belt a pocket-sized device with a scanning slot, as small as a pager. While he carried the credit cards and the bills from the table to the cash register, he swiped the cards through the device, skimming the numbers. Hmimssa then used them to make counterfeit credit cards. According to the FBI, even the 11 September hijackers used credit card fraud to support themselves.

In the US, credit cards are also an easy way of raising cash. In February 1998, Richard Rode, deputy assistant director of the office of investigations, US secret service, testified before the Senate Committee on Terrorism that several members of Middle Eastern terror groups had applied for and received as many as 40 credit cards each. He also added that this scheme costs financial institutions in excess of $4.5 million.[21] 'The ease with which these individuals can obtain false identification or assume the identity of someone else and then open bank accounts and obtain credit cards make these attractive ways to generate funds,' added Dennis Lormer, chief of the FBI's Financial Crime Unit.[22]

SMUGGLING

Though fraud is a considerable source of income, terror's most important income-generating activity is smuggling, which is also a crime.[23] Contraband ranges from cigarettes and alcohol to diamonds. Daniel Pearl, the journalist from the *Wall Street Journal* assassinated allegedly by Jaish-I-Mohammed (Army of Mohammad) while investigating the ATTA trade in Pakistan, wrote just before he was kidnapped that 'beyond providing potential revenues to those in charge, smuggling offers employ- ment to poor inhabitants of tribal areas along the Afghan border'.[24] Much of the economics of contraband is summarised in this sentence. Smuggling is an industry, but it supports armed groups, criminal organisations and state-shells and because of that it is the largest entry in the terror balance of payments. Pakistan's tribal belt is a good example of this phenomenon. Merchants set the volume of smuggled goods via the ATTA to Pakistan at a staggering 80 per cent of total Pakistani imports. These include Chinese and Korean textiles as well as cars dismantled in Afghanistan, carried in pieces across the border and reassembled on the other side.[25] One of the main markets in Pakistan is the Karkhano Bazaar in Peshawar, where 600 merchants, most of them from Afghanistan, supply a wide variety of foreign goods. In 1999, a United Nations study estimated that 'illegal' exports from Afghanistan to Pakistan amounted to almost $1 billion, and from Afghanistan to Iran to $140 million. The Taliban's cut in these businesses, in effect an export duty, is estimated by the UN at $36 million, while the World Bank puts it at $75 million.[26]

On the other side of the world, Ciudad del Este, a major contraband centre, is the hub of a smuggling business that generates over $12 billion per year. Situated in Paraguay, where the country intersects with Brazil and Argentina, this area is also known as the Triangle or Triple Border. A duty-free port, Ciudad del Este is a Mecca for terror and crime organisations. About 200 murders are committed every year in a population of 100,000. Sixteen foreigners enter Paraguay illegally every week through the airport and many more by land, paying $5,000 in advance.[27] Until 11 September, border controls were non-existent. A false or stolen passport in the streets of this town costs $5,000, while bribing a customs official requires as little as $500. All types of goods are smuggled through this city, from Colombian narcotics to computers from Miami to stolen cars from Brazil. Officials estimate that more than half of the automobiles on the road in Paraguay were stolen in Brazil and shipped via Ciudad del Este. According to the International Intellectual Property Alliance, in 2000 Brazil lost $300 million in sales of CDs due to Ciudad del Este's booming contraband in pirated CDs.[28] Terror organisations are part of the contraband economy and make a generous profit from it. Ali Khalil Mehri, a Lebanese-born businessman and naturalised Paraguayan citizen, sold millions of dollars' worth of pirated software and used the proceeds to fund the Hizbollah. When the police raided his house in Ciudad del Este, they found CDs and videos of suicide bombers, which he used for propaganda and fundraising activities.[29] According to the police, documents found during the raid disclosed that Mehri was also linked to an organisation that raised money for families of 'martyrs and prisoners'. Records of money transfers received from several countries, including Canada, Chile, the US and Lebanon, were also found. Over the past seven years, as much as $50 million is believed to have been sent from Ciudad del Este to the Hizbollah accounts.[30]

Ciudad del Este has a population of 20,000 Muslims, about one in every 30 residents, and hosts a variety of radical Islamist groups. A Hizbollah cell operating in the city is believed to have masterminded the 1992 bombing of the Israeli Embassy and the Jewish Community Centre in Argentina.[31] In October 2001, 20 people were arrested and accused of having links with Hamas. At the same time the authorities froze $22 million in over 40 accounts used to channel money to various Middle Eastern armed groups.[32] The presence of Islamist groups is no secret; for example, both the Hizbollah and Islamic Jihad train local recruits in the *mato grosso*, the jungle and outback near the

Iguacu Falls, not far from the city. Support from the local Muslim population is also strong. At the mosque in Foz do Iguacu, on the Brazilian side of the border, Shiite and Sunni Muslims pray together and talk 'openly about blowing up the United States'.[33] 'Hizbollah is a legitimate resistance group, struggling against invaders in historically Arab land,' explained Sheikh Mounir Fadel, the mullah of Ciudad del Este. 'You can't go around calling people terrorist sympathisers if they support organisations such as the Hizbollah. These are not such simple lines to draw. Not in the Middle East, and certainly not in Paraguay.'[34]

Middle Eastern money brokers linked to Islamist groups are believed to be involved in the laundering of Latin America's narcotics profits. Drug gangs from Peru, Colombia and other South American countries converge in Ciudad del Este to ship drugs and wash their money. Illegal profits are washed through the CC5 account offered by the Central Bank of Brazil to foreigners in Ciudad del Este. Originally this special account was set up to speed up the conversion and transfer of Paraguayan money to Brazilian banks. The whole operation takes less than a day. However, contraband and money laundering are not the sole attractions of Ciudad del Este. The city is also a major hub for Latin American armed organisations to relax and do business at the same time. Members of the IRA, ETA and FARC are regular visitors.[35]

The benefits of contraband for armed groups are manifold. Not only is it a healthy source of income, it also erodes the infrastructure of traditional economies and in doing so it facilitates the breeding of the economics of war. A study from the National University of Colombia estimated that sales from San Andresino, the largest smuggling market in Colombia, accounted for 13.7 per cent of the country's GNP in 1986 and as much as 25.6 per cent in 1996.[36] In Colombia, smuggling from Panama is putting local tobacco and import companies out of business. Smuggling also has a negative impact upon the country's fiscal revenues. In 1996 total shipments from Panama were worth about $1.7 billion, of which Colombian customs only reported imports worth $166 million. The difference of $1.5 billion, which entered the country illegally, represents a net fiscal loss for the government.[37]

Smuggling is also an excellent vehicle for the recycling of funds. According to the US Treasury Department's Financial Crime Enforcement Network, contraband is 'the primary money laundering system used by Colombian drug cartels and the single most effective and extensive money laundering system in the Western hemisphere'.[38] The way it works is simple. Colombian drug traffickers accumulate large amounts of dollars, which they need to reconvert and launder in pesos. Therefore, they sell dollars in the US at a discount to peso brokers. For $1 million they receive the equivalent of $750,000 in pesos. The brokers then use the money to purchase goods that can generate cash very quickly. They buy primary smuggling products, cigarettes, alcohol, electronics, etc., and ship them to Aruba, Panama's duty-free zone. Alternatively they ship cases full of cash directly to Aruba and purchase the goods from local wholesalers. From Panama the goods sail to Colombia, where they are sold at a considerable discount, often at prices lower than in the country of origin, to speed up the money-laundering cycle. Smuggling, therefore, makes accessible a vast range of products that would otherwise be too expensive for large sections of the local population. Politically it is very hard to eradicate this type of business.[39]

THE SUSURLUK AFFAIR

Contraband is also one of the economic terrains where state-shell economies interact with criminal and traditional economies. On 3 November 1996 a car crash near Susurluk, in Turkey,[40] shocked the country. Travelling together was a very unusual group of people: Abdullah Catli, a member of the right-wing armed group Grey Wolves, his girlfriend Gonca Us, the former vice-director of security of Istanbul, Huseyin

Kocadag and Edip Bucak, commander chief of the 'village guards'[41] of Siverek and a member of the Turkish parliament for DYP (True Path Party); Bucak was the sole survivor. During a lengthy investigation it emerged that the passengers were all involved in the smuggling of drugs to Europe. Between 70 and 80 per cent of the narcotics that enter Europe transit through Turkey. According to Human Rights Watch, in the late 1990s the annual narcotics budget of the Turkish mafia was about $50 billion, slightly higher than the annual budget of the Turkish government ($48.4 billion). High-ranking politicians are also involved in this illegal trade. In 1997, the Italian anti-mafia commission objected to the visit of the Turkish Interior Minister Tansu Ciller, who was believed to have close links with the Turkish mafia. Drug money is recycled by Turkish banks abroad. From 1991 to 1995, the German Federal Criminal Police (BKA) investigated 500,000 bank accounts and discovered that 150 billion Deutschmarks, most of which came from drug trafficking, had been transferred to Turkey. Today the bulk of the money enters Turkey in suitcases carried by couriers.

OIL SMUGGLING

Oil smuggling is another business where terror, criminal and legitimate economies interact. Smugglers from Iraq used to charter cargoes that sail from southern Iraq and immediately entered Iranian waters. For a $50/ton of oil toll, the Iranian Revolutionary Guards, who patrol the waters, not only let them go but provided them with false papers as well. The crude oil then travelled from the Straits of Hormuz to Saudi Arabia, the United Arab Emirates, Oman, etc., from where it was sold on the international market.[42] This was profitable business for smugglers. It was also lucrative for Iran, which levied a tax on virtually all the Iraqi oil smuggled across its waters. '[The Iraqis] offer oil to smugglers at a much discounted price, a price of about $95 per metric ton. This

. . . enables a smuggler to purchase the oil for that price, pay the Iranians $50 a metric ton . . . and then sell the oil at their destination for around $205 a metric ton and thereby make $50 to $60 a metric ton in profit.'[43] Another way to contraband Iraqi oil was to declare only part of the oil purchased legally. According to Chiladakis Theofanis, the captain of the Liberian oil tanker *Essex*, Transfigura, a privately owned commodities trading company registered in the Netherlands, chartered the *Essex* twice to buy Iraqi oil under the UN oil-for-food agreement from Ibex, a company registered in the Bermudas with subsidiaries in France and the British Virgin islands. On both occasions, as soon as the inspectors left the cargo at the port of Mina al-Bakr, in Iraq, Transfigura loaded additional tonnage, which went undetected. Both cargoes sailed to the Caribbean where the oil was then sold. The end buyers were Koch Oil, a US trading firm, and PDVSA, a Venezuelan state oil company.[44] Iraqi oil was also smuggled via Turkey and Jordan, where oil is transported by trucks, or to Syria through the pipeline; this was a much smaller business. For Saddam any of these deals were advantageous because they allowed the sale of tonnage that otherwise could not leave the country. Overall the oil smuggling business generated an additional $2–3 billion a year, monies that went undetected by the UN. Therefore, profits from oil smuggling were particularly valuable for Saddam Hussein, who used them to buy arms or finance research on new weapons. Payments for contraband oil were deposited in accounts controlled by the Iraqi leader; in the case of Transfigura, for example, a payment of $10 million for 500,000 barrels of Iraqi oil made through Ibex ended up in a numbered Swiss bank account.[45]

TRANSFER OF DOMESTIC ASSETS

Armed groups also fund themselves via transfer of domestic assets, which can assume various forms: looting, robbery, extortion and pillage. This method is extremely damaging for the traditional economy because it preys directly upon its resources. In the 1970s, the ETA's policy of extortion and robbery depleted the wealth of the Basque region, forcing industrialists and their families to emigrate, as we saw in chapter 3. In Southern Lebanon, the Hizbollah's main revenues originate from the extortion of traders, merchants, businessmen, restaurant owners and shopkeepers, mostly in the Bekaa Valley. Both ETA and the Hizbollah classify their criminal acts as 'revolutionary tax', payments owed to them as administrators of the territory.

Given its nature, therefore, domestic asset transfer is a limited source of revenue, especially in countries riddled by civil war. When the Sudanese government used the Bagara militia from the north to pillage villages in the south, the stronghold of the SPLA (Sudanese People's Liberation Army), the outcome was famine in southern Sudan. The militia was responsible for widespread cattle-rustling, which destroyed the sustenance economy of the local population and led to the famine.[46]

To summarise, terror revenues can be divided into three main categories according to their origins: legitimate business (these are activities which are not considered illegal per se), illegal revenues which break or circumvent legislation, and criminal activities. Legitimate business includes profits from companies or state-shells controlled by armed groups, donations from charities and individuals, asset transfer and legally approved aid from foreign countries. Illegal revenues originate from covert aid from foreign governments and smuggling. Criminal activities are many and include kidnapping, blackmail, theft, fraud, piracy and money laundering.

These are the positive entries, the inflows, of the balance of payments of armed groups. The negative, the outflows, will be discussed in chapter 16.

16. State-Shell Economics

*'Keep it up, die in dignity because surrender would be the end
of resistance and intifada.'*

Sheikh Ahmed Yassin, leader of Hamas, to Yasser Arafat

In the southern suburbs of Beirut, a shanty town known as the
Belt of Misery houses hundreds of thousands of refugees from
Palestine, mostly poor Shiite peasants and farmers. There are
no street signs, no pavements, no public lighting; a web of cables
hangs above the 28 km of unfinished houses, derelict buildings
and winding alleyways. This is rich recruitment ground for the
Hizbollah. The monotonous landscape of bricks and cement is
broken only by multicolour murals depicting Khomeini and
Hizbollah's martyrs; black flags of mourning alongside the green
and yellow flags of Islam that hang from balconies and windows,
remind the rare visitors of the destiny of its inhabitants; the
few streets which have been named by the residents bear the
names of local suicide bombers, people hardly known outside
the Belt of Misery. In a modest house, four-year-old
Mohammad watches a video with his baby sister; a bleak landscape provides the background to a row of buildings. This is a
snapshot of a place which could be anywhere in the Third
World. Suddenly, the screen is filled with a blast; debris, flames,
shards of steel explode in a fashion reminiscent of a gigantic
firecracker. The young boy jumps up in excitement and screams:
'My daddy, my daddy!'[1]

Mohammad's father, Salah Ghandour, was a suicide bomber.
On 25 May 1995, he attacked an Israeli convoy and blew himself

up with 450 kg of explosives, killing 12 Israeli soldiers. The Hizbollah filmed the attack and presented it to his family, a token of his sacrifice. Although it is unusual for a married man and a father to carry out a suicide mission, Salah had always wanted to be a martyr and eventually convinced the leadership of the Hizbollah to let him fulfil his ambition. His wife and family approved of his decision:'I was filled with joy because he had died while carrying out such an operation,' said his wife Maha. 'It is something for us to be proud of, something that makes us hold our heads high with pride, especially because he succeeded in alarming and startling Israel like he did.'[2] Astonishingly, Salah's last wishes were for his son Mohammad to follow in his footsteps.

In this deadly conflict, becoming a martyr is the highest moral achievement available to some of the refugees. Death, paradoxically, restores the dignity lost with the land, along with the political identity attached to it. Refugees are obsessed with dignity; like exposed bodies in a fully clothed society they search frantically for something to cover their nakedness. Martyrdom is the best protection they can get: it ends a life of misery and grants social status, a very high one, something to be proud of for the entire family.

A COST-BENEFIT ANALYSIS OF SUICIDE BOMBERS

For those who manage to achieve such a death, young men like Mohammad's father, life is ultimately an asset to dispose of; Salah traded his for the future of his community. 'Many people come to the Jihad and they are willing to lay down their souls,' explained Shehadeh Salah, 'which is the most precious thing a man has.'[3] For armed groups martyrdom is primarily an asset, a weapon like missiles, and thus suicide bombers figure as assets in the terror balance of payments. In the words of Abdel Aziz Rantisi, one of Hamas's leaders in Gaza, 'Hamas uses these tactics and means of struggle because it lacks F-16s, Apaches, tanks and missiles . . . It is not just for Paradise, or the virgins, but because we are under occupation and we are weak.'[4] Suicide bombing is an offensive weapon. The Liberation Tigers of Tamil, the armed group that has perfected this art, admits that it was devised to compensate for their numerical inferiority and military weakness.[5] In this macabre business people's lives are merchandise. 'Suicide bombers are a commodity that can be passed from hand to hand,' explained a senior Israeli official. 'Say you are in a terrorist cell in Bethlehem and you convince someone, or someone comes to you ready to carry out a suicide attack. You have got a treasure and you can trade it with another cell – say in Ramallah – for money, or for weapons.'[6]

If suicide bombers are assets, their missions represent expenditures. The costs of martyrdom are many and they vary from place to place. Logistical costs should not be undervalued. Equipment such as bombs and explosives can be quite accessible even in the occupied territories of Palestine. Militants from Hamas and al-Aqsa Martyrs' Brigades maintain that to construct a bomb costs as little as $5. Fertiliser, sugar, metal fragments and plastic tubing are all that is required. Planning, on the contrary, can be quite expensive; targets have to be identified and filmed and the dynamics of the attack need to be studied in meticulous detail. This requires manpower and equipment. Finally, the cost of transportation can be steep. Today, the highest logistical cost of a suicide attack inside Israel is to take the bomber to his final destination. This can be as high as $100–200[7] because most of the would-be martyrs live inside the occupied territories and Israel has set up a series of checkpoints to spot them.

Moreover, collateral costs need to be taken into consideration. The Israelis have reintroduced a technique used in 1999 whereby they destroy the family homes of suicide bombers.

Often, this is the only asset the families possess. This ruthless policy has borne some fruit; since its introduction families have been reluctant to let young people follow the path of martyrdom. Overall, the most important cost is the compensation to the family for the loss of a loved one. How to quantify the life of a child? Impossible. In the occupied territories, families receive about $30,000 for each son or daughter's death from outside sponsors such as charitable organisations, groups of sympathisers or foreign regimes such as Saudi Arabia and until recently that of Saddam Hussein in Iraq. Since compensation for families generally comes from money raised abroad, the organisers of the suicide missions do not have to fund it entirely by themselves. In addition, Saudi Arabia pays for the families' pilgrimage to Mecca.[8]

Nevertheless, even taking into consideration all these costs, including the collateral ones, suicide operations still remain the most cost-effective terror attacks. For S. Thamilchelvam, the political leader of the Liberation Tigers of Tamil in Sri Lanka, suicide attacks 'ensure maximum damage done with minimum loss of life'.[9] Following 11 September, for example, the Israeli population has been terrified; immigration is down 40 per cent while migration from Israel is considerably up.[10] Suicide missions also hit hard at the economy of the enemy. Excluding compensations to the families of the hijackers, 11 September cost as little as $500,000. In sharp contrast, the total costs for the US in terms of property loss, cleaning up and federal government bailouts will be in excess of $135 billion.[11]

In Grozny, a city that resembles Dresden after the air raids of the Second World War, the cost of martyrdom is much lower, sometimes as low as the price of the explosives, mainly because no compensation is given to the relatives, as suicide bombers often come from families already wiped out by Russian troops. The policy pursued by Moscow is simple: when a rebel is captured or killed, the army goes after his family, men are killed or taken away, houses are burned or blown up, women and

children are left to fend for themselves. Today, after a decade
of war, Chechnya is a country where 60,000–100,000 Russian
soldiers fight Islamist armed groups and a handful of survivors,
mostly women and teenagers; death for these people is a relief.
As pointed out by Zulikhan Bagalova, head of the Moscow
Centre for Chechen Culture, the women who participated in
the seizure of the Moscow theatre at the end of October 2002
were all in their early twenties; they belonged to a generation
which had grown up during the war, mostly uneducated, for
whom war is life and life is permanent fear. They are confronted
daily with death squads, rape, torture, killings and mutilation;
for them death is a much better option than life.[12] 'I personally know several women who were raped by troops in front
of their fathers, brothers and husbands,' said Bagalova. 'After
such treatment women either die, go mad or become kamikazes.
There are lots of girls who are ready to become the next
kamikaze and there will be more. Life has lost all sense for
them after this humiliation.'[13]

CHECHNYA: AN EXAMPLE OF
PREDATORY WAR

In the bleak universe of the economics of terror, Chechnya is
the victim of a predatory war.[14] During the last decade, Russian
troops have carried out the progressive destruction of the traditional economy, a phenomenon that has contributed to the
radicalisation of the conflict and eventually paved the way for
Islamist armed movements. This is a process that dates back to
1862 when, after half a century of resistance, the Chechens
were forced to become part of the Russian Empire. They finally
gained a brief interval of *de facto* independence in 1918, only
to have the Red Army march into Chechnya in 1920 and annex
it to the Union of the Soviet Republics. In 1944, Stalin ordered
the deportation of all Chechens – half a million at that time

– to Siberia and the destruction of villages and towns. It was only in the 1950s that the survivors were allowed to return, after the famous denunciation of Stalin's policies by his successor, Nikita Khrushchev. In 1990, when the Soviet Union disintegrated, the Chechen national conference, which included all political groups, declared independence. Russia rejected this decision and in 1994 launched the first Chechen war.

The economic motives of Russian domination are related to the strategic role that Chechnya plays in Russian politics and, more recently, in the Russian oil and gas pipeline which crosses Chechnya.[15] In 1999, Russia reinvaded Chechnya, this time also for reasons related to the escalation of violence created by the war, to stop the spread of terror attacks in Moscow, the hostage taking, the incursion of Chechen fighters into Dagestan, etc. The toll of the two wars is shocking: about 100,000 civilians have been killed, equivalent to 10 per cent of the pre-war population; over 200,000 people have been made refugees and the country is littered with mines and weapons. Eventually, the state collapsed and in the vacuum created by its failure warlords and armed groups blossomed. Until then, there had been a few Arabs in Chechnya – traditionally a secular state – though populated by a majority of Muslims.

The collapse of the state opened the gates to Islamist armed organisations, including bin Laden's followers, which soon modified Chechnya's secular resistance into radical fundamentalism; Russian troops have transformed a country once rich in natural resources into a cluster of state-shells which act as transhipment points for the drugs and arms trade. For the last decade Chechnya has survived on a subsistence predatory war economy. Warlords, Islamist armed groups and Russian troops prey on what is left of the population. The progressive criminalisation of the economy, i.e. drug trade, smuggling, money laundering, kidnapping, etc., has become the main source of subsistence. The impact on the population has been tragic: massive displacement, destitution and death.

Predatory, guerrilla and commercial war economies are part of the new wars. These conflicts are waged by armed groups, state-shells as well as legitimate states and are fought outside the international rules of war. Often, the perpetuation of these wars becomes an end in itself, as in Afghanistan. When this happens, being at war legitimises, in the eyes of armed groups, the use of violent means to create and sustain economic profits and political power. In the 1990s, Afghanistan was a country without a state structure, divided into two main state-shells at war with each other; the Taliban and the Northern Alliance ruled thanks to a war economy based on the production of narcotics, smuggling, arms dealings and external support. War, therefore, creates alternative systems of profit, power and protection. The Afghan narcotics industry, the largest in the world, was assembled during the anti-Soviet Jihad by the ISI in co-operation with the Mujahedin to fund the war against Moscow. When Sendero Luminoso moved to Selva Alta, it created an economic stronghold, an area under its control. To finance its war against the Peruvian government, the *Senderistas* used the profits from the coca production.

DIAMONDS-FOR-ARMS TRADE

In countries rich in natural resources, such as gold and diamonds, state-shells prey on those assets to keep the war economy going. This was the case with the Revolutionary United Front (RUF) in Sierra Leone, one of the largest producers of diamonds in the world. In 1991 the RUF, guided by Foday Sankoh, invaded the country from Liberia and gained control of the mining fields. In 2000, estimates of RUF diamond revenues ranged between $25 million and $125 million a year.[16] The diamond trade has also been supporting and enriching former armed groups' leaders, now heads of states: Charles Taylor, president of Liberia, and Blaise Compaore, ruler of

Burkina Faso. In the early 1990s, Taylor, Compaore and Ibrahim Bah, a Senegalese who fought in the anti-Soviet Jihad, helped Sankoh gain control of Sierra Leone's diamond mines.[17] Together, they ran an illicit diamonds-for-arms trade, which kept the RUF and its friends well armed. Arms and ammunition were shipped to Burkina Faso or Liberia and then smuggled to the RUF; payments were in diamonds. People like Victor Bout, a former Soviet air force officer-turned-arms dealer, have been smuggling weapons into and diamonds out of Africa for over a decade. The figures for this illicit trade are staggering. In 1999, for example, diamonds worth $75 million were exported via these channels; these are untaxed and unrecorded export revenues which bought the RUF and its partners arms, ammunition, food, fuel and medicine.[18]

The RUF war economy is not limited to its African neighbours; it is very much a part of the New Economy of Terror. In 1998, Ibrahim Bah brokered a deal with members of the bin Laden network. Bah introduced Abdullah Ahmed Abdullah to Sam Bokerie, better known as Mosquito, a leading RUF commander. Through the deal, uncut diamonds, worth tens of millions of dollars, were traded for arms and cash. In this way al-Qaeda was able to launder drug money with highly liquid assets. Aziz Nassour, a Lebanese diamond broker, sold a share of the diamonds for $6 million on the international market.[19] Between December 2000 and September 2001, Nassour is believed to have set up a courier system to buy $300,000 worth of diamonds. Couriers travelled from Antwerp to Abidjan on Sabena flights. From Abidjan they reached Monrovia in Liberia, chartering small planes from Weswua airlines. In Monrovia they met the commanders of Sierra Leone who carried the diamonds.[20]

The diamonds that have not been sold have been kept as a safeguard in the event that Western governments freeze accounts used by bin Laden's network.[21] According to Belgian sources, just before 11 September, bin Laden's associates converted $10

million into precious stones for precisely this reason.[22]
Diamonds are not the sole highly liquid assets used as a hedge
against the actions of Western governments. Reports confirm
that bin Laden's men have been buying Tanzanite, a dark blue
stone similar to but not as hard as diamonds, mined only in a
small corner of Tanzania, to resell it on the international market
or to store it.[23] Up to 90 per cent of Tanzanite production is
smuggled out of the country. In 1997, the FBI seized the diary
of Wadih el Hage, an associate of bin Laden, who had been
selling smuggled Tanzanite in London. The diary contained
evidence of the role played by the gemstone in money laundering and financing bin Laden's network.[24]

PREYING ON HUMANITARIAN AID: THE EXAMPLE OF SUDAN

In the absence of commercial natural resources, state-shells'
economies feed primarily on the humanitarian aid generated
by war. This happens when armed groups, sustained by predatory war economies, fight one another. In these circumstances,
groups use war to divert international aid from their victims.
In Sudan, the population of the south has been depleted of its
assets by the government of the north; a coalition of the military, merchants and politicians has absorbed most of this wealth.
The policy of asset transfer has been implemented by promoting
famine and preventing relief and aid from reaching their destination. 'Economic resources given to the displaced [in the south]
to promote their self-sufficiency have invariably ended up in
the hands of exploiting groups.'[25] However, the southern population is also the victim of the Sudan People's Liberation Army
(SPLA), an armed group led by John Garang, and other
Sudanese armed groups at war with the government of
Khartoum and sponsored by the United States.[26] Far from being
a liberation army, the SPLA is a *de facto* occupying force. The

SPLA uses the same tactics as Khartoum to prey on the population. The 1998 famine in Sudan, for example, was precipitated by the US-sponsored SPLA offensive in the Bahr al-Ghazal area.[27] In a courageous denunciation, Monsignor Caesar Mazzolari, a Roman Catholic bishop, accused the SPLA of diverting 65 per cent of the food aid supplied to populations trapped inside areas controlled by the rebels in southern Sudan. According to relief workers, 'much of the relief food going to more than a million famine victims in rebel-held areas in southern Sudan is ending up in the hands of the SPLA'.[28]

To maximise the exploitation of the population, state-shells engaged in predatory war economies may even establish economic cooperation. In this case an agreement is reached between the groups to maximise the looting of the population, as happened in Sierra Leone. When the army withdraws from a village, it leaves arms and ammunition for the terror groups to use to raze villages and towns and loot them for cash. The population abandons the houses and takes refuge in the countryside, thus emptying the towns. As soon as the armed groups move out, the army moves in and loots the villages a second time, collecting property, items which are difficult for the rebels to dispose of.[29] This reflects the conditions of war in which state-shells survive, reminiscent of medieval wars in which booty was an integral part of the conflict. The rules of war allow victorious soldiers to confiscate public property when required by the necessity of war.[30]

PAYING FOR THE WAR

The primary victims of the new war economies are civilians. As pointed out by Mary Kaldor in her book *New and Old Wars*, at the beginning of the twentieth century, 85–90 per cent of casualties in wars were military. In the Second World War, approximately half of all war deaths were civilians. Today more than 50 per cent of war casualties tend to be civilians.[31] Territorial control is often achieved by physically suppressing the opposition. According to Human Rights Watch: 'In such places as the commune of Nyakizu, in Southern Rwanda, local officials and other killers came to "work" to kill Tutsi. They went home "singing" at quitting time . . . The "workers" returned each day until the job had been finished – that is until the Tutsi had been killed.'[32]

State-shells are economic entities at war and their balance of payments reflects this reality. Cost of arms and ammunition is paramount and represents their major expenditure. According to Aaron Karp, former director of the Arms Transfer Project at the Stockholm International Peace Research Institute and an expert in how weapons reach armed groups, 'it costs about 75 million dollars a year to equip a militia army of 10,000 troops with light arms'.[33] Legitimate and covert state sponsorship is often required to bear part of these costs. US foreign policy still includes the sponsoring of armed groups, using either legitimate or covert operations. In 2001, for example, the US Congress voted to supply the SPLA with millions of dollars. Previously, the group had been sponsored via covert operations. In 1996, the Clinton administration sent the SPLA more than $20 million in military equipment via Eritrea, Ethiopia and Uganda.[34]

Iran is another country engaged in similar activities. In 1993, a ship sailing under a Panamanian flag was seized in the Mediterranean. It carried surface-to-surface missiles, 25,000 machine guns and 7 million rounds of ammunition from Iran heading for Muslim fighters in Bosnia. A year earlier, at Zagreb airport, an Iranian Boeing was confiscated; it was carrying thousands of machine guns and 40 Iranian volunteers.[35] More recently, in 2002, a shipment of Iranian arms to the PLO was discovered while en route to the occupied territories. According to Aaron's estimate, in the early 1990s, the 'arms trade just to non-state actors, to insurgent groups, ethnic nationalists, terrorist cells . . . little sub-state groups . . . [was] worth at the most about 2.5 to 3 billion dollars per year'.

Banks and financial institutions are also part of the activities related to sponsoring arms purchases. The Iraqis used Credit Lyonnais in France and Banca Nazionale del Lavoro (BNL) in the United States and Italy to fund their weapons expenditures. During the Iran–Iraq war, the BNL branch in Georgia, Atlanta, loaned money to Saddam Hussein to build up his military arsenal. The bank was used as a covert source of funding for the Iraqi weapons programmes by the US; overall the Iraqis were able to get as much as $5 billion out of BNL. Ironically, the US taxpayer has reimbursed part of the money because the US government had guaranteed some of the loans on which Iraq eventually defaulted.[36] Naturally, when state sponsors cover the cost of arms, what is generally a net cost for the terror balance of payments becomes an asset. This was the case with the Stingers given to the Mujahedin in Afghanistan by the US in the 1980s. Most of them were not used, as it was impossible to carry them across the harsh terrain of Afghanistan; over the years they were resold on the black market at ten times the original price. Iran, for example, bought several and, in 1987, used them from Iranian gunboats to fire at US Navy helicopters in the Persian Gulf. To avoid a repetition of this scenario, the US government has even tried to repurchase the Stingers, offering, in the mid-1990s, more than $100,000 for missiles initially sold for $23,000. However, this offer was well below the black market price of over $200,000, so the US was unable to complete the purchase.

BLACK MARKETEERS

The black market is where most state-shells and armed groups buy arms and ammunition. According to Aaron, 'where there's warfare, there's a demand',[37] and where there is demand there is supply. Ironically, it is the United States that is one of the principal suppliers of the illegal market. There are numerous examples of American companies involved in these businesses. A Los Angeles trading firm, for example, smuggled 87 US helicopters, which could easily be adapted for war purposes, to North Korea. During the Iran–Iraq war, a contraband ring based in the US supplied US-made F-14 aircraft and their parts to Iran for over $10 million. Between 1982 and 1988, the US Customs Service, FBI and other law enforcement groups seized over 6,000 US-manufactured weapons and military items for a total value of half a billion dollars, which people had tried to smuggle out of the country.[38]

In the 1990s, Victor Bout masterminded an international web of arms smuggling, selling stockpiles of redundant Soviet arms to state-shells and armed groups across the world. According to Belgian authorities, his fleet of Soviet-era ships supplied the RUF in Sierra Leone, Unita in Angola and the extremist Hutu militia in Rwanda, among others.[39] More recently, he became one of the main arms dealers for the Taliban. Bout, like most black market arms suppliers, relies largely on barter. While in Sierra Leone he was paid in diamonds; in Afghanistan it was narcotics.[40]

SMUGGLING IRAQI OIL, AFGHANI NARCOTICS AND UKRAINIAN WEAPONS

In the absence of state sponsors, or in conjunction with them, state-shells and terror groups use smuggling to meet the high costs of arms, to avoid embargoes and sanctions imposed by the international community. According to the UK government, Saddam Hussein stockpiled chemical, biological and conventional weapons using a $2 billion per year illicit sale of oil. Oil is smuggled via neighbouring Arab and Islamic countries. Over 500 companies have been involved in the oil-for-arms deal.[41]

State-shell war economies often depend on the ability to develop a 'healthy' contraband industry. Afghanistan, for example, has survived on smuggling for two decades. Smuggling replaces the domestic and export industry. In so doing it offers large sections of the population the possibility of earning enough money to survive and a much smaller group of people opportunities for the accumulation of wealth. Two-way smuggling, where one product is taken out and another brought in, is the most common method. In Afghanistan drugs-for-weapons deals were the most popular.

Following the laws of economics, experienced smugglers from neighbouring countries were attracted by the Afghan narcotics business; people like Mansour Shahab, an Iranian bandit and professional smuggler of Arab origins from Ahvaz. In 1996 Shahab met an Arab-Afghan who sold him drugs in exchange for 150 Kalashnikovs. The man invited him to visit Afghanistan. Shahab went, and set up a healthy smuggling business for the Taliban. His route cut across the Iraq–Iran border, along which Shahab and his gang of bandits smuggled everything, from narcotics to electronic equipment to arms and ammunition.[42]

To avoid capture, smugglers utilise the most ingenious techniques. To cross the Iranian desert, for example, they use camels addicted to opium; the animals carry their loads of illicit goods unaccompanied, travelling from one fix to the next.[43] Smuggling routes are the arteries of the New Economy of Terror; they feed terror's current account with an endless supply of cash, goods and migrants. Like the old Silk Route, smugglers also travel in caravans across hostile territories, far from the highways of civilisation.

On the supply side, the disintegration of the Soviet Union has greatly boosted the international contraband of arms. The disappearance of the Soviet central government, which co-ordinated the supply and demand for weapons, has left its three largest producers of arms – Russia, Ukraine and Belarus – in need of new markets. In 2001, these three countries exported $5 billion worth of weapons, a figure that excludes undisclosed and illegal deals. While Russia is in a better position, supplying large clients like China and India, the other two are not as fortunate and have to rely on demand from state-shells. Thus Ukraine is one of the major suppliers for the RUF in Sierra Leone. Arms are shipped to Liberia or Burkina Faso, legitimate countries, and from there smuggled to Sierra Leone. In addition, stockpiles of arms and ammunition left over from the Soviet era have been flooding the illegal market. For a decade, inside the New Economy of Terror there has been no shortage of weapons; on the contrary, the buoyant supply has been boosting demand.

The analysis of the balance of payments of armed organisations has shown a vast range of economic activities within reach of state-shells and armed groups. Some of them are directly linked to the war economies that sustain terror; others are related to criminal activities and a small percentage refer to legitimate activities. All of them, however, belong to the New Economy of Terror, a parallel economic system to the traditional and legitimate one. The final question to answer is: how big is this illicit economic system and how much does it overlap with the world economy?

17. The Globalisation of the New Economy of Terror

'If [the United States] enters into a conflict with the sons of the two holy mosques, America will forget the horrors of Vietnam. This, indeed, was the case; praise God. What is to come is even greater, God willing.'

Osama bin Laden on al-Jazeera TV channel,
21 December 2001

In November 2001, at an international conference held in Bonn on the future of Afghanistan, Hamid Karzai was elected prime minister *ad interim*. Since then a lot has been written about him, from his patriotic fight against the Taliban to the style of his clothes. Yet very few people remember that during the 1990s Karzai was involved in negotiations with the Taliban regime for the construction of a Central Asian gas pipeline from Turkmenistan through western Afghanistan to Pakistan. At that time he was a top adviser and lobbyist for Unocal, the California-based oil company which was negotiating the right to build the pipeline across Afghanistan. Even fewer people remember that as leader of the Pashtun Duri tribe during the anti-Soviet Jihad, Karzai was a member of the Mujahedin. In the early 1990s, thanks to his excellent contacts with the ISI, he moved to the US where he cooperated with the CIA and the ISI in supporting the Taliban's political adventure.[1]

President Bush's special envoy to the newly formed Afghanistan state is a man named Zalmay Khalilzad, another former employee of Unocal. In 1997, he produced a detailed analysis of the risks involved in the construction of the Central

Asian gas pipeline. Khalilzad also worked as a lobbyist for Unocal and therefore knows Karzai very well.[2] In the 1980s, during the anti-Soviet Jihad, President Reagan named Khalilzad special adviser to the State Department; it was thanks to his influence that the US accelerated the shipment of military aid to the Mujahedin.

THE CENTRAL ASIAN PIPELINE

Karzai and Khalilzad's involvement with the Taliban on behalf of Unocal took place at a time when Mullah Omar was preaching the benefits of the Sharia law, when women in Afghanistan were banned from social life and plans were under way to blow up the ancient statues of the Buddha at Bamiyan. Somehow, the backwardness and cruelty of the Taliban regime could be overlooked by the West when one of the deals of the century was at stake. Unocal was about to write a new chapter in the long history of 'The Great Game', the phrase immortalised by Rudyard Kipling in *Kim*.[3]

One of the earth's richest oil and gas fields is located on the eastern shore of the Caspian Sea, north of Afghanistan,[4] in the territories belonging to the Central Asian republics. The cheapest way to link these fields with the international market is with a pipeline across Iran. From the Iranian coast oil and gas can be shipped via the existing Iranian network. However, US companies are prevented from using this route by the Iran–Libya Sanctions Act (ILSA), which prohibits commercial ventures with these two countries. The longer route, through Afghanistan to the Pakistani coast, is more expensive, but considerably more advantageous for the US. It would eliminate the need to deal with Iran, a country towards which Washington nurtures deep antipathy and resentment, and give the US and its partners control of the new supply of energy. Since the mid-1990s, the Americans have been pursuing this avenue.

'Impressed by the ruthlessness and willingness of the then-emerging Taliban [movement] to cut a pipeline deal,' writes Ahmed Rashid, 'the State Department and Pakistan's Inter-Services Intelligence agency agreed to funnel arms and funding to the Taliban in their war against the ethnically Tajik Northern Alliance. Until 1999, US taxpayers paid the entire annual salary of every single Taliban government official.'[5]

The Unocal deal was also regarded as the jewel in the crown of what was known in Washington as 'the strategy of the Silk Route'. This policy pursued the exclusion of Russia from the Asian pipelines: the energy highways that travel from the basin of the Caspian Sea westwards, and from Central Asia south and eastwards. Finally, by establishing a strong presence in these areas, the US wanted to lock Iran and China out of the energy business in the region, since Washington feared they could assist the Central Asian republics in setting up their own oil companies. In the months before the Taliban came to power, former US Assistant Secretary of State for South Asia, Robin Raphael, waged an intense round of shuttle diplomacy between the powers with possible stakes in the Unocal project. 'Robin Raphael was the face of the Unocal pipeline,' said an official of the former Afghan government who was present at some of the meetings with her. '. . . In addition to tapping new sources of energy, the [project] also suited a major US strategic aim in the region: isolating its nemesis Iran and stifling a frequently mooted rival pipeline backed by Tehran.'[6]

The rise of the Taliban was the outcome of an alliance between the US and its Muslim partners, Pakistan and Saudi Arabia. The involvement of Islamabad and Riyadh was part of the policy of Islamist colonisation discussed in chapter 9. Washington's motivations were exclusively economic. As pointed out by Professor William O. Beeman, an anthropologist specialising in Middle Eastern studies at Brown University, US support for the Taliban had 'nothing to do with religion or ethnicity, but only with the economics of oil'.[7] The Unocal consortium feared that as long as the country was split among squabbling warlords, the pipeline would never be built. Political stability was required to implement the $4.5 billion project and the US believed that the Taliban regime would be the most suitable government to achieve such a goal. Thus, in the aftermath of the Taliban's conquest of Kabul in 1996, the State Department avoided criticising the methods the Taliban used to establish control over the country; instead, it comfortably declared that the US found 'nothing objectionable' in the introduction of the Sharia law in Afghanistan. This statement was echoed by the Chairman of the Senate Foreign Relations Subcommittee on the Near East and South East, Senator Hank Brown, who said, 'the good part of what has happened is that one of the factions [the Taliban] at least seems capable of developing a new government in Afghanistan'.[8]

The alliance between American capitalism and Islamist fundamentalism was not limited to the creation of the Taliban; it also produced business ventures designed to extract favours from the new regime. To strengthen its bargaining power with the newly formed Islamist state, Unocal joined the Saudi Delta Oil Corporation to create a consortium called CentGas.

Ironically, it was through the CentGas consortium that people close to bin Laden came to work with people close to the Bush family. The feasibility study of the Central Asian pipeline project was performed by Enron, the US oil giant which, in 2002, filed for bankruptcy; Enron CEO Ken Lay was an old Bush family friend; Donald Rumsfeld, the current US Secretary of Defense, was a large stockholder in Enron; and Thomas White, former vice-chairman of Enron, is President Bush's Secretary of the Army. 'A chief benefactor in the CentGas deal [was going to be] Halliburton, the huge oil pipeline construction firm that also had its eye on the Central Asian oil reserves. At the time, Halliburton was headed by Dick Cheney,'[9] the US vice-president.

The CentGas deal never came to fruition. The Taliban's inability to commit to any agreement, coupled with public recognition of the exploitative nature of their regime, contributed to its failure. For years, the Taliban skilfully conducted simultaneous negotiations with two potential oil companies: the Argentinean Bridas and Unocal/CentGas. Both companies showered the Taliban with gifts and money, flying their delegations to the US to win them over. On one occasion, a group of Taliban met high-ranking executives of Unocal in Texas. Parties, dinners and trips to the local shopping malls were organised. At that time, Zalmay Khalilzad, who was working for Unocal, lobbied the Clinton administration to 'engage' with the Taliban.[10] The press reported some of these 'informal' meetings between US officials and the rulers of Afghanistan: 'Senior Taliban leaders attended a conference in Washington in mid-1996 and US diplomats regularly travelled to Taliban headquarters,' wrote the *Guardian*.[11] But these reports aroused very little interest.

The major impediment to the deal, however, was political: the Taliban demanded official recognition from the White House, something concrete to endorse their rule. This was not feasible. Strong social pressure from US women's organisations, which strenuously lobbied their congressmen and the nation against the inhuman treatment of women in Afghanistan, exposed Americans to the facts of the brutality of the Taliban regime. 'The United States wants good ties [with the Taliban] but can't openly seek them while women are oppressed,' reported CNN.[12] None the less, negotiations carried on more or less openly until 1998, when bin Laden's associates bombed US embassies in Africa. At that point relations broke down. Clinton launched cruise missiles at bin Laden's supposed whereabouts in Afghanistan, an act that convinced the oil lobby that, for the moment, the pipeline deal could not go ahead.

OIL ECONOMICS

Clinton's belligerent attitude towards bin Laden and the Taliban regime did not reflect a shift in policy. Corporate America continued to do business with people who supported Islamist insurgency. The oil industry, in particular, continued to be run by a very small group of American and Saudi families with close financial relations. Among them were the Bush family, the bin Laden family and Osama bin Laden's Saudi sponsors. The ties among these people go back a long way. In 1979, when George W. Bush was attempting to break into the big league of Texas's oil businessmen, he received $50,000 from a family friend, James Bath, in exchange for 5 per cent of his firm Arbusto Energy. At the time Bath represented the US business interests of Salem bin Laden, brother of Osama and head of the bin Laden family. For several years, George Bush Sr has been the senior adviser of the Carlyle Group, a Washington-based merchant bank specialising in buyouts in the defence and aerospace industry. Former members of the Reagan and Bush administrations are also Carlyle 'advisers': James Baker, former Secretary of State, and Frank Carlucci, former Secretary of Defense. John Major, former British prime minister, is also a Carlyle adviser, as are Fidel Ramos, former president of the Philippines, and Anand Panyarachun, the former Thai premier. Among the investors in the Carlyle group are members of the Saudi elite, including the bin Laden family, which sold its stock after 11 September.

Naturally, as soon as George W. Bush was elected president, Unocal and BP-Aramco, which had in the meantime bought Bridas, the Argentinean rival, started once again to lobby the administration, among whom were several of their former employees. Unocal knew that Bush was ready to back them and resumed the consortium negotiations. In January 2001, it began discussions with the Taliban, backed by members of the Bush administration among whom was Under Secretary of

State Richard Armitage, who had previously worked as a lobbyist for Unocal. The Taliban, for their part, employed as their PR officer in the US Laila Helms, niece of Richard Helms, former director of the CIA and former US ambassador to Iran. In March 2001, Helms succeeded in bringing Rahmatullah Hashami, Mullah Omar's adviser, to Washington. Apparently, he even brought a carpet as a gift for George W. Bush from the Taliban leader.[13] As late as August 2001, meetings were held in Pakistan to discuss the pipeline business. At one of these, which took place in Islamabad on 2 August, Christina Rocca, in charge of Asian affairs at the State Department, met the Taliban ambassador to Pakistan, Abdul Salam Zaeef.

While negotiations were under way, the US was secretly making plans to invade Afghanistan. The Bush administration and its oil sponsors were losing patience with the Taliban; they wanted to get the Central Asian gas pipeline going as soon as possible. The 'strategy of the Silk Route' had been resumed. US academics, journalists and intellectuals denounced the White House's new approach. 'The US had quietly begun to align itself with those in the Russian government calling for military action against Afghanistan and has toyed with the idea of a new raid to wipe out bin Laden,'[14] wrote Frederick Starr, head of the Central Asian Institute at Johns Hopkins University, in December 2000. Paradoxically, 11 September provided Washington with a *casus belli* to invade Afghanistan and establish a pro-American government in the country. When, a few weeks after the attack, the leaders of the two Pakistani Islamist parties negotiated with Mullah Omar and bin Laden for the latter's extradition to Pakistan to stand trial for the 11 September attacks, the US refused the offer.[15] Back in 1996, the Sudanese Minister of Defence, Major General Elfatih Erwa, had also offered to extradite Osama bin Laden, then resident in Sudan, to the US. American officials declined the offer at that time as well. Instead, they told General Erwa to ask bin Laden to leave the country. 'Just don't let him go to Somalia,' they added. In 1993, 18 US soldiers had been brutally killed in Somalia in street riots involving al-Qaeda supporters and the US feared that bin Laden's presence in the country would create further unrest. When Erwa disclosed that he was going to Afghanistan, the American answer was 'let him go'. Is it possible that the US did not want to bring bin Laden to 'justice'? Could it be because he has too many tales to tell?

For Gore Vidal, 'the conquest of Afghanistan had nothing to do with Osama. He was simply a pretext for replacing the Taliban with a relatively stable government that would allow Union Oil of California [Unocal] to lay its pipeline for the profit of, among others, the Cheney-Bush junta.'[16] Vidal's view might not be far from the truth. Karzai's role during the interim government is clearly that of a mediator of the interests of the US oil companies in the pipeline business. Kalilzad has a similar task. Two small oil companies, Chase Energy and Caspian Energy Consulting, have already obtained permission from the governments of Turkmenistan and Pakistan to resume the pipeline negotiations. These companies acted on behalf of much bigger oil corporations whose identity has been kept secret; however, the fact that S. Rob Sobhani, president of Caspian Sea Consulting, has worked for BP-Aramco as a consultant for Central Asia[17] might throw some light on the mystery.

THE ECONOMICS OF US FOREIGN POLICY

The Unocal consortium saga outlines the degree of interaction that exists between traditional and state-shell economies even in the domain of 'legitimate' businesses. This exchange transcends the lack of 'full political status' of state-shells. Although the US refused to recognise the Taliban regime, it did engage with it in high-level negotiations for the construction of the Central Asian pipeline. The administration was willing to ignore the regime's brutal treatment of women, the breaching of human rights and the cruelty of the Afghani rulers, provided the Taliban agreed to a deal that would have given US oil companies the upper hand in the Great Game. In the post-Cold War era the economic interests of a sector of American industry, and not a policy of international equilibrium, forged US foreign policy towards state-shells. Behind a façade of principles and ideological propaganda, relationships between Washington and state-shells harbouring Islamist terror groups have been formulated according to the narrow principles of self-interest.

The relations between the Clinton administration and Sudan are a good example of the subordination of politics to economics. In November 1997, Washington imposed economic sanctions on Khartoum, a regime that according to the US was still hosting training camps for Islamist armed groups. A number of American companies which imported gum arabic objected to the sanctions and asked for an exemption. Among them were trade giants such as the 'Newspaper Association of America, [the] National Soft Drinks of America, [the] National Food Processors Association, [the] Grocery Manufacturers of America and the Non-prescription Drug Manufacturers Association'.[18] All these companies depended on imports of gum arabic from Gum Arabic Co. of Khartoum, a company controlled by Osama bin Laden, of which the Sudanese government held only a 30 per cent stake. Sudan is the largest exporter of gum arabic and US importers are its biggest buyers. Indeed, they receive better treatment than French importers, the second largest buyers, who pay higher prices. The consequences of the embargo for US companies would have been disastrous. Since importing from Chad or Nigeria was not viable due to the poor quality of the product, American importers would have had to buy gum arabic from their French competitors at much higher prices. Eventually, the US Gum Arabic lobby won their appeal and the product was excluded from President Clinton's economic sanctions. To justify this decision, the State Department issued the following statement: 'We have no information that bin Laden controls gum arabic exports from Sudan.'[19] Therefore, trade between Gum Arabic Co. of Khartoum and the US continued as usual even in the summer of 1998, in the shadow of the cruise missiles launched by Clinton.

Washington's policy towards Saudi Arabia has been shaped by similar constraints. The high dependency of America upon Saudi oil was, until recently, at the root of the determination of post-oil-shock US administrations to keep the House of Saud in control of the largest oil reserves in the world. This commitment often required turning a blind eye to a strong and growing connection between the Saudi elite and Islamist armed groups. As long as America was safe, this policy went almost undetected. Prior to 11 September the FBI had attempted unsuccessfully to investigate a Muslim organisation, the World Assembly of Muslim Youth (WAMY), which was suspected of having links with terror groups. Two of Osama bin Laden's brothers were actively involved in it: Abdullah bin Laden, who was the US director of the charity, and his brother Omar. The WAMY was founded in 1972 with the aim of blocking 'Western corruptive ideas'. By 2002 it was controlling 450 organisations in 34 countries. In the early 1990s, it began acting as a channel for Saudi donations to radical Islamist groups. Among them was the Student Islamic Movement of India, which supports Islamist armed groups in Kashmir and seeks to transform India into an Islamist state.[20] In the late 1990s, the Philippine military denounced the WAMY for its funding of Islamist insurgency. However, an FBI investigation into the WAMY and its Saudi connection was repeatedly blocked by the US administration. 'The FBI wanted to investigate these guys,' admitted Joe Trento, a US national security expert, '. . .they weren't permitted to.'[21] Restrictions increased when President Bush was elected to the point where agents were specifically told to 'back off'.

Today, the United States is no longer safe; the illusion of keeping political violence outside its borders has evaporated. So has the notion that Washington could manipulate Islamist armed groups to its own advantage. What remains is its high energy dependency – Americans' addiction to oil. As long as it lasts, Washington's foreign policy is likely to be forged by Texan interest groups. A clear indication of this reality is the fact that in the aftermath of 11 September the Saudi elite has continued to benefit from the protection of the White House; WAMY accounts were not frozen and all the members of the bin Laden family were whisked out of America on a privately chartered flight back to their country of origin, Saudi Arabia, where US investigators cannot reach them. It took the US more than one year to begin to criticise the Saudi regime and this took place only when the evidence of the degree of Saudi involvement in Islamist terror could no longer be denied. It took the Bush administration a further year to pull US troops out of Saudi Arabia, a decision taken only after securing the rich oil fields of Iraq.

SMUGGLING ELECTRONICS IN ASIA

The interdependency between some US business interests, Islamic states and state-shells is particularly strong in the domain of 'illegal businesses'. State-shells, for example, offer attractive outlets for consumer-product multinationals, companies whose financial well-being depends on the exploitation of new markets. Smuggling offers a very good example of the nature of this relationship. According to the late Daniel Pearl, Sony Corporation used a contraband network in Asia as part of its overall marketing strategy in the region. The economics of smuggling are based on the avoidance of high import duties, barriers to trade levied by governments of the developing world. In Pakistan, a legally imported 21-inch Sony Wega TV costs almost $500; the identical TV smuggled in would cost 25 per cent less. Sony, however, receives the same amount of money (about $220) from either the smugglers or legal distributors. Naturally, smuggled goods sell better because they are cheaper; therefore demand for them is higher. By 1996, as many as half a million televisions were smuggled into Pakistan, 70 per cent of which were Sony.[22] According to the Pakistan Electronics Manufacturers Association, in 1997 for every TV imported legally two were smuggled. Most of the smuggled electronic items come from distributors in the Gulf. 'Sony Gulf's author-ised distributor in Dubai sells [TV] sets to traders who often ship them to the Iranian port of Bandar Abbas. From there some of the goods head northeast to the Afghan border near Herat, then southeast on the highway to Kandahar, on to Jalalabad and then typically enter Pakistan illegally along the Khyber Pass near Peshawar.'[23] Dealers in Pakistan confirmed that the Sony distributor in Dubai supplied the Pakistani market with smuggled products along with a service guarantee. Although in 1997 Sony did not import or assemble any product in Pakistan, it did offer service guarantees. Data Electronics in Lahore provides repair under the Sony guarantee for products sold in the Middle East and used in Pakistan. The company has been regularly reimbursed by Sony for services offered to 'smuggled TVs'.[24]

CRIMINAL MONEY

Smuggling of goods is only one aspect of the close relation-ship that exists between state-shells' criminal and legitimate economies. Illegal capital flights, tax evasion and other crim-inal activities are others. Globalisation has provided criminal and armed organisations with the opportunity to build and share international economic infrastructures: Islamic banks, offshore tax havens and state-shell economies described in the

previous chapters are part of it. So are money-laundering institutions in the West. They are all key elements of the same body:
the international illegal economy.

Organised trafficking in drugs, weapons, goods and people
constitutes a large section of this economy, which can be defined
as the 'criminal economy'. Narcotics generate a turnover of
about $400 billion a year; another $100 billion is produced by
the smuggling of people, weapons and other goods, such as oil
and diamonds; and 90 per cent of this money is recycled outside
the country of origin. Out of the $400 billion from the narcotics
business, for example, as little as $1.4 billion stays in the country
of production.[25] Raymond Baker, a senior fellow at the Center
for International Policy in Washington and a leading expert on
money laundering, believes that most of the money generated
by violent criminal activity is recycled in the West, particularly
in the US. 'When it comes to large deposits from overseas, far
too often American banks assume a "don't ask, don't tell" philosophy,' he said. 'In fact, the Treasury Department estimates that
99.9 per cent of the criminal money presented for deposit in
the United States is accepted into secure accounts. It's a sad
fact, but American banks, under the umbrella of conflicting
American laws and policies, will accept money from overseas
even if they suspect that it has been illegally obtained.'[26]

ILLEGAL CAPITAL FLIGHT

Another component of the international illegal economy is
represented by illegal capital flight. This refers to money that
moves from country to country illegally, undetected and
unrecorded. Illegal capital outflow can be generated by tax
evasion, payments of kickbacks and bribes, earnings from falsi-
fied invoices and other sham transactions. As a phenomenon
of the globalisation of the illegal economy, it has the most
damaging effect on the domestic economies of countries where

the money is generated and taken out, as it depletes them of their wealth. According to Baker nearly 40 per cent of Africa's aggregate wealth has been transferred abroad and between $200 billion and $500 billion left Russia in the 1990s. Sierra Leone offers a good example of the negative impact of illegal capital outflow; the bulk of the foreign exchange produced by the contraband of diamonds, estimated between $25 million and $125 million a year, is used to buy weapons for the Revolutionary United Front (RUF) and its partners in the smuggling business. Little of this wealth is redistributed inside the country.

Asset transfer is another component of illegal capital outflow that results in the impoverishment of countries. In 2001 about $68 billion were given in aid to countries which produce drugs, such as Afghanistan, or are drug transhipment points, such as Chechnya. The bulk of this money never reached the needy, but went to sustain the drugs, smuggling and terror industries, which in turn shipped or spent the profits outside the country of origin. According to Baker, in the late 1990s developing and transitional economies received a capital inflow of $50 billion a year from foreign aid (from the US, OECD and World Bank). During the same period, the outflow of money that illegally left these countries due to mispricing in arm's-length trade and the proceeds of corruption was $100 billion,[27] twice the inflow. 'In addition there are transfers of pricing by multinational corporations dealing with their own subsidiaries and affiliates, all criminal money, all illegal asset swaps, all falsified transfers that are not attached to any trade. The total figure of dirty money out of poor countries is $500 billion per year.'[28]

GROSS CRIMINAL PRODUCT

Raymond Baker calculated that overall illegal capital flight is equivalent to about half a trillion dollars a year.[29] Therefore, together with criminal money, it amounts to a staggering $1 trillion a year, higher than the nominal GDP of the United Kingdom. Other estimates of the size of illicit financial transactions, also known as the 'Gross Criminal Product', are very similar and set the value at between $600 billion and $1.5 trillion, about 2–5 per cent of the world gross national product, of which narcotics range from $300 billion to $500 billion, smuggling of arms, other goods, people and counterfeiting between $150 billion and $470 billion and proceeds from computer crimes at $100 billion.[30]

This torrent of money runs from developing and transitional economies to Western countries. It represents a considerable wealth, a yearly injection of cash equivalent to 5 per cent of world GDP, which is regularly washed through the international money-laundering system. Many financial institutions provide this service. In 1995, a report of the Australian Financial Intelligence Unit, Austrac, estimated that 3.5 billion Australian dollars were recycled through Australia every year. As little as 1 per cent of this money was seized by the police. Turkish Cyprus is another laundering paradise where banks and financial institutions wash about $1 billion a month from Russia.[31] In recent years Thailand has also become a favourite destination for money launderers. In 1996 Bangkok's Chulalongkorn University estimated that $28.5 billion went through the country's money-laundering system, the equivalent of 15 per cent of Thai GDP.[32]

By far the largest and most important market for the recycling of dirty money is the US. Baker is adamant that the bulk of the money to be laundered goes through US and European institutions. Criminal and terror money enters the system in the guise of corrupt or tax-evading money. Though US anti-money laundering legislation requires the registration of cash deposits, 'Treasury Department officials have stated on multiple occasions that it is US policy to attract flight capital out of other countries, with little or no heed paid to whether or not it is tax evading.'[33] Corruption is another field where the law is highly

ambiguous. Until the end of 2001, while US businessmen were
prohibited from bribing foreign government officials, US banks
were allowed to assist them in moving money without asking
any questions about the origins. 'What the US law conveys
. . . to American business people, financial advisers and bankers,'
writes Baker, 'is do not bribe foreign officials; however, if
wealthy foreign officials are encountered, including those
suspected of being corrupt, then the United States wants their
money.'[34] The Bank of New York, for example, has been under
investigation about a laundering scheme that shipped $10 billion
out of Russia. Members of the Russian mafia, business and
government officials linked to it have masterminded the
outflow, which included money given in aid from the
International Monetary Fund.[35] In October 2001, in the Patriot
Act, handling the proceeds of corruption was finally made an
offence under US anti-money laundering law, 25 years after
the Foreign Corrupt Practices Act was passed. However, crim-
inalising the handling of the proceeds of corruption does not
change the fact that there remain many ways of getting around
the law.[36]

Money laundering comes at a price. In the 1980s it was only
6 per cent; by the end of the 1990s it had jumped to 20 per
cent of the sum to be recycled,[37] and it is still rising. 'This is
the percentage charged on the total amount to be laundered,'
explains Baker. 'For drugs dealers, this is a cost easily absorbed.
The price of drugs has in fact been falling in the US at the
same time that the cost of laundering has been rising. This
clearly reflects the ready supply of drugs and the lower costs
of smuggling, enabling the laundering tab to be paid easily.'[38]
Laundering is not only getting riskier and therefore more
expensive, it also requires more sophisticated techniques.
According to Raymond Baker every $100 billion processed by
the laundering machine corresponds to $400 billion to $500
billion of 'dirty money'.[39] If this figure is correct, out of $1
trillion every year about $200 billion are 'washed' by Western

money-laundering institutions and enter the world money supply as 'clean money'.

THE NEW ECONOMY OF TERROR

Armed groups do not finance themselves solely with illegal money, they also have access to legal sources of revenue. The 11 September attacks, for instance, were financed with clean money. Profits from legitimate businesses, money collected by Muslim charities and mosques, independent donations made to Muslims that end up supporting armed groups are not 'dirty money'. Unocal's $25 million 'donations and gifts' to the Taliban to win the Central Asian pipeline contract came out of the company's legal budget. In essence this is the main difference between criminal money and the financing of terror: assets and profits acquired by legitimate means and even declared to tax authorities can be used to finance terror. Thus, when compared with the international illegal economy, the New Economy of Terror has this additional financial source, which could be estimated at between one-third and half a trillion dollars per year.[40]

Together with the illegal economy, the New Economy of Terror amounts to nearly $1.5 trillion, well over 5 per cent of the world economy. This constitutes an international economic system parallel to the legitimate one. It generates a river of money, which flows towards traditional economies and essentially poisons them. It increases dependency upon illegal monetary sources and weakens the system of control for money laundering. The outflow depletes developing and transition countries, where much of this wealth originates. It impoverishes legitimate economies and boosts illegal and terror economies. This process weakens states and encourages the formation of state-shells; entities created around the economics of armed conflict sustained by terror groups. As this process evolves, the size of this alternative economic system will increase and with it Western dependency on it.

The final question to answer is: how big is the pool of resources that feeds the world illegal economy? How large is the amount of money in circulation inside this economic system? In monetary terms, a very rough indicator is provided by the stock of US dollars held abroad, that is US currency used outside the United States.[41] Because the means of exchange of the illegal economy is the US dollar, it is reasonable to assume that the bulk of the stock of dollars held outside the US is part of this economy. Recent studies have shown that from 1965 to 1998 the share of US currency permanently held abroad has risen about 60 times.[42] This is a very basic indicator of the growth of the illegal economy over this period of time. Today about two-thirds of the US money supply, M1,[43] is held outside the US and the percentage is still growing. This value gives us a rough indicator of the incremental growth of the world illegal economy. A comparison of the issue of $100 bills from 1965 to 1998 shows that the growth of foreign stock has been much higher than that of the domestic one. More and more dollars leave the country where they are issued and never return; they are used for transactions, held as a security, deposited in foreign banks in monetary safe havens. The implications for the US economy are considerable and outline the degree of dependency between the legal and illegal economies.

US currency held abroad is a considerable source of revenue to the US treasury because of signorage, the government's gain in converting valuable metal into more valuable coins.[44] 'If the amount of currency held abroad is around 200 billion dollars [1996 figure], and the three-month Treasury bill rate is 5.2 per cent . . . the amount of seigniorage (and taxpayer saving) from externally circulating currency, calculated as the product of these two figures, would be more than 10 billion dollars.'[45]

The degree of interdependence between the two systems is already too advanced to consider severing all ties. Could Western capitalism afford to lose a yearly cash injection of $1.5 trillion? Could we live without the oil of Muslim countries? The answer, for the time being, is no. Recolonising those regions where Islamist terror is breeding is not feasible, even if this is what the Bush administration is effectively attempting to do. The era of Western colonisation is gone. The difficulties encountered in rebuilding Afghanistan, the reluctance of world leaders to back the US invasion of Iraq, the political instability of the new Iraq, the split between the US and new Europe and old Europe are all signs of the danger looming ahead. The threat of terror, forever present in the minds of Western policy-makers, is a constant reminder that major changes in Western foreign policy are needed. War is not the best option. Ironically, any conflict will boost the New Economy of Terror, which feeds on conflicts; so will economic embargoes and any commercial straitjackets imposed upon countries that harbour terror groups. Closing channels to the legitimate international economic system will only open up new ones to the illegal one.

18. Globalisation, Terror's Unwilling Ally

'Injustice is inflicted on us and on you [western people]
by your politicians'

Osama bin Laden

Days after the 11 March attacks in Madrid, al-Qaeda distributed through the Internet a new terror manual. 'Strikes within
cities are a type of military diplomacy,' stated the document.
'This type of attack is often written with blood, embellished
with body parts and perfumed with gunpowder.'[1] The manual
is a chilling reminder of the reasons why, since the tragic events
of 11 September, the incidence of terror attacks in Muslim and
Western cities has increased exponentially. 'Strikes bear a political meaning related to the conflict in ideology. They are considered as messages sent to multiple parties, thus choosing the
targets is done with extreme precision. Those bombings – such
as the CIA building bombing, the East Riyadh operation –
were well executed and were the sparks to awaken the struggling youth.'[2] The lexicon of Islamist armed groups is encrypted
in their urban terror actions; these attacks bear a double message:
a deadly political warning for the enemies and a powerful revolutionary call for the followers.

Among al-Qaeda's primary aims is the destruction of the
economy of western countries. The aim is 'to create a disrup-
tion in the stability required for moving the economic sector
towards development',[3] summarises the terror manual. It is in
this context that one has to analyse the sabotage of oil wells
and pipelines in Iraq; they were ad hoc measures to keep Western

economic interests at bay and to damage the interests of Western oil companies. Iraqi oil revenues are managed by the Fund for the Development of Iraq, which is controlled by a committee of the Provisional Coalition Authority, headed by Paul Bremer, and composed of seven Americans and one British and one Australian representative in addition to the foreign minister of Iraq and the President of the committee (both appointed by Bremer).[4] 'Another goal is to withdraw, or force the withdrawal of, foreign capitals from the local market. [...] As a result of the blessed strikes in Madrid, for instance, the entire European economy suffered. This was a double strike to the economy of the governments of the Crusaders, the Jews or the apostates.'[5] Indeed, following the Madrid bombings and the disinformation campaign of the Aznar government – who initially blamed ETA for the bombings – the markets reacted badly: the euro fell *vis-à-vis* all major currencies, European stocks plummeted all over the world and a climate of uncertainty tainted the confidence of international market operators in the Spanish economy.

THE ECONOMIC CONSEQUENCES OF SEPTEMBER 11

Islamist terror groups have an in-depth knowledge of the functioning of Western capitalism. Not only did they successfully speculate before the 11 September[6] and the 11 March attacks,[7] they were able to predict the markets' long-term reaction to such tragic events. Thus, beyond the symbolism of the destruction of the World Trade Center lies the assault against the real enemy; al-Qaeda's final objective is to inflict a mortal blow to the hegemony of the US economy. Indirectly, the attack also hit hard at countries linked to the US. The closure of the markets, for example, had tremendous consequences for foreign institutional and private investors; the Saudis alone lost $24 billion.[8] But the most profound impact was felt by the US economy. A study conducted by a group of OECD economists confirms that 11 September contributed to the fall in the value of the US dollar which in turn slowed down the American economy.[9] While the immediate impact of the Bush war on terror was positive – the dollar in fact rallied – the medium- to long-term reaction was negative. As early as November 2001, 'the markets showed signs of nervousness and lack of confidence towards the American economy and went elsewhere to invest,' explained a Wall Street broker.

Contrary to what many believe, the weakening of the dollar began well before the US budget deficit was even an issue of concern in the international financial markets. The lack of confidence in US foreign policy precipitated the decline in activity in the US financial markets, which in turn reduced the global demand for dollars. Oil-producing investors were, understandably, among the first to show concern. 'People no longer have any confidence in the US economy or in the US foreign policy,' admitted a financial consultant based in Riyadh to the BBC in October 2002.[10] A few months earlier the Iranian government had admitted to be considering switching crude oil sales from dollars to euros for fear of further depreciation in the American currency.[11] In 2002, Iranian oil revenues were about $10 billion, equivalent to 80 per cent of its foreign income.[12]

Islamist terror groups also understand the interdependencies of the tightly knitted global economy. The weakening of the dollar initiated a chain effect which affected negatively some of America's trade partners, i.e. its main exporters. Several of those countries had been already targeted by the Islamists, for example Indonesia. A weaker dollar reduced US imports from South East Asia, which in turn curbed economic growth. In addition, the war in Iraq produced a drastic fall in the volume of foreign direct investments in the region. It is against this background that the October 2002 Bali bombing took place. The attack was part of a global strategy to destroy the traditional economy of Indonesia and to create the necessary socio-economic void for the Islamists and their sponsors to take over – to build their shell-state. The economic impact of the Bali bombing confirms this analysis: its immediate effect was a 10 per cent drop in the Jakarta Stock Exchange and a drastic reduction in the yearly $5 billion tourist industry. In the long term, it reduced Indonesia's GDP, which, for the whole of 2002, experienced a 1 per cent drop.[13]

Unlike Islamist terror groups, Western governments seem to have a limited knowledge, if any, of terror economics; at the same time, they are conditioned by the maintenance of a dereg-ulated global market, which implies as few controls as possible. These are the two main factors which so far have hindered the financial war on terror. The last UN Security Council report on the finances of al-Qaeda,[14] produced in December 2003, states that since 11 September, a modest $150 million of terror funds have been frozen across the world.[15] Seventy per cent of the money was held in bank accounts in the West, predomin-antly by charities used as fronts by armed organisations; virtually nothing was frozen in 2003 because terror funds had vanished from areas under Western jurisdiction. By the time Western authorities started to follow al-Qaeda's money trail, the organisation had relocated and decentralised most of its wealth in the Muslim world and was using the informal banking system, e.g. the *hawala*; terror money was simply out of reach.

Before 11 September, al-Qaeda restructured its portfolio: it closed several bank accounts held in the West – predominantly in the US – and used the funds to invest heavily in commod-ities, e.g. diamonds and gold; it decentralised its operational and financial network and shifted its offshore activities to the Old Continent. The organisation has turned to the *hawala* as well as to couriers to move money around the world. $50,000 of the $150,000 used to fund the November 2003 bombing in Turkey were delivered by an al-Qaeda courier to the cell that carried out the attack, the balance was provided by funds which were already in Turkey.[16] The objective of the restructuring was twofold: to shield the organisation's wealth from the counter-terrorism measures which al-Qaeda anticipated would inevitably follow the 11 September attacks, and to profit from market changes generated by their economic consequences. These changes are now apparent to us all. The invasion of Afghanistan and the war in Iraq, milestones in the war on terror, accelerated the fall of the dollar *vis-à-vis* the euro and the Swiss franc, the other two widely traded currencies. From the end of 2001 to March 2003, an almost perfect correlation exists between the depreciation of the dollar and the appreciation of these two currencies. Over the same period, a similar correlation characterised the relationship between the price of gold and the value of the dollar. Is it feasible to say that, thanks to its remarkable knowledge and understanding of the world's financial markets, al-Qaeda predicted the economic consequences of the Bush war on terror? While this thought may be repulsive to many, it is a distinct possibility which needs to be considered and analysed.

The UN report also laments the inability of the West to track profits of legitimate businesses which are diverted to terror groups, as well as the difficulties encountered in blocking funds generated by business empires managed by Islamist terror sympathisers, as, for example, that of Youssef Nada.[17] These difficulties sprang from the idiosyncrasies of the globalised financial market. Until December 2003, Nada, an Egyptian national living in Switzerland, designated as a terror financier by the UN and subjected to sanctions (including a travel ban), travelled freely in Europe, where he had access to most of his wealth.[18] Nada used the flexibility of the financial markets to liquidate several companies by appointing himself as liquidator and relocating the funds elsewhere and out of reach of the authorities. The Financial Action Task Force (FATF), an international organisation based in Paris which is attempting to block dirty and terror money from flowing into legitimate economies, blames the lack of cooperation and poor information-sharing practices among countries for the failure to cut off terror finances from the Western financial system.[19] However, often, counter-terrorism officers have little to share, especially when money travels through the offshore banking system. The FATF agrees with the UN that targeting Islamist charities has also proved very difficult. Often those closed in one country reappear after a few months under a new name or move to another country. Al Haramain, which in 2002 had been found guilty of acting as a front for al-Qaeda in its Bosnian and Somalian branches, opened an Islamic school in Jakarta[20] in December 2003. A FATF officer admitted that charities can be relocated as quickly as money can be wired from one place to the next. The speed at which offices are moved from country to country is also a by-product of globalisation and deregularisation. So far, globalisation seems to have been more of an obstacle than an advantage in tracking terror money.

Almost three years since 11 September, the Islamist religious colonisation is still in full swing and charitable organisations are its most powerful tool in penetrating new markets. Africa is today the new frontier; Wahhabism is rapidly spreading in both East and West Africa. In East Africa: Somalia, Kenya and Tanzania are among the countries targeted by Saudi terror financiers. Funds are used to build new mosques and *madaris*. A Wahhabi follower from Tanzania admitted to *Time* magazine that Saudi Arabian and Yemeni charities regularly send money to his country. 'Officially, the money is used to buy medicine, but, in reality, the money is given to us to support our work and buy guns.'[21] In West Africa: Saudi Arabia and Sudan are the major sponsors. Thanks to their money, Islamist insurgency has exploded in Senegal, Gambia, Niger, Mauritania and Chad. In Nigeria, the introduction of the Sharia law is spreading from region to region; bin Laden has even declared that the country is 'ready for liberation'.[22]

In Africa, as in South East Asia, the colonisation forces have found a fertile terrain in the failure of the domestic political economies.[23] Corruption, unemployment, slow economic growth, poverty, inequitable distribution of wealth – these are all-too-familiar economic factors boosting the spread of Islamist insurgency. In Africa, as in South East Asia, the Islamist religious colonisation is promoted by Arab economic forces; Saudi financiers and Yemeni businessmen, for example, represent the driving economic backers of Islamist terror in South East Asia. Centuries ago, traders and merchants from the Southern tip of the Arabian Peninsula, a region that today belongs to Yemen, brought Islam to South East Asia. Thus religious, as well as trading and commercial, ties between these two regions go back several centuries. This explains why Yemeni businessmen have a strong presence in South East Asia and why they are among the major investors in the region; unfortunately some of them control joint ventures which operate as fronts for al-Qaeda.[24]

THE PATRIOT ACT

In October 2001, the US Congress approved the Patriot Act, the first financial counter-terrorism measure. The Act is based on the conviction that money laundering and a lack of financial transparency have facilitated the financing of global terrorism. At a macro level, the Patriot Act targets three areas of the financial system which are believed to have been exploited by terror groups: offshore banking, correspondent banking and the private banking service. The Act specifically prohibits US banks from doing business with shell banks, e.g. to let them open correspondent accounts, and from entertaining relations with foreign banks which do business with them. *De facto* the Patriot Act has banished shell banks from the US banking system, explains Raymond Baker.[25] Shell banks are banks which do not have a physical presence in any country; often they are nothing more than a name registered offshore.

They are the hard core of offshore banking: unregulated, elusive and often without a street address.

Domestically, the Patriot Act also regulates the businesses of private banks. Following the shocking revelation that the September 11 hijackers used ATM machines to withdraw money, the US government launched a full investigation of their bank accounts. It emerged that the 19 hijackers had opened 24 accounts in the US at large branches of four well-known US banks. These accounts never held more than $5,000 at any given time. According to the testimony of Dennis Lormer, chief of the FBI financial crime unit, to the House Financial Services Committee, the hijackers kept their deposits at relatively low levels to remain below the financial radar screen.[26] To open the accounts they used visas issued by Saudi Arabia or the United Arab Emirates, as they did not have social security numbers or permanent addresses. All the accounts were joint accounts, with three or four members entitled to use them. These discoveries prompted the introduction of a series of restrictions in the US banking system to reinforce the 'know your customer' requirement. Thus, today, opening a bank account in the US requires several checks on the identity of the account holder and on the origins of the cash deposited.[27]

The Patriot Act goes against the principles of deregularisation of the international financial markets, which call for the abolition of any restriction to the movement of funds. It departs from the spirit of globalisation and deregularisation which has characterised Western economies since the early 1990s. Therefore, it has not been welcomed by the international banking community. For a start, it puts tremendous pressure upon US banks and US-registered foreign banks. The act makes criminal the failure of any American and US-registered foreign banks to report to the US authorities 'suspicious' activities or transactions. Its implementation is costly; banks have to train their staff, at their own expense, to make sure they know how to comply with the Act. Many bankers feel that certain provisions have produced excessive and costly paperwork and others regard the new legislation as an intrusion in to the privacy of their customers.[28] However, the most serious impact of legislation such as the Patriot Act, which limits the degree of freedom of foreign banks, is the growing belief among the international banking community that America has become unfriendly to foreign investors.[29] This perception is reinforced by the passing of other measures which clearly discriminate against foreign investors, for example Bush's tax bill, which reduces tax on capital gains for US taxpayers while maintaining a high with-holding tax on foreign investors' dividends. These legislations, coupled with the lack of confidence in the US created by the 11 September attacks, have prompted a decline in private foreign investments held in US dollars, which, in turn, is one of the factors that has weakened the dollar. So far, the immediate beneficiary of these changes has been the euro. As the inter-national economy moves closer and closer to a dual-currency standard, i.e. the dollar and the euro, private foreign invest-ments gravitate toward Europe. In December 2003, a UK banker admitted to me that several merchant banks operating in Asia and Africa had detected a tendency of legitimate investors to shift away from the dollar towards the euro. Amid the uncer-tainty of the war on terror, the euro seemed a more secure reserve currency where to 'park' capitals.

To curb money-laundering activities, capital flight and terror transactions, the Patriot Act monitors money transfers denom-inated in dollars all over the world. This measure reduces the flow of illegal and terror money into the US. However, because similar legislation has not been implemented in Europe, since 11 September illegal capital flows have headed for the Old Continent, from where they penetrate the legality of Western economies. I recently interviewed a South African businessman who used to circumvent the South African foreign-exchange controls. With the help of 'friendly' local banks he converted funds denominated in Rand[30] into US dollars, which ended up in US dollar accounts in the US. Since the introduction of the Patriot Act, he admitted to having been unable to do so. 'American authorities are watching closely dollar flows into the US,' he explained. 'South African banks are very wary of such screening and refuse to cooperate with businessmen like me who want to take money out of the country.' Today, the most common way to break the foreign-exchange control is to purchase diamonds and gold and smuggle them out of the country for sale in Europe. The profits are then deposited in euro-denominated bank accounts in European offshore centres, from where they find their way into the European economy. It is likely that al-Qaeda is following the same strategy.

THE BLACK MARKET PESO EXCHANGE

The Patriot Act and other counter-terrorism financial measures, for example those imposed by the FATF, have had a very limited impact, if any, in reducing the activities of both drug traffickers and terror groups handled through the informal banking system. This system can be described as a series of alternative and unregulated networks, through which money moves from country to country. One of these networks is the Black Market Peso Exchange, another one is the *hawala*. The Black Market Peso Exchange is the system of money laundering most commonly and widely used by the Colombian and other South American drug cartels. The *hawala*, which is very popular in the Muslim world, is predominantly used by Islamist terror groups. Both networks are extremely elusive to traditional monetary controls because they do not involve the physical movement of cash from one country to another. Ironically both systems function according to principles of globalisation and deregularisation: they are truly transnational, they are self-regulated (failure to deliver the cash often results in death) and they are fast (the *hawala* operates in real time).

In the early days of the Medellin drug cartel, cash was flown back to Colombia by the same planes which took the drugs to America. Once in Colombia, dollars had to be converted into pesos with the help of corrupt bankers. But the process was slow and the drug traffickers had to store huge amounts of cash. Cash storage created several problems. One Colombian drug trafficker, for example, buried so much cash on his property that occasionally, when it rained heavily, the resultant floods washed US dollars downstream, clogging the sewage system.[31] According to Marci Forman, who directs the US custom services financial investigation unit, in Colombia today there are still warehouses full of US currency.[32] US dollars are of no use to the Colombian drug cartel or to FARC, the terror group which is acting as its militia, or to Sendero Luminoso in Peru. Members of these organisations live in secluded areas where they use local currencies and never travel abroad. They need domestic money to pay the growers, to buy protection, to corrupt politicians, to recruit and to purchase arms and explosives. In the 1990s, to avoid storage problems and guarantee a steady flow of local currency, drug traffickers and terror groups successfully infiltrated the currency black market and transformed it into their own illegitimate and informal banking system.[33]

The way the Black Market Peso Exchange works is fairly simple. The drug traffickers hand over bulk cash to a money broker in the US, who agrees to exchange it at a discount to the official rate, generally around 40 per cent. The cash is handed over in boxes, suitcases or even inside the trunk of a car and the corresponding pesos are delivered in Colombia a few weeks later. The broker distributes the cash among its vast staff of runners, who deposit it in small amounts into thousands of US bank accounts. Once the money is in the bank, it can be easily manipulated. At the same time the broker has an office in Colombia where legitimate businessmen go to buy foreign products, ranging from US cigarettes to TV sets and pay in pesos. The purchases are done with an exchange rate which generally is 20 per cent above the official exchange rate. The broker buys the goods in the US, often from companies which know the origins of the money, ships them to Colombia and uses legitimate pesos to pay back the drug traffickers. The purchases are always in cash and below the $10,000 limit imposed by the IRS. The technique of breaking down large sums of deposits into several transactions of less than $10,000 is also illegal. In January 2003, two Miami-Dade women were sentenced to six years in prison for using their company, Pride International, an appliance export business, to money launder $5 million of drug money.[34]

The Black Market Peso Exchange is also used by South American professionals, as well as politicians, to send dollars to their children studying in the US. Thus, it functions in a fashion similar to the *hawala*. It presents the same advantages: it is faster, cheaper and avoids any type of monetary controls.

According to the IRS, from 1999 to 2003, the volume of money laundered via the Black Market Peso Exchange has risen from $1 to $6 billion.[35] According to Raymond Kelly, Commissioner of the US Custom Service, the Back Market Peso Exchange is 'the ultimate nexus between crime and commerce, using global trade to mask global money laundering.'[36]

THE HAWALA

In 2001, the restructuring of al-Qaeda's finances involved the movement of large quantities of gold out of Afghanistan. This was achieved using both couriers and the *hawala* system. From Afghanistan and Pakistan, al-Qaeda successfully transferred gold to Dubai from where it was redirected around the world to sustain the organisation's elusive network. For the *hawaladors*, transferring either currencies or gold is not a problem; they use gold to balance the books from one country to another, therefore they hold gold reserves around the world. *De facto*, the *hawala* system operates on a strict gold standard; currency exchange rates, for example, are set according to the value of the metal. In the developing world, gold is often the most reliable means of exchange. *Hawaladors* are, therefore, intimately interlinked with gold brokers; in Kashmir, for example, they operate from Srinagar's main gold market, Lal Chowk.[37] There is virtually no limit to the amount of gold that a big gold broker can handle using the *hawala* system. 'If you say you want 100 kilos of gold, I can give it to you wherever you want in 12 hours' admits one of Dubai's largest gold bullion dealers.[38]

It is through the *hawala* system that gold becomes a highly liquid commodity, one that can be converted into any type of currency in a very short time. Thus the decision to convert a considerable amount of al-Qaeda wealth into gold was facilitated by the efficiency of the system for transforming gold into cash; in turn, this boosted the volume of transactions handled via the *hawala*. Naturally, the other great advantage of this informal system is its widespread presence in areas where Islamist terror is blossoming and where the banking system is weak. In Pakistan, it is estimated that on a yearly basis between $2 and $5 billion of foreign remittances pass though the *hawala* system,[39] as compared with as little as $1.2 billion which are transferred via the banking system. In South East Asia, for example, the *hawala* is the most common system of foreign exchange remittances; in downtown Manila's Ermita District, there are block after block of *hawaladors*, which handle on a yearly basis about $350 million of remittances from the 1.4 million Filipinos who work in the Middle East.[40] In India, where Indira Gandhi pursued a strong campaign to eradicate it, the *hawala* is believed to handle transactions equivalent to as much as 40 per cent of the country's gross national product.[41]

Foreign exchange controls is another factor that increases the popularity of the *hawala*. In 1998, when the Malaysian government imposed capital controls to prevent capital flights the *hawala* became the principal source of foreign exchange.

Western terror backers also resort to the *hawala* to send money to Islamist armed groups. In the summer of 2002, the Indian police unmasked a scheme through which money raised by a pro-Kashmiri British charity group, was transferred to Kashmiri terror organizations. A *hawalador* delivered the money to the UK charity's contact in India. The man then deposited it in a bank account as funds for his magazine. He then wrote several cheques, transferring the money into other bank accounts. Eventually the funds reached a bank in Kashmir from where he withdrew the money and delivered it in person.[42]

EUROPE: TERROR'S NEW FINANCIAL AND LOGISTICAL HOTBED

Far from being defeated or even seriously wounded, since 11 September al-Qaeda and its global network of affiliates, cells and sleepers, have grown exponentially and today are more elusive than ever. Islamist terror has shown a remarkable ability to adapt to counter-terrorist measures. In response to the closure of the training camps in Afghanistan, Sudan and the Balkans, for example, al-Qaeda began training its followers 'virtually'. It uses documents containing military training courses, such as manuals on how to build bombs, which can be downloaded from the Internet only at a set time. 'The documents are never online for longer than an hour,' explains Nick Fielding, the *Sunday Times* investigative journalist specialising in Islamist terror, 'but it is enough time for thousands of people across the world to download them. These manuals contain all the necessary information to train people in the "art of terror".'[43] The manuals also have information about the intended targets. According to Indira Singh, an event-risk architect who designs econometric models to offset the impact of exceptional events, such as 9/11, for major banks, messages related to when and where to launch an attack are often hidden in pictures. 'This technique is called steganography, linguistic steganography,' explains Ms Singh. 'It mixes letters and words of some text within the millions of pixels of a picture; the mixture is done using specific softwares.'[44]

Al-Qaeda has been able to exploit the different approaches that the US and Europe have towards terror financing. For example, while the US adopted a zero-tolerance approach *vis-à-vis* charities that are somehow linked to terror organisations, the European Union protected organisations which perform humanitarian work and worried about affecting their valuable activity.[45] However, the biggest advantage that Europe has offered terror finances is the absence of a homogenous legislation similar to the Patriot Act.

The limits of the EU financial counter-terrorism policies range from the lack of EU-wide definition of terrorism, which some states have yet to introduce, to the failure to introduce monitoring of bank accounts or to implement measures such as the pan-European arrest warrant, approved two years ago. The European inefficiency in tracking terror money is outlined by the modest amount of funds frozen since 11 September – about $40 million. From South Cyprus to the British Channel Islands, European offshore facilities are still fully operational. It was only after the Madrid bombing that the EU decided to address the role that offshore Gibraltar plays in funding terror.

In Europe, shell banks and offshore facilities are the primary channels used by terror sponsors to move money. Italian magistrates have discovered that Islamist cells operating in Italy have received funds from Arab countries via British offshore facilities. An intercepted conversation inside a mosque in Milan confirmed the identity of the sponsors. 'The thread begins in Saudi Arabia,' said an unidentified Arab visitor to the Imam. 'Do not even worry about money because Saudi Arabia's money is your money.'[46] Once the money has successfully entered the

European banking system it can be wired and withdrawn anywhere. Members of terror groups operating in Europe use ATM machines, as the 11 September hijackers did, to access the cash made available by their sponsors. ATM machines were also used by those who participated in the Bali, Istanbul and Madrid attacks.[47]

Undoubtedly, since 11 September, the appreciation of the euro *vis-à-vis* the dollar boosted the appeal that Europe presents to money launderers and terror sponsors. According to Raymond Baker, it takes between six months and one year to launder dirty money.[48] During this period the launderers hold cash. If the currency they have depreciates, this amounts to an additional cost. In 2003, the dollar lost significantly *vis-à-vis* the euro. If one adds this extra cost to the rising fees for money laundering in US dollars due to the restrictions imposed by the Patriot Act, the total cost of washing dirty money in US dollars may be so expensive as to reduce the profits generated by the illegal/criminal activity.

The introduction of a common European currency has facilitated the activity of laundering bulk cash in Europe. In Italy, customs police have recently busted a major operation run by the 'ndrangeta, the Calabrian organised crime group, where drug money was laundered through real estate transactions in Brussels. The cash was shipped in bulk inside containers to Brussels, where it was used to buy existing properties or to fund the construction of new ones. The Italian police estimate that the 'ndrangeta bought an entire section of Brussels using this method. Since 9/11, both the Mafia and the 'ndrangeta are increasingly laundering drug money in Europe. The principal countries where this activity takes place are Belgium and Holland. Total earnings of the four major criminal organizations, i.e. mafia, camorra, 'ndrangeta and sacra corona unita, amounts to 10 per cent of Italian GDP (euro 100 billion).[49]

If Italian organised crime is increasingly using euros to conduct its drug-trade activities, this means that the euro is also used along the drug route. 'It is unfeasible to think that couriers are paid in dollars', explains an Italian anti-drug covert agent, 'when the sales and the money laundering in Europe is conducted in euros.' The agent also confirmed that the bulk of the drugs sold in Europe comes from Afghanistan and Central Asia and that drug smuggling is an area where crime and terror have forged a joint venture. In December 2003, for example, the US navy blocked a cargo sailing in the Persian Gulf. When they inspected it they discovered that it was carrying two tons of hashish and that it was operated by suspected al-Qaeda affiliates. The drug was stored in 54 bags, which weighed about 70 pounds each. Its street value ranges from $8 to $10 million dollars.[50] Drug smuggling is not the sole commercial link between Islamist terror and organized crime. According to an FBI report handed over to the 11 September commission in the US, before the attacks on the Twin Towers, bin Laden had approached Cosa Nostra to purchase false US passports.[51]

THE EUROPEAN MOSQUE NETWORK

In August 2002, the relatives of the victims of 11 September launched a legal action against several members of the Saudi elite, Sudan and a number of Gulf banks and charities accused of having funded al-Qaeda. A few days before the lawsuit was filed, $200 billion of Saudi assets held in the US left the country. The bulk of the money was reinvested in Europe in equities, bonds and real estate. Overall, Saudi financiers are believed to have had about $750 billion invested in the US.[52] According to the UN, Saudi funds still find their way to support Islamist terror groups in the Muslim world and in Europe.[53]

European counter-terrorism is adamant that the presence of large Saudi investments in Europe facilitates the funding of mosques and *madaris* in the Old Continent. The mosque network is perceived as the most powerful instrument for recruiting, funding and coordinating the activity of cells and armed groups linked to Islamist terror in Europe and abroad. Spanish counter-terrorism officers have defined European mosques as 'havens for al-Qaeda planning and fund-raising'.[54] Until the Madrid bombing, counter-terrorism intelligence may have undervalued the role played by the European mosque network in bankrolling Islamist terror during the preparatory stages of 11 September. Spanish magistrates have recently discovered that a Spanish cell, Soldiers of Allah, which started in Madrid's Abu Baker mosque in 1994, provided support and money to the Hamburg cell which partic-ipated in the 11 September attack.[55]

The European network is also recruiting European Muslims to carry out suicide missions. The two British suicide bombers who last year carried out attacks in Tel Aviv were residents of Hounslow and Derby. Italian magistrates have revealed that Italian mosques supplied several suicide bombers to Iraq, including those who participated in the attack against the hotel Rashid during the visit of Paul Wolfowitz. Some of the funds used to recruit and *forge* came from Arab sponsors and reached Italy via Britain and were denominated in euros.[56]

The man in charge of the supply of European suicide bombers to Iraq is known as 'Mullah Fouad', described as the 'gatekeeper' of Iraq.[57] Mullah Fouad was born Mohammed Majid and is an Iraqi Kurd member of Ansar al-Islam, the Iraqi Islamist terror group linked to al-Qaeda. Before fleeing to Syria in 2003, he resided in Parma for several years. From Syria he is supervising the smuggling of European suicide bombers into Iraq.[58] According to Jean-Louis Bruguiere, the French anti-terrorism investigative magistrate, since the summer of 2003, dozens of new European recruits have reached Iraq.[59] In a conversation intercepted by the Italian authorities, Mullah Fouad asked a member of the Italian cell to send more people 'like those that were in Japan',[60] clearly using the analogy with kamikaze. Mullah Fouad is the right-hand man of Abu Musab al Zarqawi, a Jordanian born 37-year-old; the man whom the European counter-terrorism forces believes is at the centre of a network of cells, sleepers and terror groups in the Old Continent. Al Zarqawi is believed to have masterminded the attacks in Casablanca, those against the UN and the Red Cross in Iraq as well as the Istanbul bombing; he also had links with the people who participated in the Madrid bombing. Ironically, the first time the world heard his name was in February 2003, when Colin Powell accused him of being the link between Saddam Hussein and al-Qaeda. Far from being a go-between, al Zarqawi is an ingenious terror manager, a representative of a new generation of Islamist leaders.[61]

European mosques are also the headquarters of radical Islamist preachers, people who in the last decade have successfully obtained political asylum in European countries because of persecution in their own. Several of them are linked to al Zarqawi, including Mullah Krekar, one of the founders of Ansar al-Islam. Krekar, who was born in Iraqi Kurdistan, took refuge in Norway 13 years ago to escape Saddam Hussein's executioners. In 2001, the Dutch authorities arrested him when they found him in possession of an inventory of Ansar al-Islam fighting capabilities, including small arms and explosives. He was put on trial in Norway and acquitted soon after on terrorist charges on the grounds that he was waging war against Saddam's regime, an action which cannot be considered terrorism. This incident highlights the need to find a proper definition of terrorism, one which will be embraced universally. Presently, Krekar is being held by the Norwegian authorities for organising two attacks in Iraq using suicide bombers recruited and trained through the mosque network in Norway.[62]

EASTERN EUROPE

The European Islamist terror network uses Eastern European countries as bases for their activities. The lack of controls, i.e.

efficient counter-terrorism activity, coupled with porous borders, makes it easy for them to move freely. Operating on the eastern fringes of the EU presents other advantages. An investigation by the *Observer*, published in January 2004, showed that Islamist cells based in Eastern Europe have established contacts with the Balkan mafia to purchase arms and explosives. This is a very important fact as acquiring explosives in Western Europe presents serious difficulties due to the controls of the police. The explosive used in the Madrid bombing, for example, was collected over a period of one year by a worker in a coal-mine in Asturia. He stole small amounts almost daily so that the theft would not be discovered through the routine checking of the inventories. The explosive was swapped with drugs, hashish and Ecstasy by the Madrid cell.[63]

Porous borders in Eastern Europe make it also easy to move to and from Iraq; the two British suicide bombers who carried out the attacks in Tel Aviv travelled via the Balkans to Syria from where they entered Israel. Another route is through the Mediterranean Sea. According to Italian magistrates, Italian cells linked to al Zarqawi and Ansar al-Islam smuggled European suicide bombers into Iraq by sea from Syria from where they entered North West Iraq.

Eastern Europe is also the most important and efficient supplier of false identities. Nick Fielding of the *Sunday Times* has successfully obtained several fake European identities by answering an ad in a UK-based Russian language newspaper that offered 'help' with passports. He was contacted by a former KGB agent who resides in London and who became the go-between with the supplier. The false passports and driving licences were manufactured in Bulgaria and sold to him by a gang of criminals from Eastern Europe operating in the UK. According to Fielding these false identities are produced in 'factories' in Eastern Europe and are extremely authentic and very cheap, costing as little as £600 each, while on the black market forged passports cost £7,000.[64]

FUNDING THE EUROPEAN NETWORK

The European network continues to rely upon the financial support of al-Qaeda, however, this organisation is today acting more like a venture capitalist of terror than as an organiser of terror attacks. This metamorphosis is apparent when comparing 11 September with the bombings in Bali, Istanbul and Madrid. The 11 September attack was planned, funded and executed under the direct supervision al-Qaeda,[65] the most recent bombings were the work of separate groups loosely linked to al-Qaeda. As in the venture capital model, al-Qaeda provided part or most of the funds and a sort of supervision; the decision to back one attack instead of another is taken upon a detailed analysis of the cost benefits of the bombing, as has emerged from the investigation into the Bali bombing. Once the attack has been successfully implemented, the leadership of al-Qaeda officially endorses it. In an April 2004 tape of Osama bin Laden, where he offered a truce to the Europeans, he specifically refers to the Madrid bombing as an al-Qaeda attack.[66]

Since 11 September, Islamist armed groups across the world have successfully developed several techniques to self-finance themselves and no longer have to rely upon the funding of al-Qaeda. The Madrid bombing was almost entirely self-financed. Following the model of al-Qaeda, the Islamist terror network is shaping a life of its own. In Europe the mosque network represents a strong backer; another is direct sponsorship from Arab sympathisers. Groups use a mixture of legitimate and criminal activities. In Spain and in Italy, members of Islamist armed groups worked as mechanics and waiters to support themselves and to reduce the financial borders of the organisation. However, crime remains the most important source of revenues. Farid Belaribi, an Algerian immigrant jailed in England in the summer of 2003, helped raise $250,000 through an international fraud network. He admitted to having defrauded banks and credit-card companies though he denied knowing the money was used for terrorist purposes.[67] Credit-card fraud was conducted with skimming devices. The credit-card numbers were used throughout Europe and in Dubai. In 2002 credit-card losses due to fraud accounted for $424 million.[68] Experts are adamant that these type of frauds bankroll crime and terrorism.

The European network also funds itself by smuggling drugs, as was the case in the Madrid bombing – bankrolled through the sale of hashish and Ecstasy – and revenues from petty crime.[69] The link between al Zarqawi and Ansar al-Islam, which is involved in the smuggling of drugs from Afghanistan, confirms that European Islamist groups benefit from the sale of illegal narcotics in Europe.

Three years after 11 September, the Islamist terror network has evolved throughout the world. Emulating al-Qaeda's military actions, appealing to similar sponsors and utilising the techniques of self-financing, it is becoming a global organism with a life of its own. Modtada al-Sadr has been bankrolled by Iraqi money-changers who hope that when he gains control of the holy cities of Iraq he will hand them the monopoly of currency exchanges. With millions of Shia pilgrims travelling to those shrines each year, profits will be plentiful. Al Zarqawi's European network is sustained by mosques and charities.

Not only have Western counter-terrorism policies been unable to stop the financing of terror, they have failed to curb the distribution of wealth inside the network, a key element in the spreading of Islamist terror. Paradoxically, the new generation of Islamist terror leaders, those who eventually will replace Osama bin Laden, understand globalisation and are using its tools: virtual training courses, ATM machines, offshore bank accounts. They also complement them with ancient instruments, heritage of their culture and religion, such as the *hawala* or the *Zakat*. What we are facing today is a powerful enemy, one who has an in-depth knowledge of our world: an enemy we hardly know.

Conclusions

Outside the Finsbury Park Mosque in London, it was possible until recently to buy videos of Islamist propaganda. Among the bestsellers were films showing the last hours in the lives of suicide bombers. In a basement just a few blocks away from the mosque, Jewish amateur actors staged plays to raise money for Israeli victims of suicide bombers. This is the world we live in. Our daily life carries on in the shadow of political violence. For the North London Muslim and Jewish communities, who live next to each other and share the same butchers', there is no other reality. 11 September has only extended it to the rest of the world.

Regardless of what we call it – terrorism, terror, armed struggle, political violence – the use of violence for political aims, the targeting of civilians and the state of sheer fear that it creates have all been part of our world for over 50 years. Due to its highly emotional charge, this phenomenon has been greatly manipulated. In North London, depending upon which side of the street you walk, a suicide bomber is a martyr and a hero or a terrorist and an assassin. With so many deaths and so much suffering on both sides, building a political bridge between these two interpretations at the present time is impossible. Political analysis is tainted by resentment and skewed by hatred. Economics offers a more dispassionate tool for an investigation into the forces that make and sustain armed organisations. Economics may, in the end, even offer a viable solution.

In this book I have tried to circumvent the trap of politics, using an economic analysis to trace the birth and evolution of the New Economy of Terror – a web based on terror, crime, corruption and deceit. This is not an isolated network created by the interaction between armed and criminal organisations, it is an international economic system linked to both legitimate and illegitimate sectors of traditional economies. Like any economic system, the New Economy of Terror has grown through evolutionary stages to take on a life of its own. The principal stages have been: the wars by proxy of the Cold War era, the foreign sponsorship of armed groups, the privatisation of terror, the birth of state-shells and the Modern Jihad.

Retracing the economics of armed organisations has unveiled their phenomenal growth. Fuelled by political violence, organised crime and common greed, the New Economy of Terror is today twice the size of the GNP of the United Kingdom and three times the size of the US money supply, and is still growing. At present, its main engine is the Modern Jihad, a brew of Islamist revolutionary ideology, the Muslim search for identity and the socio-economic aspirations of the Muslim world.

The Modern Jihad feeds into a network of economies run by Islamic states, state-shells and armed organisations; its economic lifelines are many and range from legitimate to criminal businesses. The export of gum arabic, the transfer of wealth from rich Muslims via charitable organisations, the smuggling of arms and narcotics and money laundering are all part of a drive to achieve economic self-sufficiency. Islamist state-shells want to reap the benefits of this network, the network embraces them, and the system expands.

Today the declared aim of the Modern Jihad is the destruction of the State of Israel and of its Western imperialist allies – political entities identified by their religious creeds, i.e. Judaism and Christianity. However, its true targets are others: those regimes, such as the House of Saud in Saudi Arabia as well as Gaddafi in Libya, that block the formation of pure Islamist states, preventing the birth of the new Caliphate which will re-appropriate the rich resources of Muslim lands. Once the shield of religion is removed, the true enemies are revealed: foreign and domestic powers that economically exploit the Muslim masses.

What we are witnessing today is a clash between two
economic systems, one dominant and the other subordinate.
This is the root of the conflict between Islamist terror and the
West. Retracing the economics of armed groups has exposed
a wealth of real forces behind Islamist terror – commercial
and financial entities that have been kept at the periphery of
the world economy by their Western counterparts. The fall
of the Soviet Union, however, opened up new opportunities
for these Islamic forces in countries with large Muslim populations. The Islamic financial colonisation of former members
of the Soviet system was made possible by the alliance of
these commercial and financial entities with Wahhabism, the
strictest religious interpretation of Islam.

In the global village of international economics, sections of
the New Economy of Terror inevitably interact with the
economies of Western countries. Money laundering, legal businesses run by armed organisations, charitable aid – these are
just some of the links between the two systems. Their degree
of interdependency is astonishingly high. The West is the
primary consumer of narcotics and the major seller of arms –
the largest revenue and expenditure items, respectively, in the
balance of payments of armed organisations. Western financial
institutions recycle the bulk of the money generated by the
world's illegal economy, about $1.5 trillion a year. When I asked
a well-known English economist what would happen if this
liquidity was suddenly taken out of the system, he admitted
that it would plunge Western economies into a deep recession.

The economic analysis of the interdependency between the
New Economy of Terror and Western economies suggests that
the first step in fighting terror is to identify its channels of
interaction with the economies of the West and progressively
sever them – close its avenues into the free market and the
world of capitalism. This is a decision that must be made at a
government level but enacted at the grass roots, and can only
be accomplished if we, as citizens of democratic nations, take

hold of the greatest privilege offered us by an open society – the opportunity to be informed about and to participate in the economic decisions that shape our lives.

As long as we allow anyone to walk into a bank in Florida with a suitcase full of cash and deposit it without being questioned as to its origin, as long as we insist on living and driving in ways that increase our dependence on foreign oil, and as long as we invest in corporations which meddle in the politics of independent states and take profit without regard to human cost, we engage in our own destruction.

These are issues of economics, but they involve individual and collective self-discipline and a willingness to make hard choices. Similar hard choices have been required of us before during wartime. The threat to us now is more diffuse, but the consequences of inaction may be more fateful, and more global, than at any other time in our history.

Groups

Abu Nidal: Founded on 22 November 1974, the group was headed by Abu Nidal, from whom it takes its name, and consisted of 200 Palestinians from France, Italy, Spain and Austria. Its aim was to free Palestine and to establish a new Palestinian state to replace the Zionist state, i.e. Israel. Abu Nidal was originally a member of al-Fatah, but he left the organisation while he was its representative to Iraq and founded his own group.

Abu Sayyaf: Literally the 'Bearer of the Sword', the group is also known as al-Harakat al-Islamiya. Founded in 1991 and originally sponsored by Libya, Abu Sayyaf is a splinter faction of the Moro National Liberation Front run by Abdouradjik Aboubakar Janjalani. Its aim is to establish an Islamist state in Mindanao, an island in the southern Philippines. At the end of 2002, its membership was estimated at several hundred active fighters and a thousand supporters. Its main activities are extortion, bomb attacks, kidnappings and assassinations.

Al-Fatah: Founded in 1957 by Palestinians in exile in Kuwait, the group has been headed for decades by Yasser Arafat. From the outset, al-Fatah was committed to the independence of Palestinians. Its aim was direct military confrontation with Israel in order to win back lost land from the Jews. Al-Fatah undertook its first armed action against Israel in January 1965. After the Six Days War in 1967 and the Israeli occupation of the territories conquered, numerous Palestinian refugees in the neighbouring countries encouraged the development of the group which became the armed wing of the PLO. Until the Gulf War, al-Fatah was financially supported by moderate Arab countries such as Saudi Arabia and Kuwait. The rapprochement between Yasser Arafat and Saddam Hussein at the outbreak of the Gulf War led to the interruption of this financial support. Al-Fatah was also materially supported by the former Soviet Union, Czechoslovakia, China and North Korea. Leaving behind the military line followed in the 1950s and 1960s, in recent years al-Fatah has changed strategy and adopted a political approach in order to obtain a democratic state in Palestine. During the second Intifada, however, some of its factions resumed armed attacks against Israel. Al-Fatah's potential is estimated at 6,000–8,000 active members (www.fateh.net).

Al-Muhajiroun: The Syrian Sheikh Omar Bakri Mohammad founded it as an anti-Saudi pressure group in 1983 in Jeddah. However, in 1986, he was forced to leave the country and now the group's headquarters are in London. It is based on an ideological Islamic movement and believes that changing thoughts and concepts in accordance with Islam is the only way for the correct revival and progress of Muslim culture (www.almuha jiroun.com).

Al-Muqatila: An Islamist fundamentalist armed group, al-Muqatila was founded in Libya in the years following the end of the anti-Soviet Jihad by Arab-Afghans linked to Osama bin Laden's network. In 1996, in cooperation with Osama bin Laden's followers, the group attempted to assassinate Gaddafi, considered an infidel by its members.

Al-Qaeda: Literally meaning the scroll or the base, it was originally formed around 1988 by Osama bin Laden and Abu Ubaydah al-Banshiri, bin Laden's top military commander, to maintain a record of the Arabs who volunteered to fight in the anti-Soviet Jihad. Al-Qaeda also helped to finance, recruit and train Sunni Islamic extremists for the Afghan resistance. Soon, it became a multi-ethnic Sunni Islamist insurgent organisation which remained active well beyond the end of the Afghan war.

Its primary aim is the establishment of a pan-Islamist Caliphate throughout the Muslim world and therefore it seeks the collaboration of other Islamist armed organisations to overthrow existing regimes regarded as 'non-Islamic' and to expel Westerners and non-Muslims from Muslim countries. In 1998, it merged with the Egyptian Islamic Jihad (al-Jihad). Its membership is thought to be anywhere between several hundred and several thousand people.

Al-Tawhid: A Palestinian Islamic group (apparently a sub-group within the al-Qaeda network), al-Tawhid is reportedly headed by Mohammad Sarkawi or, according to other sources, Abu Mussab al-Zarqawi. The group has arranged false documents for more than 100 al-Qaeda fighters who escaped from Afghanistan during the 2001 war. It also provided them with funds and a safe haven (near Teheran), and then organised their movement out of Iran to other areas in the Middle East and the West.

Ansar al-Islam: Literally translated as 'Supporters or Partisans of Islam', this is an Islamist armed group founded in September 2001 in northeast Kurdistan, northern Iraq. Initially, the group was led by al-Mullah Kreker, also known as Mala Kreker, who was arrested in Amsterdam in January 2003. Ansar al-Islam's goal is to create an Islamist state in Kurdistan modelled upon the former Taliban regime in Afghanistan.

Autodefensas Unidas de Colombia (AUC): The United Self Defence Forces of Colombia is an armed organisation founded in 1997; it has its roots in the paramilitary armies built up by Colombian drug lords and landlords. Its base is in northern Colombia and its leader is Carlos Castanos. In recent years, the AUC has extended its reach and now operates throughout central and western Colombia and also in several cities. It has an estimated army of 8,000 members and is growing rapidly. The AUC provides the landowners who finance it with some social services and defence against leftist insurgents. According to US Drug Enforcement Administration's officials the group is involved in – and profits from – the drug trade (www.colombia-libre.org/colombialibre/pp/asp).

Bader–Meinhof/Red Army Faction (RAF): Born out of the student protest movement in the 1960s in Germany, the group was founded by Andreas Baader and Gudrun Ensslin. Its ideology propounded a commitment to violence in the service of the class struggle. It developed an extensive network of underground 'urban guerrillas' and left-wing sympathisers who claimed to be motivated by disgust at what they considered the mindless materialism and fascist tendencies of German society. The Red Army Faction operated in West Germany, but used East Germany as a safe haven. It carried out several armed attacks against US and NATO targets, including bombings, assassinations, kidnappings and robberies. However, by 1997, German authorities announced that the Red Army Faction was no longer a serious terrorist threat. In April 1998, the RAF itself announced that it was disbanding.

Barbagia Rossa: Considered the Sardinian column of the Red Brigades, the group first became prominent on 27 March 1978, when it took responsibility for an incendiary assault against a van that was carrying detainees. Later that year, the group assaulted a radio-goniometric station of the army and got hold of several arms. From January 1979 it began its campaign against the 'militarisation of the territory' and carried out numerous assaults against army barracks.

Christian Phalange in Lebanon: Founded in 1936 by Pierre Jumayyil (also spelt as Gemayel), the Phalange or Phalanxes (*Kataib* in Arabic) was mostly a Maronite organisation whose followers were known as Phalangists. Its policies were Western-oriented and right wing. Its powerful militia, supported by Israel, participated actively on the Christian side in the 1975 Lebanese civil war. In the late 1970s, as its militia led by Pierre's son, Bashir, seized control of other Christian forces, it became known as the Lebanese Forces (LF). By the mid- to late 1980s, however, after Bashir's assassination and Pierre's death, the Phalange's power ebbed and it lost control of the LF.

Contras: This was a Nicaraguan counter-revolutionary armed group that opposed the elected Sandinistas' government of Nicaragua. The Contras was created by the US in the early 1980s from the supporters of the deposed right-wing government of Anastasio Somoza Debayle, exiled in Honduras and Costa Rica. Members included several thousands of former officers of Somoza's National Guard. Initially, the group was known as Fuerza Armadas Revolucionarias de Nicaragua (Nicaraguan Armed Revolutionary Forces) or FARN, but later it split into several groups, which became known as Contras. The group was financially dependent on the US who supplied official and covert aid, mostly through the CIA. Among the most famous covert operations in favour of the Contras is the 'Irangate' scandal, whereby the CIA sold, through the brokerage of Israel, arms to Iran. Part of the profit from the sale was used to fund the Contras.

Egyptian Islamic Jihad: The group is a terror movement derived from the Muslim Brotherhood. The Islamic Jihad was founded in 1979 by Abd el Salam Faraj and is presently led by Abbud al-Zoumar but, according to the Gama'a al-Islamiya, Egypt's largest militant group, it considers Sheikh Omar Abdel Rahman as its spiritual leader. Its most famous action was President Anwar Sadat's murder in October 1981 by Lieutenant Khaled al-Islambouli. It has an activist membership of about 3,000, many of whom fought in the anti-Soviet Jihad. It is set up mainly near Cairo and in High Egypt. Recently, the group founded a faction called the Tala'ah al-Fatah (avant-garde of the conquest) headed by Dr Ayman al-Zawahiri. Its terror activities are mainly concentrated against people holding important posts in the political or military hierarchy. The group did not agree to the cease-fire decided by the Gama'a al-Islamiya and in 1998 it merged with al-Qaeda.

Ejercito de Liberacion Nacional (ELN): The National Liberation Army is a Colombian Marxist armed group formed in 1964 by Fabio Vásquez Castaño and other urban intellectuals inspired by Fidel Castro and Che Guevara. The ELN used economic terror against oil companies, attacking pipelines and oil operations. From 1982 to 1999 it carried out 691 attacks of this kind, forcing Colombia, a large oil producer, to become an oil importer in 1992. Its activities are mainly kidnappings, hijackings, bombing, extortion and guerrilla ambushes. Its membership is estimated at around 3,000–5,000 active members and an unknown number of supporters. Since 1999 Bogota's central government has made several attempts to initiate dialogue with the group, but has remained unsuccessful (www.web.net/eln/).

ETA: ETA stands for Euskadi ta Askatasuna, which means 'Basque Fatherland and Liberty' in the Basque language. It is an armed group fighting for the independence of the Basque country from Spain. ETA originates from the EKIN, a nationalist group that changed its name to the Euskadi ta Askatasuna in 1958. The group's initial activities involved planting explosives in Basque cities such as Bilbao. In 1961, ETA carried out its first military action after the death of General Francisco Franco. In the following years it intensified its violence by targeting security forces and politicians. The group is still active in Spain and maintains ties with armed groups all over the world. Its membership is believed to be quite small, perhaps no more than 20 hard-core activists and several hundred supporters, and its headquarters are believed to be in the Basque provinces of Spain and France.

Farabundo Marti Liberation National (FMLN): Formed on 10 October 1980, the FMNL was made up of Salvadorian peasants who were trained as guerrilla fighters. Many were adept at using explosives, firearms and setting booby-traps. The group turned away from guerrilla warfare in 1992 to become a political party (www.fmnl.org.sv).

Fenian Brotherhood: The Brotherhood was a secret Irish-American revolutionary society founded in the United States by John O'Mahony in 1858. Its aim was to form a league of Irishmen in all parts of the world against British rule in Ireland.

Fretelin: Also known as the Revolutionary Front for an Independent East Timor, Fretelin was formed in 1974. Its aim was to achieve the full independence of East Timor from Indonesia. It was the main resistance party during the Indonesian occupation, which came to an end in 2001.

Fuerzas Armadas Revolucionarias de Colombia (FARC): Founded in 1964 by Manuel Marulanda Vélez and other members of the Central Committee of the Communist Party of Colombia (Partido Comunista de Colombia – PCC), the FARC is an armed organisation with a Marxist bent whose aim is to overthrow the government. It claims to defend the rural poor against Colombia's wealthy classes and therefore opposes the American influence in Colombia, the privatisation of natural resources and the presence of multinational corporations. The group targets wealthy landowners, foreign tourists and prominent international and domestic officials. It is structured in a military fashion and its members, estimated at around 7,000 men, wear uniforms and behave as a regular army. Its importance has grown thanks to the alliance with Colombian narco-traffickers. Experts estimate that the FARC takes in between $200 million and $400 million annually – at least half from the illegal drug trade. The rest is generated through kidnappings, extortion schemes and an unofficial 'tax' levied in the countryside (www.contrast.org/mirrors/farc/).

Groupe Islamique Armè (GIA): It is an Islamist armed group believed to have been founded in March 1992 by the

Arab-Afghans who returned to Algeria after the Afghan war. It is headed by the emir Abou Abd Ahmed, also known as 'Djafaar al-Afghani'. The GIA's final aim is to overthrow the country's current military-backed government and establish an Islamist state based on the Sharia. Its membership is estimated at around 20,000–25,000 men. Since December 1993, the GIA has carried out particularly violent attacks against foreigners in Algeria as well as against Algerian citizens.

Hamas: The group was created on 14 December 1987 (five days after the beginning of the Intifada) as a Palestinian branch of the Muslim Brotherhood with the objective to establish an Islamic Palestinian state in place of Israel. The PLO's main rival in the territories occupied by Israel, Hamas has benefited from Yasser Arafat's failures on the international front, especially after the Gulf War. It considers war as the only means to free the occupied territories; it has established a direct link between Islam and the liberation of the occupied territories that limits, or even excludes, all compromises on the issue. It opposes all negotiations with Israel and is responsible for many attacks in Israel, primarily suicide bombings. Its activities are concentrated in the Gaza Strip and a few areas in the West Bank. Hamas's objectives as stated in its charter of 18 August 1988 include in addition to the liberation of Palestine and the creation of an Islamic Palestinian state, the rejection of any Western presence in Muslim countries and opposition to the secularisation and Westernisation of Arab society.

Harkat-ul-Ansar: Its original name was Hizb-ul-Mujahedin. It is a Sunni organisation formed in Karachi, Pakistan, in 1980, primarily to send volunteers to Afghanistan to help Afghan rebels fight against Soviet forces.

Harkat ul-Mujahedin (HUM): A radical Muslim movement operating in Kashmir, the group is derived from the Harkat-ul-Ansar (HUA) created in 1993 to coordinate the actions of the Islamist Pakistanis with those of the Afghan Mujahedin. Led by Fazl Rahman Khalil and Farouk Kashimiri, his second-in-command, it is responsible for the kidnappings of several Westerners in Kashmir during the summer of 1995. Described as a terrorist organisation at the end of 1997, the HUA changed its name to Harkat ul-Mujahedin. The HUM is considered to be the main movement in Kashmir and its popularity has been widely reinforced following the American bombardments of Khost on 20 August 1998.

Hizbollah: Translated as the Party of God, it is a radical Lebanese Shia group formed in 1982 in response to the Israeli invasion of Lebanon. It advocates the establishment of Islamic rule in Lebanon as happened in Iran, the liberation of all occupied Arab lands and the expulsion of non-Muslims from Muslim countries. The group is sponsored by Iran and predominantly operates in the Bekaa Valley, south of Beirut. Its membership is estimated at 40,000 men in Lebanon and several thousand supporters. It possesses heavy artillery such as multiple BM-21 rockets. A number of its members are known or suspected to have been involved in numerous anti-US armed attacks. The Hizbollah also goes by the name of Islamic Jihad, but its official armed wing is called the Islamic Resistance. The latter, created in 1983, oversees military operations in south Lebanon. It has 400 well-trained fighters and 5,000 supporters. Besides sporadic attacks (bombings or murders), it leads proper military operations against the Israeli or south Lebanon's army. Militarily organised, the Islamic Resistance's activities have become increasingly illegal since 1993. The group has tried especially to establish a popular base in south Lebanon through social aid activities, such as its Jihad al-Hoed (holy effort for the reconstruction) that finances the reconstruction of buildings destroyed by the Israeli army. It also gives $25,000 to the families of the 'martyrs' who die during its suicide operations.

Irgun (IZL): Also known as Irgun Zvai Le'umi (National Military Organisation), and in Hebrew by its acronym Etzel, the group was an underground Jewish armed organisation founded in Jerusalem in the spring of 1931 by a group of Haganah commanders, headed by Avraham Tehomi. Initially concerned with repelling Arab riots in the country, in 1939 it focused on British rule. On 1 February 1944, Irgun initiated a revolt against British rule over Palestine, demanding that the British leave the country forthwith and a Jewish state be established. Disappointed by British government policy, on 22 July 1946 the group's terror attacks culminated in the blowing up of a wing of the King David Hotel in Jerusalem which hosted the headquarters of the Palestine government and the British military command. The united fighting front disintegrated in August 1946, after the arrest of the Jewish Agency leaders, but Irgun continued to wage armed attacks on military and government personnel and property. After the Declaration of Independence of Israel, the high command of the group offered to disband the organisation and integrate its members into the army of the new Jewish state. This was achieved in September 1948. Among the Irgun leaders was Menachen Begin, who later became prime minister of Israel and the winner with Yasser Arafat of the Nobel Peace Prize.

Irish National Liberation Army (INLA): Created on 10 December 1974, it is an extreme left-wing Catholic armed group dedicated to removing British forces from Northern Ireland and unifying Ireland. A splinter faction of the Provisional Irish Republican Army (PIRA), it adopted the name People's Liberation Army (PLA) and is directed by Hugh Torney. The group acts as the armed wing of the Irish Republican Socialist Party, which accepts the use of force to achieve its political objectives, which include the creation of a socialist republic in Ireland subdivided into 32 counties. Towards the late 1980s the INLA underwent extensive restructuring and absorbed many smaller groups. It is now known as the Irish People's Liberation Organisation. Its activities include bombings, assassinations, kidnappings, extortion and robberies. The group is believed to have a membership of several dozen gunmen and bombers, plus several hundred sympathisers.

Islamic Movement of Kurdistan (IMK): Based in Halabja, northern Iraq, the IMK appears to be split three ways, with allegiances to Saudi Arabia, Iran and Turkey. The combined strength of its forces is less than 1,500 armed men.

Islamic Movement of Uzbekistan (IMU): Founded in 1999, it is a coalition of Islamic militants from Uzbekistan and other Central Asian states opposed to Uzbekistani President Islom Karimov's secular regime. Its aim is the establishment of an Islamic state in Uzbekistan and it has approximately 2,000 active armed men as members. Before 2001, the IMU concentrated its activities against the government of Uzbekistan, mainly carrying out kidnappings, hostage taking and car bombs. Since October 2001, however, many of its members seem to have been either killed or disbanded. Its military leader Juma Namangiani was allegedly killed during an air strike in November the same year in Afghanistan. The IMU financially benefits from the drug trade in Central Asia.

Islamic Salvation Front (FIS): An Islamic movement, it was founded on 10 March 1989 by Abbasi Madani, who remains its president even though he is incarcerated in a prison in Algeria. The FIS was the largest and most influential opposition group in Algeria. In January 1991 when it won 188 seats in the Algerian parliament, the elections were declared void and a military junta took control of the country. Subsequently, the FIS was banned, leading to the spread of violence and the formation of the group's military wing the 'Islamic Salvation Army'. Later, the FIS accepted amnesty while other Islamist groups, such as the GIA, continued the armed struggle (www.ccfis.org/englishdefault.asp).

Jaish-I-Mohammad (Army of Mohammad): The group emerged out of the Harkat ul-Mujahedin in the months following the hijacking of an Indian Airlines plane from Kathmandu in December 1999. Headed by Maulana Masood Azhar, it is based in Pakistan and wants to overthrow Indian rule in Kashmir.

Jamiat-ul-Ulema-e-Islam (JUI): The Jamiat-ul-Ulema-e-Islam (JUI) is a Pakistani political group led by Maulana Fazlur Rahman. Formed in 1945 after splitting from the Jamiat-ul-Ulema-e-Hind, its objective was an independent Pakistan. In 1977 the JUI contested the National Assembly elections as a component of the Pakistan National Alliance. It did not sympathise with General Zia's Islamisation programme and in 1981 joined other groups who demanded free elections. In 1990, the JUI won six seats in the National Assembly and in the 1993 national elections the JUI was the main component of the Islami Jamhoori Mahaz, which won four seats in the National Assembly. In the 2002 elections, the party won several seats as part of the Muttahida Majlis-e-Amal and Maulana Fazlur Rahman was in the running as prime minister. However, he lost and is now part of the opposition.

Japanese Red Army (JRA): Formed around 1970 after breaking away from the Japanese Communist League-Red Army Faction, its objectives are the removal of the monarchy and of the Japanese government and the advent of a global Marxist revolution. However, it operates mainly as a 'mercenary' movement. It is headed by Fusako Shigenobu. Its members have been trained in camps in the Bekaa Valley (Lebanon). During the Cold War, the JRA received support from the USSR and East Germany but, with the fall of the Soviet bloc, it seems that China took over as a sponsor in order to destabilise its main rival in the Pacific area, Japan. Japanese police efforts and ideological weariness have reduced the group's members to about 20–30 die-hards, all of whom are in exile in Lebanon, Afghanistan, Romania, North Korea and, according to some persistent rumours, even in Colombia. Today the JRA as an organisation seems to be inactive, even though its leaders (Fusako Shigenobu and Kunio Bando) are still at large and wanted by the police.

Jemaah Islamiyah: The Jemaah Islamiyah dates back to the late 1970s. It is a militant Islamist group active in several South East Asian countries; its aims include the establishment of a Muslim fundamentalist state in the region. The group has its roots in Darul Islam, a violent radical movement that advocated the introduction of Islamic law in Indonesia. Abu Bakar, an Indonesian of Yemeni descent, is thought to be the group's spiritual leader. It has an estimated membership of 2,000 armed men in Malaysia alone. It operates in South East Asia, including Indonesia, Malaysia, Singapore and possibly the Philippines and Thailand. Indonesian officials have jailed several members of the group for allegedly planning the October 2002 bombing that killed nearly 200 people in a Bali nightclub.

Komando Jihad: Komando Jihad was formed in 1977 in Indonesia with the intention to persuade men associated with previous Muslim rebellions to launch a renewed drive for an Islamic state. The Komando Jihad also aimed at discrediting the PPP, the Muslim Political Party in Indonesia.

Kopassus, Group IV: The Special Forces Command (KOPASSUS), also known as 'militer khussus' or 'milsus' (special military), was founded in 1952. The group engaged in acts of state terrorism in Indonesia. By the late 1990s its membership had reached 6,000 armed men. Part of the Indonesian security forces under Suharto and Sukarno, the KOPASSUS was divided into various groups. Group IV specifically handled intelligence operations and its members were trained in intelligence gathering, a variety of special operations techniques and sabotage.

Kosovo Liberation Army (KLA): Also known as the UCK in the Albanian acronym, it is generally considered as a guerrilla movement aiming to unite the Muslim populations of Kosovo, Macedonia and Albania into a greater Albania. The KLA does not operate like a monolithic organisation, but as small relatively autonomous units. Its members are grouped under a military-like structure, they wear uniforms and distinctive badges. Between 1995 and 1998, the KLA targeted the Serbian police and local political figures in Kosovo as well as the Kosovars suspected of collaborating with the Serbian police. Since mid-1998, the group has become better organised and better armed thanks to the pillaging of Serbian and Albanian ammunition, the financial help of Muslim and Western countries and the interaction with bin Laden's terror network. At the peak of its strength, during the Kosovo war, its membership was estimated to be around 12,000–20,000 men in arms.

Kurdistan Workers Party (PKK): The party was founded on 27 November 1978, inspired by the leftist student organisations in Turkey in the 1960s. Its ideological base was primarily created by Abdullah Ocalan and its main goal was the setting up of an independent Kurdish state in south-eastern Turkey. Until the 1980s, the group mostly conducted locally supported attacks on tribal chiefs in the Urfa province. After the military coup in Turkey on 12 September 1980, the PKK leaders moved to the Syrian-controlled Bekaa Valley. In 1982, thanks to financial assistance from Kurdish businessmen and workers in Libya, political backing from the Iraqi Kurds and training in Lebanon and Syria, the PKK expanded its activities. Between 1980 and 1984, while Ocalan established his power, some of his internal dissenters deserted him and established their own organisations, such as TEVGER (Kurdistan Liberation Movement). By 1992, the PKK was reputed to have about 10,000 militants and supporters (www.pkk.org).

Lashkar-e-Taiba: The Lashkar-e-Taiba (the Army of the Pure) envisions the expansion of the Jihad in Jammu and Kashmir to the rest of India and the creation of two independent homelands for the Muslims of South and North India. Based in Pakistan, it provides military training for its members, which includes the use of arms and ammunition, ambush and survival techniques. In January 2002, the organisation was declared terrorist by the Pakistan government and banned.

Laskar Jihad: Defined also as the Indonesian Holy Warriors, this is a paramilitary organisation that has threatened to wage Jihad against the region's Christians, especially in the Moluccas. Since 1999, the Laskar has also been linked to several raids on Christian communities in the north of the Halmahera island in which at least 200 people have been killed and many more injured.

Lebanese National Movement (LNM): The movement was formed in 1976 in Lebanon by Kamal Jumblatt to bring about political reform in the country in alliance with the PLO. When Jumblatt was assassinated in 1977, the LNM abandoned its programme of political reform and in 1980 began building bridges with the traditional Islamic leadership. Israel's invasion of Lebanon in 1982 struck a blow at both the PLO and the LNM.

Liberation Tigers of Tamil Eelam (LTTE): A separatist movement in the north of Sri Lanka, it was created as a result of the sporadic insurrectionary movement that has shook this region since 1948. The LTTE appeared in 1977 to carry out a guerrilla war in Sri Lanka. Its members are estimated at 8,000 armed men and it essentially operates within Sri Lanka, but has also conducted some operations in India, in the state of Tamil Nadu where it has many supporters. The Black Tigers, the LTTE's most violent wing, have committed some of the group's bloodiest attacks: the bomb attack that killed Indian prime minister Rajiv Gandhi (May 1991), the murder of Lalith Athulamudali, Sri Lankan opposition leader (April 1993) and the murder of Sri Lankan President Ranasinghe Premadasa (May 1993). The Black Tigers have also led two truck bomb attacks against the Central Bank in Colombo (January 1996) and the Colombo World Trade Center (October 1997). Its members are said to carry a cyanide capsule to commit suicide if they are arrested. The Black Tigers were the first armed group to use suicide bombers. The LTTE also have a naval unit, the Sea Tigers, to create problems for the Sri Lankan army's northern garrisons, which receive supplies only by sea or air. The Sea Tigers also have a suicide unit called the Black Sea Tigers. The LTTE's operations are financed by 'grants' – more or less voluntary – made by the Tamil diaspora in Western Europe and the US. It also has a significant overseas support structure for fundraising, weapons procurement and propaganda activities (www.eelam.com).

Moro Islamic Liberation Front: Based in Mindanao, this armed group was formed in 1978 when Hashim Salamat, with the support of the ethnic Maguindanaos from Mindanao, split from the Moro National Liberation Front (MNLF). It advocates a more moderate and conciliatory approach towards the government. Its membership is estimated at around 2,900 men. The group's military branch called the Bangsa Moro Islamic Liberation Front, however, is more radical than the MNLF and refuses to accept the peace treaty signed between the present and previous governments.

Movimento 19 Abril (M19): The Movimento 19 Abril was founded in 1974. In 1980 it became known for the occupation of the embassy of the Dominican Republic in Bogota. In 1990 the group abandoned the armed struggle after 16 years to form the political party Alianza Democratica M19.

Movimento Revolucionario Tupac Amaru (MRTA): A revolutionary movement with Marxist-Leninist leanings created in 1983, its name is derived from Tupac Amaru, the leader of the Indian revolt against the Spaniards in 1780. Its main operational area is around Lima and in the departments of Junin and San Martin. On 17 December 1996, a commando unit of

14 men seized the Japanese embassy and 400 of the ambassador's guests. During the negotiations conducted by President Fujimori, where he notably asked for Fidel Castro's mediation, an operation of intervention was prepared in secret. The president himself successfully directed the operation on 22 April 1997, in which a hostage lost his life. The Tupac Amaru's main financial sources are extortion, narco-traffickers' protection, kidnappings and burglary. It is believed to have 100 active armed members (www.voz-rebelde.de).

Muslim Brotherhood: This is a radical Muslim organisation, created in 1928 by Abd el-Rahman al-Banna, an Egyptian teacher. Since 1935, the Muslim Brotherhood has maintained contact with Hadj Amino Al-Husseini, Mufti of Jerusalem, and taken part in the Palestinian insurrection in 1936. In 1945, a Palestinian branch of the movement was created in Jerusalem by Saïd Ramadan. The movement quickly became successful and many of its members took part in the war of 1948. Held responsible for the murder of the Egyptian prime minister in 1948, al-Banna was murdered, probably by government agents. The organisation was declared outlaw in 1957 by Nasser, who feared an attack against himself. About 20,000 brothers were jailed. The Muslim Brotherhood's aim is the reinforcement of Islamic culture in the Muslim countries. Its Palestinian wing has generated the al-Moujamma Al-Islami in the occupied territories, from which Hamas was created. Although adhering to the final aim to free Palestine from Israeli occupation, the Muslim Brotherhood gives priority to Islam's reinforcement and growth. Its financial resources come largely from Saudi Arabia (www.ummah.net/ikhwan).

National Front for the Liberation of Libya: This is a political movement against the regime of Muammar Gaddafi in Libya. It was formed in October 1981 with the goal of ending Gaddafi's reign and establishing a constitutional and democratically elected government in Libya.

Northern Alliance: It is an Afghan Islamic rebel faction actively and belligerently opposed to the Taliban regime since their taking control of the country in September 1996 under the leadership of Mullah Mohammad Omar. It is primarily a coalition of warlords who, at that time, controlled 5 per cent of Afghanistan, while the Taliban controlled nearly all the rest. Its leader Ahmed Shah Massoud was killed by al-Qaeda on 7 September 2001. In November 2001, with the help of US military forces, the Northern Alliance defeated the Taliban and entered the country's capital Kabul.

Palestine Liberation Organisation (PLO): A Palestinian nationalist movement and the central organisation of all Palestinian movements, the PLO was created in 1964 by Ahmed Shukeiry under the auspices of Egypt. Its objective, as stated in its charter established in May 1964, is the creation of an independent Palestinian State on the territory today covered by Israel or, at least, in the occupied territories (Gaza and the West Bank). Its leader is Yasser Arafat and the organisation is divided into various subgroups: the Popular Front for the Liberation of Palestine, the Popular Democratic Front for the Liberation of Palestine, General Command and al-Fatah. Originally, its aim was the destruction of Israel and to achieve this it launched a terror campaign. However, in the 1990s the PLO decided to move towards the political arena. On 9 September 1993, in a letter to Israeli Prime Minister Rabin and Norwegian Foreign Minister Holst, Arafat committed the PLO to cease all violent and terrorist activities. However, during the second Intifada, elements of the PLO resumed armed attacks (www.pna.net).

Popular Front for the Liberation of Palestine (PFLP): The Popular Front for the Liberation of Palestine (PFLP) is a Marxist–Leninist group founded in 1967 by George Habash. It was one of the first Palestinian organisations to use political violence to draw attention to its cause. The organisation carried out a long list of armed attacks in the international arena, particularly hijackings. With the collapse of the Soviet Union, the PFLP found itself pushed to the periphery of the Palestinian armed struggle and was replaced, in the occupied territories, by Islamist groups such as Hamas. Attempting to regain the initiative after the signing of the Declaration of Principles in 1993, the PFLP joined forces with a 10-member rejection front, based in Damascus. It forbade its members to participate in the Palestinian elections in 1996. However, three years later, Abu Ali Mustafa, the designated successor of George Habash, travelled to Cairo to negotiate better terms with Yasser Arafat and in September 1999 he received permission to enter the Palestinian autonomous areas. The headquarters of the PFLP were also moved from Damascus to the Palestinian city of Ramallah. On 27 August 2001, Abu Ali Mustafa was killed in an attack carried out by the Israeli army and Ahmed Sadat was appointed general secretary on 3 October of the same year (www.pflp-pal.org).

Provisional IRA: The Provisional Irish Republican Army (PIRA) is a radical armed group formed in 1969 as a spin-off of the original Irish Republican Army whose origins date back to 1916. Its aim is the removal of British forces from Northern Ireland and the unity of Ireland. The group rose to prominence in the summer of 1969 after riots and clashes between Catholics and Protestants in Ulster. It then began conducting guerrilla ambush operations against the British Army and police. In 1981 ten IRA prisoners, lead by Bobby Sands, died as a result of a hunger strike in the Maze, a Northern Ireland prison. The provisional IRA received financial support and aid from sympathisers in the US and some of its members have received arms from Libya and training from the PLO. The IRA used bombings, assassinations, extortion, robberies, but rarely kidnappings, to raise funds. Before its 1994 cease-fire, its targets included senior British government officials, military and police in Northern Ireland and Northern Irish Loyalist paramilitary groups. Since breaking its cease-fire in February 1996, IRA operations have included bombing campaigns on train and subway stations and shopping areas on mainland Britain, attacking the British military and Royal Ulster Constabulary in Northern Ireland, and British military facilities in Europe. The IRA officially ceased its armed struggle after the Good Friday Agreement of 1998.

Red Brigades (Brigate Rosse, BR): The Red Brigades was formed in 1969 in Italy out of the student and workers' movements. Its ideology advocated violence in the service of class warfare and revolution. The Red Brigades possessed the most solid and consistent ideology among all European extreme left armed organisations of the 1970s and 1980s. The group was based in and operated from Italy and mainly targeted symbols of the establishment such as industrialists, politicians and businessmen. In 1978, in what became the hallmark of Italian political terrorism, the group kidnapped former prime minister, Aldo Moro. He was held captive for nearly two months, before his corpse was finally found in a car in the heart of Rome. The same year, *New York Times* reported that the core of the Red Brigades consisted of 400–500 full-time members. From the mid-1980s onwards, however, the Red Brigades entered a period of decline and became increasingly isolated from its working-class base and from public opinion. In 1981 the *pentiti* (repentant) legislation was issued: it encouraged defection and enhanced the powers of the security forces, helping to hasten the group's decline. In April 1984, four imprisoned leaders of the organisation published an 'open letter' in which they rejected the armed struggle as pointless in the new political context of Europe. That was the beginning of the *Battaglia della Liberta* (Struggle for Freedom) to which many former members of the group adhered. The same year the group split into two separate factions: the Communist Combatant Party (BR-PCC) and the Union of Combatant Communists (BR-UCC). Some of its members are believed to be living clandestinely in other European countries, especially in France where they have taken refuge.

Revolutionary People's Liberation Party/Front (DHKP/C): The group was formed in 1978 in Turkey under the name Devrimci Sol, or Dev Sol, a splinter faction of the Turkish People's Liberation Party/Front. However, it was given its present name in 1994 after factional infighting. It espouses a Marxist ideology and is virulently anti-US and anti-NATO. Armed robberies and extortion are its main source of funding.

Revolutionary United Front (RUF): The RUF is a rebel group formed in 1991 with support from the National Patriotic Front of Liberia and is based in Sierra Leone. The RUF uses guerrilla tactics and its aim is to topple the current government of Sierra Leone and to retain control of the lucrative diamond-producing regions of the country. The group funds itself largely through the extraction and sale of diamonds obtained in the areas of Sierra Leone under its control. A UN report on the country stated that President Charles Taylor of Liberia provides support to the RUF.

Second Soran Unit: This group, with between 350 and 400 armed men led by Asad Muhammad Hasan (Aso Hawleri), was the single largest military unit in northern Iraq within the Islamic Movement of Kurdistan (and its successor, the Islamic Unity Movement). Approximately 50–60 Arabs also fight with the group, many of whom trained in Afghanistan. In 1998, the Second Soran Unit created a political front group called the Central Islamic Faction led by Aso Hawleri, several Arabs and a Turk named Abu Khubayi Barachak (now imprisoned by the KDP on terrorism charges). After the split in the IMK and Islamic Unity Movement, the Second Soran Unit initially became independent, but eventually joined the Tawhid Islamic Front.

Sendero Luminoso: Literally translated as 'shining path', the group derives its name from Mariategui, an avowed Marxist, who once stated that Marxism was a 'shining path to the future'. Shining Path, established in the late 1960s in Peru by former university professor Abimael Guzman, arose in response to Peru's entrenched system of race- and class-based discrimination, which has deeply impoverished most of the country's population, especially citizens of indigenous descent. It seeks to topple the existing Peruvian government in favour of an Indian-run socialist system. The group's terror tactics have resulted in the deaths of between 10,000 and 12,000 people since its creation in 1970. Oscar Ramirez Durand and Judith Ramos Cuadros currently lead the group. Funding for the group continues to come primarily from robberies, crimes and drug trade, although a significant revenue source remains the 'war tax' that the group demands from local businesses and individuals. Its network consists of approximately 1,500–2,500 armed militants and a larger number of supporters, mostly in rural areas.

Stern Gang: This was an extremist group formed as a spin-off of the Irgun in 1939. Both groups were especially active during and after the Second World War against the British authorities in Palestine. Both maintained several thousand armed men until all Israeli forces were integrated in June 1948.

Ulster Defence Association (UDA): Formed in 1971 as an umbrella organisation for loyalist paramilitary groups, the UDA remained a legal group until 1992 when the British government proscribed it. It has been linked to pipe bombings and sporadic assaults on Catholics in Northern Ireland. It has an estimated membership of 2,000–5,000 armed members, with several hundred active in paramilitary operations.

UNITA (União Nacional para a Independência Total de Angola): It is an 'Africanist' party, emphasising ethnic and rural rights, formed in 1966 to fight against Angola's government.

Later, it renounced the armed struggle but, after losing the 1992 elections, UNITA took up arms again. Today, it is involved in negotiations with the government on the future of the country and an uneasy cease-fire appears to be holding.

World Islamic Front for the Jihad against Jews and Crusaders: Al-Qaeda (see above) is sometimes known by this name as well.

Glossary

Afghan Pipeline: System of shipment and distribution of supplies and cash to the Mujahedin in Afghanistan set up by the CIA and the ISI during the anti-Soviet Jihad.

Anni di Piombo: Period of most intense political violence in Italy (1969–81) waged against the state by both right- and left-wing armed groups. 'Anni di Piombo' is commonly translated as the 'years of the bullet'.

Anti-Soviet Jihad: Common definition of the Afghan war of 1979–89. The war was triggered by the Soviet invasion of Afghanistan in December 1979 and ended with the Red Army's defeat and withdrawal in February 1989.

Arab-Afghans: Term originally used to distinguish between Afghan and non-Afghan Muslim fighters in the anti-Soviet Jihad. The term Arab-Afghans now includes all Muslims who joined in the fight.

ARENA: Abbreviation for Alianza Republicana Nacionalista (Nationalist Republican Alliance) a coalition group of El Salvador. It was founded in September 1981 by rightist military officers, landowners and leaders of the death squads.

Armed Community: Expression used in the jargon of Italian armed groups to define members of armed organisations.

Asian Development Bank: Established in 1967, the bank assists in economic development and promotes growth and cooperation in Asian developing member countries. A body of 47 members, which includes both Asian and Western developed and developing countries, owns the bank.

ATTA: Abbreviation for Afghan Transit Trade Agreement. In 1950 Afghanistan, a landlocked country, signed this agreement with Pakistan guaranteeing the right to import duty-free goods through the port of Karachi. During the anti-Soviet Jihad, ATTA became synonymous to the smuggling of Afghan duty-free goods.

Bundesbank: The German central bank, with headquarters in Frankfurt; established in 1957.

Caliph: Honorary title adopted by the Ottoman sultans in the sixteenth century, after Sultan Selim I conquered Syria and Palestine, made Egypt a satellite of the Ottoman Empire and was recognised as the guardian of the holy cities of Mecca and Medina. The term derives from the Arab *Khalifa*, which means succeed; its literal translation is Prince of the Faithful. Caliph was the Muslim title for the chief civil and religious ruler, who protected the integrity of the state and of the faith. The Caliphs were the successors of Mohammad. However, they were not prophets; 'one of the fundamental tenets of Islam is that Mohammad was the Seal of the Prophets, the last of the line that included Adam, Noah, Abraham, Moses and Jesus before him'.[1]

Caliphate: Term indicating the dominion of the Caliph.

Chador: Traditional Muslim dress for women, similar to a black coat it covers the body from head to toe.

CIA: Central Intelligence Agency, United States intelligence agency.

Colombo Plan: Founded in 1951 and known as the Colombo Plan for Cooperative Economic Development in South and South East Asia until it was expanded in 1977 and became the Colombo Plan for Cooperative Economic Development in Asia and the Pacific. It is an arrangement that permits a developing member country to approach a developed member country for assistance on a one-to-one basis. Assistance may be technical or in the form of capital or commodity aid.

Contra: Short for *contra revolucionarios* (counter-revolutionary). The term defines a member of the Nicaraguan Resistance, a right-wing armed resistance movement in the 1980s supported by the United States that fought against the national Sandinistas government. The Contras were primarily former members of the National Guard of Somosa, the former Nicaraguan dictator.

Commercial War Economy: Form of war economy run by armed groups and based on the commercialisation of local resources, i.e. coca plantations and trafficking in illegal products such as narcotics, from the regions they militarily control.

Croatian Pipeline: System of shipment and distribution of supplies and cash to the Mujahedin and Muslims fighting in the former Yugoslavia.

Crusades: Military campaigns waged by Catholic European forces to reclaim the Holy Land from Muslim control. Between the eleventh and thirteenth centuries there were eight crusades. In 1085, Pope Urban II launched the First Crusade, introducing the concept of a war sanctioned by divine power. Catholic knights who took part in them believed that they were walking a new path to heaven. For the Muslims the Crusades were military campaigns to expand the domain of Christendom and eliminate Islam.

Diaspora: Term originally used to describe the Jews living in scattered communities outside Eretz Yisrael (the Land of Israel) during and after the Babylonian Captivity (sixth century BC) and, especially, after the dispersion of the Jews from the region following the destruction of the Temple by the Romans in AD 70 and the Bar-Kokhba War in AD 132–35. In modern times the word refers to the Jews living outside Palestine or present-day Israel. When the word is applied – usually in lower case – to non-Jews, such as the Palestinian Arab refugees, the word describes the situation of the people of one country dispersed into other countries.

Drug Barons: Wealthy and powerful businessmen whose power derives from trading narcotics.

Failed States: Countries with weak or non-existent central authority. States that do not enjoy state sovereignty in the modern sense, that is, 'unquestioned physical control over the defined territory, but also an administrative presence throughout the country and the allegiance of the population to the idea of state'.[2]

Faqih: An expert in religious jurisprudence, specifically a Shia cleric whose mastery of the Qur'an, the traditions of the Prophet and the Twelve Imams, and the codices of Shia Islamic law permit him to produce binding interpretations of religious laws and regulations.

Fatwa: A technical term used in Islamic law to indicate a formal legal judgment or binding religious ruling made by a qualified Islamic scholar or jurist.

Fedayeen: Literally 'he who sacrifices himself'. The name comes from the early Palestinian refugees who, displaced by the Israelis, organised themselves in armed bands in the Sinai and Gaza Strip. Throughout the 1950s, the Fedayeen raided Israel from across the border.

Fitna: Originally considered a trial, a temptation to test the believer's faith, fitna now refers to periods of unrest and internal war within the Muslim community. It is often used in Islamic history with the specific historical sense of Civil War. In Hamas's jargon fitna has become known as the violent version of the Intifada.

Gaza Strip: Former Egyptian territory occupied by Israel in the 1967 War.

Glas'nost: Russian term for public discussion of issues and accessibility of information to the public. Devised by Soviet leader Mikhail S. Gorbachev to provoke public discussion, challenge government and party bureaucrats, and mobilise support for his policies through the media.

Gross Domestic Product (GDP): The total value of goods and services produced exclusively within a nation's domestic economy, in contrast to the gross national product (GNP). Normally computed over one-year periods.

Gross National Product (GNP): The total value of goods and services produced within a country's borders plus the income received from abroad by residents, minus payments remitted abroad by non-residents. Normally computed over one-year periods.

Guerrilla: The term derives from the Spanish 'guerrilla', meaning small war. It was originally used in Spain to describe the resistance against the Napoleonic troops. It refers to the techniques of fighting used by small groups or units against a much larger regular army. For the guerrilla to succeed it is essential to be legitimated and integrated among the civilian population. It is also known as the 'war of attrition', because its tactics are aimed at demoralising and tiring the enemy more than at defeating it. After the war in Algeria and the Vietnam War, this concept of war of attrition has been extended to the political arena.

Guerrilla War Economy: Form of war economy run by armed groups and based predominantly on the exploitation of local resources. In this model armed organisations develop close ties with local populations, which tend to share their ideological and political causes.

***Hawala*:** Term indicating an alternative or parallel remittance system to the banking system. It exists and operates outside of, or parallel to, 'traditional' banking or financial channels. The components of *hawala* that distinguish it from other systems of money transfer are trust and the extensive use of connections, such as family relationships or regional affiliations. Unlike traditional banking, *hawala* makes minimal (often no) use of any sort of negotiable instrument. Transfers of money take place based on communications between members of a network of *hawaladars*, or *hawala* dealers.

***Hawaladars*:** *Hawala* dealer.

Hijra: Literally means to migrate, to sever relations, to leave
one's tribe. Throughout the Muslim world, *hijra* refers to the
migration of Mohammad and his followers to Medina in
AD 622, marking the start of the Muslim era. In this sense,
the word has come into European languages as '*hegira*' and
is usually and somewhat misleadingly translated as 'flight'.

Hizbollah: the Party of God. This is the name borne by a
major fundamentalist Shiite movement in Lebanon formed
after the 1979 Iranian Revolution.

Imam: A word used in several senses. In general use, it means
the leader of congregational prayers; as such it implies no
ordination or special spiritual powers beyond sufficient
education to carry out this function. It is also used figurat-
ively by many Sunni (*q.v.*) Muslims to mean the leader of
the Islamic community. Among Shias (*q.v.*) the word takes
on many complex meanings; in general, however, and particularly when capitalised, it indicates a particular descendant
of the Party of Ali who is believed to have been God's designated repository of the spiritual authority inherent in that
line. The identity of this individual and the means of ascer-
taining his identity have been major issues causing divisions
among Shias.

International Monetary Fund (IMF): Established with the
World Bank in 1945, it is a specialised agency affiliated with
the United Nations and responsible for stabilising international exchange rates and payments. Its main function is to
provide loans to its members (including industrialised and
developing countries) when they experience balance of
payments difficulties. These loans frequently carry conditions
that require substantial internal economic adjustments by the
recipients, most of which are developing countries.

Irredentism: Term deriving from the Italian 'Risorgimento'.
Its root comes from the word unredeemed, unrecovered. The
Irredentist movement advocated the recovery and union to
Italy of all Italian-speaking districts, which were subjects of

other countries. The modern usage refers to the unity of people speaking the same language under a common state.

ISI: Inter Services Intelligence, Pakistani military intelligence service.

Islamic: Term used to describe the belief and adherence to the preaching of Islam.

Islamist: Term used to define members of Islamic fundamentalist armed groups. It can be defined as the beliefs of groups who officially have their core in the preaching of Islam but base their practice on the armed struggle.

Jahiliyya: State of ignorance. The Arabic word is used to define the pre-Islamic period.

Jihad: This term has often been translated as 'Holy War', a concept coined in Europe in the eleventh century which refers to the Crusades and which has no equivalent in Islam. Jihad derives from the Arabic root of 'striving'; therefore a better translation would be 'striving in the cause of God'. There are two aspects of the Jihad: the greater jihad, fighting to overcome carnal desires and evil inclinations; and the lesser jihad, the armed defence of Islam against aggressors. The term Jihad has been used by different armed groups in their violent confrontations with the West; famously Osama bin Laden called for a jihad in his *fatwa* against Americans, using the term as a 'just war' against the oppressor.

Jirga: Council, assembly or meeting to discuss political or legal issues.

KGB (Komitet Gosudarstvennoy Bezopasnosti): Committee for State Security. It was the predominant Soviet security police organisation since its establishment in 1954 as the successor to the MVD (Ministerstvo Vnutrennykh Del, Ministry of Internal Affairs). In October 1991 Gorbachev decreed that the KGB should be disbanded because of its involvement in the August coup d'état. The KGB was replaced by the SVR (foreign intelligence service) and FSB (federal security service).

Khanate: Dominion or territorial jurisdiction of a Mongol khan (ruler).

Khmer Rouge: The name given to the Cambodian communists by Prince Norodom Sihanouk in the 1960s. Later, the term was applied to the insurgents of varying ideological backgrounds who opposed the Khmer Republic regime of Lon Nol. Between 1975 and 1978, it denoted the Democratic Kampuchea regime led by the radical Pol Pot faction of the Kampuchean (or Khmer) Communist Party. After being driven from Phnom Penh by the Vietnamese invasion of Cambodia in December 1978, the Khmer Rouge went back to guerrilla warfare and joined forces with two non-communist insurgent movements to form the coalition government of Democratic Kampuchea.

Kufr: Literally meaning infidelity, unbelief, atheism, the term is used to describe those who do not believe in Islam, i.e. the infidels.

Madaris: plural of *madrassah*.

Madrassah: School, college, place of education, often linked to, or associated with, a mosque.

Maghrib: The western Islamic world (northwest Africa); distinguished from the *Mashriq*, or eastern Islamic world (the Middle East). Literally, 'the time and place of the sunset − the west'. For its Arab conquerors, the region was the 'island of the west' (*jazirat al-maghrib*), the land between the 'sea of sand' (the Sahara) and the Mediterranean. Traditionally includes Morocco, Algeria, Tunisia and Tripolitania (in Libya); more recently some sources have treated Mauritania as part of the region. Also transliterated as Maghreb.

Maquis: Guerrilla fighters' units of the French underground during the Second World War. Maquis has also been used by the French to describe the indigenous partisan groups, trained by them, who fought against the communists during the First Indochina War (1946–50).

Maronites: The largest Christian sect in Lebanon, the Maronite Church is one of a group of Christian churches known as Uniate, which are in full communion with the Holy Sea of Rome, but are separately organised and adhere to an Eastern rite. Maronites settled in the mountains of northern Lebanon in the mid-seventh century; many continue to live there and in East Beirut. They have traditionally looked to the West for cultural inspiration. They tend to be better educated and wealthier than other segments of Lebanese society. Prior to the civil war, by custom, the president of the Republic of Lebanon was a Maronite.

Mare Nostrum: Literally, our sea, term used to describe the Mediterranean sea during the Roman Empire.

Martyrdom: The suffering of death, or the sacrifice of one's own life, on account of adherence to a cause and especially to one's religious faith.

Millet: In the Ottoman Empire, this term indicated the policy of governance of non-Muslim minorities. The system created autonomous communities ruled by religious leaders responsible to the central government.

Modern Jihad: Modern interpretation of the Jihad where it becomes an instrument to fight the West. The Modern Jihad is an integral part of Islamist political violence.

Money Laundering: The process through which any money which breaks anti-money-laundering laws is 'washed' or 'recycled' through legitimate institutions. In the United States, there are some 200 classes of domestic crime and if you knowingly handle money derived from one of these crimes, then you have committed a money-laundering offence. However, only some 12–15 of these types of crimes are applicable if the crime is committed outside US borders. These crimes are related to drugs, violence, bank fraud, corruption by foreign government officials and crimes that break certain treaty obligations of the United States. The exact number of overseas crimes that constitute an offence under US anti-money-laundering laws is a bit vague because several of the possible laws have not been tested in court.

Mosque Network: System of mosques around the world. The Mosque Network is used to finance and recruit for Islamist armed groups.

Mufti: Religious jurist who issues judgments and opinions on Islamic law and precedent.

Mujahedin: The term derives from the Arabic *mujahid*, literally meaning 'he who wages Jihad'. The term was applied to Muslims fighting the Red Army during the anti-Soviet Jihad in Afghanistan (1979–89) and has been translated as 'holy warriors'. Today it is used to describe Islamic guerrilla fighters, especially in the Middle East.

Mullah: Word deriving from the Arabic *mawla*: master. It was borne as a title of respect by religious figures and jurists.

Muslim Brotherhood: Founded in Egypt in 1928, this confraternity is considered the matrix of all modern Islamist movements of Sunni obedience. Present all over the world, the Muslim Brotherhood promotes a more fundamentalist and militant Islam.

Narco-terrorism: Use of terror tactics by the narco-traffickers and drug lords to protect their illegal businesses. It also describes the alliance between drug lords and armed organisations. Both have interests in destabilising governments and breaking down the established social order.

Nationalism: Term used to describe the sentiment and ideology of attachment to a nation and to its interest. The word originates from the theory that a state should be founded in a nation and that a nation should be constituted as a state. Nationalism requires the consciousness of national identity, which includes territorial integrity, common language, custom and culture.

New Economy: Term referring to the birth and development of a new economic sector created by the Internet revolution.

Nom de Guerre: Name used to hide the real identity of clandestine combatants, members of armed organisations and to project a certain image inside the armed organisation and to the outside world.

North Atlantic Treaty Organisation (NATO): Also called, particularly in official NATO publications, the Atlantic Alliance or the Alliance. Created as a defensive political and military alliance by the signing of the North Atlantic Treaty in April 1949, with 12 charter members: Belgium, Britain, Canada, Denmark, France, Iceland, Italy, Luxembourg, the Netherlands, Norway, Portugal, and the United States.

Operation X: Codename for operations in which opium was purchased from Hmong tribesmen in Laos and sold to Binh Xuyen in Saigon.

Ottoman Empire: Formed in the thirteenth and fourteenth centuries when Osman I, a Muslim prince, and his successors, known in the West as Ottomans, took over the Byzantine territories of western Anatolia and south-eastern Europe and conquered the eastern Anatolian Turkmen principalities. The Ottoman Empire disintegrated at the end of the First World War; the centre was reorganised as the Republic of Turkey and the outlying provinces became separate states.

Pax Americana: Concept describing a peaceful and secure period in mainland America produced by US domination (from 1865 to 2001).

Pax Romana: Concept encapsulating one of the positive consequences of the rule of Rome during the Roman Empire. It refers to two centuries of peace and security inside the territories controlled by Rome (from 27 BC to AD 180).

Perestroika: Literally, rebuilding. Gorbachev's campaign to revitalise the Communist Party, the Soviet economy and Soviet society by reforming economic, political and social mechanisms.

Predatory War Economy: Type of war where armed groups relate to local population and economic resources through

violence and predation. This type of political economy results
in the progressive destruction of resources. The impact on
the population is dramatic, resulting in massive displacement,
destitution and death.

***Processo Guerriglia*:** Concept introduced by the Red Brigades
defendants at the Turin trial in 1978. The idea was to transform
the trial into a violent propaganda show for the violent action
conducted by members of the Red Brigades still at large.

***Qadi*:** (pl. *qudah*) Islamic judge who presides over Sharia court.

***Qisas*:** Literally means retaliation. Pre-Islamic blood revenge
(*tha'r*) was replaced by the concept of just retaliation.

Recycling of Petrodollars: Economic process through which
the excessive dollar inflows (surpluses) of the current account
of the balance of payments of oil-producing countries, generated by the first oil shock (1973–74), were reversed with
massive dollar outflows on the capital account. This process
was made possible by channelling vast amounts of money
through international banks in the West.

Salaphism: The term derives from the word *salaf*, which means
'old'. Salafists refer therefore to the Prophet as well as to his
top three successors: Caliphs Abou Bakr, Omar and Othman.
They were expected to emulate the life of their pious fore-
bears. The Qur'an and Sunnah (the Prophet's words and
gestures) are their unique reference.

Sandinista: Originally a member of the Marxist group
attempting to overthrow the Somozas or their handpicked
president in the 1960s and 1970s. The group took its name
from Augusto Sandino, who led a guerrilla struggle against
the US occupation of Nicaragua in the 1930s. The political
arm of the group, the Sandinista National Liberation Front
(Frente Sandinista de Liberación Nacional – FSLN), was the
national government of Nicaragua from July 1979 to April
1990. After the late 1970s, the term Sandinista came to be
used to designate a member or supporter of the FSLN or as
the adjectival form of the FSLN (the 'Sandinista' government).

Signorage: Term used in the Middle Ages by the Italian lords (*Signori*) to issue gold coins, the value of the coins was equal to the value of the gold contained in it plus the signorage, the cost of producing and issuing the coins.

Sharia: The Holy Law of Islam. It contains all the rules (cultural and social) to which the Muslims must submit. The Sharia (law) derives from the interpretation of the Qur'an and the Sunnah.

Shia(s): (or Shóte, from Shiat Ali, the Party of Ali) A member of the smaller of the two great divisions of Islam. The Shia supported the claims of Ali and his line to presumptive right to the caliphate and leadership of the Muslim community, and on this issue they split from the Sunni in the first great schism within Islam. Later schisms have produced further divisions among the Shia over the identity and number of Imams (*q.v.*).

Shiites: The supporters of Ali, the Prophet's son-in-law, who refused to submit to caliph Mu'awiyya (the founder of the dynasty) thereby creating the greatest schism of Islam. A minority among the Muslims and structured on a hierarchised clergy, the Shiites (in power in Iran) believe in Mehdi, an imam who will come out of hiding at the end of time to spread justice across the earth.

Shura: The term can be translated as: consultation, counsel and consultative body. It is, generally, used to refer to the Islamic council.

Sleepers: Members of armed organisations undercover among ordinary citizens waiting to be activated. Sleepers live a seemingly normal life, yet they are ready to carry out attacks whenever they receive orders to do so.

Sophism: The mystical version of Islam whose name, '*sofis*', dates back to the eighth century and means 'wool carriers'. An individual and intimate dimension of Islam, it has been influenced by Christian, Zoroastrian and Hindu influences.

Spetsnaz (Voiska spetsial'nogo naznacheniia): Special-Purpose Forces of the Soviet armed forces or KGB, trained to attack important command, communications and weapons centres behind enemy lines.

State-shell: The result of the process through which armed organisations assemble the socio-economic infrastructure (taxation, employment services, etc.) of a state without the political one (no territory, no self-determination).

Sufism: An Islamic movement that emphasises a personal and mystical approach in the search for 'divine truth'. Sufism consists of semi-secret Sufi brotherhoods, each pursuing a different school or 'path' of mystic discipline but having a common goal.

Sultan: The supreme ruler of the Ottoman Empire. Officially called the *padishah* (Persian for high king or emperor), the sultan was at the apex of the empire's political, military, judicial, social and religious hierarchy.

Sunnah: Literally it means 'trodden path'. It is the 'customary practice' of the faithful deriving from the specific actions and sayings of the Prophet Mohammad himself.

Sunnism: The orthodox and largest section of Islam. It means 'those who adhere to the Sunnah' and opposes Shiism. After Mohammad's death, those followers who supported a traditional method of election based on community agreement became known as Sunnis; those who supported Ali as successor became known as Shias.

Tamils: Ethnic group, predominantly Hindu, who speak Tamil, a Dravidian language spoken by a minority in the Northern and Eastern provinces of Sri Lanka. Tamil is the major regional language spoken in Tamil Nadu State, southeast India. Sri Lankan Tamils are descendants of settlers and invaders and are a native minority, which represented approximately 15 per cent of the population. Indian Tamils are descendants of estate labourers imported under British sponsorship to the island primarily in the nineteenth century. The Indian Tamil population has been shrinking because of repatriation programmes to Tamil Nadu.

Terror Reaganomics: Concept explaining the process of economic independence of armed organisations from state-sponsored terrorism towards privatisation of terror. A phenomenon aimed at achieving economic self-sufficiency. It resembles Reagan and Thatcher's policies of non-government intervention in economics and their vision of private enterprises as the primary regulators of the market.

Terrorism: The calculated use of violence or threat of violence to attain goals that are political, religious or ideological in nature by an illegitimate and unestablished power against a legitimate and established state. This is done through intimidation, coercion or by instilling fear.

Transitional Economies: Term that identifies the transformation of the economies of former communist countries into market economies.

Ulema: Council of religious scholars, jurists, imams, judges, Ayatollahs. Highest religious authority in Muslim countries.

Ummah: This can be translated as the community of believers which transcends national, ethnic, political, economic differences. In the Pact of Medina, the Prophet added the Jews and the Christians. The term derives from the word *oum*, which means 'source', 'matrix' or 'mother'.

Urban Guerrilla: Form of combat developed in the big cities of Latin America. The term was first used in 1969 by Carlos Marighella in his Manual of the Urban Guerrilla. It is considered an alternative theory to the 'Theory of the Fire' of Che Guevara, where the revolution originates in the countryside. A classic example of urban guerrilla is the fight of the Tupamaros in Uruguay.

VEVAK: Revolutionary Guards and Iran's Intelligence Service. VEVAK is the Islamic revolutionary successor to the Shah's SAVAK.

Viet-Cong: Communist fighter in the Vietnam war.

Wahhabism: Name used to designate the official interpretation of Islam in Saudi Arabia. The faith is a puritanical concept of unitarianism (the oneness of God) that was preached by Mohammad ibn Abd al-Wahhab.

Wahhabist: Name used outside Saudi Arabia to designate adherents to Wahhabism (*q.v.*). Followers of the strict puritanical teachings of Ibn Abd al-Wahhab. The Wahhabist embraces a strict fundamentalism in the spirit of Ahmad b. Hanbal.

Warlord: Supreme military leader exercising through force civil power in a region, especially one accountable to nobody when the central government is weak.

Warsaw Pact: Informal name for the Warsaw Treaty Organisation, a mutual defence organisation founded in 1955, including the Soviet Union, Albania (which withdrew in 1961), Bulgaria, Czechoslovakia, the German Democratic Republic (East Germany), Hungary, Poland and Romania. The Warsaw Pact enabled the Soviet Union to station troops in the countries to its west to oppose the forces of the North Atlantic Treaty Organisation (NATO) (*q.v.*). The pact legitimised the invasions of Hungary (1956) and of Czechoslovakia (1968); it was disbanded in July 1991.

West Bank: The area of Palestine west of the Jordan River seized from Jordan by Israel in the June 1967 War. Until 1988 it remained Israeli-occupied territory and was not recognised by the US government as part of Israel. Israelis refer to this area as Judea and Samaria.

World Bank: The World Bank was established in 1945 with the primary purpose of providing loans to developing countries for productive projects. To participate in the World Bank group, member states must first belong to the International Monetary Fund.

World Trade Organisation (WTO): Established in 1995 as the successor to the General Agreement on Tariffs and Trade (GATT), aimed at liberalising and securing international trade. Formed in the Uruguay Round of trade negotiations, the WTO had 115 member nations in 1996 and 15 others applied

WTO rules to their trade policies. Administered by a general council, trade dispute negotiation panel and secretariat.

***Zaim* (pl. *zuama*):** Believed to be a vestige of feudal times, the *zaim* (Arabic for leader) is a political leader, either an officeholder or a power broker, whose followers are usually of the same religious sect. Within his district, the *zaim* is all-powerful and his clients promise electoral loyalty in exchange for favours.

***Zakat*:** Obligatory alms tax, which constitutes one of the five pillars of Islam.

Notes

PREFACE

1. 'There are two ways to study the approach to terrorism. One may adopt a literal approach, taking the topic seriously, or a propagandistic approach, construing the concept of terrorism as a weapon to be exploited in the service of some system of power. In each case it is clear how to proceed. Pursuing the literal approach, we begin by determining what constitutes terrorism. We then seek instances of the phenomenon – concentrating on the major examples, if we are serious – and try to determine causes and remedies. The propagandistic approach dictates a different course. We begin with the thesis that terrorism is the responsibility of some officially designated enemy. We then designate terrorist acts as "terrorist" just in case they can be attributed (whether plausibly or not) to the required source; otherwise they are to be ignored, suppressed, or termed "retaliation" or "self-defense".' Noam Chomsky, 'International Terrorism: Image and Reality', in Alexander George ed., *Western State Terrorism* (Cambridge: Polity Press, 1991), p. 12.

2. 'Terrorism is an anxiety-inspiring method of repeated violent action, employed by clandestine individual groups, or state actors, for idiosyncratic, criminal, or political reasons, whereby – in contrast to assassination – the direct targets of violence are not the main targets. The immediate human victims of violence are generally chosen randomly (targets of opportunity) or selectively (representative of symbolic targets) from a target population and serve as message generators. Threat- and violence-based

communication processes between terrorist [organisations] [imperil] victims and main targets are used to manipulate the main target [audience(s)], turning it into a target of terror, a target of demands or a target of attention, depending on whether intimidation, coercion or propaganda is primarily sought.' In Alex P. Schmid and Albert J. Jongman, *Political Terrorism* (Amsterdam: North-Holland Publishing Company, 1988), p. 28.

3. Noam Chomsky, *9-11* (New York: Seven Stories Press, 2002), p. 90.

4. Ibid., p. 91.

PROLOGUE

1. The following story has been adapted by the author. Names and situations have been changed and the denomination of the armed groups have been omitted to conceal and protect the identity of her sources.

2. Author's interview with former members of Italian armed groups conducted between 1994 and 1995, and in 2002.

3. Ibid.

4. Ibid.

5. Ibid.

6. Ibid.

1. THE DILEMMA OF TERRORISM: WAR OR CRIME?

1. Simon Reeve, *The New Jackals: Ramzi Yousef, Osama bin Laden and the Future of Terrorism* (London: André Deutsch, 1999), p. 139.

2. Ibid., p. 143.

3. Ibid., p. 108.

4. FBI archive online, reports by Louis J. Freeh and Dale Watson, 24 February 1998–4 February 1999. See also Simona Ardito, 'L'FBI sapeva tutto in anticipo', digilan der.libero.it.

5. Reeve, *The New Jackals*, p. 61.

6. 'Above the Law: Bush's Racial Coup d'Etat and Intelligence Shutdown', Green Press, 14 February 2002, www.green press.org. See also 'Did Bush Turn a Blind Eye to Terrorism?', BBC *Newsnight*, 6 November 2001, www.greg palast.com; and Greg Palast and David Pallister, 'FBI Claims bin Laden Enquiry was Frustrated', *Guardian*, 7 November 2001. See also Greg Palast, *The Best Democracy Money Can Buy* (London: Pluto Press, 2002).

7. John K. Cooley, *Unholy Wars. Afghanistan, America and International Terrorism* (London: Pluto Press, 2000), ch. 1.

8. 'Many Say US Planned for Terror but Failed to Take Action', *New York Times*, 30 November 2001.

9. Ibid.

10. Lawrence Wright, 'The Counter Terrorist', *The New Yorker*, 14 January 2002, p. 52.

11. 'Above the Law: Bush's Racial Coup d'Etat and Intelligence Shutdown'.

12. Ibid.

13. 'Many Say US Planned for Terror but Failed to Take Action'.

14. Laurie Mylroie, 'The World Trade Center Bomb: who is Ramzi Yousef? and Why it Matters', *The National Interest*, Winter 1995/96.

15. Ibid.

16. 'Many Say US Planned for Terror but Failed to Take Action'.

17. Reeve, *The New Jackals*, p. 245.

18. Serbo-Croat for 'the explosion'.

19. 'In un piano terroristico del 1995 la dinamica degli attacchi dell'11 settembre', CNN online, 26 February 2002.

20. Maria Ressa, 'The Quest for Asia's Islamic "Super" State', CNN online, 30 August 2002, asia.cnn.com.

21. Ibid.
22. 'In un piano terroristico del 1995 la dinamica degli attacchi dell'11 settembre'.
23. 'Above the Law: Bush's Racial Coup d'Etat and Intelligence Shutdown'.

2. THE MACROECONOMICS OF TERROR

1. Peter Harclerode, *Fighting Dirty* (London: Cassell, 2001), p. 81.
2. The secret service for unconventional warfare in Indochina.
3. Harclerode, *Fighting Dirty*, pp. 108–9.
4. Alfred McCoy, 'The Politics of Heroin in Southeast Asia, French Indochina: Opium Espionage and "Operation X"', www.drugtext.org.
5. Walter Laqueur defined state-sponsored terrorism as 'warfare by proxy'. This is the strategy that 'supports[s] dissenters, separatists, ambitious politicians, or simply malcontents inside a rival state. Sometimes this strategy was defensive, meant to forestall aggressive designs on the part of a potential enemy. At other times it was part of an offensive strategy, intended to weaken the neighbour and perhaps even to prepare the ground for invasion.' Walter Laqueur, *The New Terrorism* (Oxford: Oxford University Press, 1999), p. 156.
6. Alexander George ed., *Western State Terrorism* (Cambridge: Polity Press, 1991).
7. John F. Kennedy, 'Defense Policy and the Budget: Message of President Kennedy to Congress, March 28, 1961', in Richard P. Stebbins, *Documents in American Foreign Relations* (New York: Harpers & Row, 1962), pp. 61–3.
8. The Neutrality Act forbids the launching of any military expedition from US territory against any nation with which the United States is at peace.
9. Raymond L. Garthoff, *Reflection on the Cuban Missile Crisis* (Washington: Brookings Institute, 1987), p. 17.

10. Ibid., p. 133.

11. 'Human Factors Considerations of Undergrounds in Insurgency', DA Pamphlets, US Department of the Army, April 1976, p. 770.

12. Military commentators called the 1966–67 Guatemala campaign '*el contra terror*'. See Michael McClintock, *Instruments of Statecraft: U.S. Guerrilla Warfare, Counter-insurgency, and Counter-terrorism, 1940–1990* (New York: Pantheon Books, 1992), p. 233.

13. George, *Western State Terrorism*, p. 135.

14. Opposition inside the Soviet bloc, such as in East Germany in 1953, in Hungary in 1956 and Czechoslovakia in 1968, was contained and did not spread.

15. *Pravda*, 6 February 1965.

16. Roberta Goren, *The Soviet Union and Terrorism* (London: George Allen & Unwin, 1984), p. 98.

17. Ibid.

18. David Millbank, 'International and Transactional Terrorism: Diagnosis and Prognosis', CIA, Washington D.C., 1976, p. 21.

19. *Annual of Power and Conflict, 1973–74* (London: Institute for the Study of Conflict).

20. Goren, *The Soviet Union and Terrorism*, p. 138.

21. Ercolano Ilaria, 'I rapporti tra il Partito Socialista Tedesco Unitario (SED) e il medioriente durante gli anni sessanta e settanta', dissertation in *Storia delle relazioni internazionali*, 8 March 2001.

22. United Nations, ECLA, *Economic Survey of Latin America, 1981* (Santiago: Chile, 1983), pp. 391–3, 397–8, 402.

23. Goren, *The Soviet Union and Terrorism*, p. 178.

24. Joaquìn Villalobos, *The War in El Salvador, Current Situation and Outlook for the Future* (San Francisco: Solidarity Publications, 1990), p. 17.

25. CRS Report for Congress, 'El Salvador, 1979–1989: A Briefing Book on US Aid and the Situation in El Salvador', Library of Congress, Congressional Research Service,

Foreign Affairs and National Defense Division, 28 April 1989, p. 26.

26. Economic violence is the systematic sabotage of the economy as a deliberate strategy against the enemy. Philippe Le Billon, 'The Political Economy of War: What Relief Agencies Need to Know', Network Paper no. 33, Overseas Development Institute, www.odihpn.org.uk.

27. In the guerrilla war economy model armed groups can count predominantly on local resources and therefore they develop close ties with local populations which tend to identify with their causes.

28. Hugh Byrne, *El Salvador's Civil War, a Study of Revolution* (Boulder, Co.: Lynne Rienner Publishers Inc., 1996), p. 34.

29. 'El Salvador 1980–1994, Human Rights Washington Style', excerpts from *Killing Hope* by William Blum, www.third worldtraveler.com.

30. James K. Boyce, *Economic Policy for Building Peace, The Lessons of El Salvador* (Boulder, Co.: Lynne Rienner Publishers Inc., 1996), p. 42.

31. Nationalist Republican Alliance (Alianza Republicana Nacionalista) ARENA was formed in September 1981 by rightist military officers and landowners as well as leaders of the death squads. The volatile and charismatic Roberto D'Aubuisson quickly became the party's leader. During the 1980s, ARENA was characterised by a hard-line approach to dealing with the guerrilla insurgency. Time and again, ARENA rejected meaningful negotiations with the FMLN. In 1985, D'Aubuisson stepped down as party president in an apparent effort to moderate the party's image. His replacement, Alfredo Cristiani, was a wealthy coffee grower who had been considered D'Aubuisson's protégé. D'Aubuisson was named ARENA's 'president for life' and he continued to wield considerable influence in the party until his death. With the declining popularity of the Christian Democrats and the improved image of ARENA

cultivated by Cristiani, the US, which had once seen an ARENA presidential victory as a catastrophe, came to accept the new ARENA government which took power in 1989.

32. Le Billon, 'The Political Economy of War: What Relief Agencies Need to Know'.

33. Dominique Lapierre and Larry Collins, *O Jerusalem* (Paris: Robert Laffont Editions, 1971), p. 69.

34. James Adams, *The Financing of Terror* (New York: Simon & Schuster, 1986), p. 239.

35. In 1974, after the first oil shock (caused by an unprecedented large increase in oil prices), oil-producing countries received a massive inflow of revenues. This money went into their current accounts and tilted the balance of payments. To bring it back into equilibrium, these countries had to generate capital outflow. Money flew to US and European banks which invested it predominantly in Western countries. This process became known as the recycling of petrodollars, mostly because the flow of money was initially generated in the West and returned to the West via Western banks after transiting in the oil-producing countries' balance of payments.

36. Adams, *The Financing of Terror*, p. 241.

37. Ibid., p. 66.

38. The following story is from Muhammad Haykal, *Iran, the Untold Story* (New York: Pantheon Books, 1982), pp. 112–15. See also John Cooley, *Unholy Wars. Afghanistan, America and International Terrorism* (London: Pluto Press, 2000), ch. 1.

39. Cooley, *Unholy Wars*, ch. 1.

40. In February 1960, Cuba and the Soviet Union signed a trade agreement in which the Soviet Union agreed to buy sugar and other items from Cuba and to supply Cuba with crude oil. Soon after, American oil firms in Cuba were advised by the State Department to stop refining Soviet oil. In retaliation, Cuba nationalised all its refineries.

President Dwight D. Eisenhower cancelled most of the Cuban sugar quota (prior to 1960, Cuban sales to the US were 3 million tons a year, equivalent to about half of Cuba's total crop). Cuba then expropriated all US property in the island, valued at about $1 billion and discriminated against imports of US products. Michel Krinsky and David Golove, *United States Economic Measures against Cuba: Proceedings in the United Nations and International Law Issues* (Northampton, MA: Aletheia Press, 1993). See also Richard Newfarmer ed., 'Relations with Cuba', in *From Gunboats to Diplomacy: New Policies for Latin America*, papers prepared for the Democratic Policy Committee, US Senate, June 1982. See also Anna P. Schreiber, 'Economic Coercion as an Instrument of Foreign Policy: US Economic Measures against Cuba and the Dominican Republic', *World Politics*, 25 April 1973, pp. 387–413.

41. The convertible rouble was a paper currency used in the Soviet economic system (which included Eastern Europe and any communist country trading with the USSR). The value of the currency was pegged to the value of the Soviet rouble. Imports and exports were all cleared in convertible roubles, often balancing each other.

42. Adams, *The Financing of Terror*, p. 19.

43. For details, see Mitchell Bard, *The Lebanon War*, www.us-israel.org.

44. Adams, *The Financing of Terror*, p. 49.

45. Ibid.

46. Ibid., p. 239.

47. 'The Soviet–Cuban Connection in Central America and the Caribbean', State Department documents, March 1985.

48. Stockwell ran a CIA intelligence-gathering post in Vietnam, was the taskforce commander of the CIA's secret war in Angola in 1975 and 1976 and was awarded the Medal of Merit before he resigned. John Stockwell, *In Search of Enemies: A CIA Story* (New York: W.W. Norton, 1979).

49. Adams, *The Financing of Terror*, p. 20.

50. In 1986 it was discovered that the Reagan administration had sanctioned a scheme to sell arms to Iran and then use the profits to bankroll paramilitary attacks on Nicaragua. This was a direct violation of the will of Congress, which stated explicitly in the 1984 Boland Amendment that no US funds should be expended on further overt or covert military activities in Nicaragua.

51. Money flowed to the Contras even from the Pentagon's own covert fund. This latter was part of the Black Budget, originally set up during the Second World War by President Franklin D. Roosevelt to finance 'Project Manhattan', the covert operation which gave birth to the two atomic bombs dropped on Hiroshima and Nagasaki. See Cooley, *Unholy Wars*, p. 178.

52. Al Martin is America's foremost whistleblower on government fraud and corruption. He lives in hiding. He can be reached via www.almartinraw.com.

53. Al Martin, *The Conspirators* (Montana: National Liberty Press, 2001), p. 28.

54. The foundations had 501(c)(3) status, which grants the status of non-profit organisation to institutions which are not churches or their integrated auxiliaries and public charities whose annual gross receipts are normally less than $5,000. For more information, see www.irs.gov.

55. Al Martin, *The Conspirators*, pp. 60–2.

56. Ibid., pp. 55–7. See also *United States* vs. *Richard Second*, Civil Division, 1st Eastern District of Virginia, File no. 1202-A.

57. Noam Chomsky, *9–11* (New York: Seven Stories Press, 2002), p. 86.

58. 'Spring to Fall 2000: News from the People's War in Peru', *Revolutionary Worker*, No. 1082, 10 December 2000, www.rwor.org.

59. Alison Jamieson, *Terrorism and Drug Trafficking in the 1990s* (Dartmouth: Research Institute for the Study of Conflict and Terrorism, 1994), p. 86.

60. Le Billon, 'The Political Economy of War: What Relief Agencies Need to Know', p. 8.
61. Ibid.
62. Gabriela Tarazona Sevillano, *Sendero Luminoso and the Threat of Narcoterrorism* (New York: Praeger, 1990), ch. 6.

3. THE PRIVATISATION OF TERROR

1. James Adams, *The Financing of Terror* (New York: Simon and Schuster, 1986), p. 135, see also *Irish Times*, 19 January 1978.
2. Ian Geldard and Keith Craig, *IRA, INLA: Foreign Support and International Connections* (London: Institute for the Study of Terrorism, 1988), p. 53.
3. Ibid., p. 59.
4. Adams, *The Financing of Terror*, p. 136.
5. Geldard and Craig, *IRA, INLA: Foreign Support and International Connections*, p. 55.
6. Ibid.
7. Ibid., p. 57.
8. For figures on smuggling and tax exploitation, see *Special Report of the Court of Auditors of the European Economic Community* (no. 85/C/215/01, 26 August 1986); see also *Sunday Times*, 6 October 1985.
9. Ibid.
10. Adams, *The Financing of Terror*, p. 165.
11. 'The Gun Existed', *Newsweek*, 16 January 1984, p. 52; see also *The Times*, 17 and 23 May 1985; *Sunday Times*, 2 June 1985.
12. Adams, *The Financing of Terror*, p. 166.
13. Liam Clarke and David Leppard, 'Photos Link More IRA Men to Colombia', *Sunday Times*, 28 April 2002.
14. 'IRA Suspects Move to Danger Prison', BBC News, 23 August 2001, www.news.bbc.co.uk.
15. Sandra Jordan, 'Dispatches', Channel 4, 26 May 2002.

16. Patrick Seale, *A Gun for Hire* (London: Hutchinson, 1992), p. 74.

17. Neil C. Livingstone and David Halevy, *Inside the PLO* (New York: William Morrow, 1990), pp. 168–9.

18. The Chairman's Secret Fund is a fund whose source and expenditures are secret and hidden. It is controlled entirely by Arafat.

19. Reports of the total range from $30 million to $600 million.

20. Norris McWhirter ed., *Guinness Book of Records*, 26th edn (London: Guinness Superlatives Ltd., 1979), p. 192.

21. This story was told to the author by a Lebanese businessman. See also *8 Days Magazine*, 4 August 1979, pp. 6–10; Jonathan Randal, *The Tragedy of Lebanon* (London: Chatto & Windus, 1983), pp. 98–104; Adams, *The Financing of Terror*, pp. 93–4.

22. Abu Iyad was Arafat's right-hand man. He was head of the Intelligence and Security Apparatus and was responsible for the PLO's and al-Fatah's covert and clandestine units. Ali Hassan Salameh was the operational chief of Black September and later the head of Force 17.

23. Livingstone and Halevy, *Inside the PLO*, pp. 192–3.

24. Ibid., p. 166.

25. 'El Supremo recopila testimonios y sentencias para actuar contra "Ternera"', *La Razon Digit@l*, 19 September 2002, www.larazon.es. See also 'El 'impuesto revolucionario', *La Financacio*, www.el-mundo.es and 'El Supremo Confirma La Condena De "Antxon" A Diez Años De Cárcel Como Dirigente De Eta', *Terra/Agencias*, 4 July 2002, www.terra.es.

26. Adams, *The Financing of Terror*, p. 211.

27. John Sullivan, *El Nacionalismo Vasco Radical* (Madrid: Alianza Universidad, 1987), p. 57.

28. Roberta Goren, *The Soviet Union and Terrorism* (London: Unwin Hyman, 1984), pp. 173–4.

29. Florencio Dominguez Irabarren, *ETA: Estrategia Organizativa y Actuaciones, 1978–1992* (Servicio Editorial de la Univesidad del Pays Vasco, 1998), pp. 136–44.

30. Franco ruled Spain from 1936 until his death in 1975. In 1939 he was recognised by the US as the head of state.

31. Claire Sterling, *The Terror Network, The Secret War of International Terrorism* (London: Weidenfeld & Nicolson, 1981), p. 181.

32. French francs and Spanish pesetas have been converted at 1990s exchange rates with the dollar, www.bank-banque-canada.ca/en/exchform.htm.

33. Florencio Dominguez Irabarren, *ETA: Estrategia Organizativa y Actuaciones, 1978–1992* (Servicio Editorial de la Univesidad del Pays Vasco, 1998), pp. 145–52.

34. Ibid.

35. Philippe Le Billon, 'The Political Economy of War: What Relief Agencies Need to Know', Network Paper No. 33, ODI, p. 8. www.odihpn.org.uk.

36. Alberto Abadiesand and Javier Gardeazabal, *The Economic Costs of Conflict: A Case-Control Study for the Basque Country* (Cambridge, MA: National Bureau of Economic Research, 2001), www.nber.org.

37. Neil C. Livingstone and David Halevy, 'The Perils of Poverty', *National Review*, 21 July 1986.

38. Associated Press file, 20 March 1984. See also *New York Times*, 21 March 1984, *Washington Post*, 21 March 1984.

39. '2500 Metric Tons of Cocoa Leaf', *Financial Times*, 13 June 1985.

40. Alison Jamieson, *Terrorism and Drug Trafficking in the 1990s* (Dartmouth: Research Institute for the Study of Conflict and Terrorism, 1994), p. 82.

41. *The Times*, 30 May 1984; see also *International Herald Tribune*, 23 June and 26 July 1984.

42. Adams, *The Financing of Terror*, p. 218.

43. Ibid., p. 245.

44. 'The Cuban Government Involvement in Facilitating International Drug Traffic', US Government Printing Office, serial no. J-98–36, 1983.

45. Adams, *The Financing of Terror*, p. 223.

46. He was in power from 1982 to 1986.

47. Adams, *The Financing of Terror*, p. 226.

48. 'A Colombian', *Washington Post*, 17 March 1983.

49. Author's interview with Raymond Baker.

50. Livingstone and Halevy, *Inside the PLO*, pp. 162–3.

51. Farid el Khazen, *The Breakdown of the State in Lebanon 1967–1976* (London: I.B. Tauris, 2000), ch. 27.

52. Ibid., p. 373.

53. Livingstone and Halevy, *Inside the PLO*, p. 192; see also Adams, *The Financing of Terror*, p. 96.

54. Adams, *The Financing of Terror*, p. 99.

55. Livingstone and Halevy, *Inside the PLO*, p. 191.

56. *The Times*, 5 and 6 July 1985.

57. On 5 August 1981 violence surged in Tripoli. Bloody clashes between the local militias left 20 dead and 40 injured.

58. Adams, *The Financing of Terror*, p. 100.

59. Livingstone and David, *Inside the PLO*, pp. 169–73.

60. See chapter 5.

61. *Miami Herald*, 9 November 1986; *The Record*, Hackensack, N.J., 6 November 1986.

62. Bob Woodward, *Veil: The Secret Wars of the CIA 1981–1987* (New York: Simon & Schuster, 1987), p. 413.

63. *The Iran–Contra Arms Scandal: Foreign Policy Disaster* (New York: Facts on File Publications, 1986).

4. TERROR REAGANOMICS

1. Ecevit's government lasted from 5 January 1978 to 12 November 1979.

2. James Adams, *The Financing of Terror* (New York: Simon & Schuster, 1986), p. 85.

3. Rachael Ehrenfield, 'Intifada Gives Cover to Arafat's Graft and Fraud', News World Communication Inc., *Insight on the News*, 16 July 2001, p. 44.

4. Adams, *The Financing of Terror*, p. 85.

5. Ehrenfield, 'Intifada Gives Cover to Arafat's Graft and Fraud'.

6. Alejandro Reuss, 'US in Chile, Third World Traveler', www.thirdworldtraveler.com.

7. There are many forms of foreign influence: ideological, financial, logistical, diplomatic support for opposition movements; armed support against security forces, head of states and against civilians.

8. Mark Curtis, 'US and British Complicity in Indonesia 1965', *Znet*, 21 October 2002, www.zmag.org.

9. Ibid.

10. Brian Evans III, 'The Influence of the United States Army on the Development of the Indonesian Army (1954–1964)', in *Indonesia*, Cornell Modern Indonesia Programme, April 1989, pp. 42–3.

11. Noam Chomsky, *9–11* (New York: Seven Stories Press, 2002).

12. The decolonisation process began in 1974. In 1975 Suharto began the invasion of East Timor knowing that he had the full approval of the White House. William Burr and Michael L. Evans eds, *Ford, Kissinger and the Indonesian Invasion: 1975–1976*, National Security Archive Electronic Briefing Book no. 62, 6 December 2001, www.gwu.edu.

13. Ibid.

14. In 1989, Australia negotiated a treaty with Indonesia for the joint exploration and exploitation of reserves in a 24,000 square mile area of seabed known as the Timor Gap. Kieran Cooke, 'World: Asia-Pacific Oil: Saviour of East Timor?', BBC News, 7 October 1999, www. news.bbc.co.uk.

15. George Alexander ed., *Western State Terrorism* (Cambridge: Polity Press, 1991), p. 198.

16. Noam Chomsky defined Carter's conduct as time off from his human rights-based foreign policy.

17. Neil C. Livingstone and David Halevy, *Inside the PLO* (New York: William Morrow, 1990), p. 208. For armed groups conventions, see Claire Sterling, *The Terror Network. The Secret War of International Terrorism* (London: Weidenfeld & Nicolson, 1981). She describes the Tricontinental Conference held in Havana in 1966 (p. 14). Adams, in *The Financing of Terror*, also lists 28 meetings between 1970 and 1984.

18. Originally formed in 1978 as Devrimci Sol, or Dev Sol, the Turkish Revolutionary People's Liberation Front was a splinter faction of the Turkish People's Liberation Party or Front. Renamed in 1994 after factional infighting, it espouses a Marxist ideology and is virulently anti-US and anti-NATO. The group finances its activities chiefly through armed robberies and extortion.

19. Author's interview with a former member of the Red Brigades.

20. Sterling, *The Terror Network*, p. 284.

21. Robert Fisk, 'In on the Tide, the Guns and Rockets that Fuel this Fight', *Independent*, 29 April 2002.

22. 'PLO Operates Airport Shops', *Los Angeles Times*, 31 December 1985.

23. *Pentito* is a repentant, a member of the armed community who has rejected the principles of the armed struggle and decided to collaborate with justice in exchange for a reduced sentence.

24. 'Panorama', 16 June 1980; see also Sterling, *The Terror Network*, p. 285.

25. Author's interview with Italian magistrates.

26. Author's interview with a former member of the Red Brigades.

27. According to Mario Moretti, former leader of the Red Brigades, in the 1970s the monthly stipend of a member of the organisation was around 220,000 lire, equivalent to the salary of an unskilled worker.

28. The above figures are from Sterling, *The Terror Network*, pp. 301–2.

29. Author's estimate.

30. Expropriation in the jargon of the Red Brigades referred to the right of the proletariat to 'expropriate' the capitalists. Bank robberies, for example, a primary source of financing in the early 1970s, were seen as an expropriation of money that belongs to the proletariat. See Alberto Franceschini, *Mara, Renato ed Io* (Milano: Mondadori, 1988), p. 47.

31. Author's interview with former members of the Red Brigades.

32. *Corriere della Sera*, 1 December 1978.

33. Patrick Seale, *Abu Nidal: a Gun for Hire* (London: Hutchinson, 1992), p. 138.

34. Ibid., p. 203.

35. Ibid., p. 113.

36. Ibid., p. 204.

37. Ibid., pp. 129–30.

38. Livingstone and Halevy, *Inside the PLO*, p. 224.

39. Ibid., p. 216.

40. For a summary of the evidence, see Peter Scowen, *Rogue Nation, The America The Rest of the World Knows* (Toronto: McClelland & Stewart Ltd., 2002), p. 67.

41. The report on Terpil and Wilson's activity comes from Adams, *Financing of Terror*, pp. 66–8. For a comprehensive account of the lives of Terpil and Wilson, see Joseph C. Goulden, *The Death Merchant* (New York: Simon & Schuster, 1984). See also *Sunday Times*, 21 December 1981, *Los Angeles Times*, 28 August 1981, *New York Times*, 26 and 30 August 1981.

42. *Small Arms Survey, 2001* (Oxford: Oxford University Press, 2001), p. 103.

43. *International Herald Tribune*, 30 July 1983.

44. *Small Arms Survey, 2001*, p. 103.

45. Sources vary about how much money OPEC paid Carlos. Sterling claims it was as much as $5 million. Sterling, *The Terror Network*, p. 147.

5. *THE BIRTH OF THE TERROR STATE-SHELL*

1. Figures taken from Neil C. Livingstone and David Halevy, *Inside the PLO* (New York: William Morrow, 1990), ch. 5.
2. GDP is measured in Purchasing Power Parity; World Bank/Euromonitor.
3. The state-shell model is a hypothesis, an interpretation of a phenomenon which is still taking place. For the definition of state-shell, see also Cheryl Rubenberg, *The Palestine Liberation Organization, its Institutional Infrastructure* (Belmont, MA: Institute of Arab studies Inc., 1983), p. 58.
4. Maggie O'Kane, 'Where War is a Way of Life', *Guardian*, 15 October 2001.
5. Ibid.
6. War requires a solid socio-economic structure, people and resources. Thus a member of the Laskar Jihad, the Indonesian Holy Warriors, described his group's mission as follows: to provide social work, Muslim education and defence, i.e. armed struggle. Interestingly, the socio-economic structure on which the war rests, which includes Islamist indoctrination, is mentioned before the actual conflict. What a state-shell lacks is a proper political infrastructure and external recognition. This shortcoming is due to the fact that a state-shell is assembled from the outside-in, as opposed to the inside-out process of nationalism. In the absence of sovereignty and the right to self-determination, state-shells are held together by the complex infrastructure of war. The Laskar is a full service religious army. It supplies medicine, food and help to refugees, teaches the Koran and gives Muslims a focus, an objective to reach.

Seth Mydans, 'Indonesian Conflict May be Breeding the Terrorists of Tomorrow', *International Herald Tribune*, 10 January 2002.

7. Ibid.

8. Christopher Pierson, *The Modern State* (London: Routledge, 1996); see also Anthony Giddens, *The Nation-State and Violence* (Cambridge: Polity Press, 1985).

9. 'Spectrum: International Terror Incorporated', *The Times*, 9 December 1985.

10. Livingstone and Halevy, *Inside the PLO*, p. 175.

11. Cheryl Rubenberg, *The Palestine Liberation Organization, its Institutional Infrastructure* (Belmont, MA: Institute of Arab Studies Inc., 1983).

12. James Adams, *The Financing of Terror* (New York: Simon & Schuster, 1986), p. 88.

13. Ibid., p. 89.

14. Ibid., p. 28.

15. Ibid., p. 33.

16. Rubenberg, *The Palestine Liberation Organization, its Institutional Infrastructure*.

17. Livingstone and Halevy, *Inside the PLO*, p. 175.

18. 'Spectrum: International Terror Incorporated'.

19. Livingstone and Halevy, *Inside the PLO*, p. 176.

20. *Wall Street Journal*, 10 April 1984. See also Adams, *The Financing of Terror*, pp. 99–100.

21. 'Spectrum: International Terror Incorporated'.

22. Livingstone and Halevy, *Inside the PLO*.

23. 'US Government, Foreign Broadcast Information Service', Near East and South Asia report, 3 October 1988.

24. Livingstone and Halevy, *Inside the PLO*, p. 169.

25. James Clarity, 'Hard-up Lebanon Puts the Squeeze on Smugglers', *New York Times*, 6 November 1986.

26. The following information on Hamas comes from Steven Emerson, 'Meltdown: the End of the Intifada', *New Republic*, 23 November 1992.

27. Dean Andromidas, 'Israeli Roots of Hamas are Being Exposed', *Executive Intelligence Review*, 18 January 2002, www.larouchepub.com.

28. Ben Barber, 'Saudi Millions Finance Terror against Israel', *Washington Times*, 7 May 2002.

29. Author's interview with a Hamas sympathiser.

30. Ibid.

31. www.terrorismanswer.com.

32. Yassin regained his freedom in 1997 after an attempt to assassinate one of the Hamas leaders in Jordan went terribly wrong. King Hussein demanded the release of Yassin in exchange for two captured Mossad men. Philip Jacobson, 'Warlord of the Jihad', *Sunday Times Magazine*, 26 January 2003.

33. Steven Emerson, *Americam Jihad, The Terrorist Living Among Us* (New York: Free Press, 2002), p. 88.

34. Mousa Abu Marzook, head of Hamas's political bureau, gave the HLF cheques for $200,000 in 1992. David Firestone, 'Mideast Flare-up: The Money Trail', *New York Times*, 6 December 2001.

35. 'Crackdown on Charities Irks Arab-Americans, May Strain Coalition', *Bloomberg News*, 6 December 2002.

36. Steve Feldman, 'No One Knows why Hamas Graced Philly with its Presence', *Ethnic News Watch*, Jewish Exponent, 13 December 2001.

37. Jim Bronskill and Rick Mofina, 'Hamas Funded by Canadian Agency: Report: Aid Organization Accused of Sending Money to U.S. Charity Shut Down for Alleged Hamas Ties', *Ottawa Citizen*, 6 December 2001.

38. Firestone, 'Mideast Flare-up'.

39. Emerson, *American Jihad, The Terrorist Living Among Us*, p. 101.

40. William Gaines and Andrew Martin, 'Terror Funding', *Chicago Tribune*, 8 September 1998.

41. 'World Affair: "A Mafia State"', *Newsweek International*, 19 June 2000.

42. Danny Rubinstein, 'Protection Racket, PA-Style', *Ha'aretz Daily Newspaper*, Tel Aviv, 3 November 1999.

43. Ibid.

44. Ibid.

45. Noam Chomsky, 'The Colombian Plan: April 2000', *Z magazine*, June 2000.

46. On 24 October 1999, 2 million Colombians demonstrated against the civil war under the slogan, '*No Mas*' (enough).

47. Maurice Lemoine, 'En Colombie, Un Nation, Deux Etats', *Le Monde Diplomatique*, May 2000.

48. Ibid.

49. George Monbiot, 'To Crush the Poor', *Guardian*, 4 February 2003.

50. Ibid.

51. 'I Hope The Peace Process Will Be Irreversible', an interview with Colombia's President Andres Pastrana, 23 February 2001, *Napue Zurcher Zeitung*, www.nzz.ch.

52. 'Enemies of the State, Without and Within', *Economist*, 6 October 2001.

53. Ibid.

54. Lemoine, 'En Colombie, Un Nation, Deux Etats'.

55. Ibid.

56. Monbiot, 'To Crush the Poor'.

57. 'I Hope The Peace Process Will Be Irreversible', an interview with Colombia's President Andres Pastrana.

6. TOWARDS A NEW WORLD DISORDER

1. Adkin Mark and Mohammed Yousaf, *The Bear Trap: Afghanistan's Untold Story*, (London: Cooper, 1992), pp. 78–9.

2. Bob Woodward, *Veil: The Secret Wars of the CIA 1981–1987* (New York: Simon & Schuster, 1987), pp. 78–9.

3. Ibid.
4. Michael Chossudosky, 'Who is Osama bin Laden?', Centre for Research on Globalisation, 12 September 2001.
5. Baneriee Dipankar, 'Possible Connections of ISI with the Drug Industry', *India Abroad*, 2 December 1994.
6. Mark and Yousaf, *The Bear Trap*.
7. Dilip Hiro, 'Fallout from the Afghan Jihad', *Inter Press Services*, 21 November 1995.
8. The Parties were based in Pakistan and Iran. They were four fundamentalist/extremist parties and three moderate parties based in Pakistan (Sunni Muslim) and six religious parties based in Iran (Shiite Muslim).
9. Mark and Yousaf, *The Bear Trap*, p. 83.
10. Ibid., p. 107.
11. Ibid., p. 106.
12. John K. Cooley, *Unholy Wars. Afghanistan, America and International Terrorism* (London: Pluto Press, 2000), p. 176.
13. Ibid.
14. Fred Halliday, 'The Un-Great Game: the Country that Lost the Cold War, Afghanistan', *New Republic*, 25 March 1996.
15. Cooley, *Unholy Wars*.
16. Ibid., ch. 5.
17. Richard Thompson, 'CIA Used Bank in Covert Operations', *Independent*, 15 July 1991.
18. Cooley, *Unholy Wars*, p. 187.
19. Thompson, 'CIA Used Bank in Covert Operations'.
20. Ibid.
21. Jonathan Beaty and S.C. Gwynne, 'The Dirtiest Bank of All', *Time Magazine*, 29 July 1991.
22. Ibid.
23. Ibid.
24. Jonathan Beaty and S.C. Gwynne, *The Outlaw Bank, A Wild Ride into the Secret Heart of BCCI* (New York: Random House, 1993), pp. 118–19.
25. Cooley, *Unholy Wars*, p. 190.

26. Ahmed Rashid, 'The Taliban: Exporting Extremism', *Foreign Affairs*, November 1999.

27. Arundhati Roy, 'The Algebra of Infinite Justice', www.nation-online.com.

28. In 1984 alone, 13 majors and two brigadiers were charged with drug-related crimes.

29. Alfred McCoy, 'Drug Fallout, the CIA's Forty-Year Complicity in the Narcotics Trade', *The Progressive*, 1 August 1997.

30. With the exception of the North-West Frontier territories.

31. Dipankar, 'Possible Connections of ISI with the Drug Industry'.

32. United Nations Office on Drugs and Crime, global drugs trend report 2000.

33. Chris Smith, 'Areas of Major Concentration in the Use and Traffic of Small Arms', in Jayantha Dhanapala et al., *Small Arms Controls: Old Weapons, New Issues* (Aldershot: Ashgate, 1999).

34. Mark and Yousaf, *The Bear Trap*, p. 106.

35. Author's interview with a former Mujahid.

36. Chossudosky, 'Who is Osama bin Laden?'

37. Ibid.

38. Steve Coll, 'Anatomy of a Victory: CIA's Covert Afghan War: $2 billion Programme Reversed Tide for Rebels', *Washington Post*, 19 July 1992.

39. Halliday, 'The Un-Great Game'.

40. In 1945 at Yalta, Crimea, British prime minister Winston Churchill, US president Franklin Delano Roosevelt and Soviet premier Joseph Stalin met to discuss the terms of peace after the Second World War. Yalta marked the beginning of a new world order and what became known as the 'Cold War'.

7. ISLAMIST ECONOMICS

1. K. Subrahmanyam, 'Pakistan is Pursuing Central Asian Goals', *India Abroad*, 3 November 1995.
2. International Press Service, 22 August 1995.
3. Figures on the ATTA from Ahmed Rashid, 'The Taliban: Exporting Extremism', *Foreign Affairs*, November 1996.
4. Ahmed Rashid, *Jihad, the Rise of Militant Islam in Central Asia* (New Haven: Yale University Press, 2002), p. 53.
5. BBC World Wide Monitoring, Former Soviet Union, from *Nezavisimaya Gazeta*, 3 February 2000.
6. Ibid.
7. Ibid.
8. Rashid, *Jihad, the Rise of Militant Islam in Central Asia*, p. 165.
9. Steve Levine, 'Critics Say Uzbekistan's Crackdown on Radicalism May Fuel Fervor', *Wall Street Journal*, 3 May 2001, see also 'Tajik, Russian Officials Suggest Tajikistan is Developing into Drug Production Center', *Eurasia Insight*, 14 August 2001.
10. Rashid, *Jihad, the Rise of Militant Islam in Central Asia*, p. 163.
11. Douglas Keh, 'Drug Money in a Changing World', Technical document No. 4, 1998, Vienna UNDCP, p. 4. See also Richard Lapper, 'UN Fears Growth in Heroin Trade', *Financial Times*, 24 February 2000.
12. Keh, *Drug Money in a Changing World*.
13. Banerjee Dipankar, 'Possible Connections of ISI with the Drug Industry', *India Abroad*, 2 December 1994.
14. Graduate Institute of International Studies, *Small Arms Survey, 2001* (Oxford: Oxford University Press, 2001).
15. The Hizbul Mujahedin was established in 1989 by Ihsan Dar and Muhammed Abdullah Bangro. The outfit was created to substitute the secular Jammu & Kashmir Liberation Front.

16. Ibid.
17. The JUI was part of Bhutto's ruling coalition. See Ahmed Rashid, *Taliban: The Story of the Afghan Warlords* (London: Pan, 2001).
18. Steve Coll, 'Anatomy of a Victory: CIA's Covert Afghan War: $2 billion Programme Reversed Tide for Rebels', *Washington Post*, 19 July 1992.
19. Ibid.
20. According to Yossef Bodansky, director of the US Congress Task Force on Terrorism and Unconventional Warfare, the war in Chechnya had been planned during a secret summit of Hizbollah International held in 1996 in Mogadishu.
21. Coll, 'Anatomy of a Victory'.
22. Ibid. See also Rohan Gunaratna, *Inside al-Qaeda* (New York: Columbia University Press, 2002), p. 135.
23. Kitovani was a former defence minister of Georgia. He was sentenced to eight years in prison for setting up a para-military group. Later, he was released for health problems.
24. Graduate Institute of International Studies, *Small Arms Survey*, p. 178.
25. Michael Chossudovsky, 'Who is Osama bin Laden?', Centre for Research on Globalisation, 12 September 200. See also BBC *Newsnight*, 29 September 1999.
26. Chossudovsky, 'Who is Osama bin Laden?'
27. Graduate Institute of International Studies, *Small Arms Survey*, p. 180.
28. *Daily News*, Ankara, 5 March 1997. See also Michael Chossudovsky, 'The KLA: Gangsters, Terrorists and the CIA', www.historyofmacedonia.org.
29. Jerry Seper, 'KLA Rebels Train in Terrorist Camps', *Washington Times*, 4 May 1999.
30. *Geopolitical Drug Watch*, No. 35, 1994, p. 3.
31. Brian Murphy, 'KLA Volunteers Lack Experience', *Associated Press*, 5 April 1997.

8. TERROR JIHAD: THE ISLAMIST CRUSADES

1. The following quotes in Pope Urban II's speech have been taken from Steven Runciman, *A History of the Crusades*, Volume I (London: Folio, 1994), pp. 89–90.

2. The following quotes are taken from 'Declaration of War against the Americans Occupying the Land of the Two Holy Places, A Message from Osama bin Muhammad bin Laden unto his Muslim Brethren all over the World Generally, and in the Arab Peninsula specifically', www.islamic-news.co.uk.

3. Aziz Atiya, *Crusade, Commerce and Culture* (Bloomington: Indiana University Press, 1962), p. 167.

4. Ibid., pp. 167–8.

5. Ibid., p. 169.

6. Nasser courted the West and the Soviets without committing fully to any of them. It was Anwar Sadat who openly embraced Western values and allied Egypt to the US.

7. Malcolm Barber, *The Two Cities. Medieval Europe 1050–1320* (London: Routledge, 1992), p. 26.

8. Text of the *Fatwa* urging Jihad against Americans, published in *Al-Quds al-'Arabi* on 23 February 1998.

9. The following quotes are taken from 'Declaration of War against the Americans Occupying the Land of the Two Holy Places'.

10. Runciman, *A History of the Crusades*, p. 95.

11. Lal Khan, *Pakistan, Futile Crusades of a Failed State*, www.marxist.com.

12. Ibid.

13. 'The Italians [for example] received extensive trading concession comparable to the privileges enjoyed by the Venetians at Constantinople.' Christopher Tyerman, *The Invention of the Crusades* (London: Macmillan, 1998), pp. 62–3.

14. 'Wahhabiyyah preaches a return to what they [its followers] view as a fundamentalist state in modern Middle East. Wahhabiyyah aims at purifying religion from all "satanic"

influences, including most facets of modernity, including for some the use of cameras and modern electronic gadgets.' As'ad Abukhalil, *Bin Laden, Islam and America's New 'War on Terrorism'* (New York: Seven Stories Press, 2002), p. 63.

15. John Sloan, *Crusades in the Levant (1097–1291)*, www.xenophongroup.com.

9. ISLAMIST FINANCIAL COLONISATION

1. Stefan Wagstyl, 'Frontline States Seek Place on World Map', *Financial Times*, 22 November 2001.

2. EBRD, Transition Report, 'The First Ten Years: Analysis and Lessons for Eastern Europe and the Former Soviet Union, 2001', p. 8.

3. James Lamont, 'Africa's Trade Flows Clogged up at Dockside', *Financial Times*, 8 January 2002.

4. All figures on poverty are from the World Bank data.

5. In certain circumstances, the proliferation of state-shells is also related to other factors specific to the countries where they emerged such as the prevailing feudal land tenancy structure.

6. For a breakdown by countries see EBRD, Transition Report, 'The First Ten Years: Analysis and Lessons for Eastern Europe and the Former Soviet Union, 2001', pp. 8–9.

7. In 1988 only one in every 60 people in the transition economies had per capita income below $1 a day. Ten years later one in 20 people earned less than $1 a day.

8. Tariq Ali, *The Clash of Fundamentalism* (London: Verso, 2002), p. 267.

9. Nicholas D. Kristok, 'Behind the Terrorists', *New York Times*, 7 May 2002.

10. Secular nationalism has been displaced by Islamist groups, which is why the pattern of the formation of states has been altered.

11. 'Global Development Finance, Financing the Poorest Countries', World Bank, 2002, p. 90.
12. Ibid., p. 56.
13. These three countries received over half of FDI.
14. 'Global Development Finance, Financing the Poorest Countries', p. 39.
15. International Transaction Accounts, www.bea.com.
16. Nasdaq composite – price index, datastream.
17. Wagstyl, 'Frontline States Seek Place on World Map'.
18. Ibid.
19. 'Global Development Finance, Financing the Poorest Countries'. See also Claudia Buch and Gayle De Long, 'Cross-Border Bank Mergers: What Lures the Rare Animal?', Kiel working paper No. 1070, Kiel Institute of World Economics, August 2001, pp. 36–7.
20. 'Global Development Finance, Financing the Poorest Countries', p. 64.
21. Stephen Wagstyl and Eric Jansson, 'Extremists May be Only Winners as Serb Voters Shun Election', *Financial Times*, 15 October 2002.
22. Following the first oil shock in 1973–74, Western banks feared similar actions from Arab financial institutions.
23. 'The revival of Islamic banking coincided with the world-wide celebration of the advent of the 15th Century of Islamic calendar (Hijra) in 1976. At the same time financial resources of Muslims, particularly those of the oil producing countries, received a boost due to the rationalisation of oil prices, which had hitherto been under the control of oil corporations. These events led Muslims to strive to model their lives in accordance with the ethics and philosophy of Islam.' The Institute of Islamic Banking and Insurance, www.islamic-banking.com.
24. Roland Jacquard, *In the Name of Osama bin Laden* (Durham, NC: Duke University Press, 2002), p. 132.
25. Susan Sachs, 'An Investigation in Egypt Illustrates al-Qaeda's Web', *New York Times*, 21 November 2001.

26. Ibid.

27. Ibid.

28. 'Arms for Drugs in the Balkans', *International Herald Tribune*, 6 June 1996.

29. Christopher Deliso, *Bin Laden, Iran and the KLA*, 19 September 2001, www.antiwar.com.

30. Ibid.

31. Also known as Green Crosscut. See Milan V. Petkovic, *Albanian Terrorists*, 1998, www.balkania.net.

32. Alex Standish, 'Albanians Face Ruin as Cash Pyramids Crumble', *European*, 28 November 1996.

33. 'Hope and Danger for Ethnic Albanians', *Economist*, 29 March 1997.

34. The various pseudo-banks that succeeded in absorbing funds from almost every Albanian household with the promise of exorbitant interest payments before going bankrupt.

35. 'Hope and Danger for Ethnic Albanians'.

36. In 2001 Indonesia's exports totalled $56.5 billion.

37. Shawn Donnan, 'Indonesian Ties with the Arabs Highlighted', *Financial Times*, 17 October 2002.

38. Anon, *Through Our Enemies' Eyes* (Washington: Brassey's Inc., 2002), p. 106.

39. Ibid.

40. Edward Said, 'When Will We Resist?', *Guardian*, 25 January 2003.

41. Anon, *Through Our Enemies' Eyes*, pp. 105–6.

42. John Pilger, 'This War is a Fraud', *Daily Mirror*, 29 October 2001.

43. Ahmed Rashid, 'The Taliban: Exporting Extremism', *Foreign Affairs*, November 1999.

44. Embargo on deliveries of weapons and military equipment imposed by UN Resolution 713 in September 1999.

45. Revolutionary Guards and Iran's intelligence service, known as VEVAK, the Islamic revolutionary successor to the Shah's SAVAK.

46. Michael Chossudovsky, *Guerra e Globalizzazione* (Torino: EGA, 2002), p. 44.

47. 'Iran Gave Bosnia Leader $500,000, CIA Alleges: Classified Report Says Izetbegovic Has Been "Co-Opted," Contradicting U.S. Public Assertion of Rift', *Los Angeles Times*, 31 December 1996.

48. Third World Relief Agency (TWRA), a Sudan-based, fake humanitarian organisation which has been a major link in the arms pipeline to Bosnia. See 'How Bosnia's Muslims Dodged Arms Embargo: Relief Agency Brokered Aid From Nations' Radical Groups', *Washington Post*, 22 September 1996; see also 'Saudis Funded Weapons For Bosnia, Official Says: $300 Million Program Had U.S. "Stealth Cooperation"', *Washington Post*, 2 February 1996.

49. Congressional Press Release, Republican Party Committee, US Congress, 'Clinton-approved Iranian Arms Tranfers Help Turn Bosnia into Militant Islamic Base', 16 January 1997, www.globalsearch.ca. For original document, see www.senate.gov.

50. A great Albania where US and German companies could freely exploit energy resources.

51. Alija Izetbegovic was the Muslim president of Bosnia.

52. 'Bosnian Leader Hails Islam at Election Rallies', *New York Times*, 2 September 1996.

53. Cees Wiebes, *Intelligence and the War in Bosnia, 1992–1995* (Amsterdam: Netherlands Institute for War Documentation, 2002).

54. Rashid, 'The Taliban: Exporting Extremism'.

55. Richard McGregor, 'Uighur Training Angered Beijing', *Financial Times*, 18 October 2001.

10. THE ECONOMIC FORCES OF ISLAMIST COLONISATION

1. Jean Charles Brisard and Guillaume Dasquie, *La Verita' Negata* (Milano: Marco Tropea, 2001).
2. Richard Thomson, 'CIA Used Bank in Covert Operations', *Independent*, 15 July 1991.
3. The loans were unsecured, backed exclusively by the shares bought in the companies. Clearly they were never going to be repaid. However, in return for the loans, the BCCI got *de facto* ownership and control of strategic companies and banks in the US.
4. Jonathan Beatty and S.C. Gwynne, 'The Dirtiest Bank of All Time', *Time Magazine*, 29 July 1991.
5. Banks can lend only a proportion of their deposits, whose amount is regulated by the central bank of the country in which they operate. This is because they must maintain a certain degree of liquidity to repay depositors whenever they demand their money back. Exceeding the limit creates accountancy irregularity in the treasury department; in the case of the BCCI this was covered up with money generated by additional deposits.
6. Beatty and Gwynne, 'The Dirtiest Bank of All Time'.
7. James Ring Adams and Douglas Frants, *A Full Service Bank* (London: Simon & Schuster, 1992), p. 92.
8. For further information, see Carey Sublette, 'Dr. Abdul Qadeer Khan', www.nuketesting. enviroweb.org.
9. Ibid., p. 192.
10. This is a special type of steel, which is resistant to very high temperatures, mostly used in weapons manufacture.
11. Brisard and Dasquie, *La Verita' Negata*, p. 12.
12. Ibid., pp. 65–6.
13. Isabel Kershner, 'Behind the Veil', *Jerusalem Report*, 3 June 1993.
14. Ibid.

15. Ibid.

16. Mateen Siddiqui, 'Differentiating Islam from Militant Islamist', *The San Francisco Chronicle*, 21 September 1999.

17. 'The principal judge and *Amir* of the courts was Sheikh Abu Umar from Buraydah in the Qasseem region of the Arabian Gulf. Sheikh Abu Umar studied Islam in the Arabian Gulf under some of the notable scholars in the region such as Sheikh Muhammad bin Saleh al-Uthaimeen. In the Islamic university examinations, he came first. Sheikh Abu Umar came to Chechnya in 1995 and joined the ranks of the Mujahedin there under the leadership of Ibn-ul-Khattab, the *Amir* of the foreign Mujahedin in Chechnya, also from the Arabian Gulf. He underwent training and, at the same time, set about teaching Islam with the correct *aqeedah* [faith] to the Chechen Mujahedin, many of whom held incorrect and distorted beliefs about Islam.' *Global Muslim News*, December 1997, www.islam.org.au.

18. *Global Muslim News*.

19. Borzou Daragahi, 'Financing Terror', *Time*, November 2001. See also *Money*, Vol. 30, No. 12, November 2001.

20. The Tadamon Islamic Bank was founded in 1981 and is the second largest banking institution in Saudi Arabia. It is represented in the whole Sudanese territory by 21 branches. In 1998 its main shareholders were the companies National Co. for Development and Trade of Khartoum (15 per cent), the Kuwait Finance House, the Dubai Islamic Bank, the Bahrain Islamic Bank as well as several individual shareholders, most prominent among which was the Social Affairs Minister of the United Arab Emirates. Tadamon has several branches in Sudan, mainly in the agricultural, industrial and property sectors. According to the report, since 1991 the Tadamon Islamic Bank's shareholding has not evolved remarkably. The only change has been the Faisal Islamic Bank's replacement in the board of directors with its branch, the National Company for Development

and Trade. The Faisal Islamic Bank, established in 1997, is directed by Prince Mohammad Saoud el Faisal, King al-Saud's son and King Fahd's cousin-german (Bette Stern, 'La Toile Financière d'Oussana ben Laden s'etend du pays du Golfe à l'Europe', *Le Monde Interactif*, 24 September 2001). In 1998, 15 per cent of its stocks were controlled by the National Company for Development and Trade of Khartoum. Tadamon has 21 operative branches in Saudi Arabia and a considerable banking network in Sudan, where it is particularly active in the agricultural, industrial and real estate sectors (Brisard and Dasquie, *La Verita' Negata*, p. 73). Among its shareholders are several Islamic institutions from the Gulf, such as the Bahrain Islamic Bank, Kuwait Finance House and the Dubai Islamic Bank, one of the largest shareholders of the BCCI ($81.7 million) (Ahmad Mardini, 'Gulf-Economy: BCCI Deal Buoys UAE Stocks', *Inter Press Services*, 6 February 1995). Over the last two decades, the Dubai Islamic Bank has been involved in numerous scandals in the Middle East. Among its shareholders are the governments of Dubai and Kuwait. The bank also holds large stakes in the Bahrain Islamic Bank and the Islamic Bank of Bangladesh.

21. Members of the bin Laden family sit on the board of directors of the Faisal Bank. Interestingly, these two banks are among the largest stockholders of the al-Shamil Islamic Bank.

22. Jonathan Wells, Jack Meyers and Maggie Mulvihill, 'War on Terrorism, Saudi Elite Tied to Money Groups Linked to bin Laden', *Boston Herald*, 14 October 2001.

23. Ibid.

24. Brisard and Dasquie, *La Verita' Negata*, p. 71.

25. Mark Huband, 'Inside al-Qaeda, Bankrolling bin Laden', *Financial Times*, 29 November 2001.

26. David Pallister and Owen Bowcott, 'Banks to Shut Doors on Saudi Royal Cash', *Guardian*, 17 July 2002.

27. Greg Palast, *The Best Democracy Money Can Buy* (London: Pluto Press, 2002), p. 145.

28. Ibid.

29. Wells, Meyers and Mulvihill, 'War on Terrorism, Saudi Elite Tied to Money Groups Linked to bin Laden'.

30. Neil Mackay, 'John Mayor Link to bin Laden Dynasty', *Sunday Herald*, 7 October 2001.

31. Robin Allen and Roula Khalaf, 'Al-Qaeda: Terrorism after Afghanistan', *Financial Times*, 21 February 2002.

32. 'Financial Chain, Funds Continue to Flow Despite Drive to Freeze Network's Assets', *Guardian*, 5 September 2002.

33. United Nations, S/20021050/Corr.1 Second Report of the Monitoring Group pursuant to resolution 1390 (2002).

34. In 1991, Qadi was accused of having transferred by wire from a Swiss account $820,000 for investment purposes. The transaction was intended to conceal the source of the money, namely, that it was from Qadi. According to the US government, part of this money was used by Hamas to purchase weapons and reorganise the group in the occupied territories. Jeff Gerth and Judith Miller, 'A Nation Challenged: On the List, Philanthropist or Fount of Funds for Terrorists?', *New York Times*, 13 October 2001.

35. 'Financial Chain, Funds Continue to Flow Despite Drive to Freeze Network's Assets', *Guardian*, 5 September 2002.

36. Edward Alden, 'The Money Trail: How a Crackdown on Suspect Charities is Failing to Stem the Flow of Funds to al-Qaeda', *Financial Times*, 18 October 2002.

37. Charles Clover, 'Return of the "Afghans" Puts Spotlight on Kuwaiti Divisions', *Financial Times*, 17 October 2002.

38. Mark Huband, 'Inside al-Qaeda, Bankrolling bin Laden', *Financial Times*, 29 November 2001.

39. Yael Shahar, 'Tracing bin Laden's Money, Easier Said than Done', ICT, 21 September 2001, www.ict.org.

40. Allen and Khalaf, 'Al-Qaeda: Terrorism after Afghanistan'.

41. Borzou Daragahi, 'Financing Terror', *Time*, November 2001.

42. Sam Vaknin, 'Analysis: Hawala, the Bank that Never Was', United Press International, 17 September 2001, www.upi.com.

43. Kimberly I. Thachuk, 'Terrorism's Financial Lifeline: Can It Be Severed?', Strategic Forum, Institute for the National Strategic Studies National Defense University, Washington D.C., No. 191, May 2002, p. 5.

44. Jimmy Burns, Harvey Morris and Michael Peel, 'Assault on America Terrorists Funds', *Financial Times*, 24 September 2001.

45. Vaknin, 'Analysis: Hawala, the Bank that Never Was'.

46. Ibid.

47. United Nations, Security Council Committee pursuant to resolution 1267 (1999), 22 September 2002, p. 15.

48. Ibid.

49. Richard McGregor, 'Rumours Rule the Money Pit', *Financial Times*, 24 November 2001.

50. Karl Vick, 'The Taliban's Good-Bye: Take the Banks' Millions and Run', *Washington Post*, 8 January 2001.

51. Vaknin, 'Analysis: Hawala, the Bank that Never Was'.

52. This figure has been calculated using the constant 1995 US dollar price. Purchasing Power Parity figures are naturally higher at $213 billion for 1998. Source: World Development Indicators database.

53. Douglas Farah, 'Al-Qaeda's Road Paved with Gold; Secret Shipments Traced through a Lax System in United Arab Emirates', *Washington Post*, 17 February 2002.

54. 'Financial Chain, Funds Continue to Flow Despite Drive to Freeze Network's Assets', *Guardian*, 5 September 2002.

55. Ibid.

56. Ibid.

57. Marcus Walk, 'In the Financial Fight against Terrorism, Leads are Hard Won', *Wall Street Journal*, 10 October 2001.

58. 'Correspondent Banks, the Weakest Link', *Economist*, 29 September 2001.

59. David Leppard and Michael Sheridan, 'London Bank Used for bin Laden Cash', *Sunday Times*, 16 September 2001.

11. THE MOSQUE NETWORK

1. Nick Fielding, 'Al-Qaeda Issues New Manifesto of Revenge', *Sunday Times*, 17 November 2002.
2. Roy MacCarthy and Richard Norton-Taylor, 'Kashmir Militants Plan New Attacks', *Guardian*, 25 May 2002.
3. Ibn Saud pushed out the Hashemites and in 1926 was recognised as ruler of the Kingdom of Hijaz and Najd. In 1932 this became the United Kingdom of Saudi Arabia.
4. www.islamicweb.com. See also Anthony H. Cordesman, *Economic, Demographic and Security Trends in the Middle East* (Washington D.C.: Center for Strategic and International Studies, January 2002).
5. The Khanate was the state or jurisdiction of a khan. The Uzbek Khanate was a group of tribes, a sort of confederation.
6. CBT TV, *The National*, 29 July 2002.
7. Jason Burke, 'You Have to Kill in the Name of Allah until You are Killed', *Observer*, 26 January 2002.
8. Ibid.
9. CBT TV, *The National*, 29 July 2002.
10. 'Suicide Blast: Briton Named', *Manchester Guardian Weekly*, 10 January 2001.
11. Daniel McGrory, 'UK Muslims Volunteers for Kashmir War', *The Times*, 28 December 2000.
12. Jeevan Vasagar and Vikram Dodd, 'British Muslims take Path to Jihad: Kashmir Terror Group Claims Suicide Bomber was from Birmingham', *Guardian*, 29 December 2000.
13. Salah Shehadeh was killed on 23 July 2002 by a bomb dropped by the Israel Defence Forces (IDF) on his house in Gaza.

14. 'Inside a Terrorist's Mind', interview with Salah Shehadeh, The Middle East Media Research Institute, Special Dispatch Series, No. 403, 24 July 2002, www.memri.org.

15. Suzanne Goldberg, 'The Men Behind the Suicide Bombers', *Guardian*, 12 June 2002.

16. Daniel Benjamin and Steven Simon, *The Age of Sacred Terror* (New York: Random House, 2002), pp. 28–9.

17. 'Indian Agency Says British Muslims Support Kashmiri Militants Financially', *BBC Monitoring International Reports*, 13 January 2002.

18. 'London Cleric Told Followers "to Kill"', *Sunday Times*, 17 November 2002.

19. Yahya Kocoglu, 'Hizbullah: The Susurluk of the Southeast', *Turkish Daily News*, 27 January 2000.

20. Ersel Aydinli, 'Implications of Turkey's anti-Hizbullah Operation', Washington Institute for Near Policy, 9 February 2000.

21. Kocoglu, 'Hizbullah: The Susurluk of the Southeast'.

12. WEAK STATES: TERROR BREEDING GROUND

1. Charles Smith, 'China and Sudan: Trading Oil for Humans', *Worldnetdaily*, 19 July 2000, www.worldnetdaily.com.

2. Robert I. Rotberg, 'The New Nature of Nation-State Failure', *Washington Quarterly*, Summer 2002.

3. Ibid.

4. Richard Haass, *Intervention: The Use of American Military Force in the Post-Cold War World* (Washington: Brookings Institution Press, 1999), p. 84.

5. 'Let us imagine a map of each country in which the areas covered by blue would designate those where there is a high degree of presence of the state (in terms of a set of reasonably effective bureaucracies and of the effectiveness

of properly sanctioned legality), both functionally and territorially; the green color would indicate a high degree of territorial penetration but a significantly lower presence in functional/class term; and the brown color a very low or nil level in both dimensions.' Guillermo O'Donnell, 'On the State, Democratization and Some Conceptual Problems', working paper No. 192 (University of Notre Dame, The Helen Kellogg Institute for International Studies, April 1993).

6. Ibid., p. 10.
7. John Aglionby, 'The Secret Role of the Army in Sowing the Seeds of Religious Violence', *Guardian*, 16 October 2002.
8. Bernie Hecht, 'Irgun and the State of Israel', www.jewishmag.com.
9. Rotberg, 'The New Nature of Nation-State Failure', p. 90.
10. 'Colombia-Weapons, Colombian Arms Dealer who Purchased Arms for FARC Arrested', *Financial Times*, 8 May 2002.
11. Graduate Institute of International Studies, *Small Arms Survey, 2001*, (Oxford: Oxford University Press, 2001), p. 187.
12. Ray Takeyh and Nicholas Gvosdev, 'Do Terrorist Networks Need a Home?', *Washington Quarterly*, Summer 2002.
13. Ibid.
14. 'Report: bin Laden Linked to Albania', *USA Today*, 1999, www.usatoday.com.
15. Ibid.
16. John Burton, 'Islamic Network "is on a Mission"', *Financial Times*, 16 October 2002.
17. According to Russian law enforcement agencies, profits generated by the Afghan opium trade are used by bin Laden and his followers to arm, train and support Islamist terror groups in Asia, including the IMU, the Uighurs in the Chinese province of Xinjiang and the Chechen resistance,

in Takeyh and Gvosdev, 'Do Terrorist Networks Need a Home?'

18. Yael Shahar, 'Tracing bin Laden's Money: Easier Said than Done', ICT, 21 September 2001, www.ict.org.

19. Wimar Witoelar, 'Terror Has Deep Roots in Indonesia', *Guardian*, 16 October 2002.

20. Jason Burke, 'Revealed: the Quiet Cleric behind Bali Bomb Horror', *Observer*, 20 October 2002.

21. Burton, 'Islamic Network "is on a Mission"'.

22. Witoelar, 'Terror Has Deep Roots in Indonesia'. These 'dark forces' include the Kopassus Group IV, or ex-Kopassus, known as 'militer khussus' or 'milsus' (special military), such as Tim Mahwar (Rose Team), which kidnapped and in some cases 'made disappear' activists and students ahead of Suharto's fall from power; also 'Tidar Boys' and some officers who trained Laskar Jihad, the Islamist armed group at Bogor. For a comprehensive description of Islamist groups in Indonesia, see Damien Kingsbury, *Power Politics and the Indonesian Military* (London: Routledge Curzon, 2003).

23. The Laskar Jihad was funded, armed and paid for by elements within the Tentara Nasional Indonesia (TNI), the Indonesian military. They had close ties with the FPI, which in turn had some association with the MMI (Majelis Mujahidin Indonesia or Indonesian Mujahideen Council) headed by Bashir.

24. Aglionby, 'The Secret Role of the Army in Sowing the Seeds of Religious Violence'.

25. Shawn Donnan, 'Bombing to Test the Fabric of Indonesia Society', *Financial Times*, 14 October 2002.

26. Shawn Donnan, 'Blast May Reverberate across the Economy', *Financial Times*, 15 October 2002.

13. FROM MODERN JIHAD TO THE NEW ECONOMY OF TERROR

1. Peter Finn and Sarah Delaney, 'Sinister Web Links Terror Cells across Europe', *International Herald Tribune*, 23 October 2001.
2. Author's interview with Dr Saad al-Faqih.
3. United Nations, Security Council Committee established pursuant to resolution 1267 (1999), 20 September 2002.
4. Giles Foden, 'Australian "Crusaders" Targeted by bin Laden', *Guardian*, 16 October 2002.
5. Author's interview with Dr Saad al-Faqih.
6. PBS interview with Dr Saad al-Faqih, www.pbs.org.
7. Jason Burke, 'Revealed: the Quiet Cleric behind Bali Bomb Horror', *Observer*, 20 October 2002.
8. Ibid.
9. Anon., *Through Our Enemies' Eyes* (Washington D.C.: Brassey's Inc., 2002), p. 49.
10. Ibid., p. 102.
11. Abu Mahmud is the *nom de guerre* of one of bin Laden's lieutenants who fought during the anti-Soviet Jihad.
12. Jamal Khashuqji, 'Al-Qaeda Organization: Huge Aims without Programs or Cells', *Al-Hayah*, 12 October 1998.
13. 'The Great Game', www.aliyev.com.
14. Heydae Aliyevich Aliyev is a former member of the KGB and of the Soviet politburo. He gained power in a military coup in 1993.
15. 'Over 6 billion dollars in contract "signing bonuses" were paid to the Aliyev regime in Baku – by far more than all aid and investments in Georgia and Armenia combined – yet Azeris still live in refugee camps, worse off than even Georgians and Armenians.' 'The Great Game', www.aliyev.com.
16. Ibid.
17. Ahmed Rashid, *Taliban: The Story of the Afghan Warlords* (London: Pan, 2001), pp. 135–6.

18. Jean-Charles Brisard and Guillaume Dasquie, *La Verita' Negata* (Milano: Marco Tropea Editore, 2001), ch. 9.
19. Ibid., p. 82.
20. Samuel P. Huntington, 'The Age of Muslim Wars', *Newsweek Special Issue*, 2002.
21. Francis Fukuyama and Nadav Samin, 'Heil Osama, The Great Reformer', *Sunday Times*, 29 September 2002.
22. Samuel P. Huntington, 'The Clash of Civilization?', *Foreign Affairs*, Summer 1993.
23. Huntington, 'The Age of Muslim Wars'.
24. Finn and Delaney, 'Sinister Web Links Terror Cells across Europe'.
25. Fukuyama and Samin, 'Heil Osama, The Great Reformer'.
26. Francis Fukuyama, *The End of History and the Last Man* (London: Penguin, 1993).
27. Fukuyama and Samin, 'Heil Osama, The Great Reformer'.
28. 'Osama bin Laden Talks Exclusively to Nida'ul Islam about the New Powder Keg in the Middle East', *Nida'ul Islam*, No. 15, October–November 1996, www.islam.org.au.
29. Ladan and Roya Boroumand, 'Terror, Islam and Democracy', *Journal of Democracy*, Vol. 13, No. 2, April 2002.
30. Ibid.
31. Roland Jacquard, *In the Name of Osama bin Laden: Global Terrorism and the bin Laden Brotherhood* (Durham, NC: Duke University Press, 2002).
32. Farish A. Noor, 'The Evolution of "Jihad" in Islamist Political Discourse: How a Plastic Concept Became Harder', www.ssrc.org.
33. Nick Fielding, 'Al-Qaeda Issues New Manifesto of Revenge', *Sunday Times*, 17 November 2002.
34. Ladan and Roya Boroumand, 'Terror, Islam and Democracy'.
35. Lew Scudder, 'A Brief History of Jihad', www.rca.org.
36. 'Ansar Al-Islam Activists Leave Norway After Increased Pressure on Their Leader', 12 September 2002, Kurdishmedia.com.

37. David I. Phillips, 'The Next Stage in the War on Terror', *International Herald Tribune*, 23–24 March 2002.

38. Ewen MacAskill and John Aglionby, 'Suspicion Turns on Indonesia's Islamist Militants', *Guardian*, 14 October 2002.

39. Jeffrey Goldberg, 'The Great Terror', *New Yorker*, 25 March 2002.

14. TERROR'S LEGITIMATE BUSINESS

1. Roula Khalaf, 'Al-Qaeda Recruiting Ground Offers Tough Challenge in War of Terror', *Financial Times*, 22 February 2002.

2. Judith Miller and Jeff Gerth, 'Trade in Honey is Said to Provide Money and Cover for bin Laden', *New York Times*, 11 October 2001.

3. Ibid.

4. James Adams, 'The Financing of Terror', in Paul Wilkinson and Alastair M. Stewart eds, *Contemporary Research on Terrorism* (Aberdeen: Aberdeen University Press, 1987).

5. Ibid., p. 88.

6. Giles Foden, 'The Former CIA "Client" Obsessed with Training Pilots', *Guardian*, 12 September 2001.

7. Lou Dolinat, 'A Focus on Their Smaller Crimes', *Newsday*, 5 October 2001, www.newsday.com.

8. Robin Wright and Joseph Meyer, 'America Attacked; Mapping a Response', *Los Angeles Times*, 12 September 2001.

9. Kimberly L. Thachuk, *Terrorism Financial Lifeline: Can it be Severed?*, Strategic Forum, Institute for the National Strategic Studies, National Defense University, Washington D.C., no. 191, May 2002, pp. 5–6.

10. Roland Jacquard, *In the Name of Osama Bin Laden* (Durham, NC: Duke University Press, 2002), p. 134.

11. Grant Ringshow, 'Profits of Doom', *Sunday Telegraph*, 23 September 2001.

12. Robert Fisk, 'Talks with Osama Bin Laden', *The Nation*, 21 September 1998.

13. 'Jihad against Jews and Crusaders', World Islamic Front Statement, 23 February 1998, www.fas.org.

14. Jacquard, *In the Name of Osama Bin Laden*, pp. 110–11.

15. Ibid., p. 96.

16. John Mintz, 'Bin Laden's Finances are Moving Target', *Washington Post*, 28 August 1998; see also Yael Shahar, 'Tracing bin Laden's Money', ICT, 21 September 2001, www.ict.org.

17. Jacquard, *In the Name of Osama Bin Laden*, p. 128.

18. Simon Reeve, *The New Jackals: Ramzi Yousef, Osama bin Laden and the Future of Terrorism* (London: André Deutsch, 1999), p. 178

19. Ibid., ch. 9.

20. Yael Shahar, 'Tracing bin Laden's Money: Easier Said than Done', ICT'.

21. Jacquard, *In the Name of Osama Bin Laden*, p. 128.

22. Ibid., pp. 127–8.

23. Ringshow, 'Profits of Doom'.

24. John Hooper, 'Terror Made Fortune for bin Laden', *Guardian*, 23 September 2001.

25. Ringshow, 'Profits of Doom'.

26. Thachuk, *Terrorism Financial Lifeline: Can it be Severed?*

15. TERROR'S BALANCE OF PAYMENTS

1. 'As late as 1997 Washington chose to include the [KLA] on the State Department's list of terrorist organizations', from 'The US, the KLA and Ethnic Cleansing', World Socialist web-site, 29 June 1999, www.wsws.org.

2. 'Albanian-Americans Help Fund the KLA', AFP, 20 February 1999, www.members.tripod.com.

3. Milan V. Petkovic, 'Albanian Terrorists', 1998, www.balcania.net.

4. 'Albanian-Americans Help Fund the KLA'.

5. Stacy Sullivan, 'Albanian Americans Funding Rebels' Cause', *Washington Post*, 26 May 1998.

 6. Petkovic, 'Albanian Terrorists'.
 7. Michael Chossudovsky, 'Osamagate, Role of the CIA in Supporting International Terrorist Organizations during the Cold War', Canadian Business and Current Affairs, Brandon University, November 2001.
 8. Noam Chomsky, *9–11* (New York: Seven Stories Press, 2002), p. 91.
 9. Eric Lichtblau, 'US Indicts Head of Islamic Charity in Qaeda Financing', *New York Times*, 10 October 2002.
10. Ibid.; see also Edward Alden, 'The Chicago Charity Accused of Defrauding Donors', *Financial Times*, 18 October 2002.
11. In 1996, the magazine *Watan al-Arabi* reported that bin Laden had admitted to being one of Muwafaq's supporters. David Pallister, 'Head of Suspects Charity Denies Link to bin Laden', *Guardian*, 16 October 2001.
12. 'Assault on Charities is Risky Front for the US', *Wall Street Journal*, 16 October 2001.
13. Mark Duffield, 'The Political Economy of Internal War: Asset Transfer, Complex Emergencies and International Aid', in Joanna Macrae and Anthony Zwi eds, *War and Hunger: Rethinking International Responses* (London: Zed Press, 1994).
14. Oliver Burkeman, 'US "Proof" over Iraqi Trucks', *Guardian*, 7 March 2002.
15. Mary Kaldor, *New and Old Wars, Organized Violence in a Global Era* (Cambridge: Polity Press, 1999), ch. 5.
16. Ahmed Rashid, 'They're Only Sleeping. Why Militant Islamists in Central Asia aren't Going to Go Away', *New Yorker*, 1 July 2002.
17. BBC, *The Money Programme*, 21 November 2001.
18. Mike Ingram, 'UK Admits Hostages in Chechnya Were Asked to Report Sensitive Information', World Socialist web-site, 21 January 1999, www.wsws.org.
19. Statement of Dennis M. Lormer, chief of the terrorist financial review group in the FBI before the senate judiciary committee's subcommittee on Technology,

Terrorism and Government Information, 9 July 2002, www.fbi.gov.

20. Deborah Tetley, 'Terrorists Active in Canada', *Calgary Herald*, 1 October 2001.

21. Testimony of Richard A. Rode before the subcommittee on Technology, Terrorism and Government Information of the senate committee on the judiciary, 24 February 1998, www.fas.org.

22. Todd Lighty and Ray Gibson, 'Suspects Blend in, Use Credit Swindles to Get Easy Money', *Tribune*, 4 November 2001.

23. Smuggling produces foreign exchange and requires the physical movement of products from one country to another. This is why it can be equated to exports of merchandise.

24. Daniel Pearl and Steve Stecklow, 'Taliban Banned TV but Collected Profits on Smuggled Sonys', *Wall Street Journal*, 9 January 2002.

25. Michela Wrong, 'Smugglers' Bazaar Thrives on Intrepid Afghan Spirit', *Financial Times*, 17 October 2002.

26. Pearl and Stecklow, 'Taliban Banned TV but Collected Profits on Smuggled Sonys'.

27. 'Commandos Terroristas se Refugian en la Triple Frontera', *El Pais Internacional* S.A., 9 November 2001.

28. Sebastian Junger, 'Terrorism's New Geography', *Vanity Fair*, December 2002.

29. Blanca Madani, 'Hezbollah's Global Finance Network: the Triple Frontier', *Middle East Intelligence Bulletin*, Vol. 4, No. 1, January 2002.

30. Junger, 'Terrorism's New Geography'.

31. Jack Sweeney, 'DEA Boots its Role in Paraguay', *Washington Times*, 21 August 2001. See also Junger, 'Terrorism's New Geography'.

32. Anthony Faiola, 'US Terrorist Search Reaches Paraguay; Black Market Border Hub Called Key Finance Center for Middle East Extremists', *Washington Post*, 13 October 2001.

33. Junger, 'Terrorism's New Geography'.

34. Ibid.

35. Ibid.

36. Douglas Farah, 'Money Cleaned, Colombian Style: Contraband Used to Convert Drug Dollars', *Washington Post*, 30 August 1998.

37. Ibid.

38. Ibid.

39. Ibid.

40. The information about Turkey comes from the archives of the Kurdish Human Rights Association of Rome.

41. Villagers were armed and paid by the Turkish government to fight the PKK. 'Turkey No Security without Human Rights', www.amnesty.org.

42. Mark Devenport, 'Iraqi Oil Smuggling Warning', 24 March 2000, www.news.bbc.co.uk.

43. Charles Recknagel, 'Iraq: Mystery Surrounds Iran's About-Face on Oil Smuggling', 21 June 2000, www.rferl.org.

44. Carola Hoyos, 'Oil Smugglers Keep Cash Flowing back to Saddam', *Financial Times*, 17 January 2002.

45. Ibid.

46. David Keen, 'A Disaster for Whom? Local Interests and International Donors during Famine among the Dinka of Sudan', *Disaster*, Vol. 15, No. 2, June 1991.

16. STATE-SHELL ECONOMICS

1. Hala Jaber, *Hizbollah, Born with a Vengeance* (New York: Columbia University Press, 1997).

2. Ibid., p. 5.

3. 'Inside a Terrorist's Mind', interview with Salah Shehadeh, The Middle East Media Research Institute, Special Dispatch Series No. 403, 24 July 2002, www.memri.org.

4. Suzanne Goldberg, 'The Men behind the Suicide Bombers', *Guardian*, 12 June 2002.

5. The Tamil population comprises one-quarter of the Sinhalese population of Sri Lanka. Amy Waldman, 'Master of Suicide Bombing: Tamil Guerrillas of Sri Lanka', *New York Times*, 14 January 2003.

6. Ibid.

7. James Dunnigan, 'The Rise and Fall of the Suicide Bomber', 21 August 2002, www.strategypage.com.

8. Goldberg, 'The Men Behind the Suicide Bombers'.

9. Waldman, 'Master of Suicide Bombing: Tamil Guerrillas of Sri Lanka'.

10. Ibid.

11. Kimberly I. Thachuk, *Terrorism's Financial Lifeline: Can it be Severed?*, Strategic Forum, Institute for the National Strategic Studies Defense University, Washington D.C., No. 191, May 2002, p. 7.

12. Chris Kline and Mark Franchetti, 'The Woman behind the Mask', *Sunday Times*, 3 November 2002.

13. Ibid.

14. See chapter 3.

15. During the Soviet era, the oil pipeline linked the port of Baku to Tikhoretsk and crossed Chechnya, right through Grozny. In 1994, Moscow started a war against Chechnya to defend the pipeline threatened by the Chechen rebels. In 1999, Russia invaded Chechnya after the pipeline was temporarily blocked by the rebels who had invaded Dagestan.

16. Greg Campbell, *Blood Diamonds* (Boulder, CO: Westview Press, 2002). See also Ewen MacAskill and David Pallister, 'Crackdown on "Blood" Diamonds', *Guardian*, 20 December 2000.

17. Douglas Farah, 'An "Axis" Connected to Qaddafi, Leaders Trained in Libya Have Used War to Safeguard Wealth', *Washington Post Foreign Service*, 2 November 2001.

18. Campbell, *Blood Diamonds*, p. 184.

19. Ibid., ch. 8.

20. Amelia Hill, 'Terror in the East: bin Laden's 20m dollar African "Blood Diamond" Deals', *Observer*, 20 October 2002.

21. Mark Doyle, 'Sierra Leone Rebels Probe al-Qaeda Link, The RUF is Worried by Claims of al-Qaeda Link', *BBC News Online*: World: Africa, 2 November 2001.

22. Hill, 'Terror in the East: bin Laden's 20m dollar African "Blood Diamond" Deals'.

23. 'Man Pleads Not Guilty in Terror-funding Investigation', *The Bulletin*, 16 November 2001.

24. Glenn Simpson, 'Terrorist Grid Smuggled Gems as Early as '95, Diary Suggests', *Wall Street Journal*, 17 January 2002.

25. Philippe Le Billon, 'The Political Economy of War: What Relief Agencies Need to Know', Network Paper No. 33, ODI, p. 16, www.odihpn.org.uk.

26. 'The SPLA has been supported by the Clinton administration. Arms, land mines, military training and funds have been allocated to it. Most of the help has been received via Uganda.' 'Sudan; USAID Boss under Fire on Sudan Policy', *Africa News*, 13 November 2001.

27. 'In late January 1998, Kerubino Kuanyin Bol, a SPLA commander, led a rebel attack on the city of Wau in Bahr al-Ghazal. This attack, and the fighting that followed it, led to a drastic deterioration in the security and food distribution situation of the region.' Ibid.

28. Ibid.

29. David Keen, 'When War Itself is Privatised', *Times Literary Supplement*, December 1995.

30. In theory, this refers only to public property; private property must be returned to the legitimate owners at the end of the war. Lesley Green, *The Contemporary Law of Armed Conflict* (Manchester: Manchester University Press, 2000), pp. 152–5.

31. Mary Kaldor, *New and Old Wars: Organized Violence in a Global Era* (Cambridge: Polity Press, 1999), ch. 5.

32. Ibid., p. 99. See also 'Playing the Communal Card:

Communal Violence and Human Rights', *Human Rights Watch*, 1995.

33. Robert Block and Leonard Doyle, 'Drug Profits Fund Weapons for Balkans', *Independent*, 10 December 1993.

34. 'Sudan; USAID Boss under Fire on Sudan Policy', *Africa News*, 13 November 2001.

35. Block and Doyle, 'Drug Profits Fund Weapons for Balkans'.

36. 'Arms Sales to Saudi Arabia and Taiwan', 28 November 1993, www.cdi.org.

37. Ibid.

38. Ibid.

39. 'Hunting the Merchants of Destruction', *Sunday Times*, 17 February 2002.

40. Ibid.

41. David Leppard, 'Dossier will Reveal Iraq's Poison Cache', *Sunday Times*, 22 September 2002.

42. Jeffrey Goldberg, 'The Great Terror', *New Yorker*, 25 March 2002.

43. Guy Dinmore, 'General Declares War on Desert Traffickers', *Financial Times*, 10 January 2002.

17. THE GLOBALISATION OF THE NEW ECONOMY OF TERROR

1. Michael Chossudovsky, *Guerra e Globalizzazione* (Torino: Edizioni Gruppo Abele, 2002), p. 95.

2. Karen Talbot, 'US Energy Giant Unocal Appoints Interim Government in Kabul', *Global Outlook*, Spring 2002, Vol. 1, No. 1, p. 70.

3. The Great Game is the name given to the struggle between Victorian Britain and Tsarist Russia, a secret war fought to control Central Asia and its resources.

4. Estimates of barrels of crude oil beneath the Caspian in 'proven' reserves range from 68 billion to over 100

billion barrels, worth approximately $2 trillion at current prices.

5. Ted Rall, 'It's All about Oil', *San Francisco Chronicle*, 2 November 2001.

6. Ahmed Nafeez Mosaddeq, *The War on Freedom, How and Why America was Attacked,* (CA: Tree of Life Publications, 2002) p. 45; see also Agence France Presse, 'US Gave Silent Blessing to Taliban Rise to Power: Analysis', 7 October 2001.

7. William O. Beeman, 'Follow the Oil Trail – Mess in Afghanistan Partly Our Government's Fault', *Jinn Magazine* (online), Pacific News Service, 24 August 1998, www.pacificnews.org.

8. Ahmed Rashid, *Taliban: The Story of the Afghan Warlords* (London: Pan, 2001), p. 166.

9. Wayne Madsen, 'Afghanistan, the Taliban and the Bush Oil Team', *Globalresearch.ca*, January 2002.

10. Jonathan Wells, Jack Meyers and Maggie Mulvihill, 'US Ties to Saudi Elite may be Hurting War on Terrorism', *Boston Herald*, 10 December 2001.

11. Ahmed Nafeez Mosaddeq, 'Afghanistan, The Taliban and the United States. The Role of Human Rights in Western Foreign Policy', January 2001, www.institute-for-afghan-studies.org.

12. CNN, 6 October 1996.

13. Madsen, 'Afghanistan, the Taliban and the Bush Oil Team'.

14. Gore Vidal, 'The Enemy Within', *Observer*, 27 October 2002.

15. John Pilger, 'This War of Lies Goes On', *Daily Mirror*, 16 November 2002.

16. Vidal, 'The Enemy Within'.

17. Chossudovsky, *Guerra e Globalizzazione*, pp. 96–7.

18. Peter Benesh, 'Did US Need for Obscure Sudan Export Help Bin Laden?', *Investor's Business Daily*, 21 September 2001.

19. Ibid.

20. Gregory Palast, 'FBI and US Spy Agents Say Bush Spiked Bin Laden Probes before 11 September', *Guardian*, 7 November 2001.

21. Gregory Palast, 'Did Bush Turn a Blind Eye on Terrorism?', *BBC Newsnight*, 6 November 2001.

22. Daniel Pearl and Steve Stecklow, 'Taliban Banned TV but Collected Profits on Smuggled Sonys', *Wall Street Journal*, 9 January 2002.

23. Ibid.

24. Ibid.

25. $1.4 billion is the average value of drugs produced in 1999–2001 at constant 2001 prices for the seven major drug-producing countries: Afghanistan, Bolivia, Burma, Colombia, Laos, Mexico, Peru. This figure has been calculated on the basis of the value of the drugs at the first point of sale, which is different from the cost of production (how much did it cost the farmer to produce the harvest). This indicator is based on potential production of drugs as estimated by the United Nations. Seizures and damage to crops at harvest time has been taken into consideration.

26. 'Q&A, Dirty Money: Raymond Baker Explores the Free Market's Demimode', *Harvard Business School Bulletin*, February 2002, www.alumni.hbs.edu.

27. Raymond Baker, 'Money Laundering and Flight Capital: The Impact on Private Banking', Senate Committee on Governmental Affairs, permanent Subcommittee on Investigations, 10 November 1999, http://www.brook.edu.

28. Author's interview with Raymond Baker.

29. Baker included in this calculation the *zakat* and money sent abroad with the *hawala*.

30. Kimberly L. Thachuk, *Terrorism's Financial Lifeline: Can it be Severed?*, Strategic Forum, Institute for the National Strategic Studies Defense University, Washington D.C., No. 191, May 2002, p. 2.

31. Mike Brunker, 'Money Laundering Finishes the Cycle', *MSNBC News*, 31 August 2002, msnbc.com/news.

32. 'That Infernal Washing Machine', *Economist*, 26 July 1997.

33. Author's interview with Raymond Baker.

34. Baker, 'Money Laundering and Flight Capital: The Impact on Private Banking'.

35. Brunker, 'Money Laundering Finishes the Cycle'.

36. Author's interview with Raymond Baker.

37. 'That Infernal Washing Machine'.

38. Author's interview with Raymond Baker.

39. Ibid.

40. This estimate is based on the author's research and calculation of the size of the legal business of terror organisations.

41. According to the Federal Reserve, 'foreigners use high-denomination bank notes primarily as a store of value, while countries with unstable economies may choose to use the dollar as a medium of exchange'. Federal Reserve Board, *Currency and Coin*, www.federalreserve.gov/paymentssystems/coin/.

42. This is the component of 'US currency that is in continual circulation, or permanently held abroad. We assume, as an identifying assumption, that there is a permanent and transitory component to foreign-held currency. As a matter of definition the permanent component reflects currency which is in continual circulation abroad and hence does not flow through Federal Reserve cash offices. We assume that currency held temporarily abroad, say due to tourism or business travel, returns to the United States . . . with the same transit time as currency in domestic circulation.' Richard G. Anderson and Robert H. Rasche, *The Domestic Adjusted Monetary Base*, working paper 2000–002A, Federal Reserve Bank of St. Louis, www.research.stlouisfed.org/wp/2000/2000–002.pdf.

43. Cash and short-term deposits.

44. Each time the government issues money due to the demand for money it creates wealth. Signorage was the term used

in the Middle Ages by the Italian lords (*signori*) to issue gold coins, the value of the coins was equal to the value of the gold in it plus the signorage, the cost of issuing the coins. All US currency, including that held externally, can be thought as a form of interest-free Treasury borrowing and therefore as a saving to the taxpayer.

45. Richard D. Porter and Ruth A. Judson, *The Location of US Currency: How Much is Abroad?* (Federal Reserve of St. Louis, 1996).

18. GLOBALISATION, TERROR'S UNWILLING ALLY

1. Al Battar training camp, Northeast Intelligence network, March 2004. www.homelandsecurityus.com

2. Ibid.

3. Ibid.

4. *Venduto dal CPA Petrolio per 7,5 Miliardi di Dollari*, Manifesto 15, April 2004.

5. Al Battar training camp, Northeast Intelligence network, March 2004. www.homelandsecurityus.com.

6. See chapter 10.

7. Author's interview with a Wall Street trader.

8. 'Losses inflicted on Saudi investors following September 11th attacks in the US', *Arabic news.com*, 21 November 2001, www.arabicnews.com.

9. OECD details.

10. 'Saudi Investors "pull out of US"',*BBC News*, 21 August 2002, www.news.bbc.co.uk.

11. Marc Tran, 'Dollar falls as Saudi Investors "withdraw billions"', *Guardian*, 21 August 2002.

12. Ibid.

13. Zachary Abuza, *Militant Islam in South East Asia, crucible of terror*, Lynne Rienner, London, 2003, ch. 1.

14. UN Security Council, monitoring group established pursuant to resolution 1363 (2001), report S/2003/1070, 2 December 2003, www.un.org.

15. Ibid.

16. 'Al-Qaeda Cash', *Associated Press*, 29 December, 2003.

17. Douglas Farah, 'Al-Qaeda's Finances Ample, Say Probes. Worldwide Failure to Enforce Sanctions Cited', *Washington Post*, 14 December 2003.

18. Ibid.

19. Claes Norgren and Jamie Caruana, 'Wipe Out The Treasuries of Terror,' *Financial Times*, 7 April 2004.

20. UN Security Council, monitoring group established pursuant to resolution 1363 (2001), report S/2003/1070, 2 December 2003, www.un.org.

21. Paul Marshall, 'Radical Islam's Move to Africa', *Washington Post*, 16 October 2003.

22. Ibid.

23. Zachary Abuza, *Tentacles of Terror: Al-Qaeda's Southeast Asian Networks*, Four Corners, 28 October 2002, www.abc.net.au.

24. Zachary Abuza, 'Militant Islam in Southeast Asia, Crucible of Terror', Lynne Rienner, London, 2003.

25. Author interview with Raymond Barker.

26. Cliff Stephenson and Tom Crook, *Pressure from all Sides*, Critical Technology Management Information, 7 October 2002, www.banktech.com.

27. S. Louise Mitchell, 'The Implication of the USA Patriot Act on Foreign Banking Institutions', Speech delivered at the National Anti Money Laundering Training Seminar, 24 May 2002, St. Vincent and the Granadines.

28. Richard W. Rahn, 'How Far will the Dollar Fall?', *Washington Times*, 30 December 2003.

29. Ibid.

30. South African currency.

31. Oriana Zill and Lowell Bergman, *The Black Peso Money Laundering System*, www.pbs.org.

32. *The Black Market Peso Exchange*, Underworld Economy, 12 November 2001.

33. See chapter 10.

34. Black Market Peso Exchange: two women jailed, 22 January 2003, www.forum.transnationale.org.

35. Ibid.

36. Ibid.

37. Zachary Abuza, 'Militant Islam in Southeast Asia, Crucible of Terror', Lynne Rienner, London, 2003, p. 21, see also Zachary Abuza, *Tentacles of Terror: Al-Qaeda's Southeast Asian Networks*, Four Corners, 28 October 2002, www.abc.net.au.

38. Douglas Farah, 'Al-Qaeda's Road Paved with Gold', *Washington Post*, 17 February, 2002.

39. Douglas Frantz, 'Secretive Money Moving System Scrutinized for bin Laden Funds', *International Herald Tribune*, 3 October 2001.

40. Zachary Abuza, *Tentacles of Terror: Al-Qaeda's Southeast Asian Networks*, Four Corners, 28 October 2002, www.abc.net.au.

41. Scott Baldauf, 'The War on terror's Money', *Christian Science Monitor*, 22 July 2002.

42. Ibid.

43. Author's interview with Nick Fielding.

44. Author's interview with Indira Singh.

45. Anne C. Richard, 'Europe Can Do More to Shut Down Terrorist Funds', *International Herald Tribune*, 18 March 2004.

46. Targets Inside Cities, section of the al-Qaeda document translated by Site Institute, the search for international terrorist entities, www.siteinstitute.org.

47. Ibid.

48. Ibid.

49. Money Laundering: Vigna on Counterstrategies, Agenzia Giornalistica Italia, 5 April 2004, www.agi.it.

50. 'Navy Makes Persian Gulf Drug Blast,' *CBSNews*, 19 December 2003.

51. *Bin Laden voleva allearsi con Cosa Nostra*, Messaggero, 13 April 2004.

52. 'Saudi Investors "pull out of US"', *BBC News*, 21 August 2002, www.news.bbc.co.uk.

53. UN Security Council, monitoring group established pursuant to resolution 1363 (2001), report S/2003/1070, 2 December 2003, www.un.org.

54. Neil Mackay, 'Was it ETA or al-Qaeda? The confusion over who was behind the Madrid bombing obscures intelligence predictions of an enhanced terror threat', *Sunday Herald*, 14 March 2004.

55. Ibid.

56. 'Tentacles of Terror: Ansar al-Islam goes international, causing tremors', *Daily Star*, 17 January 2004, www.lebanon wire.com.

57. Anthony Barnett, Jason Burke and Zoe Smith, 'Terror cells regroup and now they target Europe', *Observer*, 11 January 2004.

58. 'Tentacles of Terror: Ansar al-Islam goes international, causing tremors', *Daily Star*, 17 January 2004. www.lebanonwire.com.

59. Ibid.

60. Anthony Barnett, Jason Burke and Zoe Smith, 'Terror cells regroup and now they target Europe', *Observer*, 11 January 2004.

61. Rodolfo Casadei, *Connection Europa*, N6 Anno 10, www.tempi.it.

62. 'Terror Network', *Newsnight*, BBC News, 27 January 2004, news.bbc.co.uk.

63. Dale Fuchs, 'Spain Gives details on Terror Cell', *International Herald Tribune*, 15 April 2004.

64. Author's interview with Nick Fielding.

65. Yosri Fouda and Nick Fielding, *Masterminds of Terror, the truth behind the most devastating terrorist attack the world has ever seen*, Mainstream Publishing, London, 2003.

66. Full Text: 'bin Laden tape', *BBC News*, 15 April 2004, www.bbc.co.uk.

67. Jacqui Walls, Man Jailed for Raising Terrorism Funds, The Press Association Limited, 10 July 2003.
68. 'Credit Card Fraud', *Evening Gazette*, 2 July 2003.
69. Dale Fuchs, 'Spain Gives Details on Terror Cell', *International Herald Tribune*, 15 April 2003.

GLOSSARY

1. James Wasserman, *The Templars and the Assassins* (Rochester, NY: Inner Traditions, 2001), p. 70.
2. Jeffrey Herbst, 'Responding to State Failure in Africa', *International Security*, Vol. 21, No. 3 (Winter 1996–97), pp. 121–2.

Bibliography

ARTICLES

'2500 Metric Tons of Cocoa Leaf', *Financial Times*, 13 June 1985

'*8 Days Magazine*', 4 August 1979

'A Colombian', *Washington Post*, 17 March 1983

'Above the Law: Bush's Racial Coup d'Etat and Intelligence. Shutdown', *Green Press*, 14 February 2002, www.greenpress.org

'Ansar Al-Islam Activists Leaves Norway after Increased Pressure on their Leader', 12 September 2002, www.Kurdishmedia.com

'Arms for Drugs in the Balkans', *International Herald Tribune*, 6 June 1996

'Arms Sales to Saudi Arabia and Taiwan', 28 November 1993, www.cdi.org

'Assault on Charities is Risky Front for the US', *Wall Street Journal*, 16 October 2001

'Bosnian Leader Hails Islam at Election Rallies', *New York Times*, 2 September 1996

'Colombia-Weapons, Colombian Arms Dealer who Purchased Arms for FARC Arrested', *Financial Times Information*, EFE News Service, 8 May 2002

'Commandos terroristas se refugian en la triple frontera', *El Pais Internacional S.A.*, 9 November 2001

'Correspondent Banks, the Weakest Link', *Economist*, 29 September 2001

'Crackdown on Charities Irks Arab-Americans, May Strain Coalition', *Bloomberg News*, 6 December 2002

CRS Report for Congress, 'El Salvador, 1979–1989: A Briefing Book on US Aid and the Situation in El Salvador', the Library of Congress, Congressional Research Service,

Foreign Affairs and National Defense Division, 28 April 1989

'Declaration of War against the Americans Occupying the Land of the Two Holy Places, A Message from Osama bin Muhammad bin Laden unto his Muslim Brethren all over the World Generally, and in the Arab Peninsula Specifically', islamic-news.co.uk

'El Salvador 1980–1994. Human Rights Washington Style', excerpts from Blum William, *Killing Hope*, www.thirdworld traveler.com

'El Supremo Confirma La Condena De "Antxon" A diez Anos De Carcel Como Dirigente De Eta', *Terra*, 4 July 2002, www.terra.es

'El Supremo recopila testimonios y sentencias para actuar contra "Ternera"', *La Razon Digit@l*, 19 September 2002, www.larazon.es

'Enemies of the State, Without and Within', *Economist*, 6 October 2001

'Financial Chain, Funds Continue to Flow Despite Drive to Freeze Network's Assets', *Guardian*, 5 September 2002

'Global Development Finance, Financing the Poorest Countries', World Bank 2002

'Hope and Danger for Ethnic Albanians', *Economist*, 29 March 1997

'How Bosnia's Muslims Dodged Arms Embargo: Relief Agency Brokered Aid from Nations, Radical Groups', *Washington Post*, 22 September 1996

'Hunting the Merchants of Destruction', *Sunday Times*, 17 February 2002

'I Hope the Peace Process Will Be Irreversible, An Interview with Colombia's President Andres Pastrana', *Napue Zurcher Zeitung*, 23 February 2001, www.nzz.ch

'In un piano terroristico del 1995 la dinamica degli attacchi dell'11 settembre', *CNN on line*, 26 February 2002

'Indian Agency Says British Muslims Support Kashmiri

Militants Financially', *BBC Monitoring International Reports*, 13 January 2002

'Inside a Terrorist's Mind', Interview with Salah Shehadeh, The Middle East Media Research Institute, *Special Dispatch Series – No. 403*, 24 July 2002, www.memri.org

'Iran Gave Bosnia Leader $500,000, CIA Alleges: Classified Report Says Izetbegovic Has Been "Co-opted", Contradicting U.S. Public Assertion of Rift', *Los Angeles Times*, 31 December 1996

'Jihad against Jews and Crusaders, World Islamic Front Statement', 23 February 1998, www.fas.org

'La Financacio. El "impuesto revolucionario"', www.el-mundo.es

'London Cleric Told Followers "To Kill"', *Sunday Times*, 17 November 2002

'Man Pleads Not Guilty in Terror-Funding Investigation', *Bulletin's Frontrunner*, 16 November 2001

'Many Say US Planned for Terror but Failed to Take Action', *New York Times*, 30 November 2001

'Osama bin Laden Talks Exclusively to Nida'ul about the New Power Keg in the Middle East', *Nida'ul*, No. 15 October–November 1996, www.islam.org

'Playing the Communal Card: Communal Violence and Human Rights', Human Rights Watch, 1995

'PLO Operates Airport Shops', *Los Angeles Times*, 31 December 1985

'Q&A, Dirty Money: Raymond Baker Explores the Free Market's Demimode', *Harvard Business School Bulletin*, February 2002, www.alumni.hbs.edu

'Report: bin Laden Linked to Albania', *USA Today*, 1999, www.usatoday.com

'Saudis Funded Weapons for Bosnia, Official Says: $300 Million Program Had U.S. "Stealth Cooperation"', *Washington Post*, 2 February 1996

Special Report of the Court of Auditors of the European Economic Community (no. 85/C/215/01, 26 August 1986)

'Spectrum: International Terror Incorporated', *The Times*, 9 December 1985

'Spring to Fall 2000: News from the people's war in Peru', *Revolutionary Worker* #1082, 10 December 2000, www.rwor.org

'Sudan; USAID Boss Under Fire on Sudan Policy', *Africa News*, 13 November 2001

'Suicide Blast: Briton Named', *Manchester Guardian Weekly*, 10 January 2001

'Tajik, Russian Officials Suggest Tajikistan is Developing into Drug Production Center', *Eurasia Insight*, 14 August 2001

'That Infernal Washing Machine', *Economist*, 26 July 1997

The Cuban Government Involvement in facilitating International Drug Traffic, US Government Printing Office, serial no. J-98–36, 1983

'The Gun Existed', *Newsweek*, 16 January 1984

The Iran–Contra Arms Scandal: Foreign Policy Disaster, Facts on File Publications (New York, 1986)

The Soviet–Cuban Connection in Central America and the Caribbean, State Department Documents (March 1985)

'The US, the KLA and Ethnic Cleansing', *World Socialist Web Site*, 29 June 1999, www.wsws.org

'Turkey no Security without Human Rights', *Amnesty International*, www.amnesty.org

'*United States vs. Richard Second*', Civil Division, 1ˢᵗ Eastern District of Virginia, File no. 1202-A

'US Gave Silent Blessing to Taliban Rise to Power: Analysis', *Agence France Presse*, 7 October 2001

'US Government, Foreign Broadcast Information Service', Near East and South Asia Report, 3 October 1988

ARTICLES 2

Abadies, Alberto and Gardeazabal, Javier, *The Economic Cost of Conflict: A Case-Control Study for the Basque Country* (Cambridge, MA: National Bureau of Economic Research, September 2001), www.nber.org

AFP, 'Albanian-Americans Help Fund the KLA', *AFP*, 20 February 1999, www.members.tripod.com

Aglionby, John, 'The Secret Role of the Army in Sowing the Seeds of Religious Violence', *Guardian*, 16 October 2002

Alden, Edward, 'The Chicago Charity Accused of Defrauding Donors', *Financial Times*, 18 October 2002

Alden, Edward, 'The Money Trail: how a crackdown on suspect charities is failing to stem the flow of funds to al-Qaeda', *Financial Times*, 18 October 2002

Allen, Robin and Khalaf, Roula, 'Al-Qaeda: Terrorism after Afghanistan', *Financial Times*, 21 February 2002

Andromidas, Dean, 'Israeli Roots of Hamas are being Exposed', *Executive Intelligence Review*, 18 January 2002, www.larouchepub.com

Ardito, Simona, 'L'FBI sapeva tutto in anticipo', www.digilander.libero.it

Baker, Raymond, 'Money Laundering and Flight Capital: The Impact on Private Banking', Senate Committee on Governmental Affairs, Permanent Subcommittee on Investigations, 10 November 1999

Baneriee, Dipankar, 'Possible Connections of ISI with Drug Industry', *India Abroad*, 2 December 1994

Barber, Ben, 'Saudi Millions Finance Terror against Israel', *Washington Times*, 7 May 2002

Bard, Mitchell, 'The Lebanon War', www.us-israel.org

BBC News, 'IRA Suspects Move to Danger Prison', 23 August 2001, www.news.bbc.co.uk

BBC World Wide Monitoring, Former Soviet Union, *Nezavisimaya Gazeta*, 3 February 2000

BBC, *The Money Programme*, 21 November 2001

Beatty, Jonathan and Gwynne, S.C., 'The Dirtiest Bank of All', *Time Magazine*, 29 July 1991

Beeman, William O., 'Follow the Oil Trail – Mess in Afghanistan Partly Our Government's Fault', *Jinn Magazine* (online) *Pacific News Service*, San Francisco, 24 August 1998, www.pacificnews.org

Benesh, Peter, 'Did US Need For Obscure Sudan Export Help Bin Laden?', *Investor's Business Daily*, 21 September 2001

Bin Laden, Osama, 'Letter to America', *Observer Worldview*, 24 November 2002, www.observer.co.uk

Block, Robert and Doyle, Leonard, 'Drug Profits Fund Weapons for Balkans', *Independent*, 10 December 1993

Boroumand, Ladan and Boroumand, Roya, 'Terror, Islam and Democracy', *Journal of Democracy*, Vol. 13, No. 2, April 2002

Bronskill, Jim and Mofina, Rick, 'Hamas Funded by Canadian Agency: report: Aid organization accused of sending money to U.S. charity shut down for alleged Hamas ties', *Ottawa Citizen*, 6 December 2001

Brunker, Mike, 'Money Laundering Finishes the Cycle', *MSNBC News*, 31 August 2002, www.msnbc.com/news

Buch, Claudia and De Long, Gayle, 'Cross-Borders Bank Mergers: What Lures the Rare Animal', Kiel Working Paper No. 1070, Kiel Institute of World Economics, August 2001

Burke, Jason, 'Revealed: the quiet cleric behind Bali bomb horror', *Observer*, 20 October 2002

Burke, Jason, 'You Have to Kill in the Name of Allah until You are Killed', *Observer*, 26 January 2002

Burkeman, Oliver, 'US "Proof" over Iraqi Trucks', *Guardian*, 7 March 2002

Burns, Jimmy, Morris, Harvey and Peel, Michael, 'Assault on America Terrorists Funds', *Financial Times*, 24 September 2001

Burr, William and Evans, Michael L. ed., 'Ford, Kissinger and the Indonesian Invasion: 1975–1976', National Security Archive Electronic Briefing Book, No. 26, 6 December 2001, www.gwu.edu

Burton, John, 'Islamic Network "is on a Mission"', *Financial Times*, 16 October 2002

Carella, Antonio, 'Mammar el Gheddafi. Un Leone del Deserto Fratello dell'Occidente', www.members.xoom.virgilio.it

CBT TV, *The National*, 29 July 2002

Chomsky, Noam, 'The Colombian Plan: April 2000', *Z magazine*, June 2000

Chossudovsky, Michael, 'The KLA: Gangsters, terrorists and the CIA', www. historyofmacedonia.org

Chossudovsky, Michael, 'Osamagate: role of the CIA in supporting international terrorist organizations during the Cold War', *Canadian Business and Current Affairs*, Brandon University, November 2001

Chossudovsky, Michael, 'Who is Osama bin Laden?', Montreal Center for Research on Globalisation, 2001

Clarity James, 'Hard-up Lebanon Puts the Squeeze on Smugglers', *New York Times*, 6 November 1986

Clarke, Liam and Leppard, David, 'Photos Link More IRA Men to Colombia', *Sunday Times*, 28 April 2002

Clover, Charles, 'Return of the "Afghans" Puts Spotlight on Kuwaiti Divisions', *Financial Times*, 17 October 2002

Coll, Steve, 'Anatomy of a Victory: CIA's Covert Afghan War: $2 billion programme reversed tide for rebels', *Washington Post*, 19 July 1992

Congressional Press Release, Republican Party Committee, US Congress, 'Clinton Approved Iran Arms Transfers Help Turn Bosnia into Militant Islamic Base', 16 January 1996, www.senate.gov

Cooke, Kieran, 'World: Asia–Pacific Oil: saviour of East Timor?', *BBC News*, 7 October 1999, www.news.bbc.co.uk

Curtis, Mark, 'US and British Complicity in Indonesia 1965', *Znet*, 21 October 2002, zmag.org

Daragahi, Borzou 'Financing Terror', *Money*, Vol. 30, No. 12, November 2001

Deliso, Christopher, 'Bin Laden, Iran and the KLA', 19 September 2001, www.antiwar.com

Department of the Army, *Human Factors Considerations of Undergrounds in Insurgency*, DA Pamphlet (US Department of the Army), April 1976

Devenport, Mark, 'Iraqi Oil Smuggling Warning', 24 March 2000, www.news.bbc.co.uk

Dinmore, Guy, 'General Declares War on Desert Traffickers', *Financial Times*, 10 January 2002

Dipankar, Baneriee, 'Possible Connections of ISI with Drug Industry', *India Abroad*, 2 December 1994

Dolinat, Lou, 'A Focus on Their Smaller Crimes', *Newsday*, 5 October 2001, www. newsday.com

Donnan, Shawn, 'Blast May Reverberate across the Economy', *Financial Times*, 15 October 2002

Donnan, Shawn, 'Bombing to Test the Fabric of Indonesia Society', *Financial Times*, 14 October 2002

Donnan, Shawn, 'Indonesian Ties with the Arabs Highlighted', *Financial Times*, 17 October 2002

Doyle, Mark, 'Sierra Leone Rebels Probe al-Qaeda Link, The RUF is Worried by Claims of al-Qaeda Links', *BBC News Online: World: Africa*, 2 November 2001

Dunnigan, James, 'The Rise and Fall of the Suicide Bomber', 21 August 2002, www.strategypage.com

Ehrenfield, Rachael, 'Intifada Gives Cover to Arafat's Graft and Fraud', *News World Communication Inc.*, Insight on the News, 16 July 2001

Emerson, Steven, 'Meltdown: the end of the Intifada', *The New Republic*, 23 November 1992

Engel, Matthew, 'Drama in Court as Maussaoui Sacks Lawyers', *Guardian*, 23 April 2002

Ercolano, Ilaria, 'I rapporti tra il Partito Socialista Tedesco Unitario (SED) e il medioriente durante gli anni sessanta e settanta', *Storia delle Relazioni Internazionali*, 8 March 2001

Ersel, Aydinli, 'Implications of Turkey's anti-Hizbullah Operation', Washington Institute for Near Policy, 9 February 2000

Esposito, John L., 'Political Islam: beyond the green menace', *Current History*, Vol. 93, Nos 579–87, January–December 1994

Evans III, Brian, 'The Influence of the United States Army on the Development of the Indonesian Army (1954–1964)', in *Indonesia*, Cornell Modern Indonesia Programme, April 1998

Faiola, Anthony, 'US Terrorist Search Reaches Paraguay: black market border hub called key finance center for Middle East extremists', *Washington Post*, 13 October 2001

Farah, Douglas, 'Al-Qaeda's Road Paved with Gold: secret shipments traced through a lax system in United Arab Emirates', *Washington Post*, 17 February 2002

Farah, Douglas, 'An "Axis" Connected to Gaddafi: leaders trained in Libya have used war to safeguard wealth', *Washington Post Foreign Service*, 2 November 2001

Farah, Douglas, 'Money Cleaned, Colombian Style: Contraband used to convert drug dollars', *Washington Post*, 30 August 1998

Feldman, Steve, 'No One Knows why Hamas Graced Philly with its Presence', *Ethnic News Watch*, 13 December 2001

Fielding, Nick, 'Al-Qaeda Issues New Manifesto of Revenge', *Sunday Times*, 17 November 2002

Fielding, Nick, 'The British Jackal', *Sunday Times*, 21 April 2002

Finn, Peter and Delaney, Sarah, 'Sinister Web Links Terror Cells Across Europe', *International Herald Tribune*, 23 October 2001

Firestone, David, 'Mideast Flare-Up: The Money Trail', *New York Times*, 6 December 2001

Fisk, Robert, 'As My Soccer Said: Thank Mr. Clinton for the fine words', *Independent*, 22 August 1998

Fisk, Robert, 'In on the Tide, the Guns and Rockets that Fuel this Fight', *Independent*, 29 April 2002

Fisk, Robert, 'Talks with Osama bin Laden', *The Nation*, 21 September 1998, www.thenation.com

Foden, Giles, 'Australian "Crusaders" Targeted by bin Laden', *Guardian*, 16 October 2002

Foden, Giles, 'The Former CIA "Client" Obsessed with Training Pilots', *Guardian*, 12 September 2001

Fukuyama, Francis and Samin, Nadav, 'Heil Osama, The Great Reformer', *Sunday Times*, 29 September 2002

Gaines, William and Martin, Andrew, 'Terror Funding', *Chicago Tribune*, 8 September 1998

Gerth, Jeff and Miller, Judith, 'A Nation Challenged: On the list, philanthropist or fount of funds for terrorists?', *New York Times*, 13 October 2001

Goldberg, Jeffrey, 'The Great Terror', *New Yorker*, 25 March 2002

Goldberg, Suzanne, 'The Men behind the Suicide Bombers', *Guardian*, 12 June 2002

Haass, Richard, *Intervention: The Use of American Military Force in the Post-Cold War World* (Brookings Institute Press, 1999), www.brookings.nap.edu

Halliday, Fred, 'The Un-Great Game: the Country that Lost the Cold War, Afghanistan', *The New Republic*, 25 March 1996

Hecht, Bernie, 'Irgun and the State of Israel', www.jewishmag.com

Herbst, Jeffrey, 'Responding to State Failure in Africa', *International Security*, Vol. 21 No. 3, Winter 1996–97

Hill, Amelia, 'Terror in the East: bin Laden's $20m African "Blood Diamond" dials', *Observer*, 20 October 2002

Hiro, Dilip, 'Fallout from the Afghan Jihad', *Inter Press Services*, 21 November 1995

Hooper, John, 'Terror Made Fortune for bin Laden', *Guardian*, 23 September 2001

Hoyos, Carola, 'Oil Smugglers Keep Cash Flowing back to Saddam', *Financial Times*, 17 January 2002

Huband, Mark, 'Special Report, Inside al-Qaeda Bankrolling bin Laden', *Financial Times*, 29 November 2001

Huntington, Samuel P., 'The Age of Muslim Wars', *Newsweek*, Special Issue 2002

Huntington, Samuel P., 'The Clash of Civilization?', *Foreign Affairs*, Summer 1993

IBRD, 'Transition Report, The First Ten Years: Analysis and Lessons for Eastern Europe and the Former Soviet Union', 2001

Ingram, Mike, 'UK Admits Hostages in Chechnya were Asked to Report Sensitive Information', *World Socialist Web Site*, 21 January 1999, www.wsw.org

Jacobson, Philip, 'Warlord of the Jihad', *Sunday Times Magazine*, 26 January 2003

Jones, Stephen and Israel, Peter, 'Others Unknown', *Publicaffairs*, New York, 2001

Jordan, Sandra, 'Dispaches', *Channel 4*, 26 May 2002

Junger, Sebastian, 'Terrorism's New Geography', *Vanity Fair*, December 2002

Keen, David, 'A Disaster for Whom? Local Interests and International Donors During Famine among the Kinka of Sudan', *Disaster*, Vol. 15, No. 2, June 1991

Keen, David, 'When War Itself is Privatized', *Times Literary Supplement*, December 1995

Keh, Douglas, *Drug Money in a Changing World*, UNDCP Technical document no. 4 (Vienna, 1998)

Kelley, Jack, 'Saudi Money Aiding bin Laden: businessmen are financing front groups', *USA Today*, 29 October 1999

Kershner, Isabel, 'Behind the Veil', *Jerusalem Report*, 3 June 1993

Khalaf, Roula, 'Al-Qaeda Recruiting Ground Offers Tough Challenge in War of Terror', *Financial Times*, 22 February 2002

Khan, Lal, 'Pakistan, Futile Crusades of a Failed State', www.marxist.com

Khashuqji, Jamal, 'Al-Qaeda Organisation: Huge Aims without Programme or Cells', *Al-Hayah*, 12 October 1998

Kline, Chris and Franchetti, Mark, 'The Woman Behind the Mask', *Sunday Times*, 3 November 2002

Kocoglu, Yahya, 'Hizbullah: The Susurluk of the Southeast', *Turkish Daily News*, 27 January 2000

Kristof, Nicholas D., 'Behind the Terrorists', *New York Times*, 22 November 2002

Lamont, James, 'Africa's Trade Flows Clogged up at Dockside', *Financial Times*, 8 January 2002

Lapper, Richard, 'UN Fears Growth in Heroin Trade', *Financial Times*, 24 February 2000

Le Billon, Philippe, 'The Political Economy of War: what relief agencies need to know', *Network Paper* No. 33, ODI www.odihpn.org.uk

Lemoine, Maurice, 'En Colombie, Un Nation, Deux Etats', *Le Monde Diplomatique*, May 2000

Leppard, David, 'Dossier will Reveal Iraq's Poison Cache', *Sunday Times*, 22 September 2002

Leppard, David and Sheridan, Michael, 'London Bank Used for bin Laden Cash', *Sunday Times*, 16 September 2001

Levine, Steve, 'Critics Say Uzbekistan's Crackdown on Radicalism May Fuel in Fervor', *Wall Street Journal*, 3 May 2001

Liam, Clarke and Leppard, David, 'Photos Link More IRA Men to Colombia', *Sunday Times*, 28 April 2002

Lichtblau, Eric, 'US Indicts Head of Islamic Charity in Qaeda Financing', *New York Times*, 10 October 2002

Lighty, Todd and Gibson, Ray, 'Suspects Blend in, Use Credit Swindles to Get Easy Money', *Tribune*, 4 November 2001

Livingstone, Neil C. and Halevy, David, 'The Perils of Poverty', *National Review*, 21 July 1986

MacAskill, Ewen and Aglionby, John, 'Suspicion Turns on Indonesia's Islamist Militants', *Guardian*, 14 October 2002

MacAskill, Ewen and Pallister, David, 'Crackdown on "Blood" Diamonds', *Guardian*, 20 December 2000

MacCarthy, Roy and Norton-Taylor, Richard, 'Kashmir Militants Plan New Attacks', *Guardian*, 25 May 2002

Mackay, Neil, 'John Mayor Link to bin Laden Dynasty', *Sunday Herald*, 7 October 2001

Madani, Blanca, *Hezbollah's Global Finance Network: the Triple Frontier*, Middle East Intelligence Bulletin, Vol. 4, No. 1 (January 2001)

Madsen, Wayne, 'Afghanistan, the Taliban and the Bush Oil Team', January 2002, www.Globalresearch.ca

Mardini, Ahmad, 'Gulf-Economy: BCCI deal buoys UAE stocks', *Inter Press Service*, 6 February 1995

Martinelli, M., 'IBR alla sbarra rivendicano il delitto Biagi', *Il Messaggero*, 29 March 2002

McCoy, Alfred, 'Drug Fallout: the CIA's forty-year complicity in the narcotics trade', *The Progressive*, 1 August 1997

McCoy, Alfred, 'The Politics of Heroin in Southeast Asia, French Indochina: opium espionage and "Operation X"', www.drugtext.org

McGregor, Richard, 'Rumours Rule the Money Pit', *Financial Times*, 24 November 2001

McGregor, Richard, 'Uighur Training Angered Beijing', *Financial* Times, 18 October 2001

McGrory, Daniel, 'UK Muslims Volunteers for Kashmir War', *The Times*, 28 December 2000

Miller, Judith and Gerth, Jeff, 'Trade in Honey is Said to Provide Money and Cover for bin Laden', *New York Times*, 11 October 2001

Mintz, John, 'Bin Laden's Finances are Moving Target', *Washington Post*, 28 August 1998

Monbiot, George, 'To Crush the Poor', *Guardian*, 4 February 2003

Murphy, Brian, 'KLA Volunteers Lack Experience', *Associated Press*, 5 April 1997

Mydans, Seth, 'Indonesian Conflict May be Breeding the Terrorists of Tomorrow', *International Herald Tribune*, 10 January 2002

Mylroie, Laurie, 'The World Trade Center Bomb: Who is Ramzi Yousef? and why it matters', *The National Interest*, Winter 1995/96

NaFeez Mosaddeq, Ahmed, 'Afghanistan, the Taliban and the United States. The Role of Human Rights in Western Foreign Policy', January 2001, www.institute-for-afghan-studies.org

Newfarmer, Richard ed., 'Relations with Cuba', in *From Gunboats to Diplomacy: New Policies for Latin America.* Papers prepared for the Democratic Policy Committee, US Senate, Washington, June 1982 (Johns Hopkins University Press, 1984)

Noor, Farish A., 'The Evolution of "Jihad" in Islamist Political Discourse: how a plastic concept became harder', www.ssrc.org

O'Donnell, Guillermo, 'On the State, Democratization and Some Conceptual Problems', working paper No. 192 (University of Notre Dame: The Helen Kellogg Institute for International Studies, April 1993)

O'Kane, Maggie, 'Where War is a Way of Life', *Guardian*, 15 October 2001

Palast, Gregory, 'Did Bush Turn a Blind Eye on Terrorism?', *BBC Newsnight*, 6 November 2001

Palast, Gregory and Pallister, David, 'FBI Claims bin Laden Enquiry was Frustrated', *Guardian*, 7 November

Pallister, David, 'Head of Suspects Charity Denies Link to bin Laden', *Guardian*, 16 October 2001

Pallister, David and Bowcott, Owen, 'Banks to Shut Doors on Saudi Royal Cash', *Guardian*, 17 July 2002

Pearl, Daniel and Stecklow, Steve, 'Taliban Banned TV but Collected Profits on Smuggled Sonys', *Wall Street Journal*, 9 January 2002

Petkovic, Milan V., 'Albanian Terrorists', *Balknianet*, 1998, www.balkania.net

Phillips, David, 'The Next Stage in the War on Terror', *International Herald Tribune*, 23–24 March 2002

Pilger, John, 'This War is a Fraud', *Daily Mirror*, 29 October 2001

Pilger, John, 'This War of Lies Goes on', *Daily Mirror*, 16 November 2002

Rall, Ted, 'It's all about Oil', *San Francisco Chronicle*, 2 November 2001

Ranstrorp, Magnus and Xhudo, Gus, 'A Treat to Europe? Middle East Ties with the Balkans and their Impact upon Terrorist Activity throughout the Region', in *Terrorism and Political Violence*, Vol. 6, No. 2, Summer 1994

Rashid, Ahmed, 'The Taliban: Exporting Extremism', *Foreign Affairs*, November 1999

Rashid, Ahmed, 'They're Only Sleeping. Why Militant Islamists in Central Asia aren't going to go away', *The New Yorker*, 14 January 2002

Recknagel, Charles, 'Iraq: mystery surrounds Iran's about-face on oil smuggling', 21 June 2000, www.rferl.org

Ressa, Maria, 'The Quest for the Asia's Islamic "Super" State', *CNN on line*, 30 August 2002, www.asia.cnn.com

Reuss, Alejandro, 'US in Chile', in *Third World Traveller*, www.thirdworldtraveler.com

Ringshow, Grant, 'Profits of Doom', *Sunday Telegraph*, 23 September 2001

Rotberg, Robert I., 'The New Nature of Nation-State Failure', *The Washington Quarterly*, Summer 2002

Roy, Arundhati, 'The Algebra of Infinite Justice', www.nation-online.com

Rubinstein, Danny, 'Protection Racket, PA-Style', *Ha'aretz Daily Newspaper*, Tel Aviv, 3 November 1999

Sachs, Susan, 'An Investigation in Egypt Illustrates al-Qaeda's Web', *New York Times*, 21 November 2001

Said, Edwar, 'When We Will Resist?', *Guardian*, 25 January 2003

Schreiber, Anna P., 'Economic Coercion as an Instrument of Foreign Policy: U.S. Economic Measures against Cuba and the Dominican Republic', *World Politics*, Vol. 25, April 1973

Scudder, Lew, 'A Brief History of Jihad', www.rca.org

Seper, Jerry, 'KLA Rebels Train in Terrorist Camps', *Washington Times*, 4 May 1999

Shahar, Yael, 'Tracing bin Laden's Money: easier said than done', *ICT*, 21 September 2001, www.ict.org

Siddiqui, Mateen, 'Differentiating Islam from Militant Islamist', *San Francisco Chronicle*, 21 September 1999

Simpson, Glenn, 'Terrorist Grid Smuggled Gems as Early as '95, Diary Suggests', *Wall Street Journal*, 17 January 2002

Sloan, John, 'Crusades in the Levant (1097–1291)', www.xenophongroup.com

Smith, Charles, 'China and Sudan: trading oil for humans', *Worldnetdaily*, 19 July 2000, www.worldnetdaily.com

Standish, Alex, 'Albanians Face Ruin as Cash Pyramids Crumble', *The European*, 28 November 1996

Stern, Babette, 'La Toile Financière d'Oussana ben Laden s'etend du pays du Golfe à l'Europe', *Le Monde Intercatif*, 24 September 2001

Sublette, Carey, 'Dr. Abdul Qadeer Khan', www.nuke testing.enviroweb.org

Subrahmanyam, K., 'Pakistan is Pursuing Central Asian Goals', *India Abroad*, 3 November 1995

Sullivan, Stacy, 'Albanian Americans Funding Rebels' Cause', *Washington Post*, 26 May 1998

Sweeney, Jack, 'DEA Boots its Role in Paraguay', *Washington Times*, 21 August 2001

Takeyh, Ray and Gvosdev, Nicholas, 'Do Terrorist Networks Need a Home?', *The Washington Quarterly*, Summer 2002

Talbot, Karen, 'US Energy Giant Unocal Appoints Interim Government in Kabul', *Global Outlook*, Vol. 1, No. 1, Spring 2002

Tetley, Deborah, 'Terrorists Active in Canada', *Calgary Herald*, 1 October 2001

Thachuk, Kimberly L., *Terrorism's Financial Lifeline: Can It Be Severed?*, Strategic Forum, Institute for the National Strategic Studies National Defense University, Washington D.C., No. 191, May 2002

Thompson, Richard, 'CIA Used Bank in Covert Operations', *Independent*, 15 July 1991

Vaknin, Sam, 'Analysis: Hawala, the bank that never was', *United Press International*, 17 September 2001, www.upi.com

Vasagar, Jeevan and Dodd, Vikram, 'British Muslims take Path to Jihad: Kashmir terror group claims suicide bomber was from Birmingham', *Guardian*, 29 December 2000

Vick, Karl, 'The Taliban's Good-Bye: take the banks' millions and run', *Washington Post*, 8 January 2001

Vidal, Gore, 'The Enemy Within', *Observer*, 27 October 2002

Wagstyl, Stefan, 'Frontline States Seek Place on World Map', *Financial Times*, 22 November 2001

Wagstyl, Stefan and Jansson, Eric, 'Extremists may be Only Winners as Serb Voters Shun Election', *Financial Times*, 15 October 2002

Waldman, Amy, 'Master of Suicide Bombing: Tamil Guerrillas of Sri Lanka', *New York Times*, 14 January 2003

Walk, Marcus, 'In the Financial Fight against Terrorism, Leads are Hard Won', *Wall Street Journal*, 10 October 2001

Weiser, Benjamin, 'The Trade Center Verdict: The Overview: "mastermind" and driver found guilty in 1993 plot to blow up Trade Center', *New York Times*, 13 November 1997

Weizman, Steve, 'Bush Decries Arafat, to Meet Sharon', Associated Press, Worldstream, 6 May 2002

Wells, Jonathan, Meyers, Jack and Mulvihill, Maggie, 'War on Terrorism: Saudi elite tied to money groups linked to bin Laden', *Boston Herald*, 14 October 2001

Witoelar, Wimar, 'Terror has Deep Roots in Indonesia', *Guardian*, 16 October 2002

World Affair, 'A Mafia State', *Newsweek International*, 19 June 2000

Wright, Lawrence, 'The Counter-Terrorist', *New Yorker*, 14 January 2002

Wright, Robin and Meyer, Joseh, 'America Attacked: mapping a response', *Los Angeles Times*, 12 September 2001

Wrong, Michela, 'Smugglers' Bazaar Thrives on Intrepid Afghan Spirit', *Financial Times*, 17 October 2002

BOOKS

Abukhalil, As'as, *Bin Laden, Islam and America's New 'War on Terrorism'* (New York: Seven Stories Press, 2002)

Adams, James, *The Financing of Terror* (New York: Simon & Schuster, 1986)

Adams, James Ring and Douglas, Frants, *A Full Service Bank* (London: Simon & Schuster, 1992)

Adkin, Mark and Mohammed, Yousaf, *The Bear Trap: Afghanistan's Untold Story* (London: Cooper, 1992)

Ajami, Fouad, *The Arab Predicament* (New York: Cambridge University Press, 1981)

Alexander, George ed., *Western State Terrorism* (Cambridge: Polity Press, 1991)

Annual of Power and Conflict, 1973–74 (London: Institute for the Study of Conflict, 1975)

Anon., *Through Our Enemies Eyes* (Washington D.C.: Brasseys, 2002)

Atiya, Aziz, *Crusade, Commerce and Culture* (Bloomington: Indiana University Press, 1962)

Aydinli, Ersel, *Implications of Turkey's anti-Hizbullah Operation* (Washington Institute for Near Policy, 9 February 2000)

Barber, Malcolm, *The Two Cities. Medieval Europe 1050–1320* (London: Routledge, 1992)

Beaty, Jonathan and Gwynne, S.C., *The Outlaw Bank, A Wild Ride into the Secret Heart of BCCI* (New York: Random House, 1993)

Benjamin, Daniel and Simon, Steven, *The Age of Sacred Terror* (New York: Random House, 2002)

Bobbitt, Philip, *The Shield of Achilles* (London: Penguin Books, 2002)

Boyce, James K., *Economic Policy for Building Peace, The Lessons of El Salvador* (Boulder, CO: Lynne Rienner Publishers, 1996)

Brisard, Jean Charles and Dasquie, Guillaume, *La Verita' Negata* (Milano: Marco Tropea Editore, 2001)

Byrne, Hugh, *El Salvador's Civil War, a Study of a Revolution* (Boulder, CO: Lynne Rienner Publishers, 1996)

Campbell, Greg, *Blood Diamonds* (Boulder, CO: Westview Press, 2002)

Chomsky, Noam, *9–11* (New York: Seven Stories Press, 2002)

Chossudovsky, Michael, *Guerra e Globalizzazione* (Torino: Edizioni Gruppo Abele, 2002)

Cooley, John K., *Unholy Wars. Afghanistan, America and International Terrorism* (London: Pluto Press, 2000)

Cordesman, Anthony H., *Economic, Demographic and Security Trends in the Middle East* (Washington D.C.: Center for Strategic and International Studies, January 2002)

Duffield, Mark, 'The Political Economy of Internal War: asset transfer, complex emergencies and international aid', in Joanna Macrae and Anthony Zwi eds, *War and Hunger: Rethinking International Responses* (London: Zed Press, 1994)

El Khazenm, Farid, *The Breakdown of the State in Lebanon 1967–1976* (London: I.B. Tauris, 2000)

Emerson, Steven, *American Jihad, The Terrorist Living Among Us* (New York: Simon & Schuster, 2002)

Franceschini, Alberto, *Mara, Renato ed Io* (Milano: Mondadori, 1988)

Friedman, Thomas, *The Lexus and the Olive Tree* (New York: Farrar, Straus & Giroux, 1999)

Fukuyama, Francis, *The End of History and the Last Man* (London: Penguin Books, 1993)

Garthoff, Raymond L., *Reflection on the Cuban Missile Crisis* (Washington D.C.: Brookings Institute, 1987)

Geldard, Ian and Craig, Keith, *IRA, INLA: Foreign Support and International Connections* (London: Institute for the Study of Terrorism, 1988)

Gilbert, Paul, *Terrorism, Security and Nationality* (London: Routledge, 1994)

Goren, Roberta, *The Soviet Union and Terrorism* (London: Hyman, 1984)

Goulden, Joseph C., *The Death Merchant* (New York: Simon & Schuster, 1984)

Graduate Institute of International Studies, *Small Arms Survey, 2001* (Oxford: Oxford University Press, 2001)

Green, Lesley, *The Contemporary Law of Arm Conflicts* (Manchester: Manchester University Press, 2000)

Griffin, Michael, *Reaping the Whirlwind* (London: Pluto Press, 2002)

Gunaratna, Rohan, *Inside al-Qaeda* (New York: Columbia University Press, 2002)

Harclerode, Peter, *Fighting Dirty* (London: Cassell, 2001)

Hardt, Michael and Negri, Antonio, *Impero* (Milano: Rizzoli, 2000)

Hopkirk, Peter, *The Great Game* (Oxford: Oxford University Press, 1990)

IRA, *INLA: Foreign Support and International Connections* (London: Institute for the Study of Terrorism, 1988)

Irabarren, Florencio Dominguez, *ETA: Estrategia Organizativa y Actuaciones, 1978–1992* (Servicio Editorial de la Universidad del Pays Vasco, 1998)

Jaber, Hala, *Hizbollah, Born with a Vengeance* (New York: Columbia University Press, 1997)

Jacquard, Roland, *In the Name of Osama bin Laden, Global Terrorism & the bin Laden Brotherhood* (Durham, NC: Duke University Press, 2002)

Jamieson, Alison, *Terrorism and Drug Trafficking in the 1990s* (Dartmouth: Research Institute for the Study of Conflict and Terrorism, 1994)

Jones, Stephen and Israel, Peter, *Others Unknown: The Oklahoma City Bombing & Conspiracy* (New York: PublicAffairs, 1998)

Juergensmeyer, Mark, *Terror in the Mind of God* (Berkeley: University of California Press, 2000)

Kaldor, Mary, *New and Old Wars: Organized Violence in a Global Era* (Cambridge: Polity Press, 1999)

Kartha, Tara, *South Asia – A Rising Spiral of Proliferation,* Background paper (Geneva: Small Arms Survey, 2000)

Kennedy, John F., 'Defense Policy and the Budget: Message of President Kennedy to Congress, March 28, 1961', in Richard P. Stebbins, *Documents in American Foreign Relations, 1961* (New York: Harper & Row, 1962)

Kingsbury, Damien, *Power Politics and the Indonesian Military* (London: Routledge Curzon, 2003)

Krinsky, Michael and Golove, David, *United States Economic Measures against Cuba: Proceedings in the United Nations and International Law Issues* (Northampton, MA: Aletheia Press, 1993)

Lapierre, Dominique and Collins, Larry, *O Jerusalem* (Paris: Editions Robert Laffont, 1971)

Laqueur, Walter, *The New Terrorism: Fanaticism and the Arms of Mass Destruction* (Oxford: Oxford University Press, 1999)

Lewis, Bernard, *Assassins, A Radical Sect in Islam* (London: Weidenfeld & Nicolson, 2001)

Livingstone, Neil C. and Halevy, David, *Inside the PLO* (New York: William Morrow, 1990)

Martin, Al, *The Conspirators: Secrets of an Iran Contra Insider* (Pray, MO: National Liberty Press, 2001)

McClintock, Michael, *Instruments of Statecraft: U.S. Guerrilla Warfare, Counter-insurgency, and Counter-terrorism, 1940–1990* (New York: Pantheon Books, 1992)

McWhirter, Norris ed., *Guinness Book of Records* (London: Guinness Superlatives Ltd., 26th edition, 1979)

Millbank, David, *International and Transnational Terrorism: Diagnosis and Prognosis* (Washington D.C.: CIA, 1976)

Moretti, Mario, *Brigate Rosse, Una Storia Italiana* (Milano: Anabasi, 1994)

Muhammad, Haykal, *Iran, the Untold Story* (New York: Pantheon Books, 1982)

Nafeez Mosaddeq, Ahmed, *The War on Freedom, How and Why America was Attacked, September 11, 2001* (CA: Tree of Life Publications, 2002)

Palast, Gregory, *The Best Democracy Money Can Buy* (London: Pluto Press, 2002)

Pierson, Christopher, *The Modern State* (London: Routledge, 1996)

Polito, Ennio, *Arafat e Gli Altri* (Roma: Data News, 2002)

Randal, Jonathan, *The Tragedy of Lebanon* (London: Chatto & Windus, 1983)

Rashid, Ahmed, *Jihad, the Rise of Militant Islam in Central Asia* (New Haven, CT: Yale University Press, 2002)

Rashid, Ahmed, *Taliban: The Story of the Afghan Warlords* (London: Pan, 2001)

Reeve, Simon, *The New Jackals: Ramzi Yousef, Osama bin Laden and the Future of Terrorism* (London: André Deutsch, 1999)

Rivers, Gayle, *War Against Terrorism: How to Win it?* (New York: Charter Books, 1986)

Rubenberg, Cheryl, *The Palestine Liberation Organization, its Institutional Infrastructure* (Belmont, MA: Institute of Arab Studies Inc., 1983)

Runciman, Steven, *A History of the Crusades*, Volume I (London: Folio, 1994)

Scowen, Peter, *Rogue Nation, The America The Rest of the World Knows* (Toronto: McClelland & Stewart, 2002)

Seale, Patrick, *Abu Nidal: a Gun for Hire, the Secret Life of the World's Most Notorious Arab Terrorist* (London: Hutchinson, 1992)

Sevillano, Tarazona Gabriela, *Sendero Luminoso and the Threat of Narcoterrorism* (New York: Praeger, 1990)

Small Arms Survey, 2001 (Oxford: Oxford University Press, 2001)

Smith, Chris, 'Areas of Major Concentration in the Use and Traffic of Small Arms', in Jayantha Dhanapala et al., *Small Arms Controls: Old Weapons New Issues* (Aldershot: Ashgate, 1999)

Sterling, Claire, *The Terror Network, The Secret War of International Terrorism* (London: Weidenfeld & Nicolson, 1981)

Stockwell, John, *In Search of Enemies: A CIA Story* (New York: W.W. Norton, 1979)

Sullivan, John, *El Nationalismo Vasco Radical* (Madrid: Alianza Universidad, 1987)

Tariq, Ali, *The Clash of Fundamentalism* (London: Verso, 2002)

Tibi, Bassam, *The Challenge of Fundamentalism* (Berkeley: University of California Press, 1998)

Tyerman, Christopher, *The Invention of the Crusades* (London: Macmillan Press, 1998)

United Nations, ECLA, *Economic Survey of Latin America, 1981* (Santiago: United Nations Chile, 1983)

Villalobos, Joaquìn, *The War in El Salvador, Current Situation and Outlook for the Future* (San Francisco: Solidarity Publications, n.d.)

Wasserman, James, *The Templars and the Assassins* (Rochester, NY: Inner Traditions, 2001)

Wiebes, Cees, *Intelligence and the War in Bosnia, 1992–1995* (Amsterdam: Netherlands Institute for War Documentation, 2002)

Woodward, Bob, *Veil: The Secret Wars of the CIA 1981–1987* (New York: Simon & Schuster, 1987)

Index